THE CHRÉTIEN LEGACY

The Chrétien Legacy

Politics and Public Policy in Canada

Edited by

LOIS HARDER AND STEVE PATTEN

Published for the Centre for Constitutional Studies
by
McGill-Queen's University Press
Montreal & Kingston • London • Ithaca

© McGill-Queen's University Press 2006
ISBN-13: 978-0-7735-3095-9   ISBN-10: 0-7735-3095-9 (cloth)
ISBN-13: 978-0-7735-3107-9   ISBN-10: 0-7735-3107-6 (paper)

Legal deposit second quarter 2006
Bibliothèque nationale du Québec

Printed in Canada on acid-free paper that is 100% ancient forest free
(100% post-consumer recycled), processed chlorine free

McGill-Queen's University Press acknowledges the support of the
Canada Council for the Arts for our publishing program. We also
acknowledge the financial support of the Government of Canada
through the Book Publishing Industry Development Program (BPIDP)
for our publishing activities.

This book originated as a special issue of *The Review of Constitutional
Studies/Revue d'études constitutionnelles.*

Library and Archives Canada Cataloguing in Publication

   The Chrétien legacy : politics and public policy in Canada / edited by
Lois Harder and Steve Patten.

Originally published as a special issue of the Review for constitutional
studies, vol. IX, nos. 1 & 2.
Includes bibliographical references.
ISBN-13: 978-0-7735-3095-9   ISBN-10: 0-7735-3095-9 (bnd)
ISBN-13: 978-0-7735-3107-9   ISBN-10: 0-7735-3107-6 (pbk)

   1. Chrétien, Jean, 1934–. 2. Canada—Politics and government—1993–.
1. Harder, Lois, 1966– 11. Patten, Steve, 1961– 111. Title: Review of
constitutional studies.

FC635.C48 2006   971.064'8   C2006-900953-8

Typeset by Jay Tee Graphics Ltd. in 10.5/13 Sabon

For Janine Brodie: teacher, mentor, friend.

Contents

Introduction

LOIS HARDER

This collection of essays was originally compiled during the spring and summer of 2003 and published as a special issue of the *Review of Constitutional Studies* in 2004. At its inception, Prime Minister Chrétien was on the brink of retirement, his succession by Paul Martin was assured, and it seemed appropriate to engage in a sustained and critical reflection on the previous decade of Canadian politics. Of course, at that time the contributing authors were only beginning to hear the rumblings of what would eventually become the sponsorship scandal. The full articulation of that incident's impact on the Liberal Party and, indeed, on Prime Minister Chrétien's political legacy would not be fully manifested at least until the autumn of 2005 and, subsequently, not until after an ensuing federal election. The potential impact of Justice John Gomery's inquiry into the federal sponsorship program was such that we invited contributors to revisit their chapters to consider whether the Gomery report had any notable effect on their assessments of the Chrétien legacy in their chosen area of policy analysis. The current collection is thus a revised and updated set of analyses from those originally published in 2004.

In the wake of the January 2006 federal election, it is evident that the sponsorship scandal had a significant electoral impact on the Liberal party, though perhaps not as significant as some might have anticipated during the campaign. In the short term, it is clear that Paul Martin paid the biggest political price for the scandal, having had his prime ministerial dreams curtailed by a voting public that viewed his Liberal Party as more of what had come before. Yet in terms of Jean Chrétien's impact on

Canadian politics, the sponsorship scandal is unlikely to be the defining feature of his decade of leadership. As the chapters in this book elaborate, the political program of the Chrétien Liberals will have a far more lasting effect on the shape of Canadian governance and the future of public policy than the misuse of public funds in the promotion of the federal government's relevance to Québec. And even if Paul Martin's opportunity to put his prime ministerial stamp on Canada was short-lived, his tenure as Jean Chrétien's Minister of Finance will certainly be recorded as having implemented a sea change in the structure and processes of Canadian governance.

Despite Chrétien's well-documented preference for pragmatic and cautious policy-making over the articulation of a grand vision, thorough and far-reaching policy changes were enacted over his three terms of leadership. The chapters in this volume cut a wide swath through most of the policy areas in which these reforms and initiatives took place. The collection begins with Reg Whitaker's overview of the Chrétien governments, which argues that Chrétien's skills as a political broker will ultimately garner him a positive legacy. As Whitaker recounts, the absence of a narrow ideological agenda within the Liberal Party and the fracturing of the party system that accompanied the demise of the Progressive Conservatives created prime conditions for just the kind of leadership style that Chrétien embraced. Deficit-fighting through cost-cutting was undertaken out of a sense of necessity rather than a penchant for small government – a posture that Canadians found more palatable than grandiose but ultimately empty rhetoric.

Similarly, the Liberals' post-1993 embrace of NAFTA might also be assessed in terms of expediency. Chrétien's task on this front was, as Whitaker argues, to help Canadians come to terms with the new economic reality and to appreciate that Canada's position in the global economy was directly tied to its access to the North American market. Of course, striking the right balance in the narrower terms of the Canada-U.S. relationship is a perennial challenge for Canadian political leaders. For Chrétien, the challenges of the relationship were particularly acute in the aftermath of September 11, 2001. The need to retain economic access to U.S. markets required sensitivity and overt responsiveness to American security concerns. If joining the U.S. in a coalition invasion of Iraq was too much for Canada, participating in peace-making efforts in Afghanistan was a required compromise.

On the home front, Whitaker argues that, in general, Chrétien's interactions with the provinces had a similar tenor of shrewd expediency, thus forging a more amicable federalism than had been characteristic of his prime ministerial predecessors. The notable and important exception to this assessment lies with Chrétien's approach to post-referendum relations with Quebec. On this file, Chrétien abandoned pragmatism in favor of a much more forthright course of action. The secession reference, the Clarity Act, the policies incorporated within Plan A (carrot) and Plan B (stick), and perhaps a cyclical character to sovereignty's appeal all led to the restoration of support for federalism in Québec by the time Chrétien left office. Whether or not the sponsorship scandal and Justice Gomery's findings would set the sovereignty cycle on spin remained an open question even after the 2006 election.

The next five chapters might be conceptualized in terms of the significance of space and place during the Chrétien era. Robert Young examines the Chrétien legacy with regard to Québec and shares much of Whitaker's assessment. Having nearly "lost the country" in the 1995 referendum, Chrétien ended his prime ministerial tenure with support for sovereignty at 40 percent, more Liberal than BQ seats in the commons, and a 59 percent job approval rating from Quebecers. Young traces the developments on the Quebec file beginning with Chrétien's unwillingness to provide any incentives to Québec to increase the appeal of the federal option in the lead-up to the referendum and the opportunities this lack of action provided to sovereignists in framing their alternative vision for the Québec nation. Canada and Chrétien received a stay-of-execution, but the Prime Minister could not disregard the precipitous edge of the guillotine's cold blade. The course of action subsequently laid out to address future articulations of sovereigntist aspirations would attest to a remarkable strategic shift. Young concludes with a provocative, post-Gomery postscript, asserting that while Chrétien was responsible for the sponsorship program, responsibility for scandal might be judged to lie elsewhere.

Caroline Andrew considers the Chrétien government's urban policies. While noting failures in social housing and more positive developments with regard to infrastructure, Andrew argues that Liberal initiatives in the realm of postsecondary education are the most significant elements of the 1993–2003 policy agenda with regard to the vitality of Canada's urban spaces. Andrew begins her analysis by outlining broad trends affecting cities over the Chrétien tenure. These trends included increased urbanization, intensified polarization between and within cities, and the concentration of recent immigrants in Canada's largest metropolitan centres. Andrew's discussion of federal infrastructure funding points to divisions in focus between sewers and roads and support the development of a knowledge economy. Much of the investment in the latter realm has been channeled through postsecondary institutions under programs ranging from the 13 Canadian Institutes for Health Research, to Canada Research Chairs, to the Canada Foundation for Innovation. And while this funding has certainly affected the institutions through which it is channeled, it has also effected the urban centres in which postsecondary institutions are housed. Ultimately, Andrew concludes, Chrétien's urban legacy, like his legacy in many other areas, is a mixed bag, with many of the positive developments occurring more incidentally than as the direct objective of a considered urban policy.

The chapters by Christina Gabriel and Laura Macdonald, Stephen Clarkson and Erick Lachapelle, and Tom Keating consider the Chrétien legacy with regard to Canada's place in the world. Gabriel and MacDonald argue that Chrétien's approach to North American integration required a precarious balancing act in which Canadians' ambivalence towards their southern neighbour needed to be weighted against the Canadian economy's dependence on the U.S. market. During Chrétien's first two terms as Prime Minister, this balancing act was played out in the Liberals' decision to endorse NAFTA despite Red Book promises to renegotiate some of its key provisions, Lloyd Axworthy's successful negotiation of an international land mines treaty to which the U.S. did not become a signatory, and efforts to establish a "seamless border" between Canada and the U.S. Even attempts to foster stronger ties with Mexico were undertaken, at least in part, in an effort to counter U.S. power within the trilateral relationship. Nonetheless, historical and economic ties ensured that, from the Canadian perspective, the U.S.-Canada relationship would remain primary. Gabriel and Macdonald observe that the election of George W. Bush and the terrorist attacks of September 11, 2001 further intensified the "pragmatic ambivalence" with which the Chrétien government approached the U.S. Chrétien implemented security legislation that extended the power of the state into people's lives in unprecedented ways, in part because addressing U.S. security concerns was integral to maintaining the bilateral economic relationship. Nonetheless, Chrétien was unsupportive of the Bush doctrine and rejected the invitation to join a coalition invasion force for Iraq. Gabriel and Macdonald conclude that Chrétien's posture vis-à-vis its North American partners was less the product of the man and more a necessity produced by the contradictory forces of Canadian public opinion, international trade, and global security – forces that remain to challenge his successors.

Clarkson and Lachapelle's discussion focuses on the Canada-U.S. economic relationship under Chrétien's stewardship. They assess both the narrow economic indicators of the partnership as well as the broader implications of trade liberalization for Canada's culture and legal and political institutions. In examining the record of economic integration with regard to trade and investment, Clarkson and Lachapelle observe some positive benefits for Canada resulting from tariff reductions and currency devaluation, but note that the price of these benefits has been paid through increased reliance on a single market. With regard to foreign investment in Canada, post-NAFTA developments have seen a decrease in the rate of foreign direct investment in Canada, while Canadian investment in the U.S. has increased. The latter phenomenon, they argue, is, in fact, the result of the failure of the NAFTA to ensure secured access to the U.S. market, thus compelling Canadian firms to establish plants in the U.S. to shield themselves from U.S. protectionism. With regard to employment, after initial increases in the unemployment rate, the Canadian economy adjusted to the new reality of a continental marketplace. Nonetheless, they argue, the quality of jobs has generally declined and the promised parity with the American standard of living has not been delivered. In terms of social and cultural policy, Clarkson and Lachapelle note the strains that job losses placed on Canada's social programs and tax revenue, and remind us of the blow to Canada's efforts to protect its cultural sovereignty that was struck by the WTO in its response to a U.S. challenge to Canadian magazine policies. Similar disappointment is registered in the areas of labour and the environment. Despite the NAFTA side agreements negotiated by the Clinton administration, neither the North American Commission on Labour Co-operation nor the North American Commission for Environmental Co-operation have been able to counter NAFTA's primary logic of trade and investment. On balance, Clarkson and Lachapelle assert, Chrétien's legacy on trade is one of ongoing confusion and intensified vulnerability to the U.S. market.

Tom Keating's chapter engages Chrétien's foreign affairs legacy. As Keating notes, foreign policy scholars are divided in their assessments of the Chrétien era, with some claiming an activist tradition for at least part of his mandate, while others lament Canada's squandered reputation and collapsed integrity on the international stage. In Keating's assessment, however, Chrétien is best characterized as a passive internationalist. The chapter proceeds to consider the impact of high-profile international summits in compelling national leaders to articulate at least some sense of their global obligations. In this regard, Chrétien could be enticed to assert the need to protect human rights and promote human security, most notably in Africa, but for the most part, the inspiration for these claims would rarely compel his sustained attention. Further, while Chrétien supported the role of the United Nations in peacekeeping, Canada's financial and troop commitments to UN operations fell precipitously over the course of his mandate. More contradictions in the Chrétien foreign policy file can be found in the context of Canada-U.S. relations, which, as previous chapters argued, witnessed both a rhetorical distancing between the two countries and a simultaneous economic binding. Of course, Chrétien's trade initiatives were not solely focussed on the U.S. and North America, with the Team Canada missions to China, Latin America, and South Asia and the pursuit of a Free Trade Area of the Americas attesting to at least some interest in diversifying Canada's trade partnerships. Of course, Canada did engage in a number of significant international undertakings during Chrétien's decade in office. The establishment of the International Criminal Court, the land mines treaty, and participation in the NATO invasion of Kosovo are notable examples. Yet, as Keating argues, while much hype accompanied these initiatives, a steady and significant decrease in funding for Canada's international diplomatic and military capacity weakened the country's reputation among the community of nations.

The following six chapters consider the relationship between the Chrétien governments and the people they governed. Yasmeen Abu-Laban addresses immigration policy, arguing that over the course of Jean Chrétien's terms as Prime Minister, Canada became less open to newcomers. Evoking a neo-liberal policy rationale, ideal immigrants were increasingly described in terms of their capacity to integrate quickly into Canadian society, their self-sufficiency, and their lack of threat to continentalized formulations of security. The result, Abu-Laban argues, is that relative to other countries, Canada's immigration policies continue to uphold a humanitarian reputation, but contrasted to an ideal of openness or even the decades since the introduction of the point system in 1967, the immigration policy legacy of the Chrétien Liberal governments was one of growing exclusivity. Abu-Laban traces the effects of an emphasis on integration in the areas of settlement services and the Metropolis project. In the latter context, she observes that integration has become a key word of this multimillion dollar, multicentered research initiative. And while the use of the term appears to indicate an emphasis on inclusion, it has also tended to invoke a presumption that successful integration occurs when immigrants are largely indistinguishable from the dominant group. Integration thus becomes a near-synonym for assimilation. Abu-Laban then explores the Chrétien government's increased emphasis on attracting "self-sufficient" immigrants to Canada. This policy has been manifested through the reduced admission of family and refugee/humanitarian immigrant classes and increased numbers of independent/economic immigrants, the introduction of a right-of-landing fee, and increased emphasis on education and fluency in English and/or French in immigrant eligibility determination. The exclusivity trend in integration and immigration requirements was further exacerbated by the events of September 11, 2001. As other authors in this collection observe, Canada's primary concern in the wake of the attacks was to ensure access to the American market. As a result, Canada's humanitarianism took a further blow in an effort to address U.S. concerns regarding a perceived laxness of Canadian immigration controls.

Michael Murphy examines Chrétien's long involvement with Aboriginal policy, from his early days as Pierre Trudeau's Minister of Indian Affairs and the development of the 1969 White Paper on Indian policy through his tenure as Prime Minister. Murphy argues that, in the early period of his leadership, Chrétien supported a number of promising developments in Aboriginal-state relationships. His government subsequently retreated from these ambitious goals, pursuing the problematic *First Nations Governance Act* (FNGA) and, subsequently, efforts to improve the quality of life for Indigenous peoples. Upon election, the new Liberal government quickly moved to recognize the inherent right of Aboriginal self-government, not through renewing constitutional negotiations, but by asserting that this right had already existed under section 35 of the *Constitution Act, 1982*. The establishment of the Saskatchewan Treaty process and an official apology for the actions of past governments in their treatment of Indigenous peoples (from which the Prime Minister was absent) were also important initiatives. Yet, it was not long before these initial indications of a more promising terrain for the federal-Aboriginal relationship were reversed. The Chrétien Liberals delayed their response to the Mulroney-appointed Royal Commission on Aboriginal Peoples and ultimately rejected the Commissioners' recommendation that the report form the basis for subsequent developments in Aboriginal-state relationships. Federal rhetoric emphasized the need to look forward without looking back, a view that was then incorporated into the FNGA. In a repeat performance of the White Paper, the Prime Minister was again involved in an overhaul of the *Indian Act* and facing concerted opposition from its key constituents. An impossibly short period of consultation (rather than negotiation) with Indigenous peoples concerning their governance was a serious weakness in the process, as was the federal government's unwillingness to recognize the importance of practical sovereignty and Indigenous-led institutional reform. As with his predecessors, Chrétien was ultimately unwilling to cede federal sovereignty, rejecting the nation-to-nation formulation of the Aboriginal-state relationship, and hence losing a significant opportunity to improve the federal government's relationship to Indigenous peoples.

In assessing the impact of Chrétien era policies on women, Alexandra Dobrowolsky echoes the findings of most Canadian feminists – that the Liberals' consolidation of neo-liberal governance worsened the conditions of many women's lives while simultaneously making it more difficult for women to draw attention to the situation. Dobrowolsky notes that the negative consequences of neo-liberal policy-making were particularly intense during the deficit cutting period of Chrétien's first term in office. Subsequently, rhetoric and policy shifted from the language of cutbacks to social investment. Dobrowolsky examines illustrative institutions and policies in both periods and considers their effects on the relationship between social movement organizations and the state. The child care promises of the 1993 Red Book as well as the promise of a Social Security Review had encouraged feminists and social advocacy organizations that the Liberals would redress the stealthy demise of the welfare state that had been initiated by the Mulroney Conservatives. Instead, the Liberals promptly embraced the deficit-fighting agenda and any hopes for new programs quickly foundered. The institutions of "the women's state" were consolidated and the Canadian Advisory Council on the Status of Women was abolished with the likely result that the dramatically gendered impacts of the transformation of UI into Employment Insurance went unconsidered. Moreover, the restoration of the government's fiscal health did not bring these institutions back. Neo-liberalism had fundamentally transformed the understanding of the relationship between citizen and state. Hence, newly minted social investment programs emphasized education, innovation, health care, and children, focusing on future pay-offs and creating the conditions in which people could realize their potential. Children were a particular focus of attention, but any reflection on or awareness of the gendered dimensions of their care was markedly absent.

Michael Prince's assessment of Chrétien's social policy legacy focuses on the politics of public finance and its role in framing the Liberals' initiatives for families with children and intergovernmental programs for early learning and child care. As Prince observes, savvy political leaders tend to embrace support for social programs in the interest of acquiring votes, and this was certainly a Chrétien strategy. After the 1993 election, however, the Liberals' rapid shift to a deficit-fighting posture sapped much of the momentum propelling new social policy initiatives. Indeed, the Liberals' first substantive act in the social policy realm was the dramatic reduction in social and health care transfers to the provinces through the implementation of the Canada Health and Social Transfer (CHST). Once the country's finances were in surplus, the Liberals renewed social policy spending, but as Prince observes, these contributions were more about reparations than new investment. Important new policies were established, however, particularly around support for families with children. The creation of the Canada Child Tax Benefit, heralded at the time as the most important social policy development since medicare, involved an intergovernmental agreement (in which Québec did not participate) to augment the incomes of low-income families with children and to encourage labour market attachment among social assistance recipients. The Chrétien government also took a number of tentative steps towards increasing funding for child care and early learning, the most significant of which was the 2003 Early Learning and Child Care Services Initiative. This program was designed to funnel federal monies into child care centers, preschools, and nursery schools in order to increase spaces, reduce costs for low-income families, and improve the quality of care. As well, the specific needs of Aboriginal children also received some attention in this initiative. Thus, Prince concludes, while there are reasons to be critical of the Chrétien legacy in social policy, Chrétien's governments accomplished more than they have been credited for.

Gerard Boychuk examines the 1993–2003 period in health care policy and deems the outcome "the greatest missed opportunity" for Prime Minister Chrétien to make his mark. In Boychuk's estimation, federal initiatives in the health care field were motivated more by political gain than by a principled commitment to a universal public health care system. Although the Liberals proclaimed their support for the five principles of the *Canada Health Act* (CHA) in the 1993 election campaign and subsequently established the National Forum on Health to investigate the health of Canadians and their health care system, deficit fighting undermined these commitments. The implementation of the CHST in 1996 reduced the funding that the federal government transferred to the provinces and resulted in provincial efforts to recoup their losses through violations of the CHA. To its credit, the federal government rigorously defended the CHA and kept provincial privatization efforts at bay. In the 1997 campaign, the Liberals pledged to address funding shortfalls in primary care, home care, and prescription drugs. Again, however, the outcome fell well short of the promise, in part, because the provinces were unwilling to embark on new health care initiatives before previous funding levels were restored. Announcements and promises continued in the 2000 election, only to be followed by the appointment of the Royal Commission on the Future of Health Care in Canada (the Romanow Commission). The Senate Committee on Social Affairs, Science and Technology, headed by Michael Kirby, was engaged in a simultaneous and similar review of Canada's health care system and both reports were released in the fall of 2002. Boychuk observes that the reports were more similar than many had anticipated, with both of the investigations arguing for the retention of the CHA, greater accountability, and new programs to target issues such as catastrophic drug coverage and certain home care services. Responses to the recommendations were subsequently articulated in the 2003 and 2004 Health Care Renewal Accords which included, perhaps most significantly, a commitment to publicly and regularly report on the performance of provincial health care systems. As Boychuk concludes, the studies and agreements have certainly increased public knowledge of the health care system. Nonetheless, the fact that federal funding for health care declined by $26 billion over Chrétien's tenure offers the most profound and succinct articulation of the Chrétien health care legacy.

Kathy Brock analyzes policy developments concerning the voluntary or "third sector" during the Chrétien years. The role of community organizations in providing services for Canadians has always been important, but third sector organizations have become increasingly significant as governments have sought to reduce costs by either sharing responsibilities for public services with the nonprofit sector, or disengaging from service provision completely. Brock notes that the Liberals were attentive to these developments when they campaigned for office in 1993 and subsequently implemented a number of initiatives to define the relationships among the federal state, the for-profit sector, and third sector organizations. The most significant of these developments were the regularization of public consultations and the Voluntary Sector Initiative (VSI), which set out codes of practice for policy development and the receipt of public funding. Nonetheless, as Brock notes, the Liberals were less welcoming of advocacy groups (as distinct from service groups) and have ensured that charitable status is unavailable to community groups whose purposes are deemed "political." Such limits restrict many groups' activities, but this provision, along with regulations in Canada's post-9/11 anti-terrorism legislation, have had especially pernicious effects on Muslim and Arab community organizations. Since Chrétien's retirement, the fate of the VSI has come into some doubt. While nonprofit, community organizations will continue to make essential contributions to the well-being of Canadians, the extent to which these contributions receive federal government attention is not assured.

Ian Greene, David Docherty, and Steve Patten's contributions consider Jean Chrétien's impact on the institutional dimensions of Canadian politics. In the 1993 election campaign, part of the Liberal strategy was to remind voters of the ethical misdeeds of the Mulroney Conservatives and to promise to lead the country with integrity. According to at least one definitive account of the Chrétien Liberals' first term in office, this was not merely campaign ad copy but a deeply held commitment, certainly by Prime Minister Chrétien.[1] Nonetheless, Chrétien's governments did get ensnared in ethical quandaries, with the sponsorship debacle threatening to outstrip even Sir John A. MacDonald's Pacific scandal for the title of most spectacular example of bad judgment in Canadian political history. Ian Greene's chapter argues that many of the ethical lapses that befell the Chrétien government could have been avoided through the appointment of an independent ethics commissioner or the establishment of independent inquiries. Chrétien resisted this course of action, however, because he was unwilling to cede his own power to an unelected office and because some members of his caucus felt that this approach was too legalistic and potentially open to manipulation by political opponents. Moreover, Chrétien's commitment to old-style politics and patronage meant that he often judged a politician's efforts to manipulate the decisions of public agencies in favor of one's constituents as legitimate political activity. Greene makes his case by analyzing the responses to the ethical missteps taken by a series of ministers. Events ranging from the cancellation of the Pearson Airport privatization contract, the harsh treatment of anti-globalization protestors at the Vancouver meeting of APEC, Chrétien's efforts to secure a loan for the Auberge Grand-Mère, and the advertising contracts vetted through Public Works, describe a litany of offences for which stronger accountability measures are justly demanded. The fact that a variety of measures to ensure ethical conduct have been and continue to be established in the wake of these events can certainly be viewed as a product of the Chrétien era, though this is hardly a legacy of which one would be proud.

David Docherty argues that if Chrétien has a legacy in the area of parliamentary reform, it is the product of reaction against his style of leadership rather than the implementation of positive initiatives to increase the power and autonomy of Canada's parliamentarians. For Chrétien, personal loyalty and party discipline were the basic operating principles of government, and his expectations that these principles be respected were regularly reinforced. Legislation concerning gun control and limited compensation for people afflicted by Hepatitis C through tainted blood provide examples of his willingness to deploy the heavy hand of prime ministerial authority against internal party dissenters. As his tenure in office proceeded, however, the iron grip increasingly chafed. Indeed, by 2002 Chrétien had to resort to a threat to *remain* as Prime Minister if the party did not support his proposal for election finance reform. By the end of his tenure, Chrétien's "old school" approach to party discipline and parliamentary process had strengthened the desire for reform. The successful initiative by parliamentarians to elect committee chairs over the wishes of the Prime Minister demonstrates the force of that desire. Moreover, as Docherty asserts, this change in committee chair selection represents a procedural shift that will ensure a lasting increase in power for backbench and opposition MPs.

The scholarship on Canada's political parties has observed that the federal election of 1993 inaugurated a new party system in Canada. Of course, as Steve Patten argues, the Prime Minister bore no direct responsibility for the new terrain of party competition, but certainly the fragmented representation of a five-party Parliament was an important contributor to Chrétien's prime ministerial longevity. Patten explores three dimensions of the new party system: regionalization; the redefinition of the centre of ideological competition to market liberalism; and changes to party organization including leadership selection, the role of MPs in the House of Commons, and electoral financing. These changes had a profound effect on the way that Canadians were governed and in how they understood their relationship to the federal government. Patten observes that while Chrétien was elected as Prime Minister in a period when populism characterized party contestation in many provinces and was a central force in the Reform Party, it was the antithesis of Chrétien's leadership ethos. The little guy from Shawinigan could be trotted out as strategically necessary, but the Prime Minister's Office was firmly in control. With regard to political parties, then, an increased role for Parliamentarians and party finance reform were important, if not fully intended, outcomes of Chrétien's leadership.

"Incrementalist," "pragmatist," "agent of history," "as visionary as possible under the circumstances" – all of these assessments of Jean Chrétien's prime ministerial legacy can be found on the following pages. Perhaps this range of views reflects the precipitateness of the task, or perhaps the range of judgments is a testament to nature of the legacy itself. In any event, we hope that the collection will provide fodder for your own determinations.

Many people have contributed to the production of this book, both in its original form and its revision for McGill-Queen's University Press. First and foremost, we want to thank Judy Garber, the Executive Director of the Centre for Constitutional Studies at the University of Alberta, for her tireless efforts in organizing, compiling, and copy-editing the post-Gomery iteration of this collection. The work of Joan McGilvray of McGill-Queen's, Janna Promislow, Tsvi Kahana, Matt Woodley, Darin McKinley, Rahab Sharkawi, Margarete Daguela, Jennine Schreiber, and numerous anonymous reviewers is much appreciated, as is the support of Richard Bauman and the Management Board of the Centre for Constitutional Studies and the Alberta Law Foundation. We are, of course, very much indebted to the contributors of this volume. Their keen insights and deft analysis are the strength of the collection. And their unfailingly good humor in the face of Canada's changeable political weather has made the project much more manageable than we might have anticipated. Finally, we want to thank Curtis Clarke and Marcia Nelson – for all the other things.

NOTES

Associate Professor, Department of Political Science, University of Alberta.

1   Edward Greenspon and Anthony Wilson-Smith, *Double Vision: The Inside Story of the Liberals in Power* (Toronto: Doubleday, 1996).

THE CHRÉTIEN LEGACY

The Chrétien Legacy

REG WHITAKER

INTRODUCTION

When Jean Chrétien left office after more than a decade as Prime Minister, he left a distinctive legacy. His personal stamp on the country's consciousness will never match the extraordinary stature of his Liberal predecessor, Pierre Elliott Trudeau. Neither will it match the controversial memory of his Conservative predecessor, Brian Mulroney. Together, these three Quebecers dominated Canadian politics for over three and a half decades. Chrétien's tenure represents a kind of synthesis of the antinomies of the Trudeau and Mulroney years. Bearing a synthetic legacy, Chrétien's profile may be blander, less sharp-hewn. Nonetheless, his legacy may be as enduring.

RESTORING BROKERAGE: THE VITAL CENTRE

One way of summarizing Chrétien's record is to say that he restored what had once been a central element of Canadian politics: *brokerage*. By this I mean more than the brokerage model of political parties, although Chrétien's Liberals certainly match the specifications of this model (pragmatic, non-programmatic, aggregating and articulating inputs from outside the party system rather than defining issues from the inside out). I also mean brokerage as a method of governing, and of negotiating the boundaries between the state and civil society. Trudeau challenged brokerage on all fronts, pushing his party and the political system to test

their limits, which is why, in memory, he towers over other prime ministers, and why his death generated such a remarkable response. Mulroney
seemed, in contrast, to be the perfect brokerage politician, at home in the
practice of elite accommodation and the arts of backroom political dealing – constraints that Trudeau chafed at, and consistently evaded by
direct appeals to the public. Yet at the end of the day, Mulroney's was the
brokerage that failed; indeed, it failed so catastrophically that his own
party was shattered, until in 2004 it was merged, as junior partner, with
its old rival Reform/Alliance.

When Chrétien assumed office in 1993, the impact of that failed
Mulroney brokerage was evident everywhere. The "two-party plus"
system was gone, replaced by a new multiparty system with two new
programmatic, ideological parties that had arisen out of the ashes of the
Conservatives. A secessionist party formed the Official Opposition in
Parliament. Federalism had sustained two debilitating upheavals in the
failed Meech Lake and Charlottetown constitutional initiatives. Within
two years, the second referendum on Québec sovereignty would come
within a paper-thin margin of defeat. Despite the Conservative promise
of economic recovery through free trade and neo-liberal restructuring,
the federal government was far deeper in red ink than when Mulroney
had come to office, and the competitive performance of the Canadian
economy seemed on a downward trajectory. Less tangibly, but omi-
nously, the Canadian people were in a sour and disillusioned mood,
deeply distrustful of their elites, scornful of their institutions, quarrel-
some and divisive. Although the Liberals possessed a working majority,
their political challenge was unenviable. And Chrétien's leadership qualities were, at the outset, in doubt.

As Prime Minister, Chrétien lacked some of the basic communication
skills of his predecessors, certainly the intelligence and eloquence of Trudeau, and even the polished salesmanship of Mulroney. Throughout his
years in office, Chrétien has consistently failed to find the appropriate
words for the occasions when words are required of a leader. One would
have to hark back to the dour Alexander Mackenzie in the 1870s to find
a prime minister as resolutely prosaic in public utterance. His off-the-cuff
remarks are notoriously inarticulate in both official languages. One
searches in vain in his speeches for even hints of the expression of a vision
for the country.

On these counts, his leadership might seem wanting. Yet it has been his
special skill to turn these very flaws into strengths. After the wrenching
conflicts over the fundamentals of the political community from the

1960s through the 1980s, the country had grown weary and suspicious of big ideas and grand words. Change, real and threatened, had become too insistent, too unrelenting. Both Chrétien predecessors had been, in different ways, aggressive and articulate advocates of change. If Theodore Roosevelt used the U.S. Presidency as a bully pulpit from which to preach to the nation, Chrétien's predecessors had similarly exploited the office of Prime Minister. But there were limits to the tolerance of Canadians for being lectured. After 1993, the absence of eloquence, even the very uneasiness with words, struck a sympathetic chord.

Chrétien's leadership tended to be relatively low-key, low-profile, and *managerial* in a manner not seen since the St. Laurent governments of the 1950s. This style was generally welcomed with relief after the hot-button, high-anxiety politics of the preceding years. When he did get into trouble, it was usually when he uncharacteristically said too much. Very occasionally, he sustained criticism for saying too little, too ineptly, when it seemed that words were unavoidably required to reassure and give clear voice to an anxious and confused public, as after the September 11 terrorist attacks in 2001, or during the great Ontario power blackout in August 2003. This is simply the inescapable downside of his greatest strength: his unease with words masks an *instinctive* approach to political leadership, and his instincts have, by and large, served him well. His instincts certainly kept him on the right side of public opinion, or so ten years of polling and three majority governments would strongly suggest. By neither challenging nor threatening the public, he saved himself and his party much grief sustained by Trudeau and Mulroney. Despite appearances, this did not always mean lack of leadership. Rather, it was a way of assuring that change was assimilated more effectively than through confrontation and division.

ECONOMIC LIBERALISM:
LEADING FROM THE RIGHT

Take the most outstanding achievement of the Chrétien government, the restoration of fiscal balance to federal finances, and the turnaround of the Canadian economy. The changes in ten years have been dramatic. In his last year in office, the former Prime Minister presided over what, by many measures, is the strongest performing economy in the G-8, with the healthiest current surplus, the best record in job creation, rising productivity, a strengthened currency. In the early 1990s, the *Wall Street Journal* declared Canada a fiscal basket ease, about to sink into Third World status. Today, seven years of steady surpluses and debt reduction in Canada stand in startling contrast to the red sea of borrowing in the U.S., with a $500 billion (US) deficit in 2003 and much more yet projected in future years. Moreover, the Canadian job creation record stands in sharp contrast to the shrinkage of U.S. employment under the George W. Bush administration. Even when the SARS outbreak, the mad cow scare, the rapid appreciation of the Canadian dollar, and the drag exerted by a sluggish U.S. economy combined in mid-2003 to force a sudden downturn in the Canadian economy, the government prudently maintained enough cushion to buffer the worst effects.

During Chrétien's tenure, political credit for this transformation of Canada from an image of socialist spendthrift to that of stern and efficient guardian of fiscal probity went mainly into the swollen account of his Finance Minister, Paul Martin, rather than to the Prime Minister, much to the latter's discomfort and irritation.[1] I shall return later to the Chrétien-Martin imbroglio, itself an important, even defining moment in the Chrétien years. For now, the important point is that, as Prime Minister, Chrétien was, for the most part, content to give his finance minister enough free rein to develop a distinctive fiscal policy, provide the appropriate tools to achieve the goals set, insist on the highest priority for these goals, and then let the political credit go to the minister, and thus to the party and the government more generally. This was, indeed, the general style in which Chrétien ran his Cabinet, despite the image he and the PMO have gained for excessive centralization of authority and decision making. Chrétien cut his ministers considerable slack. Some, like Brian Tobin, burned brightly for a time and then flamed out. Others, like Allan Rock, proved too accident-prone to endure as potential alternatives to Chrétien's own leadership. A few proved downright embarrassing, and these the Prime Minister was notably slow to remove. Others, certainly Martin, and his successor in the finance portfolio, John Manley, were able to carry the balls thrown them pretty far.

Although Chrétien may have ultimately regretted the scope he provided Martin, this style of prime ministerial leadership on the fiscal and economic front is not without significance. Brian Mulroney had taken on the role of front-line public policy innovator with an ideological commitment to the neo-liberal restructuring of Canada, replacing politics with markets, first by downsizing the national government through spending restraint, privatization, and deregulation, and downloading responsibilities from the federal to the provincial level; and second, by locking Canada into a wider trading arrangement that would free continental market forces from national policy constraints. Mulroney and his ministers never ducked from vivid rhetorical assertions of their intentions, but this ideological marking generated unanticipated negative consequences. Conservative economic policies were signaled as forming incremental parts of a larger pattern, which many critics viewed as following a Reaganite or Thatcherite neo-liberal agenda for subordinating the public sector to market forces. This fostered widespread mistrust about a "hidden" agenda and inspired opposition not only from those directly affected by particular policies, but from others who feared they might be targeted next, or further down the road. Generalized mistrust was particularly evident when structural change was on offer, whether the Canada-U.S. Free Trade Agreement or the Meech Lake constitutional accord. Rewriting the fundamental rules of the game, whether of North American economic relations or of federalism, raised mistrust to unprecedented levels when there was little confidence that the stated policy objectives were the "real" objectives. Provincial neo-liberal restructuring projects couched in similar ideological form, like those of the Mike Harris Tories in Ontario after 1995 and the Gordon Campbell Liberals in British Columbia after 2001, have similarly run into deep divisions, and provoked counterproductively strident extra-parliamentary opposition.

Unlike the Harris "Common Sense Revolution," the Mulroney neo-liberal project, while strong on rhetorical formulation, was weak on consistency and follow-through. This was the worst of all possible worlds: while fostering sometimes disproportionate distrust among potential sources of opposition, Mulroney's governments failed to satisfy potential supporters and sympathizers that they could produce results. The rapid rise of the Reform Party across the west in the early 1990s, culminating in its displacement of the Conservatives west of the Manitoba-Ontario border in the 1993 election, was the price exacted for Mulroney's neo-liberal rhetorical posturing. Overwhelmingly, right-wing westerners opted for a party that promised not to equivocate in implementing its neo-liberal doctrine. The Tory brokerage had failed in the west, leaving the federal fiscal problem unresolved, but at the top of the agenda of its Liberal successor.

The Chrétien-Martin fiscal regime after 1993 responded to this crisis/opportunity with subtlety and cunning. It seized the opening offered by the relative success of Reform, and the consequent rightward shift of the policy spectrum, to implement a tough deficit-elimination strategy that relied primarily on stiff reductions in government staffing and programs, and on off-loading health and education costs onto the provinces (the

1995 Canada Health and Social Transfer, or CHST). When the Finance Minister introduced the CHST as well as various cutbacks to federal programs, he was able to herd the Reform MPs in front of him like human shields. The Bloc Québecois could be expected to react negatively to shifting the fiscal burden onto the provinces, but since the BQ is a separatist party, such criticism had little resonance in the rest of Canada. The marginalization of the NDP meant that the Liberals' left flank could be left largely unprotected, at least until the fiscal situation was under control.

Significantly, the Liberals went about their business in a low-key, low-profile manner, deliberately eschewing the ideological rhetoric of their predecessors. Making no claims to a broader neo-liberal vision, downplaying the ideological antinomies of "markets" versus "politics," and avoiding rhetorical attacks on "big government" and exhortations to "free" enterprise, the Liberals instead focused on practical results. There was a distinct lowering of suspicions regarding hidden agendas, and when results were positive – as they were by 1997 with a surplus declared in the federal books – the Liberals benefited from an image of sound managerial competence, rather than any off-putting ideological triumphalism. The Liberals' post-deficit strategy since 1997 followed the same pragmatic, managerial lines. While Reform and the Conservatives on the right demanded tax cuts, the NDP on the left insisted upon new social spending, and the BQ wanted any surplus transferred to the provinces (i.e., Québec), each reflecting a distinct ideological position; the Liberals have opted instead for a balance between tax cuts, spending, and debt retirement – a classic brokerage compromise as befits a resolutely centrist party. In practice, they may not always have been able to maintain the three elements in balance, but the principle is clear, and telling. The success of this strategy was shown in the remarkable popularity during this period of Paul Martin, a cost-cutting minister managing a wrenching national readjustment, who quickly surpassed his Prime Minister in stature to become an heir apparent sufficiently powerful to force his leader into retirement. Chrétien could not be expected to appreciate the irony, but his displacement by his former finance minister is a tribute to his own fiscal stewardship.

EMBRACING GLOBALIZATION

In economic policy, the other major thrust during Chrétien's tenure has been the advancement of the economic globalization agenda via NAFTA, the project for a Free Trade Agreement of the Americas, and the broader framework of the G-8, WTO, etc. Given the memorable confrontation of Brian Mulroney by John Turner over the Canada-U.S. Free Trade Agreement in the 1988 election, the conversion of the Liberals to enthusiastic free traders requires some comment. The dexterity with which Liberals shift positions is always a source of wonder. However, although in this case the lack of any clearly articulated and attractive alternative to trade liberalization, whether to the left or the right of the Liberals, made it relatively easy for the Chrétien government to assume the free trade garb of its predecessors with remarkably little fuss or even notice. Timing was an all-important asset for Chrétien. What had appeared as novel and threatening in 1988 soon became the accepted order of things. In the 1988 election, a majority of voters supported the two parties, Liberal and NDP, that opposed the agreement. In 2003, an Ipsos/Reid poll indicated 70 percent support for NAFTA, with majorities in favour in all regions, and strongest support among the youngest group, those between eighteen and thirty-four. Twice as many believed that NAFTA had benefited Canada as believed it had hurt. Sixty-nine percent agreed that drawing the Canadian and American economies closer is a good thing (80 percent of those under the age of thirty-five).[2] There are two ways of looking at this shift in opinion in relation to the parallel shift in the Liberal view of free trade. One is simply to view the Liberals as bending to the prevailing winds. The other is to recognize the subtle interaction between government policy and public opinion, and to suggest that the Chrétien government effectively managed the transition from fear of the unknown to acceptance. Again, the low-key, relatively non-ideological manner in which Chrétien and his ministers have handled the free trade file has had something to do with this relatively smooth transition.

The emergence of articulate and impassioned "anti-globalization" movements, along with tense confrontations surrounding the 2001 Québec City and 2002 Kananaskis free trade summits, have created a new political dynamic around issues of Canada's economic relationship with the world. But Chrétien chose to play the role of traditional Pearsonian "liberal," rather than neo-liberal, statesman in international negotiations (as with his championing of the New Partnership for Africa's Development (NEPAD) project at the Kananaskis G-8 summit). In this, he could count on far more domestic support than the protesters who claim to speak for "civil society" in denouncing globalization.[3]

A serious problem for Chrétien in his third term in office was strained relations with the U.S. administration of George W. Bush, which will be examined later in more detail. Personalities do play a part in relations between national leaders, and there is no doubt that Chrétien got along much better on a personal basis with former president Bill Clinton than he did with George W. Bush (and no doubt that Liberal governments have generally had better relations with Democratic than Republican administrations). But strains in Canadian-American economic relations are more structural than personality related, and they persist despite the new "economic constitution of North America," in Ronald Reagan's words. Festering sores in the fabric of "free trade," of which the imposition of crippling duties on softwood lumber exports by the American lumber lobby is only the most egregious example, predate the Bush administration, as does narrowly parochial and bipartisan protectionist sentiment in Congress. Management of the Canadian-American dimension is one of the primary responsibilities of a Canadian prime minister, requiring not only the requisite diplomatic and political skills, but an ability to negotiate an always difficult, and never completed, safe passage between the defence of Canadian interests and sovereignty, on the one hand, and the necessity of compromise and concession to a much more powerful and influential partner, on the other.

Chrétien has been criticized from both the right and left, by both the continentalists and nationalists, for his management of Canadian-American relations within the NAFTA framework – for diametrically opposite reasons. While it would be too facile to conclude that he must have been doing something right to set off critics on both sides, it is appropriate to note that criticism of Mulroney on this score came from one direction only, from those concerned that he had willingly participated in the erosion of Canadian sovereignty. There was never any significant criticism of Mulroney's continentalism from the right. Chrétien's more ambiguous record may or may not be defensible in the longer view, but it is in keeping with the fundamental character of his leadership: the search for a middle way to broaden consensus and blunt rather than sharpen differences. In managing relations with the Americans, this kind of brokerage is inherently complex, involving tradeoffs between buying peace with the Americans and protecting vital Canadian interests. Chrétien may not have satisfied policy partisans on either side, but it is undoubtedly the case that he has built a broad popular consensus around his approach. That this has infuriated his critics on both left and right is a tribute to his brokerage skills, although not necessarily to his perspicacity in policy.

THE COMPETITIVENESS AGENDA

Another aspect of the Liberal acceptance of globalization is their "competitiveness" agenda. Too often, in the hands of neo-liberal governments, global competitiveness has been the pretext for a wholesale assault on social programs and the public sector more generally. The Chrétien government is scarcely innocent of this charge, especially during the first term attack on the deficit through cutting federal spending and federal transfers to the provinces under the CHST. However, the competitiveness agenda over which Chrétien presided has more than one face. A less neo-liberal face is the stress on the use of the federal government to promote research and development, especially in the "new economy" sectors, and on education as a key competitive resource. The latter theme has led to a series of important federal initiatives in direct support of university teaching and research. Beginning with the Millennium Scholarship Fund for undergraduate studies, and continuing with the Trudeau Scholarship program for graduate studies, the Liberals have circumvented the problem of provincial jurisdiction over education by direct payments to students to spend at universities of their own choice. Federal initiatives supporting university-based research include the Canada Research Chairs Program with $900 million to support the establishment of 2,000 of these positions at universities across the country by 2005; the Canada Foundation for Innovation, an independent corporation designed to strengthen the research and technology development capability of Canadian universities, colleges, research hospitals, and other not-for-profit institutions; and the Canadian Institutes of Health Research, which funds health research and health research trainees.[4] These initiatives have similarly evaded jurisdictional traps while making a major mark in reallocation of resources toward research promotion. The university research community has been appreciative: in an unusual show of gratitude, the research community hosted a dinner in honour of Chrétien shortly after his announced plan for retirement. In the long run, this may constitute one of the most important parts of Chrétien's legacy to Canada, the effects being mainly felt long after he has departed the scene.

NON-CONFRONTATIONAL FEDERALISM

Apart from the substance of this series of policy initiatives, what is equally significant is the relatively non-confrontational way in which an enhanced federal role in a largely provincial jurisdiction has been accomplished. Another area considered of prime importance in regard to competitiveness, manpower training, had been the object of bitter provincial complaints, especially from Québec nationalists, about the federal government elbowing them out of their proper jurisdiction. Despite initial obstinacy about permitting constitutional transfer of manpower training to the provinces, Chrétien changed course after 1995 and agreed to do just that, opening the federal government to a series of negotiations with each province on the transfer of jurisdiction. Amidst another round of abrasive conflict with the sovereigntists in Québec, Chrétien could nonetheless accommodate swift passage through Parliament of a constitutional amendment on the secularization of Québec schools (along with a similar amendment regarding Newfoundland).

In one important sense, federalism under Chrétien has been less than accommodative. The decision to put the federal books back in balance, in part via the instrument of the CHST, and the off-loading to the provinces of many of the costs of the welfare state imposed considerable burdens on the provinces. This was not confrontational federalism in the old sense of Ottawa imposing policy directions on the provincial capitals. Indeed, the areas in question – health care and post-secondary education – were clearly within provincial jurisdiction. The provinces, of course, wanted policy control but also wanted Ottawa to pay. The fact that the wealthier provinces, particularly Alberta and Ontario, had sharply cut provincial tax rates according to their own neo-liberal programs did not make their finger-pointing at Ottawa very plausible, an observation that Chrétien rarely passed up an opportunity to make. In any event, some of the damage done by the CHST has been recouped by post-surplus health care transfers, and by Ottawa's movement into the higher education field without challenging jurisdictional prerogatives. Nonetheless, there is a long-term cumulative problem of a social deficit, especially in the poorer provinces, for which Chrétien's governments cannot escape shared responsibility.

Chrétien, it is true, had abrasive relations with certain provincial premiers: notably Ontario's Mike Harris, who retired in 2002; occasionally Alberta's Ralph Klein; and, of course, always with PQ premiers in Québec until the PQ's defeat in 2003. Yet the general practice of federal-provincial relations was less volatile than in the tumultuous years under Trudeau and Mulroney. To be sure, Chrétien eschewed the constitutional agenda of his predecessors, and his governments generally avoided bold policy initiatives, at least until his last year and a half in office. There was consequently less ground for triggering provincial antagonisms. It may be said of Chrétien's tenure that intergovernmental relations returned somewhat to business as usual after the high-risk, rolling-the-dice days of the 1970s, 1980s, and early 1990s. This is evident in the field of social policy, always a jurisdictional battleground in the past between provincial responsibility and the federal spending power. The Social Union Framework Agreement signed in 1999 by all the provinces, save Québec, prevents the federal government from launching any national social policy initiatives, either cost-shared or block-funded, without prior consultation and agreement of a majority of provinces. As a leading student of social policy, Michael Prince, concluded near the end of Chrétien's leadership, the Chrétien Liberals abandoned "big bang" innovations for "directed incrementalism" – a middle-level approach to reform, stressing step-by-step advances on the basis of consensus, and thus avoiding charges of returning to the free-spending interventionism of old. "[C]hasing grand social visions," Prince wrote, "has never been the style of Prime Minister Chrétien, who has been more appropriately characterized as the ultimate step-by-step pragmatist."[5]

The Romanow Report (which Chrétien commissioned) and the high priority placed on "fixing" the health care system by both voters and politicians of all political stripes presented Chrétien with a serious challenge to incrementalism, and to co-operation with provinces willing to test national standards and the *Canada Health Act* by privatizing parts of healthcare delivery. Chrétien's conciliatory instincts in accommodating provincial preferences quickly drew fire from strong advocates of the Romanow recommendations. Whatever the outcome, the treatment of the health care system under Chrétien's watch was a much more brokered affair than was the "big bang" federal initiative of pushing the provinces into Medicare under Pearson and imposing national standards backed by the sanction of withdrawn federal funding with the *Canada Health Act* under Trudeau.

There have been two major exceptions to Chrétien's inclination to seek conciliation and consensus with the provinces (setting aside the sound and fury of Mike Harris's anti-Ottawa rhetoric and tit-for-tat Liberal ripostes, none of which signified much of substance). One was Chrétien's handling of the sovereigntist threat from Québec, which I will examine next. The other was the decision to implement the Kyoto Accord on climate change against the belligerent opposition of Alberta's Ralph Klein. The Kyoto battle was redolent of the acrimonious energy disputes between Trudeau and Lougheed and Getty governments in the 1970s and 1980s. By imposing Kyoto on an unwilling Alberta, Chrétien raised, once again, the dread spectre of the long-defunct and discredited National Energy Program, with no shortage of Alberta politicians ready and willing to invoke that spectre, with or without substantive provocation. Chrétien nonetheless braved this attack, despite the damage Kyoto might inflict on his party's future prospects in Alberta.

To be sure, a decision on Kyoto could not be ducked. The federal government had to either ratify or not ratify. The fact that the Bush administration had rejected Kyoto might have weighed even more strongly than Alberta's opposition, given concerns about maintaining Canadian industrial competitiveness in North America. But scientific opinion was strongly arrayed in favour of Kyoto, and Canadian, and Liberal, attachment to multilateralism as the foundation of good global governance, rendered a non-compliant "made-in-Canada" response to global warming an unattractive policy instrument. Perhaps more telling yet was the evidence of public opinion surveys, which showed majority support for Kyoto everywhere across Canada – save Alberta, where negative opinion was to harden following the Alberta government's campaign against ratification. The PQ government in Québec was vociferously in favour of ratification, thus providing Chrétien with an unusual but welcome ally. Although Ottawa seemed singularly ill-prepared to assess the costs of Kyoto, or even to have a clear plan for implementation, it went ahead. In so doing, the government won the admiration of environmentalists who had previously been critical of the Liberals' record in this area. (Chrétien also launched an ambitious extension of national parks, consolidating his "green" record, something that had seemed unlikely in his first two terms.) In a final ironic touch to an ill-informed and confused debate, just a few months after ratification, Klein, who had previously described Kyoto as nothing less than "the most devastating thing that has ever been contemplated by a Canadian government in the history of this country," dropped his concerns, concluding that Kyoto was not "much of a factor" in Alberta's energy plans after all.[6]

ASSERTING CLARITY IN THE SOVEREIGNTY CHALLENGE

If Kyoto pitted Ottawa against Alberta, with Québec as ally, Chrétien had earlier faced, and ultimately survived, a far more formidable challenge to federalism from Québec. From the beginning of his tenure, Chrétien had to contend with the BQ as the majority party of francophone Québec. A year after assuming office, his Québec difficulties were further compounded with the return of the PQ to power in Québec City, and in 1995, he suffered the humiliation of a near-defeat for federalism in the second sovereignty referendum. This was the lowest point of Chrétien's years in office. From the last couple of weeks of the referendum campaign when panic set into the No camp, through the confused aftermath in 1996, Chrétien and his government seemed disoriented, flailing about with various ineffectual options for winning Québec back. There were editorial calls for Chrétien's resignation, and a grim sense within Liberal ranks that Québec, Chrétien's native province, was their potential Achilles' Heel.[7] Yet by 2003, the PQ was out of office in Québec, replaced by a Québec Liberal Party firmly rededicated to federalism. The threat of sovereignty had receded, apparently almost to the vanishing point. The BQ was on the ropes, facing the prospect of marginalization and irrelevance. And Chrétien, long despised by the Québec political and intellectual class, was basking in the approval of the Québec electorate in his last days in office. How this remarkable reversal of fortunes for Chrétien and for federalism came about is a fascinating story in strategic political planning and leadership. For once, Chrétien abandoned his Mackenzie King-like caution and circumspection and instead set out on a bold gamble, à la his political mentor, Pierre Elliott Trudeau.[8] By winning this gamble, Chrétien helped change the direction of Canadian politics, and he made his historical mark among prime ministers.

In the immediate aftermath of the 1995 referendum, there were two broad options open to the federal government. The so-called "Plan A" was to continue yet again down the path that had been followed, in fits and starts, for three decades: that of seeking a general constitutional settlement that contained enough concessions to Québec nationalism to undermine the sovereigntists, while not alienating the rest of Canada. The problem was that Plan A described Meech Lake, which had secured initial unanimous agreement at the governmental level but provoked rejection in the wider English Canadian and Aboriginal communities. Following the further failure of Charlottetown in 1992, there was a general appreciation that Plan A meant gridlock.

The Meech and Charlottetown fiascos, combined with the abrasive impact of the 1995 Québec referendum, signaled a Canadian reality quite different than that envisaged in the Plan A/National Unity orthodoxy that had gripped the national political scene from Pearson through Mulroney. The English Canadian majority was no longer willing to contemplate constitutional concessions to a Québec nationalism whose

dominant voice was secessionist. From Jean Lesage through Robert
Bourassa, Québec federalist/nationalists had sought to play the separatist card as a threat that might serve to advance their dualist constitutional
program. Union Nationale Premier Daniel Johnson enunciated the strategy bluntly in the title of his 1965 book, *Égalité ou indépendance*.[9] After
Meech Lake, the late professor Léon Dion was blunter yet when he spoke
of Québec negotiating with a "knife at the throat" of English Canada.
With the PQ itself in power from 1976 to 1985, and 1994 to 2003, the
message to the rest of Canada was stark: sovereignty – in effect, an
anti-federalist Plan B for Québec alone – was the PQ's negotiating position. Increasingly, English Canadians, especially in the west, were asking
how a federal Plan A could work in any negotiation with sovereigntists
(or those willing to use sovereignty as a threat to induce concessions).
Why make concessions to save federalism if the ultimate goal of those
making the demands was secession? The idea of a federal Plan B was
born out of disillusion with the years of Plan A failure. Chrétien seized
this moment to rewrite the hitherto sacrosanct national unity position of
successive federal governments.

Here, as in fiscal policy, Chrétien borrowed – or stole, according
to one's perspective – from the ideas of the Reform party. That party,
in its first two elections, in 1993 and 1997, had gained a reputation
as "anti-Québec." While it sometimes gave that strong impression, as
with its notorious advertisement in Ontario in 1997 targeting Québec
politicians, what Reform actually said on the Québec/Canada question
was in fact more nuanced, and far less divisive, than its detractors
claimed. Reform was the first federal party to broach the idea of Québec
separation as a legitimate option. Reform's strategic plan for dealing
with this option was two-track federalism: one track if Québec stayed
and was willing to participate as one province among others, and another track if Québec were to opt for exit. Reform had a Plan B, and
English Canadians were beginning to recognize the need for just such a
plan.

To move on this front, Chrétien had to break with a long-standing
taboo of national unity orthodoxy and Liberal Party faith. It had long
been held that the federal government must never recognize that Québec
sovereignty was a real option – that to speak of such an outcome was to
create a self-fulfilling prophecy. In the 1997 election campaign, Jean
Charest, then national Conservative leader, referred to a potential secession as a "black hole," which must not be examined in advance, lest
it lose its frightening, thus discouraging, aura. All federal parties had, in

effect, tacitly endorsed Québec's abstract "right to national self-determination" simply by dint of awaiting the results of both Québec referenda before enunciating their idea of an appropriate federal response. But *de facto* recognition of the potential right to secede did not translate into any coherent Plan B to respond to a secessionist vote. Moreover, Chrétien could see very real dangers in the advance preparation of any detailed Plan B. Preparing an "English Canadian" response to a possible secession vote could open up precisely the same constitutional can of worms as Meech and Charlottetown had opened, raising all the uncomfortable questions of who spoke for the rest of Canada, and what voice would be given to provinces, First Nations, and all the other players who had wanted to get to the table for constitutional negotiations. The Chrétien Liberals were able to devise a strategy that elegantly avoided these pitfalls, while carving out a position that was distinctive in relation to their predecessors, whether Conservative or Liberal.

The Chrétien strategy began with the Supreme Court reference on secession initiated by the federal Justice Minister in September 1996.[10] The reference to the Court was by no means risk avoidance. No one could confidently predict how the justices would rule on the questions of unilateral secession and the possible conflict between national and international law. Moreover, the sovereigntists initially threatened dire consequences for federalism as a result of submitting the issue of sovereignty to a Supreme Court on which Québec judges were a minority, promising to discredit any opinion of this court as illegitimate in the eyes of Québec.

When the decision did come, it caught most of the sovereigntists off-guard, since the Court actually seemed to endorse Québec's right to national self-determination. Quickly switching gears, sovereigntists began pointing to the reference decision as a direction to Ottawa to negotiate secession after a Yes victory in a referendum. They failed to note that the Court's subtle reasoning was double-edged. Certainly a clear majority on a clear question in a democratic referendum entailed an obligation on the rest of Canada to enter into good-faith negotiations on secession. This left open the political question of what exactly would constitute a "clear" majority and a "clear" question. The crucial element in the Court's reasoning was that if the rest of Canada were under an obligation to recognize the legitimacy of a democratic mandate for secession of a part of the federation, so too sovereigntists would have to recognize that the rest of the country had an equally legitimate interest in the break-up of the federation. Unilateral secession was unacceptable.

Using this decision as a springboard, Chrétien boldly took on the
responsibility of passing federal legislation to spell out the rules for a vote
that would trigger negotiations on secession. The word "boldly" is used
here to describe very un-Chrétien behaviour of moving to seize and
define an issue in advance, rather than simply managing the crisis. It also
refers to the degree to which, on this issue, Chrétien found himself well
out in front of his party, and even some of his frontbench, including fel-
low Quebecer Paul Martin, who worried that a reckless approach would
needlessly antagonize Québec, and even provoke the so-called "winning
conditions" for the sovereigntists. All shades of opinion in Québec,
including the Québec Liberal Party, were hostile to any federal initiative
in this area. Chrétien brushed aside these qualms, gambling that he
understood Québec better than his critics.

The *Clarity Act* is a remarkable piece of legislation. It recognizes Québec's right to national self-determination, and its potential for secession
from the federation, if certain conditions are met. This is the first time that
a western democracy has formally admitted the right of a province to
secede peacefully – it should not be forgotten that the United States once
fought a bloody civil war to prevent such an outcome. On the other hand,
Québec's obligations with regard to securing a mandate for secession are
also spelled out. The referendum question must refer to Quebecers' will to
become a sovereign nation, with the issue not muddied by asking for a
mere mandate to negotiate, or offering sovereignty-association, partnership, or any other arrangement that would have to be separately negotiated with the other party. A clear majority is not spelled out precisely, but
it must be more than 50 percent plus one. The federal Parliament will
decide if the referendum question and result meet the tests. Moreover, any
negotiations must address the "division of assets and liabilities, any
changes to the borders of the province, the rights, interests and territorial
claims of the Aboriginal peoples of Canada, and the protection of minority
rights."[11] While these conditions by no means rule out negotiations culminating in lawful secession, the *Clarity Act* does insist that negotiations cannot be on terms dictated by the secessionists alone.

Politically, the *Clarity Act* was a master stroke in English Canada. The
Reform party took a look at the polls in western Canada and quickly
abandoned its initial opposition to sign on to what was, in any event, a
version of its own long-held position on the need for a Plan B. The NDP
grudgingly lined up. The Conservatives were split, as leader Joe Clark
and his handful of Québec MPs were opposed but the majority of Tory
MPs supported the bill. Chrétien had a consensus in English Canada.

It was the reaction in Québec that was critical. The angry backlash that had been threatened by the PQ and BQ never materialized. Québec francophone opinion, apart from the committed sovereignist partisans, was surprisingly calm, perhaps even indifferent. The PQ had earlier been re-elected to a second term in 1998, although it had actually gained slightly less of the popular vote than the Liberals. There was, however, no serious talk of another referendum, and the fortunes of the sovereigntists began to slide inexorably. The BQ lost ground to the Chrétien Liberals in the 2000 federal election, and the PQ was turned out of office in 2003 by the Liberals under Jean Charest, a former national party leader and an avowed federalist who, unlike his Liberal predecessors, refuses to use the threat of sovereignty as a bargaining chip. The decline of sovereignty may be cyclical, and it would be a stretch to attribute its current recession to the *Clarity Act* alone. Yet Chrétien called the sovereigntists' bluff, and he won. He had faced a near-death experience in 1995 and come out at the end of his tenure with the Québec situation fundamentally altered in favour of federalism. And he had done this while showing reasonable flexibility in managing the existing constitution, avoiding altogether opening up another round of mega-constitutional change. This is not as exciting a record as Trudeau's divisive patriation, or Mulroney's doomed rolls of the dice, but it is no mean accomplishment. Moreover, it required some courage and daring on Chrétien's part, qualities not usually associated with his political style.

SOCIAL LIBERALISM:
LEADING FROM THE LEFT

On economic policy and on Québec, Chrétien's brokerage style extended to opening up toward Reform/Alliance ideas and settling consensus on the centre-right of the spectrum. Yet Chrétien's critics on the left who have labeled his governments as simply right-wing or reactionary have failed to appreciate the subtlety – some might call it deviousness – of Liberal centrism. If Chrétien appropriated the fiscal conservatism of Reform/Alliance, thereby blunting the threat to the Liberals' right flank, there was another strain of conservatism in the new party that Chrétien was happy, indeed eager, to confront and challenge at every opportunity, to the significant political benefit of the Liberal Party. Social conservatism, stressing a Christian evangelical "family values cultural war against abortion, homosexuality, multiculturalism," and a generally "permissive" society, has been prominent in American politics for many years.

Some of the impetus toward the formation of the Reform party arose from an angry sense of exclusion from the political mainstream felt by social conservatives, directed as much at the Mulroney Tories as at the Liberals, and the desire to gain their own voice. But social conservative ideas are not only unusable by a national government committed, under the *Canadian Charter of Rights and Freedoms*, to equality among groups, but they are deeply divisive in a Canadian society now thoroughly liberal. Indeed, social conservatism turned out to be a cause for disunity on the right between the Reform/Alliance and the more socially liberal Progressive Conservatives. After merger of the two parties, continuing attachment to social conservative principles has limited the new Conservative Party's growth potential outside its core Alberta base.

Despite the presence of a small, but voluble, family-values minority in the Liberal caucus, Chrétien's Liberals have gone out of their way to highlight their differences with social conservatives and to play upon the divisions the evangelical fringe fosters among those on the right. Chrétien has been happy to depict his party as combatants on the liberal side in the cultural war.[12] In their first term, they responded to the furor set off by the massacre on 6 December 1989 of fourteen women at the École Polytechnique in Montreal by devising the National Gun Registry. The Registry has much later come under attack for its ballooning cost – itself a serious blow to the Liberal image of sound managerial competence – but it should be understood in the political context of the time. Explicitly justified in near-feminist language, gun control was presented as progressive social policy for an urban nation. Opponents were, in effect, depicted as backwoods reactionaries, an insulting image that gun control opponents were sometimes only too ready to fulfill. The pro-gun lobby has attempted to intervene in elections by backing pro-gun candidates and targeting Liberals for defeat on the issue. It was to no effect, as Reform already held seats where the anti-gun control sentiment was strong, while in the metropolitan areas, the campaign only confirmed the progressive social image the Liberals were presenting of themselves.

More recently, Chrétien has advanced further left-liberal social policy innovations, such as the reform of the marijuana laws to decriminalize possession of small amounts, despite hostile threats from the U.S. about the perils of Canada departing from punitive American practice. And in 2003, he took a further step down the path of progressive social legislation by announcing his government's intention to legalize same-sex marriage when only Belgium and the Netherlands had gone that far. To be sure, the charge on this issue had been led by the courts, and the government's only other option was the futile one of appealing three provincial court of appeal rulings to the Supreme Court. Nonetheless, Chrétien did not try to use the courts as a shield, but explained his decision in positive terms – and even earned an unusual accolade for his progressive leadership from former NDP MP and gay rights activist, Svend Robinson.

Chrétien is no social innovator, and he has never allowed himself to get so far out in front of Canadian society as to be exposed as any sort of radical. Each of the steps he has initiated have been taken with the assurance that the society has already begun to move in this direction, with government closely following. The cultural war has been won by the Left, in the first instance in the civil society, not by legislation or regulation. The role of government is to ratify the result. Controversies over multicultural policies and programs have given way to the realization that among younger Canadians, multiculturalism is simply a fact of life. Prejudices about "normal" and "abnormal" sexuality have simply fallen away, while the attention of government was elsewhere. That attention must then be refocused to give legal form to social reality. Even here, Chrétien's brokerage instincts have been to the fore. The policy objective has been to find a formula that bridges social change with some continuity to the past, while alienating opponents as little as possible. Chrétien's role in managing social change and government response is unobtrusive enough as to be missed by observers craving articulate, visionary leadership. Yet in the emotionally volatile field of cultural values, careful, cautious testing of each step ahead seems only prudent.

In the case of same-sex marriage, where the balance of opinion is only slightly on the progressive side, Chrétien moved regardless of the strong opposition, including a passionate and aggressive minority within his own caucus. On this issue, he even sparked the hostile intervention of the Roman Catholic hierarchy, thus linking himself historically with Sir Wilfrid Laurier, denounced from every pulpit in Québec (to no avail) in the election of 1896 that began the long domination of the Liberal Party in Canadian politics. Chrétien gambled that the time for change had arrived, and that, once implemented, it will work well enough that opponents will gradually become accustomed and eventually be reconciled to the new reality. It was left to his successor to finally enact legislation recognizing equal access of gay and lesbian couples to the institution of marriage, despite bitter criticism from the Conservative opposition and many of the churches. Yet this was a case in which Chrétien showed genuine leadership, and in a very challenging context.

MANAGING A WAR ON TWO FRONTS:
AFTER SEPTEMBER 11

Political leaders rarely enjoy full freedom of action to set their own agendas. Their records must also be judged by how they manage crises imposed upon them, how they respond to challenges not of their own choosing, in short, by their reactive as well as active qualities of leadership. In Chrétien's years in office, the most severe external challenge arose out of the catastrophic terrorist attacks on New York and Washington on September 11, 2001, and the radically new global and continental situation in which Canada found itself as a result.

It is the repeatedly asserted contention of the opposition, and of many media commentators, that Chrétien failed the test of September 11, and that Canada continues to pay the price for this failure in a decline in the confidence that the United States places in Canada: a situation further compounded by Chrétien's refusal to join the Americans and the British in the invasion of Iraq in the spring of 2003. Part of the explanation for this feeling of letdown is Chrétien's notorious inability to express himself in an articulate manner, a failing alluded to earlier. On occasions like September 11, there are expectations that leaders express the national mood memorably and, by their words, inspire a disoriented public to rally to a common purpose. The template here is Sir Winston Churchill in 1939–1940. By this standard, Chrétien failed. Looking back, it is clear that he said all the right things, but failed to raise his words from the level of the merely prosaic. While this is no surprise, what is surprising is the narrow partisanship of the critics, their systematic failure to look beyond the surface and assess what Chrétien's government actually has *done*, as opposed to *said*, in response to September 11, and their lack of appreciation of the complexities of the challenges facing Canada. In fact, the more closely Chrétien's post-September 11 record is examined, the better it begins to look.

Canada was not the target of the terrorist attacks, and is unlikely to be such a target in future – although that eventuality cannot be ruled out, of course. Nonetheless, the federal government acted decisively to shift its priorities towards assisting the U.S. in its war against terrorism. Chrétien as Prime Minister presided over and directed a series of actions, including: (1) the restructuring of the Cabinet architecture for decision-making with a special Cabinet security committee that, for a time, functioned as a virtual war Cabinet; (2) the reallocation of budgetary resources, with new resources for security to the tune of almost $8 billion over five years (although still niggardly on the defence side); (3) military contributions to the Afghanistan theatre of operations; (4) the provision of new and expanded legislative powers to combat terrorism, including the controversial *Anti-Terrorism Act*,[13] passed expeditiously through Parliament; (5) the restructuring of bureaucratic mechanisms in the security area; (6) placing the highest priority on the rapid negotiation of improved border security arrangements with the U.S.[14] Although mounted on a much smaller scale, Canada's efforts here compare not unfavourably with those of the U.S. in terms of structural agility and bureaucratic adaptability.[15] Moreover, Canada has avoided many of the excesses of the U.S. administration with regard to violations of civil liberties; even where draconian new anti-terrorist powers were enacted, the federal government has used them sparingly, if at all.[16]

What the critics particularly failed to appreciate is the complexity of the challenge that faced Canada. Chrétien's war was, from the start, a war on two fronts. The first was the very public face of the war on terrorism. The second was more covert, the Canadian-American front, in which Canada struggled to assure the U.S. of the security of its northern border, without sacrificing more of Canadian sovereignty than was minimally necessary to get North American commerce flowing freely across the now defended border. His government was under fierce pressure from a powerful, big business lobby to give absolute priority to securing the free flow of cross-border commerce, at whatever cost to Canadian sovereignty. Since his conservative critics, both inside and outside Parliament, regarded peace at any price with the Americans as the only legitimate objective of the Canadian government, while critics to his left tended to see every accommodation with the Americans as a sellout of sovereignty, Chrétien was operating under constant "friendly fire," a situation avoided, by and large, by President Bush, who could count on a patriotic bipartisan consensus. Chrétien had to contend with the obvious fact that Bush was indifferent, even occasionally contemptuous, toward his Canadian ally. To make matters worse, there was an embarrassing tendency for nationalists in Chrétien's camp, including his own press secretary, to let slip widely quoted anti-American insults.

Despite the provocations on both sides, Chrétien's government has, through ongoing bilateral negotiation, secured a series of sensible agreements with the U.S. on enhancing security and expediting commerce across a so-called "smart border." Critics who saw September 11 as an opportunity for thinking big and taking a window of opportunity to secure a deeper formalized integration with the U.S. in economic and security matters, have despaired at Chrétien's typical lack of vision. They ignore the dangers of entering into formal integration arrangements with an imperial power now set on a unilateralist course in international relations, unwilling to brook any limitation on its own sovereignty in relations with other nations. Chrétien deliberately eschewed thinking big, while his ministers pursued a deliberate policy of thinking small, negotiating incremental changes that cumulatively reassured the Americans while minimizing the loss of sovereignty. Canadian officials have deflected U.S. attention away from the more dangerous ground of the wider issues by engaging U.S. negotiators in a series of specific practical border problems to be solved one by one. They have been quite adroit at this.

Just how successful this incremental strategy has been was demonstrated when Chrétien was confronted by American pressure to join the so-called "coalition of the willing" in invading Iraq without UN sanction. Canada still retained a sufficient margin of independence to say no to the Americans, a position popular in all parts of the country, save Alberta, and one in strict keeping with long standing Canadian attachment to multilateralism and international institutions. Subsequent controversies over the failure to find weapons of mass destruction in Iraq, the stated *casus belli* of both the U.S. and U.K., has, if anything, only confirmed the wisdom of the Canadian choice.[17] This was an instance when Chrétien did the popular thing, but also, in terms of Canadian values, the right thing. It was not without costs, counted in threats of economic retaliation, a deepening frostiness in American attitudes to Canada (patronizingly described by the U.S. Ambassador to Canada in terms of American "disappointment" with its neighbour), and the petulant refusal of Bush to visit Ottawa while Chrétien remained in office. Yet difficult as the Iraq decision was, Chrétien showed courage and determination in following a course that preserved some measure of Canadian self-respect. The simultaneous decision to redeploy Canadian forces to Afghanistan was both a Mackenzie King-like piece of craftiness, and an affirmation of Canadian autonomy – Canadians approved of the Afghan operation as part of the war on terrorism, but rejected the logic that linked regime change in Iraq to the campaign against terrorism.

The post-September 11 world has imposed hard choices upon Canada. Chrétien has not always been able to avoid being drawn further into the Bush administration orbit than he might otherwise prefer. The apparent decision late in his watch to join the U.S. in its projected antiballistic missile defence system – despite its unfeasibility, its unilateralist implications, and its lack of any compelling justification – is a case of the inevitability of bowing to superior power, however unwisely deployed. Nevertheless, Chrétien was able to negotiate a difficult passage between the "ready, aye, ready" response of the Canadian Alliance and the unrealistic anti-American nationalism of the NDP. If post-September 11 America has set out to rewrite the global geopolitical realities, and the old Cold War alliance structure, on America First terms, which seems increasingly likely, Canada's geography and economic ties render her margin for manoeuvre very narrow indeed. Some observers have looked nostalgically back on the post-war "golden era" of Canadian diplomacy and condemned Canada's fading as an international player.[18] The enabling conditions for Canadian diplomatic activism, however, have changed drastically. In this more constricted environment, Chrétien played a limited hand with some skill and with a dogged determination to maintain some Canadian autonomy, despite intimidation.

A LONG AND VERY PARADOXICAL GOODBYE

There is a particular problem in assessing Chrétien's record, given the bizarre and unprecedented circumstances surrounding his forced retirement, not by the voters, but by his own party, inside Parliament and out. There was a general feeling that the former Prime Minister, despite his continued electoral successes, had outlived his time. For some time, opinion polls had indicated that Canadians thought Chrétien was doing a good job, but that it was time for him to retire – a paradoxical, unsettling form of voter approval. Although his policies always seemed to stay on the positive side of public opinion, the paradox might be explained by the growing impression that Liberal success was leading to one-party rule, highly centralized in the office of the Prime Minister, and that this was seriously debilitating the traditional checks and balances that maintain democracy, like Parliament and a viable opposition.

Whiffs of patronage and corruption swirled around certain ministers, and even around the former Prime Minister himself. Chrétien-era scandals became an obsessive focus of the Alliance and Conservative opposition, reaching a peak in the 2000 election campaign, perhaps for want of more substantive handles to grasp. Yet none of the scandals ever caught enough fire to do much political damage. Some, like the Human Resources Development Canada misspending allegations were over-hyped by a desperate opposition and then petered out in a series of investigations of specific cases that led nowhere significant. Others, like the sponsorship allegations, were well-founded, but deflected by government actions in response to the critics. The so-called "Shawinigate affair" that potentially drew in the former Prime Minister personally, may or may not have had solid support, but the smoking gun proved elusive, and the affair began to fade from public consciousness in Chrétien's third term of office. Scandals of this kind are hardly unprecedented, as Brian Mulroney can ruefully attest. Even if unproven, they can be cumulatively damaging to a prime minister and government over time. Perhaps the most that can be said is that Chrétien's brushes with scandal and corruption were no worse than Mulroney's, although perhaps no better either.

Rumours of scandal added to the autocratic aura of a government and leader who, even when they were doing the right things, could be seen to be doing them in the wrong way – arrogantly and unaccountably. The respected political scientist Donald J. Savoie published an influential book on the Chrétien government, *Governing from the Centre: the Concentration of Power in Canadian Politics.*[19] Canada's leading political journalist, Jeffrey Simpson, caught the mood well with his bestseller, *The Friendly Dictatorship.*[20] Could relatively good, if unimaginative, managerial government degrade the quality of Canadian democracy in the absence of effective opposition? This led to a strange conclusion, apparently widely shared: it was time for a change, but with no alternative to the Liberals available, the leader should change, yet the government should remain. But that suggested deadlock, as Liberals had no precedent of unseating a successful leader, and the very concentration of power in the PMO appeared to give him the tools to fight off any challenge. In 1999, Professor Savoie, after recalling how Prime Ministers Margaret Thatcher of Britain and Bob Hawke of Australia were shown the door by their own caucuses before their majority mandates were finished, concluded that "[t]his would be unthinkable in Canada."[21] If Chrétien himself shared this belief, he was to be shortly, unceremoniously, disabused of it.

There was, of course, a Liberal alternative-in-waiting in the hugely popular Paul Martin. Chrétien's forced, if prolonged, goodbye, can be interpreted simply as a result of the Martin forces gaining control over the Liberal Party while the former Prime Minister governed. Chrétien, so widely respected for his political instincts and skills, was oddly deserted by these when he lost control of his caucus to his rival. Mulroney, even when his standing in the polls fell to unprecedented depths in the early 1990s, always maintained the fierce loyalty of his Cabinet and caucus. Chrétien, with three successive majorities and no real threat to his party's hegemony visible on the horizon, could maintain neither the unity of his Cabinet, nor the loyalty of his caucus. This observation points to a deficiency, ultimately fatal, in his leadership capacities. Despite his reputation as a political animal, he neglected cultivating his parliamentary supporters, thus failing to establish the personal bonds that served Mulroney so well, even in adversity. Trudeau was equally aloof. But he always maintained the respect of his supporters, and moreover, he never had a serious rival, save John Turner, who left without establishing a leader-in-waiting entourage within the caucus. Martin stayed, building his support in the country and assiduously cultivating the kind of links with his colleagues that would serve him so well, once he had been forced out of the Cabinet and into open opposition. In any assessment of Jean Chrétien's leadership, his puzzling incapacity to maintain his hold over his own party must be marked down in the negative column. If Mulroney politically destroyed the vehicle that he controlled until he left on his own terms, Chrétien bequeathed to his rival a vehicle in splendid condition that had nonetheless thrown off the leader who had brought it to that state.

This is a very curious state of affairs indeed. It has also generated a striking paradox: it might be said that nothing in Chrétien's political life has become him so much as the way in which he has taken leave of it. Some of the most serious criticisms of the effects of the domination of politics by Chrétien and his Liberal Party are, surprisingly, being balanced by the demonstrated ability of the Liberal Party to hold its leader to real and effective accountability, and by the willingness of Chrétien to seize the opportunity of his sixteen-month-long goodbye to mount an ambitious legislative agenda that to some degree repairs the shortcomings of his managerial, but relatively unimaginative, decade in office. Governments grown fat in power often require defeat at the polls to permit renewal of leadership and policy. The Liberals are undergoing, instead, a two-stage renewal process, first under the outgoing leader, with time to repair the shortcomings of his past, and then under his successor, coming in with a mandate for renovation.

Some would dismiss the leadership conflict as an inconsequential personality clash, beloved by journalists, but of little lasting significance. That would be a mistake. The enormity of what the Liberal Party accomplished in driving out a successful leader, an enormity that led Professor Savoie to call such an eventuality "unthinkable," must be emphasized. If Canada really had become a one-party state, if centralization of power in the Office of Prime Minister was as awesome as the term "friendly dicta-

torship" would suggest, if opposition really was as impotent as adver-
tised, then how could the "Emperor," if determined to stay, be deposed?
Chrétien himself insisted, when challenged, that he held a personal mandate from the electorate, twice renewed, that outweighed the legitimacy
of the Liberal caucus or the Liberal Party. It was a fatal sign of *hubris*. In
point of fact, a prime minister, however powerful, is not in the Canadian
system of government a presidential bearer of a direct mandate from the
people. No one had ever voted directly for Chrétien as Prime Minister
(even his own constituents voted for him only as their local MP), but for
enough Liberal candidates to form a majority through which Chrétien
could govern. Indeed, the national voting study of the 2000 election
showed the leadership factor to be "quite small" in determining the outcome.[22] Thus the Liberal Party in Parliament shared some of that mandate, and finally chose to exercise it. Chrétien did hold a mandate
directly from the Liberal Party, derived from the leadership convention
he had won in 1990. But by the same token, the party could revoke this
mandate. When it became clear that it was prepared to do so, and when
the parliamentary party split deeply over Chrétien's leadership, it was
apparent, even to Chrétien himself, that the game was up. It is not good
enough to say that Chrétien lost and Martin won. A narrow personality
focus misses the deeper political significance of the events.

The Liberal Party, as an institution, had not been reduced to merely
formal status: it still had life, and kick, in it. Caucus was more than a rub-
ber stamp for the PMO, Parliament more than an antiquated appendage
of the executive. One of the initial skirmishes in the conflict had been
over the election of chairs of committees, as opposed to appointment by
the PMO. Chrétien lost this skirmish, and subsequently committees have
been behaving more independently than in the past.[23] Martin had provided detailed ideas to give committees, and MPs generally, more scope
under his watch. Cynics might dismiss this promise as one easily forgotten if Martin wins a majority government, but this is unlikely. Parliament's affirmation of its autonomy will stand as a reminder to future
prime ministers that it would be risky to treat MPs as "nobodies," in Trudeau's careless and unwise word long ago.

As a by-product of the leadership conflict, Liberal MPs began speaking
out freely, and often critically, on government policy and government
performance. Canadians have been treated to the highly unusual specta-
cle of debate within the ruling party being carried on publicly, indeed vol-
ubly. Partisans wince at this display of indiscipline, and opposition MPs
try vainly to suggest that the government is in disarray, but the lasting

significance of this development is surely a revitalization of democracy. If the parties across the floor of Parliament are fragmented and ineffectual, genuine debate has migrated to the government benches. This is no substitute for healthy inter-party competition, but it is better than the numbing, dead hand of one-party rule in which debate, if any, takes place behind closed doors.

Chrétien negotiated his withdrawal by buying a year and a half before relinquishing office. This might be termed a "lame duck" mandate, and signs of vigorous Liberal dissent have been interpreted as indications of Chrétien's waning grip. But the long goodbye has been the occasion for a "legacy" agenda, some of which is radical enough from a centrist Liberal perspective to make critics sit up and take notice. Indeed, many of the marks that Chrétien will leave derive from this energetic last burst (same-sex marriage and marijuana law reform, for instance). Lame duck mandates are double-edged. Obedience to the leader's directions may diminish, but on the other hand, a lame duck leader also has a freer hand, no longer constrained by constant calculations of what each initiative might cost at the next election, or in the form of the loss of future support from allies. There is some opportunity in these circumstances to simply "do the right thing," heedless of political consequences. Some of the margin for independent action that Chrétien has shown in Canadian-American relations, such as the refusal to back the Iraq invasion, might not have issued from a prime minister worrying about damaging short-run consequences, rather than the longer term, and a wider frame of reference. Critics today are scathing about Chrétien's alleged mishandling of relations with the U.S. In time, this period may rather be seen as a moment when Canada maintained a tenuous hold on its own sovereignty, while under unprecedented pressure. If so, the lame duck mandate will appear as a fortuitous circumstance.

Nowhere is the paradoxical character of Chrétien's long goodbye more striking, or the consequences more significant, than in what may be one of his most lasting contributions to Canadian democracy: Bill C-24, the political financing legislation.[24] Bill C-24 plugs most of the notorious loopholes in earlier political financing legislation. Most significantly, by banning donations from corporations and trade unions to parties, and limiting them to $1000 contributions to candidates, Bill C-24 forcefully addresses one of the most significant elements of the "democratic deficit," the power of corporate money to influence the political process. Moreover, this ban appears to come with some enforcement teeth. Public subsidies will be increased to replace corporate money. This should go some way toward severing the nexus – or perceived nexus – between private money and the public policy process.

There are some precedents for Bill C-24: Québec and Manitoba have similar laws. It is, however, rather unexpected that the party that has garnered the lion's share of corporate donations for the past decade should enact such a radical measure, apparently against its own interests. So unprecedented was it that much of the Liberal caucus and the Liberal Party were in open revolt against Chrétien. The party's president was memorably quoted in the media as denouncing the idea of banning corporate donations as being "as dumb as a bag of hammers,"[25] and he publicly lobbied against the law. Chrétien stood fast and insisted on making passage of Bill C-24 a matter of party discipline, suggesting that defeat would precipitate an immediate election. On 11 June 2003, an only slightly amended Bill C-24 was given third and final reading by the House of Commons. Paradoxically, what objectively stands as a major piece of democratic reform was imposed upon a recalcitrant party by one last exercise of perhaps somewhat undemocratic prime ministerial power. Just one more among the many paradoxes of Chrétien's extraordinary last year and a half in office.

A POSITIVE BALANCE SHEET?

I have stressed the positive aspects of Chrétien's tenure, while neglecting the more negative elements that inevitably accumulate around any prime minister's record, however successful. In part this stress is justified because familiarity breeds contempt: it is notoriously difficult to judge the virtues of an incumbent in office, as opposed to one departed from day-to-day political controversy or, even more conveniently, dead. The rating of prime ministers is usually lowest when memory of the inevitable controversies and partisan attacks is still fresh. When the Institute for Research in Public Policy recently asked a number of historians and other authorities to rank Canada's post-war prime ministers, Chrétien was placed second-last, ahead only of John Diefenbaker. The landslide winner was Lester Pearson, whose standing was not particularly high when he departed the office in 1968.[26] Chrétien's stock will likely rise with the passage of time as well.

The country that Jean Chrétien left after a decade in office was, in many ways, stronger and better off than the one he inherited. His leadership was less visible than that of his predecessors, because he neither exhorted nor inspired Canadians. His skills were predominantly those of brokerage, management, and compromise, which by their nature are invisible, easily missed, or downplayed. Yet the political vehicle of the Liberal Party he bequeathed to his successor was in a state of health and preparedness – in extraordinary contrast to the catastrophic state of the Conservative Party after a decade of Mulroney's leadership. This, in itself, is an indication of how effective Chrétien's low-profile, low-key leadership was in practice.

It would, however, be unjust to simply leave the impression that Chrétien shrank from challenges and hid behind brokerage. He did not shrug off the old adage about the buck stopping at the top. On the major achievements of his first two terms, fiscal control and the Québec sovereignty challenge, Chrétien took responsibility for action, and he insisted upon follow-through. In his third term, he handled the challenges imposed by external events like September 11 and its aftermath with greater skill and poise than he is usually given credit for, and was not shy of standing up for Canada when the U.S. pushed. On social and political reforms, he exercised his brokerage skills in smoothing the way for change, but when decisive action was required, he took strong, and relatively advanced, stands.

Chrétien reasserted brokerage as an effective instrument of governance in a diverse federation, but he could also show backbone on behalf of his own positions and values when required. Machiavelli wrote that the Prince must imitate both the fox and the lion, "for the lion cannot protect himself from traps, and the fox cannot defend himself from wolves. One must therefore be a fox to recognize traps, and a lion to frighten wolves."[27] By instinct more fox than lion, Chrétien could, if required, be lion-like enough to frighten the wolves.

ADDENDUM

The legacy of Jean Chrétien would appear to have been damaged as a result of revelations of scandal that erupted following his retirement. The scandal of the once-secret Sponsorship Program was dramatically drawn to public attention by the 2003 report of Auditor General Sheila Fraser and then by the protracted media circus of the Gomery Commission hearings, ultimately leading to the devastating first Gomery report and the subsequent fall of the Martin government in late 2005. Although Gomery specifically exonerated Paul Martin of any culpability in the affair, the scandal dogged Martin's government throughout his tenure. Given the fierce competition between Messrs. Chrétien and Martin during Chrétien's last years as Prime Minister, it is almost as if Chrétien had administered one of those "poison pills" sometimes employed in cases of hostile corporate takeover bids.

Yet for all that his successor has borne the brunt of the political fallout, the Sponsorship Program was a creation of Jean Chrétien and, thus, in the words of Mr. Justice Gomery, "he must share the blame for the mismanagement."[28] While the former Prime Minister is contesting the finding in the courts, and while he acquitted himself with wit and aplomb in his own appearance before the Commission, there can be no doubt that the sponsorship scandal casts a shadow over his legacy. Even if the courts were to find exculpatory bias in the Gomery process, and there is at least prima facie evidence of some bias, serious ramifications of the scandal will continue to reverberate in four areas.

First is the overall perception of corruption and arrogance pervading the Liberal governments since 1993. Charges of corruption against Chrétien and his successor have been a staple of opposition attacks in every election since 1997, and a favourite topic for investigative journalists, especially from the more conservative media. None of the charges really stuck – until Fraser and Gomery. The "culture of entitlement" – a phrase coined by Mr. Justice Gomery, but adopted with alacrity and employed continually by all three opposition leaders – has become an epithet for the alleged behaviour of the Liberal Party grown ethically lax in office after more a decade.

Second is the hit taken by successive Liberal governments' reputation for managerial competence. This was one of Chrétien's particular strengths as Prime Minister during his three majority governments. The ballooning cost of the national gun registry under his watch had already cast some doubt on Chrétien's reputation for relatively well-run administration. The harsh light of the sponsorship scandal has left his successor, already beset with the travails of minority government, branded with the label of Liberal waste and corruption.

Third is the degree to which the scandal and the Gomery inquiry have reopened and exacerbated the deep wounds within the Liberal Party that began with the ruthless takeover bid by the Martinites that forced Mr Chrétien into retirement. Prime Minister Martin has had the unenviable task of trying to persuade Canadians that his government was eager to "get to the bottom of" the scandal, while trying to distinguish his government from that of his predecessor, which was, after all, responsible for the program in question. He has had only very limited success, according to public opinion polling. But the Martin government's careful distancing of itself from its predecessor has enraged many close associates of the former Prime Minister, as well as Mr Chrétien himself, and may well have contributed to the lukewarm-to-absent support of some Liberals from the Chrétien wing of the party in the 2004 and 2006 elections.

These difficulties associated with the sponsorship affair may not, in the end, have lasting effects on the post-Chrétien Liberal Party. The total amount of misallocated money involved, however reprehensible, is not very large in relation to total government spending. Outside Québec, the scandal has not had strong impact on public opinion.

More serious is the devastation wrought on Liberal fortunes in Québec. The scandal is essentially a Québec-centred affair. The sponsorship program was mounted as a riposte to the near-success of the sovereigntists in the 1995 referendum – that is, as a campaign to put Canada and the federal government constantly before the eyes and ears of Quebecers to counter the sovereigntists' hegemonic cultural and ideological position within Québec society. It was kept secret and outside the usual controls over spending precisely because it was conceived as a kind of quasi-wartime emergency measure that had to be kept, for security reasons, out of the hands of advertising firms with any sovereigntist sympathies. What Quebecers saw at the Gomery Commission hearings was a sorry parade of criminal misappropriation of taxpayer dollars, kickbacks to the federal Liberal Party in Québec, and, most damaging of all, a program that was judged in and of itself to be insulting to the intelligence and dignity of Quebecers. The immediate political effect has been the precipitous decline of the Québec wing of the Liberal Party and the rapid rise of the Bloc Québécois to near-complete domination of francophone Québec. The longer-term effect is the partial discrediting of federalism and the re-emergence of sovereignty as a leading, viable option. Since Chrétien's time in office had apparently gone some way to recovering the federalist position in Québec after the great scare of the 1995 referendum, it would be ironic if the later public embarrassment of the sponsorship affair were to undermine all his efforts. If the Clarity Act was a sign that the Liberals were taking the high road in dealing with a secessionist challenge, the sponsorship program and the scandals in its administration were a sign of the low road. It would be a sad commentary on the Chrétien legacy, not to speak of a tragedy for Canadian federalism, if this low road proved to be the defining moment for the victorious resurgence of the Québec sovereignty movement.

Of course, just as sovereignty is never dead in Québec, despite reports to the contrary, neither is federalism. But Jean Chrétien's stamp on the

Sponsorship Program has certainly done neither the Liberal Party nor federalism any good in Québec. That will always remain a shadow on his legacy.

NOTES

Distinguished Research Professor Emeritus, York University, and adjunct professor of Political Science, University of Victoria.

1 On the Chrétien-Martin relationship in the first mandate, see Edward Greenspon and Anthony Wilson-Smith, *Double Vision: The Inside Story of the Liberals in Power* (Toronto: Doubleday Canada, 1996).

2 Ipsos-Reid, "Seven in ten (70%) support Canada's involvement in North American Free Trade Agreement (NAFTA)," 8 June 2003, http://www.ipsos-na.com/news/pressrelease.cfm?id=1839.

3 Matthew Mendelsohn and Robert Wolfe, "Probing the Aftermyth of Seattle: Canadian Public Opinion on International Trade, 1998–2000" (Kingston: Queen's University School of Policy Studies, Working Paper 12, 2000), conclude that governments can capture public support for globalization if they can provide a credible narrative that explains trade liberalization in non-threatening terms. This is precisely what the Chrétien Liberals did, by and large.

4 See Allan Tupper, "The Chrétien Governments and Higher Education: A Quiet Revolution in Canadian Public Policy," in G. Bruce Doern, ed., *How Ottawa Spends 2003–2004: Régime Change and Policy Shift* (Don Mills: Oxford University Press, 2003), 105–17.

5 See Michael J. Prince, "The Return of Directed Incrementalism: Innovating Social Policy the Canadian Way," in G. Bruce Doern, ed., *How Ottawa Spends 2002–2003: The Security Aftermath and National Priorities* (Don Mills: Oxford University Press, 2002), 176–95, 192.

6 Patrick Brethour, "Klein reverses Kyoto stand; now sees no peril to oil sands," *Globe and Mail*, 20 June 2003, B1.

7 Reg Whitaker, "Cruising at 30,000 Feet with a Missing Engine: The Chrétien Government in the Aftermath of the Quebec Referendum," in Gene Swimmer, ed., *How Ottawa Spends 1997–98, Seeing Red: A Liberal Report Card* (Ottawa: Carleton University Press 1997), 52–74.

8 Reg Whitaker, "King into Trudeau: Jean Chrétien Seeks Clarity," *Inroads: A Journal of Opinion* 9 (2000): 47–58.

9 (Montreal: Éditions Renaissance, 1965).

10 *Reference re Secession of Quebec*, [1998] 2 S.C.R. 217, 161 D.L.R. (4th) 385, http://www.canlii.org/ca/cas/scc/1998/1998scc63.html.

11 S.C. 2000, c. 26, s. 3(2), http://www.canlii.org/ca/sta/c-31.8/whole.html.

12 This is a point I have developed at greater length in "The Liberal Chameleon: From Red Tories to Blue Grits," in Hamish Telford and Harvey Lazar, eds., *Canada: The State of the Federation 2001, Canadian Political Culture(s) in Transition* (Montreal & Kingston: McGill-Queen's University Press, 2002), 35–50.

13 S.C. 2001, c. 41, http://www.canlii.org/ca/sta/a-11.7/whole.html/.

14 Reg Whitaker, "More or Less Than Meets the Eye? The New National Security Agenda," in Doern, *How Ottawa Spends 2002–2003*, 44–58.

15 Two years after September 11, 2001, the U.S. system was wrestling with the massive reorganization of government functions under the new Department of Homeland Security. In the summer of 2003, notice was taken in the U.S. of the need for new civil service legislation to reflect the new realities. The Canadian government, by contrast, had already passed Bill C-25, *The Public Service Modernization Act*, S.C. 2003, c. 22, http://www.canlii.org/ca/sta/p-33.4/whole.html.

16 The two most controversial new powers, preventive arrest, and investigative hearing, were so contentious that sunset clauses were added to them. Yet neither power has ever actually been exercised. On the *Anti-Terrorism Act* generally, see Kent Roach, *September 11: Consequences for Canada* (Montreal: McGill-Queen's University Press, 2003). A range of academic views on the law may be found in Thomas Gabor, Department of Criminology, University of Ottawa, *The Views of Canadian Scholars on the Impact of the Anti-Terrorism Act*, Draft Final Report (31 March 2004), http://canada.justice.gc.ca/en/ps/rs/rep/2005/rr05-1/rr05-1_03_01.html.

17 By 15 June 2003, Ipsos-Reid found that 71 percent of Canadians agreed with the decision to stay out of the Iraq war. See Ipsos-Reid, "Seven in ten (71%) now feel Prime Minister and Canada justified in not supporting U.S. coalition in Iraq military action," http://www.ipsos-na.com/news/pressrelease.cfm?id=1845.

18 See Norman Hillmer and Maureen Appel Molot, eds., *Canada Among Nations 2002: A Fading Power* (Toronto: Oxford University Press, 2002); and Andrew Cohen, *While Canada Slept: How We Lost Our Place In The World* (Toronto: McClelland & Stewart, 2003).

19 Donald J. Savoie, *Governing from the Centre: The Concentration of Power in Canadian Politics* (Toronto: University of Toronto Press, 1999).

20 Jeffrey Simpson, *The Friendly Dictatorship* (Toronto: McClelland & Stewart, 2001).

21 Savoie, *Governing from the Centre*, 362.

22 André Blais, et al., *Anatomy of a Liberal Victory: Making Sense of the Vote in the 2000 Canadian Election* (Peterborough: Broadview Press, 2002), 165–76.

23 This is exemplified in the all-party report of the fledgling committee on government operations and estimates that forced the 2003 resignation of Privacy Commissioner George Radwanski, a Liberal appointee. See Hugh Winsor, "Expect more scrutiny of government," *Globe and Mail*, 30 June 2003.

24 *An Act to amend the Canada Elections Act and the Income Tax Act (political financing)*, S.C. 2003, c. 19, http://www.canlii.org/ca/as/2003/c19/whole.html.

25 Julian Beltrame, "Dumb as a bag of hammers," *Maclean's*, 3 February 2003.

26 L. Ian MacDonald, "The Best Prime Minister of the Last 50 years – Pearson, by a Landslide," *Policy Options* 24:6 (2003): 8–12.

27 Niccolò Machiavelli, *The Prince and the Discourses* (New York: The Modern Library, 1950), 64.

28 Commission of Inquiry into the Sponsorship Program and Advertising Activities, *Who Is Responsible? Phase I Report* (Ottawa: Minister of Public Works and Government Services, 2005), 76, http://www.gomery.ca/en/phase1report/.

2

Jean Chrétien's Québec Legacy

Coasting, Then Stickhandling Hard

ROBERT A. YOUNG

INTRODUCTION

On 25 October 1993, Jean Chrétien's Liberals surged to power in Ottawa, sweeping out the Tories by capturing 176 seats in the House of Commons. But only nineteen Liberal seats were from Québec, where the sovereigntist Bloc Québécois elected fifty-four MPs with 49.3 percent of the popular vote. Chrétien's party took only 33 percent of the Québec vote. In 1997, though, the Liberals won 36.7 percent of the vote in Québec (garnering twenty-six seats), and in 2000 they took 44.2 percent of the popular vote (thirty-six seats), pulling ahead of the Bloc (at 39.9 percent of the vote). When the Prime Minister prorogued Parliament in late 2003, the federal Liberals had thirty-seven seats in the House, while the Bloc contingent had shrunk to thirty-four. As for his own leadership, Jean Chrétien received approval for his job performance from 59 percent of Quebecers in February 2002, up from 41 percent in 1995, and from 31 percent in early 1993.[1] Finally, the all-important measure of support for sovereignty in Québec stood at about 40 percent in late 2003, depending on the measure used, well down from 1995, and far below its heights in 1990 after the failure of the Meech Lake Accord.

By any conventional measure, then, and certainly by the ones most important to him, Chrétien has been successful in maintaining and building support in Québec over his tenure. It is true that, since Confederation, he is the first francophone leader of a major national party who has ever failed to carry a majority of Québec seats in a general election. But none has faced such formidable opposition in his home province. And while the party's electoral strength has lain in Ontario throughout his regime, Jean Chrétien has made consistent inroads into the support of his principal rivals in Québec: the sovereigntists.

Prime Minister Chrétien accomplished this success in Québec despite coming within a hair of losing the 1995 Québec referendum on sovereignty and having the country plunged into what would have been the worst crisis in its history. In assessing his Québec legacy, the referendum deserves very close examination: not only has it indelibly marked his prime ministership but it also raises the historic question of the extent to which the victory – or the shocking near-loss – was his responsibility. Next, the overall track record since the referendum is positive. So, having almost "lost the country" on his watch, how did Chrétien manage subsequently to gain more approval in his home province? This is the second part of his legacy. After the referendum, while making some accommodation to Québec's traditional demands, he also directed a bold fight against the sovereigntist forces. This fight was capped by the reference to the Supreme Court on Québec secession,[2] which produced an historic judgment, and by the *Clarity Act*, which legislated the principles governing Canada's stance towards a secessionist province. This fight put the sovereigntists into disarray while increasing support for Chrétien's federal Liberal government. Support may be evanescent, but the judicial and legislative residues of the struggle live on even after Jean Chrétien has left office.

THE 1995 REFERENDUM BATTLE

No single event marked Jean Chrétien's time in office more than the Québec referendum of 30 October 1995. The campaign was a struggle for Québec between the federalist and sovereigntist forces, and the fight was tough and broad and deep, penetrating every organization and family in the province and dominating public discourse for months. The final turnout – 93.5 percent of eligible voters – was unprecedented not only in Canada but in western democracies, testimony to the significance of the choice. It also reflected a terribly close contest. The No side won with 50.6 percent of the vote, and if fewer than 27,145 voters out of almost five million had switched to the Yes, the sovereigntists would have been victorious. This event rocked Jean Chrétien to the core.

The federalists faced formidable opponents. In early 1995, Jacques Parizeau, Premier of Québec, had a recent mandate and a strong Parti

Québécois (PQ) team. Brilliant though not entirely trusted in the province, he was fiercely determined to achieve sovereignty at last. The federal politician Lucien Bouchard had left the Mulroney government to found the Bloc Québécois after the Meech Lake Accord failed: it would have recognized Québec's distinctiveness and augmented the provincial government's powers. Sovereigntists were suspicious of Bouchard's commitment to the cause, given his previous role in Ottawa, but he was charismatic and many francophones placed much faith in him. Another residue of constitutional failure was the new party led by Mario Dumont, the Action Démocratique du Québec (ADQ), which rallied many disaffected members of the Québec Liberal Party (QLP). This left the QLP leader, the solid and decent Daniel Johnson, presiding over weakened forces. Under the referendum legislation in Québec, he became leader of the No side while Parizeau led the Yes troops. Jean Chrétien and his federal allies, including Jean Charest, leader of the Progressive Conservatives, participated in planning referendum strategy and tactics, and increasingly so as the campaign progressed, but they did not control the No side.

There is no need to provide here an account of the campaign.[3] Suffice it to say that in early 1995, the sovereigntists were stalled at below 45 percent support. As the Yes side's wheels spun, and the referendum was put off until the autumn, Bouchard led an historic *virage* (sharp change of direction) at the first convention of the Bloc. He argued that sovereignty was a matter of confidence, of collective self-affirmation, but he pledged that Québec would maintain an economic union with Canada after a Yes vote and would negotiate a new partnership, possibly involving common political institutions. After Bouchard made clear that he would not campaign in a losing cause, the new direction of the sovereignty movement was cemented in an agreement signed on 12 June by Parizeau, Bouchard, and Dumont.[4] This new direction of the sovereigntists' strategy proved to be exceedingly effective. It caught Jean Chrétien and his allies wrong-footed, and so it almost succeeded in putting the Yes forces over the top.

In order to assess the extent of Jean Chrétien's responsibility for the near-Yes vote in 1995, it is necessary to grasp the structure of the debate. The first big issue was the Constitution, where the federalists claimed the status quo was adequate and sufficiently flexible to accommodate Québec's genuine needs, while the sovereigntists tried to justify political independence at the same time as they argued for a new Canada-Québec arrangement. Second was national identification, where each side deployed a lot of emotionally charged discourse and essentially fought to a draw. The economic dimension was where the Yes side made gains. The promise of an economic partnership assuaged Quebecers' fears of the disruption that sovereignty might bring. One study by three reliable academics found that the shift in economic expectations between June 1995 and the end of October accounted for a 6 percent increase in the Yes vote.[5] Other studies confirm this: even though Bouchard's assumption of the Yes leadership in early October seems to have lifted both campaigners' spirits and popular support for his option, this was because of the increasing credibility of the partnership.[6]

Why did the sovereigntist gains on the economic dimension occur? Because the federalist forces were in a box. They could not say what would happen after a Yes vote. They could not bring themselves to say that a Yes would lead to secession, and yet only this admission would allow them to credibly argue that a subsequent economic and political partnership was a pipe dream. Here, Chrétien played the lead. In his first address during the campaign, he declined to say that a Yes vote would be accepted: "You're asking a hypothetical question. We have a referendum and they are proposing separation. We're going to tell Quebecers that, and Quebecers will vote for Canada."[7] While the House of Commons was in session, the Bloc deputies and Lucien Bouchard repeatedly asked whether a Yes vote would be accepted, and the Prime Minister remained noncommittal, accusing the sovereigntists of posing an ambiguous question, arguing that Quebecers simply wanted good government and predicting that they would never vote to separate.[8] He was also assailed by the Reform Party, led by Preston Manning, who pressed hard for clarity about the consequences of Quebecers' choice: "They think they can vote for separation and still enjoy the benefits of federalism. That is why we asked the Prime Minister to make clear that yes means separation and only no means federalism. I will again ask the Prime Minister sincerely, as we are not playing games here, why he is so reluctant to make that distinction crystal clear."[9] Chrétien responded famously that he would not "break up the country with one vote," and that "the scheme they have, the virage, the mirage and so on will not work. They will not succeed in fooling the people of Quebec because the people of Quebec will know when they vote 39 days from now that they will not separate. They will stay in Canada because it is their destiny, their future and their desire."[10] The issue carried through the campaign, with the sovereigntists arguing that Canadians should and would accept the democratic decision of Quebecers. As Lucien Bouchard put it at the very end, "I fully expect the rest of Canada, as all Quebecers, whatever happens, to accept the verdict of democracy."[11] But Chrétien made no such commitment. In a late-campaign television interview, asked whether he would accept a 51 percent Yes vote, he declared "No, I haven't recognized anything. You don't know the result and neither do I. People would have expressed their point of view. "After that, the mechanics are very nebulous."[12]

As a consequence, the federalists lost ground on the economic dimension. They consistently depicted sovereignty as a risky venture into the unknown, but did not spell out specific consequences. Hence, the Yes forces were able to argue that secession would be costless. Indeed, in their portrayal, every dire prediction was a bluff, designed to deter Quebecers from voting for sovereignty for fear of the economic repercussions. But after a Yes vote, they insisted, it would be irrational for people in the rest of Canada to retaliate or refuse to co-operate because this would inflict losses on themselves. So, for Bouchard, the post-Yes partnership would "impose itself after an assessment of each other's interests."[13] For Parizeau, it was "perfectly understandable that before the 30th all of these guys in Ottawa will say no, no, no, no. Well, after the 30th, they might say yes to a few things."[14] In short, economic rationality was equated by the sovereigntists with co-operation.[15] And the silence about how Canada would respond to a Yes, which only Chrétien's government could credibly break, allowed the Yes side to gain.

There are several possible reasons for the No side's silence about what would be the consequences of a Yes vote. Early on, the federalists were confident and complacent, and the *virage* towards partnership took them by surprise. Clearly, spelling out the economic consequences of a vote for sovereignty could have weakened the unity of the No side. Declarations that there would be no partnership and statements about precise consequences (loss of citizenship, mobility, market access, and so on) could have been depicted by the opponents as cruel threats or mere initial bargaining positions. Admitting the possibility of a sovereigntist victory might have made it seem more credible.[16] As well, the federalists were genuinely frustrated by a referendum question that seemed unfair and duplicitous in its reference to a "partnership." But they could not counter this without conceding that Québec might become sovereign. And this Chrétien and his closest advisors were unable to do.

Resistance to conceding the possibility of a sovereigntist victory was demonstrated early in the campaign when Lucienne Robillard, who had been brought into the Chrétien Cabinet to co-ordinate the federal referendum effort, stated: "We are in a democratic country, so we'll respect the vote."[17] Pressed immediately on this point, Daniel Johnson said:

"The people of Quebec will abide by the results – end of story."[18] But both were forced to backtrack, with Robillard stating that the government would respect "the democratic process" rather than any particular outcome, while Johnson asked "How can you break up a country on a judicial recount?"[19] Chrétien – "The Boss" – had no doubt re-asserted his line, and in a damage-control press conference he reinforced it: "There is a vote and, of course, we'll receive the result of the vote, but you're asking me a hypothetical question. I'm standing here telling you we're going to win."[20]

But polls taken around 20 October showed that the federalists were not going to win. As panic swept the No camp, pressure mounted for movement on the Constitution (and this was the only way to change, given the logic sketched above). Reluctantly, the former Prime Minister shifted his position.[21] In a speech in Québec City, Chrétien declared that Québec formed a "distinct society," and he later issued a joint declaration to this effect with Johnson.[22] He went further at a rally in Verdun, and then, in a televised speech to all Canadians, he argued for distinct-society status, a Québec constitutional veto on matters affecting its government's powers, and general decentralization.[23] This concession might have swung the electorate back; or perhaps it was Jean Charest's agreement with this position, or maybe the pro-Québec declarations made by some municipalities and provincial governments, or, improbably, the big Unity Rally held in Montreal.

In any case, Jean Chrétien bears considerable responsibility for the near-defeat of the No side. True, there were some good reasons for not specifying what would be the Canadian reaction to a Yes. And attributing responsibility always involves specifying a counterfactual – in this case, what would have happened had the Yes-side discourse been different? No one can specify this with certainty. But it seems clear that no politician other than the Prime Minister could have credibly indicated what Canada's reaction would be to a Yes vote. And it seems clear, too, that the whole federalist camp could have adopted a mixed strategy, with various leaders taking different positions on whether the vote was democratic and whether the result would be accepted; then, some would have been able to outline the negative economic consequences of a Yes decision. This strategy, in fact, would have mirrored that of the sovereigntists, who variously stressed the partnership on the one hand and the heady prospect of independence, at last, on the other.[24] But Jean Chrétien and his closest advisors, who often spoke of Québec as the "heart" or the "soul" of Canada, could not do this. They could not conceive of a sovereign

Québec. As the Prime Minister put it at the final No rally of the campaign, "For all of us, Canada without Quebec is unthinkable just as Quebec without Canada is unthinkable."[25] As a consequence of being unable to imagine Québec as a sovereign state, Chrétien, arguably, almost lost his Canada.

POST-REFERENDUM MANOEUVRES

Severely shaken by the 30 October result, Jean Chrétien nevertheless moved forward. The first initiative was to fulfill the late-campaign promises. There was not enough support in some provincial capitals to push through a constitutional amendment recognizing Québec as a distinct society, so Ottawa went it alone, passing a resolution about distinct society status.[26] This resolution was much more limited than a constitutional amendment and was derided as a "measly proposal" by Lucien Bouchard.[27] But while it did not speak to the judicial branch, and it lacked the traditional phrasing about the Québec government's power to preserve and promote its distinct society, the resolution still stands as binding on the federal government.

In short order, the government introduced a bill that would prohibit Ottawa from proposing a constitutional amendment unless it had the consent of regional majorities; in effect, the federal government was "lending" its own constitutional veto to Québec, as well as to Ontario, two western provinces with 50 percent of the regional population, and two Atlantic provinces with 50 percent of the population. This measure would apply to a limited range of matters, and it left the federal government free to define "consent."[28] The bill met resistance in the west, and was amended to provide a veto to British Columbia. It was assailed by both the Bloc and the Reform Party. But it passed, it remains in effect, and if not legislated out of existence it will have significant effects on the constitutional amendment process.[29]

These initiatives were part of what became known as Plan A measures, ones designed to meet Quebecers' aspirations, to reaffirm the benevolence of the federal government, and to strengthen popular identification with Canada. On the other side, Plan B, Ottawa aimed to counter the arguments of the sovereigntists, and to question their assumptions about the process of secession. On both prongs, the key minister was Stéphane Dion, appointed as Minister of Intergovernmental Affairs in late January 1996.

One constant preoccupation of leaders is recruitment. Chrétien's record in this regard is not unmixed, but he has attracted, supported, and retained some key ministers, and Dion is the most striking case. A scholar of public administration, he was known to his colleagues at the Université de Montréal as both brilliant and monumentally tenacious in debate. During the referendum campaign, he had made striking and brave pro-federalist interventions, and so he came to the attention of Chrétien or, some suggest, of Mrs. Chrétien.[30]

Immediately upon being sworn in, Dion released a most unusual written statement explaining why Québec's distinctiveness had to be enshrined in the Canadian Constitution. He spent several months trying to persuade his Cabinet colleagues and the various provincial premiers that such a move was advisable. He also pressed for decentralization, with more success. In the 1996 Speech from the Throne, the government committed itself to withdraw from programs in forestry, mining, and recreation, and to forge new partnerships with the provinces in food inspection, environmental management, social housing, and tourism. It would also restrict its own spending power, pledging not to establish new shared-cost programs in areas of provincial jurisdiction without the consent of a majority of the provinces.[31] On the most contentious current issue, manpower training, the Chrétien government pledged to transfer full control to the provinces, along with over $2 billion dollars in funding, and an agreement was soon signed with the Québec government.

But Dion's most striking initiatives were on the Plan B side. First, right after taking office, he suggested that Quebec might be subject to partition in the event of secession. As he put it, "You cannot consider Canada divisible but the territory of Quebec sacred"; or, again, "if Canada is divisible, Quebec is divisible too. If I give myself a right, I can't stop others from exercising the same right."[32] Prime Minister Chrétien supported the simple logic of his provocative young minister. But the sovereigntist reaction to this audacity was furious, and many moderate nationalists (and Québec Liberal Party leaders) were dismayed.[33]

Next, the 1996 Speech from the Throne asserted that the Canadian government had roles and responsibilities in any future sovereignty referendum. Again, the assumption that Québec City alone could determine the modalities of the secession process was challenged: "As long as the prospect of another Quebec referendum exists, the Government will exercise its responsibility to ensure that the debate is conducted with all the facts on the table, that the rules of the process are fair, that the consequences are clear, and that Canadians, no matter where they live, will have their say in the future of their country."[34]

The federal government now accepted that secession might occur – there was a "convention" that people could not be held against their will – but the rules had to be clear. So did the level of majority required to secede. Soon after his appointment, Dion echoed some statements made by the Prime Minister at the end of the year to the effect that a narrow majority would not be sufficient to "break" the country: the minister suggested that "for a very serious decision, that is hard to revisit, one can consider a qualified majority."[35] Again, the challenge was to the basic assumptions that the sovereigntists – and others – had shared about the right of secession and the process of achieving it.

Plan B was provocative, but, with Chrétien's support, Dion continued to press, against the doubts and hesitations of many Cabinet members, including some from Québec. The focus turned towards the legalities of secession, which were being contested by several parties, including the maverick lawyer Guy Bertrand, who argued in the Québec Superior Court that a secession accomplished unconstitutionally threatened important *Charter* rights of Canadians. The federal government intervened in the case when the Québec government's lawyers took the position that the courts had no jurisdiction over the matter, with the Attorney General of Canada arguing that there exists no right in domestic or international law for Québec to secede unilaterally.[36] This move outraged Bouchard (who had left Ottawa to become Premier of Québec), and he declared that such a position would make Canada "a prison from which we cannot escape."[37]

Ottawa was undeterred. In September 1996, using its reference power, it placed three questions about the legalities of Québec secession directly before the Supreme Court of Canada:

Under the Constitution of Canada, can the National Assembly, legislature or Government of Québec effect the secession of Quebec from Canada unilaterally?

Second, does international law give the National Assembly, the legislature or the Government of Quebec the right to effect the secession of Quebec from Canada unilaterally? In this regard, is there a right to self-determination under international law that would give the National Assembly, the legislature or the Government of Quebec the right to effect the secession of Quebec from Canada unilaterally?

Third, in the event of a conflict between domestic and international law on the right of the National Assembly, legislature or Government of Quebec to effect the secession of Quebec from Canada unilaterally, which would take precedence in Canada?[38]

This was a high-risk manoeuvre. Courts are unpredictable. Still, other cases would have reached the Supreme Court sooner or later, and through the reference the Chrétien government could control the questions at issue. There was also the possibility of inflaming Québec public opinion, which the PQ government attempted to rouse. Bouchard thundered that only the people of Québec could determine their own future, and the government declared it would ignore any ruling, for it retained the right to make a unilateral declaration of independence; later, the deputy premier attacked the Court's legitimacy by arguing that like "the Tower of Pisa" the Court "always leans the same way."[39] These views found some support in the province.[40] And as the hearing approached, the Québec minister of intergovernmental relations stayed steadfast: "No decree, no federal law, no decision from any court whatsoever can call into question or discredit this right of Quebecers to decide their future."[41]

THE SUPREME COURT DECISION AND THE *CLARITY ACT*

The reference case was heard in February 1998. Although the federal Liberals had been re-elected, the case caused dissension between them and the QLP, as both Daniel Johnson and former leader Claude Ryan held sovereignty to be a fundamentally political issue that should not have been placed before the Court.[42] Jean Charest also expressed misgivings, and the sovereigntists' rhetoric escalated, while polls showed that a majority of Quebecers felt they had the right to choose secession at the ballot box.[43] There was a real possibility of a snap Québec election on the issue, one eliminated when Daniel Johnson resigned as QLP leader ten days after the hearings concluded.

On 20 August 1998, the Supreme Court of Canada pronounced its decision in the *Reference re Secession of Quebec.*[44] The unanimous judgment was a masterful one. After asserting their jurisdiction, the justices explored at length some fundamental principles of the Canadian constitution – federalism, democracy, constitutionalism and the rule of law, and respect for minorities. Examining how these would operate "in the secession context," they proceeded in the core of the decision to eliminate two "absolutist propositions": first, that after a Yes vote, Canada must agree to Québec's secession, whatever the terms; and second, that even after a clear Yes vote on a clear question Canada would have no obligation to negotiate. Each of these propositions would ignore important constitutional principles, and each was therefore declared untenable. Having established this central position, the Court restrained itself from clarifying what amendment formula would be necessary to achieve secession, what constitutes a "clear majority" and a "clear question," what Aboriginal and minority rights were at issue, and what the substantive content of Québec-Canada negotiations would involve. These questions lay in the political realm (though later pronouncements were not ruled out). Finally, the Court rejected the argument that Quebecers have a right in international law to self-determination extending to secession and also the view that effective control of Québec territory could legitimize a unilateral declaration of independence by the provincial government.

The decision stimulated much academic comment.[45] The political impact is more important here. First, the Court's legitimacy in Québec was preserved: the even-handed ruling could not be deployed to arouse in the public a sense of humiliation or constraint.[46] Attempts by some extreme sovereigntists to assail the result as "taking away our right to decide our future" attracted little support.[47] Indeed, the sovereigntist leadership was quick to embrace parts of the decision. Parizeau argued that it would force Canada to negotiate, as the Yes side had predicted, and Bouchard was pleased to note that the "obligation to negotiate has a constitutional status."[48] In the rest of Canada, there was no assault on the decision; instead, those most confrontational towards Québec urged quick action to set out the form of the question and the level of support necessary for secession.[49]

Chrétien's government never went so far. But, after a time, it did move. On 10 December 1999 it tabled, in the House of Commons, a bill that became known as the *Clarity Act*.[50] Carefully titled, it was "to give effect to the requirement for clarity as set out in the opinion of the Supreme Court of Canada in the Quebec Secession Reference" (see Appendix). This is a truly remarkable piece of legislation. It gives legal effect to what had been asserted, at times, by some ministers of the Crown – and contradicted by other politicians: Quebecers have the right to secede. In no other advanced industrial country has there been such a stunning recognition that a portion of the citizenry cannot be kept within the polity against its will. This fundamental characteristic of the legislation is often lost sight of, but the right to secede is at the very core of the *Act*. The *Act* goes on to fill in some of the political space left by the Supreme Court. Typical of Chrétien and his approach, the emphasis is on process rather than pre-defined criteria. So the House of Commons would determine whether a referendum question about secession is clear, and it would also decide whether the results expressed a clear majority will to secede. In this process, the legislators would take into account the views of the Senate and of provincial governments, and, most important, the opinions of opposition parties in the provincial legislature that authorized the vote.[51] Finally the *Clarity Act* distinguishes between the negotiations necessary to amend the constitution to excise Québec, and those about substantive issues like the debt and borders. This the Supreme Court did not do, and it is salutary, because the participants in the two sets of negotiations would be different. So the *Clarity Act* sets out the process for the legitimate and democratic secession of Québec or any other province. As one commentator remarked, "No matter whether another referendum is called six months, six years, or sixty years from now, ordinary Canadians in all provinces and territories will be protected by fair and appropriate ground rules ensuring respect for democracy."[52]

The *Clarity Act* was fought fiercely in the House by the Bloc, and was assailed by Bouchard and the Parti Québécois.[53] But it provoked no groundswell of public opposition in Québec. In fact, there was some polling evidence in the hands of the federal government showing that Quebecers had found the 1995 question opaque, that they favoured a clear question, and that there was substantial support for requiring a majority larger than 50 percent plus one.[54] This was reflected in Québec politics. Bouchard could make no headway in rekindling the sovereigntist flame, and on 11 January 2001, he resigned as Premier and leader of the PQ. Remarkably honest, he admitted that "mes efforts pour relancer le débat sur la question nationale sont restés vains." Despite federal interventions, he said, including the Millennium Scholarships, the Canada Research Chairs program, and the *Clarity Act*, Quebecers had remained "étonnamment impassibles."[55]

Under his successor, Bernard Landry, the party and the government were beset with infighting, as splits developed between the "pur et dur" sovereignty supporters and the moderates, and also between the left and the right.[56] Party membership had fallen substantially, and the troops lacked enthusiasm, as was evident throughout a lacklustre 2003 election campaign in which Landry oscillated between the drive for sovereignty and calls for a new "confederal union" with Canada.[57] The government lost to the Liberals, now led by Charest, and while the QLP contains many strong nationalists and has adopted a program that includes stiff demands upon the central government, a federalist party was back in power in Québec City.

The Parti Québécois continues to be divided by personality and policy.[58] More generally, the sovereigntists and supporters of the broader nationalist project have been thrown back to deep questions about the weight of sovereignty in a globalizing world, the nature of identity and collective adhesion, the demographic evolution of Québec society, and, in general, whether or not collective thinking about Québec is capable "de s'exiler du paradigme qui la nourrit depuis des lustres: celui de '(in)accomplissement national.'"[59] At the level of the mass public, this has not translated into any great diminution of support for the sovereignty option, which hovers around 40 percent (depending on the question). What is quite clear, though, is that Quebecers have no interest in another referendum, in plunging into another bitterly divisive struggle: a typical poll in 2001 showed that 70 percent (including 53 percent of PQ supporters) wanted a promise from the premier not to hold a referendum for at least five years.[60] This does not mean that the drive for sovereignty is finished.[61] Linguistic insecurity, in particular, could underpin a renewed effort towards secession. The PQ could switch strategies, abandoning the referendum route, or even contemplating a unilateral declaration of independence despite the Supreme Court's ruling. But as Chrétien left office, the threat of a successful referendum certainly was in abeyance.

CONCLUSION

Apart from having almost lost the 1995 referendum and from supporting his minister's bold measures to counterattack the sovereigntists, Prime Minister Chrétien did much in Québec during ten years of office. The Liberal government supported key firms like Bombardier and sectors like pharmaceuticals, it spent substantial sums on infrastructure, it helped reinvigorate the Montreal economy (notably by cooperating with the Québec government in creating the economic development organization, Montréal International), it sprinkled funds elsewhere through the province (through the little known Economic Development Agency of Canada for Québec Regions), it provided welcome assistance during the 1996 Saguenay flood and the 1999 ice storm, and so on. All this was business as usual, and it helped maintain Chrétien's support, as did the improving economy. It is true that some anti-sovereignty efforts were extraordinary, like the embarrassing blanketing of Québec City with Canadian flags. As well, the post-referendum desperation legitimized, in the minds of Chrétien's entourage, some dubious dealings with

Liberal-oriented firms designed to propagate the federalist message.[62] And Chrétien himself was linked with questionable loans to constituents by federal agencies. But none of this is comparable to the Pacific Scandal or other memorable scandals of the past. Like the rest of the normal business, its effects will not last.

One part of Jean Chrétien's real legacy in Québec is that he almost lost the referendum of 1995. Insofar as he was responsible for the strategy, he almost lost because the federalists could not bring themselves to be clear about the consequences of a Yes vote, and so the sovereigntists could promise minimal economic disruption and a future Québec-Canada partnership. He could not be clear about the consequences of a Yes because the federalists could not admit that Québec could secede. Along with more decentralized powers, the *Clarity Act* is the second part of the legacy. It is now established in law, backed by a powerful Supreme Court decision, that Québec can secede, and a clear process is in place for it to do so. Because of this, and the sorties of Stéphane Dion, the minister Jean Chrétien chose and backed, the sovereignty movement has receded.

Chrétien once reflected that "[p]olitical life is like skating on thin ice and you never know where there will be a hole that will gobble you up and you will disappear forever."[63] In 1995, the former Prime Minister faced the abyss after coasting towards it. Then he stickhandled hard to fix the problem. On leaving office, he is still skating in Québec.

POSTSCRIPT: DECEMBER 2005

What a difference two years make!

Since this assessment was written, we have witnessed remarkable developments on the Québec file, especially in relation to the sponsorship scandal – "le scandale des commandites." First was the report of the Auditor-General, made public in February 2004. This found waste and probably worse in the distribution of advertising contracts within the program that was aimed at heightening the visible presence of the federal government in Quebec.[64] The report triggered a fevered fit of activity by Prime Minister Paul Martin, who pledged several measures to get to the bottom of the scandal, root out and punish wrongdoers, and ensure that loose contracting could not recur. Two aspects of Martin's response were notable. He fired several high-profile comrades of Jean Chrétien, including Jean Pelletier (Chair of VIA Rail), Alfonso Gagliano (Ambassador to Denmark) and André Ouellet (President of Canada Post). This was a clear effort to distance himself from his predecessor, and to absolve his "new" government from blame. Second, he established a Commission of Inquiry under Mr. Justice John Gomery to investigate the sponsorship program, and he conferred wide powers on it. Martin thereby ensured that any dirty Liberal laundry would be washed in public, day after day after day.

The consequences of the scandal continued to reverberate through the Canadian polity. In the federal election of 28 June 2004, Paul Martin's procession to a smashing majority, widely anticipated only six months earlier, failed to materialize. Instead, the Liberals were reduced to 101 seats. In Québec, the Bloc Québécois capitalized on the scandal, cleverly calling for "un Québec 'propre'," and it took 48.9 percent of the vote to the Liberals' 33.9 percent, and 54 of the 75 seats. All of Chrétien's progress against the sovereigntists was reversed by a program that was one of the several means he had used to fight them.

Over the next year, the Gomery inquiry continued to expose the machinations of a program that had gone badly out of control. Not only were funds allocated in some instances to advertising firms in return for little work, but payments and favours flowed from the firms to some people in the Québec wing of the federal Liberal party. These revelations were accompanied by a few criminal charges. More central to the issues here was the role of Jean Chrétien. Appearing before Judge Gomery, whom he felt was biased and whom he undoubtedly regarded as a twerp, Chrétien was at once dismissive and defensive. While denying any detailed knowledge of the sponsorship program's operation, he did justify the program and accepted responsibility for mounting it and also, in a general way, as head of government, for any problems with it. Subsequently, his goal was to clear his name and preserve his reputation against interpretations associated with the Commission's first report.[65]

Questions remain about the sponsorship affair, for the firms involved in Québec were not just "Liberal-friendly" companies, but federalist firms that had disproportionately funded the Progressive Conservative Party during the Mulroney government. Moreover, advertising firms outside Québec also participated in the program and gave very large donations to the federal Liberal Party.[66]

But heading into the election of 23 January 2006, Jean Chrétien's role in Québec continued to shape public opinion and political outcomes. Paul Martin faced an uphill battle to push the Bloc back from historic levels of support, and to weaken the sovereigntist camp in the provincial arena (where the Liberal government of Jean Charest seems very vulnerable). The sponsorship scandal lay at the heart of Martin's difficulties in

Québec – and elsewhere too, as the opposition parties, like the Bloc, decry "corruption" and the Liberals' "culture of entitlement." Yet as we focus on what many consider to be a big part of his legacy in Québec, it behooves us to ask the question that Jean Chrétien might well pose. There was a *sponsorship program* that went badly off the rails. And there is a *sponsorship scandal* that has badly wounded the federal Liberals in Québec, along with the whole federalist cause. Jean Chrétien was clearly responsible for the program. But who created the scandal?

APPENDIX

S.C. 2000, c. 26
An Act to give effect to the requirement for clarity
as set out in the opinion of the Supreme Court of Canada
in the Quebec Secession Reference
[Assented to 29 June 2000]

WHEREAS the Supreme Court of Canada has confirmed that there is no right, under international law or under the Constitution of Canada, for the National Assembly, legislature or government of Quebec to effect the secession of Quebec from Canada unilaterally;

WHEREAS any proposal relating to the break-up of a democratic state is a matter of the utmost gravity and is of fundamental importance to all of its citizens;

WHEREAS the government of any province of Canada is entitled to consult its population by referendum on any issue and is entitled to formulate the wording of its referendum question;

WHEREAS the Supreme Court of Canada has determined that the result of a referendum on the secession of a province from Canada must be free of ambiguity both in terms of the question asked and in terms of the support it achieves if that result is to be taken as an expression of the democratic will that would give rise to an obligation to enter into negotiations that might lead to secession;

WHEREAS the Supreme Court of Canada has stated that democracy means more than simple majority rule, that a clear majority in favour of secession would be required to create an obligation to negotiate secession, and that a qualitative evaluation is required to determine whether a clear majority in favour of secession exists in the circumstances;

WHEREAS the Supreme Court of Canada has confirmed that, in Canada, the secession of a province, to be lawful, would require an amendment to the Constitution of Canada, that such an amendment would perforce require negotiations in relation to secession involving at least the governments of all of the provinces and the Government of Canada, and that those negotiations would be governed by the principles of federalism, democracy, constitutionalism and the rule of law, and the protection of minorities;

WHEREAS, in light of the finding by the Supreme Court of Canada that it would be for elected representatives to determine what constitutes a clear question and what constitutes a clear majority in a referendum held in a province on secession, the House of Commons, as the only political institution elected to represent all Canadians, has an important role in identifying what constitutes a clear question and a clear majority sufficient for the Government of Canada to enter into negotiations in relation to the secession of a province from Canada;

AND WHEREAS it is incumbent on the Government of Canada not to enter into negotiations that might lead to the secession of a province from Canada, and that could consequently entail the termination of citizenship and other rights that Canadian citizens resident in the province enjoy as full participants in Canada, unless the population of that province has clearly expressed its democratic will that the province secede from Canada;

NOW, THEREFORE, Her Majesty, by and with the advice and consent of the Senate and House of Commons of Canada, enacts as follows:

1. (1) The House of Commons shall, within thirty days after the government of a province tables in its legislative assembly or otherwise officially releases the question that it intends to submit to its voters in a referendum relating to the proposed secession of the province from Canada, consider the question and, by resolution, set out its determination on whether the question is clear.

(2) Where the thirty days referred to in subsection (1) occur, in whole or in part, during a general election of members to serve in the House of Commons, the thirty days shall be extended by an additional forty days.

(3) In considering the clarity of a referendum question, the House of Commons shall consider whether the question would result in a clear expression of the will of the population of a province on whether the province should cease to be part of Canada and become an independent state.

(4) For the purpose of subsection (3), a clear expression of the will of the population of a province that the province cease to be part of Canada could not result from

(a) a referendum question that merely focuses on a mandate to negotiate without soliciting a direct expression of the will of the population of that province on whether the province should cease to be part of Canada; or

(b) a referendum question that envisages other possibilities in addition to the secession of the province from Canada, such as economic or political arrangements with Canada, that obscure a direct expression of the will of the population of that province on whether the province should cease to be part of Canada.

(5) In considering the clarity of a referendum question, the House of Commons shall take into account the views of all political parties represented in the legislative assembly of the province whose government is proposing the referendum on secession, any formal statements or resolutions by the government or legislative assembly of any province or territory of Canada, any formal statements or resolutions by the Senate, any formal statements or resolutions by the representatives of the Aboriginal peoples of Canada, especially those in the province whose government is proposing the referendum on secession, and any other views it considers to be relevant.

(6) The Government of Canada shall not enter into negotiations on the terms on which a province might cease to be part of Canada if the House of Commons determines, pursuant to this section, that a referendum question is not clear and, for that reason, would not result in a clear expression of the will of the population of that province on whether the province should cease to be part of Canada.

2. (1) Where the government of a province, following a referendum relating to the secession of the province from Canada, seeks to enter into negotiations on the terms on which that province might cease to be part of Canada, the House of Commons shall, except where it has determined pursuant to section 1 that a referendum question is not clear, consider and, by resolution, set out its determination on whether, in the circumstances, there has been a clear expression of a will by a clear majority of the population of that province that the province cease to be part of Canada.

(2) In considering whether there has been a clear expression of a will by a clear majority of the population of a province that the province cease to be part of Canada, the House of Commons shall take into account

(a) the size of the majority of valid votes cast in favour of the secessionist option;

(b) the percentage of eligible voters voting in the referendum; and

(c) any other matters or circumstances it considers to be relevant.

(3) In considering whether there has been a clear expression of a will by a clear majority of the population of a province that the province cease to be part of Canada, the House of Commons shall take into account the views of all political parties represented in the legislative assembly of the province whose government proposed the referendum on secession, any formal statements or resolutions by the government or legislative assembly of any province or territory of Canada, any formal statements or resolutions by the Senate, any formal statements or resolutions by the representatives of the Aboriginal peoples of Canada, especially those in the province whose government proposed the referendum on secession, and any other views it considers to be relevant.

(4) The Government of Canada shall not enter into negotiations on the terms on which a province might cease to be part of Canada unless the House of Commons determines, pursuant to this section, that there has been a clear expression of a will by a clear majority of the population of that province that the province cease to be part of Canada.

3. (1) It is recognized that there is no right under the Constitution of Canada to effect the secession of a province from Canada unilaterally and that, therefore, an amendment to the Constitution of Canada would be required for any province to secede from Canada, which in turn would require negotiations involving at least the governments of all of the provinces and the Government of Canada.

(2) No Minister of the Crown shall propose a constitutional amendment to effect the secession of a province from Canada unless the Government of Canada has addressed, in its negotiations, the terms of secession that are relevant in the circumstances, including the division of assets and liabilities, any changes to the borders of the province, the rights, interests and territorial claims of the Aboriginal peoples of Canada, and the protection of minority rights.

NOTES

Professor, Department of Political Science, and Canada Research Chair in Multilevel Governance, University of Western Ontario. I thank the Social Science and Humanities Research Council for support, Ben Elling for research assistance, and Peter Neary for advice.

1 *The Gallup Poll*, 28 January 1993; 23 January 1995; 5 February 2002.

2 *Reference re Secession of Quebec*, [1998] 2 S.C.R. 217, 161 D.L.R. (4th) 385, CanLII http://www.canlii.org/ca/cas/scc/1998/1998scc63.html.

3 See Robert A. Young, *The Struggle for Quebec* (Montreal: McGill-Queen's University Press, 1999), 13–38.

4 The agreement was very detailed, but its essence was to conflate a vote for sovereignty with "a formal proposal for a new economic and political partnership with Canada." It is found as an appendix to Bill 1, *An Act Respecting the Future of Québec* (in French, *Loi sur la souveraineté du Québec*) 1st Sess., 35th Leg., Québec, 1995. Hence flowed the question that was actually proposed to Quebecers in the referendum: "Do you agree that Québec should become sovereign, after having made a formal offer to Canada for a new Economic and Political Partnership, within the scope of the Bill respecting the future of Québec and of the agreement signed on June 12, 1995? YES or NO?"

5 André Blais, Richard Nadeau, and Pierre Martin, "Pourquoi le Oui a-t-il fait des gains pendant la campagne référendaire?" in John Trent, Robert Young,

and Guy Lachapelle, eds., *Québec-Canada: What Is the Path Ahead?* (Ottawa: University of Ottawa Press, 1996), 71–6.

6 See Guy Lachapelle, "La souveraineté partenariat: Donnée essentielle du résultat référendaire et de l'avenir des relations Québec-Canada," in Trent, Young, and Lachapelle, *Path Ahead*, 41–63; Maurice Pinard, "Le contexte politique et les dimensions sociodémographiques," in Maurice Pinard, Robert Bernier, and Vincent Lemieux, eds., *Un combat inachevé* (Sainte-Foy: Les Presses de l'Université du Québec, 1997), 277–325; and Young, *Struggle for Quebec*, 39–42.

7 Jeff Sallot, "It's official: Québec votes Oct 30," *Globe and Mail*, 12 September 1995, A3.

8 See *e.g.*, *House of Commons Debates*, 225 (18 September 1995), 14528.

9 *House of Commons Debates*, 226 (19 September 1995), 14610.

10 Ibid.

11 "Grab the chance, Bouchard urges Quebecers," *Globe and Mail*, 30 October 1995, A5.

12 Mario Fontaine, "Chrétien reste nébuleux à une victoire serrée du oui," La Presse, 27 October 1995, B5 [author's translation]. See also Jean Dion, "À l'émission Mongrain," Le Devoir, 27 October 1995, A4; and André Picard, "Beware Canada's mood, PM warns," *Globe and Mail*, 27 October 1995, A1.

13 *Globe and Mail*, 20 October 1995.

14 Philip Authier, "The Referendum: Quebec could split in 'weeks or months'," *Gazette* (Montreal), 21 October 1995, A15.

15 For a formal refutation of this, see Robert A. Young, "The Political Economy of Secession: The Case of Quebec," *Constitutional Political Economy* 5 (1994): 221–45.

16 The notion that admitting the possibility of defeat can be "a self-fulfilling prophecy" was later called one of the two "golden rules" of federalist discourse by Stéphane Dion, Minister of Intergovernmental Affairs. It consists of "never publicly admitting that the opponents might win." See Stéphane Dion, *Straight Talk: On Canadian Unity* (Montreal: McGill-Queen's University Press, 1999), xix.

17 Tu Thanh Ha, "Honour vote, Robillard urges," *Globe and Mail*, 13 September 1995, A1.

18 Ibid.

19 Ibid., A2; *London Free Press*, 13 September 1995; and *Globe and Mail*, 20 September 1995.

20 Ha, "Honour vote, Robillard urges," A2.

21 Lawrence Martin, *Iron Man: The Defiant Reign of Jean Chrétien*, vol. 2 (Toronto: Viking Canada, 2003), 128.

22 Richard Mackie, "Johnson doing damage control," *Globe and Mail*, 23 October 1995, A1.

23 Richard Mackie, "Chrétien, Bouchard to address nation," *Globe and Mail*, 25 October 1995, A1; André Picard, "PM pleads with undecided voters," *Globe and Mail*, 26 October 1995, A1.

24 Robert A. Young, "'Maybe Yes, Maybe No': The Rest of Canada and a Quebec 'Oui'," in Douglas M. Brown and Jonathan W. Rose, eds., *Canada: The State of the Federation 1995* (Kingston: Institute of Intergovernmental Relations, 1995), 47–62.

25 "Canadians rally for unity," *Gazette* (Montreal), 30 October 1995, A1.

26 *House of Commons Debates*, 267 (29 November 1995), 16971. The text reads:
Whereas the People of Quebec have expressed the desire for recognition of Quebec's distinct society;
　(1) the House recognize that Quebec is a distinct society within Canada;
　(2) the House recognize that Quebec's distinct society includes its French-speaking majority, unique culture and civil law tradition;
　(3) the House undertake to be guided by this reality;

27 Ibid., 16961; see also ibid., 16975, 16980.

28 Essentially, it covers amendments that fall under the general amending formula and that do not derogate from provincial powers: this includes, notably, the establishment of new provinces and the power, selection, and distribution of members of the Senate (as well as recognition of Québec as a distinct society).

29 *An Act Respecting Constitutional Amendments*, S.C. 1996, c. 1, http://www.canlii.org/ca/as/1996/c1/whole.html. See Andrew Heard and Tim Swartz, "The Regional Veto Formula and Its Effects on Canada's Constitutional Amendment Process," *Canadian Journal of Political Science* 30 (1997): 339–56.

30 Edward Greenspon and Anthony Wilson-Smith, *Double Vision: The Inside Story of the Liberals in Power* (Toronto: Doubleday, 1997), 354; and Martin, *Iron Man*, 143.

31 *House of Commons Debates*, 001 (27 February 1996), 4. The restrictions on the spending power were later formalized in the Social Union Framework Agreement (SUFA), to which all provinces except Québec became signatories.

32 Tu Thanh Ha, "Talk of partition heats up unity debate," *Globe and Mail*, 30 January 1996, A2; and *London Free Press*, 2 February 1996.

33 Lysiane Gagnon, "A badly coached rookie named Dion takes to the ice," *Globe and Mail*, 3 February 1996.

34 *House of Commons Debates*, 001 (27 February 1996), 5.

35 *Globe and Mail*, 31 January 1996.

36 Young, *Struggle for Quebec*, 106–7.

37 André Picard, "Bouchard rejects election option," *Globe and Mail*, 14 May 1996, A1.

38 *House of Commons Debates*, 075 (26 September 1996), 4709.

39 *Globe and Mail*, 12 May 1997; see also *London Free Press*, 27 September 1996; *La Presse*, 27 September 1996; and *Toronto Star*, 29 September 1996.

40 Lise Bissonnette, "Un an plus tard, la clarté," *Le Devoir*, 27 September 1996, A10: the 1982 constitution held Québec in a "carcan" (iron collar).

41 *London Free Press*, 19 December 1997, quoting Jacques Brassard.

42 Rhéal Séguin, "Separation not issue for top court, Ryan says," *Globe and Mail*, 3 February 1998, A5.

43 Edward Greenspon, "Liberals target Charest for views on Supreme Court reference," *Globe and Mail*, 18 February 1998, A4; and Rhéal Séguin, "Ottawa like the Titanic: Bouchard," *Globe and Mail*, 21 February 1998, A1. Parizeau declared that "the judges can decide what they want. It has no importance. We will never live under the threat of decisions taken by others."

44 *Reference re Secession of Quebec*, paras. 84–97.

45 See the issue "The Quebec Secession Reference," *Constitutional Forum constitutionnel* 10 (1) (1998); and David Schneiderman, ed., *The Quebec Decision: Perspectives on the Supreme Court Ruling on Secession* (Toronto: James Lorimer & Company, 1999).

46 See the remarks of pollster Jean-Marc Léger, *London Free Press*, 21 August 1998.

47 Josée Legault, "How to deny Quebec's right to self-determination," *Globe and Mail*, 21 August 1998, A19. This article appeared in a longer version in *Le Devoir*, yet that newspaper's editorial suggested that the Parti Québécois should "forget convoluted referendum questions." See "Cross Canada commentaries," *Globe and Mail*, 22 August 1998, A3.

48 Rhéal Séguin, "Federalist cause poisoned by ruling, Bouchard says," *Globe and Mail*, 22 August 1998, A3. See also Stéphane Dion's tart letter to Bouchard about his selective use of the decision: Dion, "Letter to Mr. Lucien Bouchard," in *Straight Talk*, 247. This letter epitomizes Dion's stance towards the sovereigntist leadership – unobsequious to the point of disdain:

Instead of concocting the question that will snatch a few thousand more votes, do your job. Explain to us Quebecers why we would be happier if we were no longer Canadians as well; why we need a smaller country that is ours alone, rather than a larger country shared with others. If you convince us, the question and the majority will follow. The referendum will then merely confirm a visible consensus. Firmly determined to separate, Quebecers could wade through the problems of the negotiations.

If this is a tall order, it is certainly not the fault of the federal government. – Quebecers have contributed tremendously to building Canada and it is in working with other Canadians that they want to take on the enormous challenges presented at the dawn of the new millennium. It is up to you to prove to them, in all clarity, that they are wrong.

49 See the remarks of Stephen Harper in Brian Laghi, "PM moves to cool off Quebec debate," *Globe and Mail*, 24 August 1998, A3.

50 S.C. 2000, c. 26, http://www.canlii.org/ca/sta/c-31.8/whole.html. The *Act* is reproduced in the Appendix to this chapter.

51 In 1995, the reaction of the leader of the Québec Liberal Party to a narrow Yes result would have been very significant, if not decisive. See Robert A. Young, *The Secession of Quebec and the Future of Canada* (Montreal & Kingston: McGill-Queen's University Press and the Institute of Intergovernmental Relations, 1995), 171–207.

52 Patrick J. Monahan, *Doing the Rules: An Assessment of the Federal Clarity Act in Light of the Quebec Secession Reference* (Toronto: C.D. Howe Institute, 2000), 37.

53 Two members of the NDP and nine Progressive Conservative MPs voted against the bill on third reading, along with forty-four Bloc members.

54 Matthew Mendelsohn, "Analyzing recent empirical trends in Quebec public opinion," (Presented to the conference on "Quebec and Canada in the New Century: New Dynamics, New Opportunities," Institute of Intergovernmental Relations, Queen's University, Kingston, 31 October-1 November 2003).

55 Lucien Bouchard, "Je regrette seulement de ne pas avoir fait mieux et davantage," *Le Devoir*, 12 January 2001, A9. ("My efforts to relaunch the debate on the national question remained fruitless"; Quebecers had remained "astonishingly imperturbable.")

56 François Cardinal, "Les purs et durs veulent le départ des ministres 'de droite'," *Le Devoir*, 24 October 2002, A1; and Rhéal Séguin, "Quebec Justice Minister resigns," *Globe and Mail*, 29 October 2002.

57 Rhéal Séguin, "Landry hits PQ with shift on sovereignty," *Globe and Mail*, 17 March 2003, A1.

58 Rhéal Séguin, "Parizeau tells BQ caucus to push for sovereignty," *Globe and Mail*, 28 August 2003, A4; and Robert Dutrisac, "Landry souhaite diriger le PQ aux prochaines élections," *Le Devoir*, 8 October 2003.

59 Jocelyn Létourneau, "Reposer la Question du Québec," *Policy Options* 24 (October 2003): 44–49 ("capable of pushing itself out of the paradigm that has long nourished it: that of national self-(non) realization") 44.

60 *Globe and Mail*, 27 October 2001.

61 See the special issue, "Is it over? Est-ce fini?" *Policy Options* 21 (June 2000).

62 *Globe and Mail*, 11 October 2001; and Canada, Office of the Auditor General, *Report to the Minister of Public Works and Government Services on Three Contracts Awarded to Groupaction* (Ottawa: Minister of Public Works and Government Services, 2002), http://www.oag-bvg.gc.ca/domino/reports. See Susan Delacourt, *Juggernaut: Paul Martin's Campaign for Chrétien's Crown* (Toronto: McClelland & Stewart, 2003), 234: the advertising agencies had been hired "to stamp the federal brand on the province of Quebec."

63 *Globe and Mail*, 14 December 2002.

64 Canada, Office of the Auditor General, "Chapter 3: The Sponsorship Scandal," *Report of the Auditor General of Canada to the House of Commons*, November 2003 (Ottawa: Minister of Public Works and Government Services, 2003), http://www.oag-bvg.gc.ca/domino/reports.nsf/html/20031103ce.html/$file/20031103ce.pdf.

65 Canada, Commission of Inquiry into the Sponsorship Program and Advertising Activities, *Who Is Responsible? Fact Finding Report* (Ottawa: Minister of Public Works and Government Services, 2005), http://www.gomery.ca/en/phase1report/ffr/.

66 Robert A. Young, "Just what is a "Liberal-friendly" ad firm?: Why the spin on the sponsorship scandal is wrong," *Inside Ottawa* 12:15 (2004), 6–7.

3

The Urban Legacy of Jean Chrétien

CAROLINE ANDREW

INTRODUCTION

It is certainly not the urban legacy of Jean Chrétien that will be his most lasting, or his most positive contribution to Canadian society. At best, it is a mixed legacy: on the negative side dominated by the withdrawal of the federal government from social housing, and on the positive side by a series of infrastructure programs offering financial assistance, through the provinces, to municipal governments. Paradoxically, and one of the major themes of this chapter, perhaps the most positive impact on urban Canada from the Chrétien era comes from the programs designed to support research in the post-secondary education system. These have not at all been seen as urban programs but, as will be argued, they can be interpreted as helping to build a knowledge-based urban society for the twenty-first century.

This summary conclusion immediately raises the question of how to judge the urban legacy of Jean Chrétien. Should the evaluation be based on the condition of cities in Canada in 2003 as compared to 1993? And, if so, is it possible to evaluate the extent of federal responsibility for these conditions? Perhaps the legacy should be judged not on the situation of Canadian cities, but on the extent to which federal policies addressed urban questions and influenced the directions of urban development. If this is the way to evaluate the urban legacy, the question of the choice of policies remains. Are we to look at explicitly urban policies or those that are implicit? And how are we to choose the implicit policies to be looked at? If we do so in terms of a vision of urban development, what is the vision being used? A final dimension that might also be used to evaluate the urban legacy is the degree to which the Chrétien government has articulated a discourse about the place of cities, and municipal government, within Canadian society and the Canadian intergovernmental system.

My choice is eclecticism and therefore our evaluation of the legacy is based on a variety of ways of looking at Chrétien's urban activity. I will begin by examining the evolution of the Canadian urban system for 1993 to 2003 with some discussion about the degree of federal responsibility for certain urban conditions. Following this I will discuss federal policy initiatives during this period, starting with the Canada Infrastructure Works Program (CIWP) of 1993 and then the federal withdrawal from social housing. My choice of federal policy initiatives is designed to discuss both programs where municipal governments were actively and officially involved (such as the infrastructure programs) and programs whose urban impact is important but not explicitly articulated. In this regard I will examine the set of federal policies for support to research in the post-secondary education system, and notably the Canada Foundation for Innovation, a federally funded arm's-length organization that gives grants to Canadian universities to develop their research capacity. I will also look at the Chrétien legacy in terms of significant additions or alterations to the built form of Canadian cities.

The last criterion I will examine is the development of an urban agenda within the federal government, the extent to which this exists and has been implemented, and the degree to which the urban agenda articulates a vision of the place of major Canadian cities in the Canadian governance system and of the role of the federal government in urban issues. In my earlier analysis of federal urban activity it was very clear that the federal government was not interested in giving itself a role in urban issues, following its own very negative evaluation of the federal urban activity of the Trudeau era.[1] But towards the end of the Chrétien era there were indications by the federal government of interest in defining a federal urban role, and it is these efforts that I wish to investigate.

Finally, it is perhaps useful to sketch out a vision of twenty-first century urban development to provide a backdrop to our evaluation of the Chrétien government's policies and programs. This description is based on the work of authors, such as Manuel Castells, who have analyzed the impact of information technology on economic development. Arguing that global economic development based on information technology created, paradoxically, a new space for cities and regions, Castells and Hall elaborated a typology of technopoles, or a "territorial concentration of technological innovation with a potential to generate scientific synergy and economic productivity."[2] Economic development in the twenty-first century was seen to be linked to cities that managed to create concentrations of innovative information technology activity. More recently, the work of authors such as Richard Florida have added to this vision by underlining the importance of the workers of these innovative activities, and therefore linking economic development to the ability of cities to attract and retain what Florida has called the creative class.[3] Creating a culturally vibrant urban centre becomes an economic development strategy. Donald and Morrow add to this a concern for social inclusion, arguing that social polarization and social exclusion can create the kind of environment that is not conducive to cultural vitality and therefore economic prosperity.[4]

This vision of urban development would, therefore, argue for public policy aimed at creating clusters of innovation and for a geographically sensitive policy that supports urban concentrations of information technology activity. In addition, public policy should support the cultural and social vitality of these urban centres. Economic growth will be concentrated in urban centres and public policy will be concerned with the cultural and social well-being of these centres. The crucial factors in this vision of economic development are that it is urban-centered, based on concentrating information technology innovation, and concerned with creating cultural and social milieux that are capable of attracting and retaining highly skilled knowledge workers.

It is with this vision of urban development in mind that I can turn to my evaluation of Chrétien's urban legacy. My first criterion for evaluation is to compare the state of Canadian cities in 2003 with what they were in 1993 at the beginning of the Chrétien era.

CANADIAN CITIES, 1993–2003

There is a certain research consensus around a number of trends relating to the evolution of Canadian cities over the period of the Chrétien government: continuing urbanization and, indeed, metropolitanization whereby the largest Canadian metropolitan areas continue to absorb an ever larger percentage of the Canadian population; growing polarization within the largest urban centres; growing ethno-cultural diversity within the largest urban centres; and a decreasing capacity of new Canadians to be integrated successfully into the Canadian economy and society.

The 2001 census figures indicated that 79.6 percent of the Canadian population was urban. The fastest-growing areas are the suburban areas surrounding the largest cities. "Despite immigration and the return of the middle class into older inner-city neighbourhoods, most growth in Toronto and Vancouver was focused in a half-dozen suburban municipalities like Markham and Vaughan (Toronto) and Surrey and Delta (Vancouver)."[5] This metropolization implies a new built form, the city-region, with very low-density residential development over an increasingly large area. This has created huge demands for increased expenditures for transportation and a very heavy use of the private automobile with consequent increases in pollution. Public interest is developing around issues of "smart growth," or public policies aimed at limiting urban sprawl and at increasing urban density. However, these debates have not developed into firm policy directions and metropolitanization continues with low-density suburban development.

The second trend in the 1993–2003 period is that of increasing polarization. Larry Bourne has described the increasing polarization, both between cities and within cities. On the overall distribution of urban growth, Bourne argues that "the contrasts between these cities that are winners and those that are losers in the national growth sweepstakes will become even more pronounced. The challenge for senior governments is to respond to the increasing variability of growth and change; but first they must recognize that the problem exists."[6] He is equally clear on the issue of increasing polarization within cities and the groups whose conditions have worsened during the 1990s.[7] The groups mentioned are "the homeless and street people, the mentally ill, and transient unemployed youth ... those on fixed or marginal incomes, those living under severe housing pressures, some recent refugees, young single mothers, the frail elderly."[8]

The concentration of recent immigration within the largest metropolitan centres is another clear trend of the 1993–2003 period. Both Toronto and Vancouver have about one-fifth of their population that has immigrated post-1981.[9] Of the 1.2 million immigrants who came to Canada between 1996 and 2001, 46.1 percent located in the Toronto region, 17.1 percent in Vancouver and 12.1 percent in Montreal. Less than a quarter of these new immigrants (24.7 percent) went to locations other than the three largest urban centres.[10] In 2001, 44 percent of Toronto's population was foreign-born as was 30 percent of Vancouver's. For Canada overall, the figure was 18 percent. What this means is that the large urban centres are increasingly different from the rest of the country in terms of ethnocultural diversity. The public policy consequences of this are not yet clear; it could be an argument for greater municipal autonomy (and resources) or for greater federal and provincial support for municipal actions.

Finally, our last trend also relates to the place of new immigrants in Canadian society, but underlines the increasing economic difficulties faced by them. Recent research indicates that immigrants arriving after 1981 are having a harder and harder time integrating successfully into the Canadian economy and society. In 1981, immigrants with a university degree, one year after arrival in Canada, were earning 20 percent more than the Canadian average, but by 1992 immigrants with a university degree, one year after arrival in Canada, were earning 30 percent less than the Canadian average.[11] One of the major differences is the much higher proportion of visible minorities among recent immigrants and the increasing requirements by employers for "Canadian experience."[12]

The question then becomes the extent to which federal policies are responsible for the conditions we have just described: increasing low-density sprawl development, increasing polarization within cities, and a decreasing capacity of recent immigrants to integrate employment successfully (specific groups marked by poverty and marginalization).

It is certainly possible to find federal programs that encourage, or do not discourage, low-density suburban development. Indeed, some critics have argued that the infrastructure programs have combined to support development based on the private car. And federal housing policy has traditionally been supportive of single-family suburban development at low densities.

Federal policies that impact on polarization are numerous and certainly many of them would not be seen as specifically urban. For instance, poverty rates among the elderly have been reduced substantially and this certainly reduces polarization based on age. However, as Anne Gauthier has demonstrated, this has not been true for child poverty rates.[13] More generally the cuts made by the federal government to unemployment insurance and to a multitude of social programs and organizations can also be seen as having added to the deterioration of the conditions of vulnerable and marginalized groups. Here the urban impact is not so obvious, except that polarization is worse in the large urban centres and therefore policies that increase or decrease polarization can be argued to have an urban impact. One of the areas where the link between federal actions and increased polarization has been asserted is that relating to the increase in the numbers of the homeless and the

relationship to the federal abandonment of social housing to the provinces.[14] We will discuss this policy at greater length, but clearly it is one of
the areas where urban conditions have deteriorated for the poor because
of federal policy decisions.

Certainly the federal government has had an important influence on
the nature of immigration and therefore on the rapidly growing ethno-
cultural diversity of the major urban centres. The federal government has
tried to develop policies for the regionalization of immigration but, in
general, these have not been successful, and immigration continues to be
highly metropolitan in destination.

The increasingly difficult integration of new immigrants into the Canadian labour market can be related, in part, to federal economic policies,
but also to the absence of policies relating to the recognition of foreign
credentials. The lack of strong policies in this area is clearly related to the
difficulties faced by immigrants in successfully integrating into the
Canadian labour market.

Canadian society is thus more urban and more metropolitan since Jean
Chrétien became Prime Minister. The largest Canadian cities are clearly
more diverse in ethno-cultural terms and, in this respect, increasingly different from the rest of Canadian society. Income polarization has grown
within Canadian cities and there are indications of the increasing persis-
tence of poverty in certain urban neighbourhoods,[15] with some of these
related to ethno-cultural communities. The increasing polarization and
deep poverty of certain urban populations have been linked to federal
policy orientations during this period, particularly those related to federal budget cutting. For instance, the fact that the federal government got
out of social housing is one factor in the increase in homelessness.
Changes in federal employment insurance have impacted particularly on
women. However these changes cannot all be related to federal policies.
The difficulties faced by new immigrants, at least in part, relate to characteristics of Canadian society that are not easily modified by public sector legislation. We turn now to the specific federal programs that had a
clear urban focus.

FEDERAL POLICY INITIATIVES 1993–2003

Moving on from this general background of urban development, what
have been the federal policy initiatives that can be seen to be urban or to
involve municipal governments? The Chrétien era began with the Canada Infrastructure Works Program and, indeed, infrastructure programs

have continued throughout the Chrétien administration. The full list is as
follows:

1993 – Canadian Infrastructure Works Program (CIWP) (with top-up
        funding announced in 1997)
2000 – Infrastructure Canada Program (ICP) and Strategic Highway
        Infrastructure Program (SHIP)
2001 – Canadian Strategic Infrastructure Program (CSIF) and Border
        Infrastructure Program (BIF)
2002 – Ten-year infrastructure program announced but February 2003
        budget only allocated an initial two-year commitment.[16]

The first program, CIWP, produced mostly traditional infrastructure
projects such as roads, sewers, and water. Examples can be found[17] of
municipalities such as North York, Ontario, that invested heavily in
"quality of life" urban amenities, but for the most part it was more the
traditional projects of municipal governments: the upgrading of basic
services. In some cases, the provincial governments played important
roles in deciding the types of projects, but overall, municipal priorities
were influential. The federal government did not play a significant role in
determining the types of projects actually built. Early federal descriptions
of the program had linked it to emerging information technology, economic development, and global competitiveness, but the actual results
were much more mundane. However this should not suggest that the
program was unsuccessful from the point of view of the federal government. Quite the opposite: "it got what it wanted out of the program: job
creation, generated activity and the sense that the Canadian intergovernmental system could function smoothly."[18] The first of the Chrétien
infrastructure programs led to others which, again, suggests that the government was pleased with the results of the program.
    The question of the extent to which the federal government is willing
to define the kinds of projects it will support is critical in evaluating the
urban impact of the various infrastructure programs. If the federal government simply allows municipal projects to be funded, the impact will
be on the improvement of basic services. In the first infrastructure program, federal technology objectives were almost non-existent in the
actual program, and so, too, the aim of increasing Canada's global competitiveness. Traditional municipal elites dominated the project choices,
and this mainly resulted in an emphasis on the basic services – roads,
water, and sewage. The Federation of Canadian Municipalities (FCM)

continues to lobby the federal government for "adequate, predictable, sustained funding"[19] for infrastructure. The municipal argument is that their fiscal resources are inadequate and that, therefore, there is a federal responsibility relating to economic development objectives, global competitiveness, and quality of life objectives. The federal pick-up on these programs has had more to do with job creation and intergovernmental harmony in the past, although it has also used the discourse of the global-local, twenty-first century, knowledge-based economy that I outlined earlier. But in practice, the infrastructure programs did not build technopoles, they built conventional roads and sewers.

There are other federal policy initiatives that can be seen as urban-related,[20] but I would argue that the most significant one, in terms of impact, is the set of policies on research support to the post-secondary education system. Several initiatives were taken during the Chrétien era, including the Canada Foundation for Innovation in 1997 (CFI), the establishing of the Canadian Institutes of Health Research (CIHR) in 2000, the creation of the Canada Research Chairs (CRC) in 2000–2001, and the earlier creation of the Metropolis research centres. These programs can be seen as implicitly urban because of the spatial location of Canadian universities and particularly that of the major research-intensive universities.

The other major federal policy that is explicitly urban was the decision, in the 1990s, to abandon social housing, or perhaps more accurately, to give over responsibility to the provinces. As Harris indicates, "the Canadian government is now less active in the housing field than that of any of the leading industrialized nations, including the United States."[21] Most of the provincial governments also cut or decentralized social housing programs, as, for example, in Ontario where the responsibility was entirely placed on municipal governments. The federal government then set up a National Homelessness Secretariat to counteract homelessness, although in part, the federal activity existed to resist pressures to get back into the social housing field. Certainly the homelessness initiative is strongly urban, with most of the federal funds being allocated to the largest urban centres. Homelessness is driven by a number of factors and public policies: de-institutionalization without adequate community supports is certainly important, but so too is public housing. As I indicated at the outset of this article, the negative side of the Chrétien urban legacy is certainly the federal decision of the 1990s to get out of social housing.

At the same time, these programs do relate to an explicit policy thrust of the Chrétien governments: support for research in post-secondary educational institutions as part of the federal government economic strategy. Some of the programs, particularly the CFI, are based on a partnership model in which other sources of funding have to be identified, and, in some cases, provincial governments have developed specific programs that relate to the federal program. In addition to the importance of partnerships, these programs are also characterized by their arm's-length relationship to the federal government. These are federal funds but not direct federal programs. The creation of the Canadian Institutes of Health Research (CIHR) was the result of a reconfiguration of the funding model for health research. The Medical Research Council (MRC) was abolished and thirteen institutes for health research were created under the CIHR. Federal funding was vastly increased, to $485 million in 2001–2002 and to $560 million in 2002–2003. Partners were to be sought in the voluntary, public and private sectors, and after intense debate and lobbying, thirteen institutes were set up. The institutes are virtual in that they bring together people from across the country and most of the programs give grants to teams that are often made up of people from a number of locations. It is, therefore, very difficult to allocate clearly the geographical location of the CIHR funds. By contrast, health research works on a clustering model. Close physical links are important between the basic research and the clinical research. So health related research has been very focussed in the largest urban centres.

The Canada Research Chairs (CRC) program, launched in 1999 for the period 2000–2005, is the one of these programs that is more easily allocated on a geographical location. Each university in Canada received an allocation for CRCs based on its recent funding from the federal granting agencies (CIHR, the Natural Science and Engineering Research Council (NSERC), and the Social Sciences and Humanities Research Council (SSHRC)). Each senior (Tier 1) CRC is given $200,000 annually from the federal government and each junior (Tier 2) CRC, is given $100,000 annually. The Metropolis research project has also been based on creating research capacity in Canadian universities. The federal government funded four such centres, in Toronto, Montreal, Vancouver and the Prairies. Metropolis is, at the same time, the Canadian arm of an international policy research network, and a set of four research centres across Canada financed jointly by Citizenship and Immigration Canada and the Social Sciences and Humanities Research Council of Canada to do policy-relevant research on immigration and integration in Canadian cities. The Metropolis project has certainly increased the knowledge about the experience of immigrant urban integration and, through the impact of its research, has influenced the overall Canadian research agenda.

In the case of the Canadian Foundation for Innovation (CFI), the projects are very often shared by researchers from a number of universities. However, the funds are given to the university that makes the application and therefore the figures for the allocation of the funds can only be seen as an approximation. It is, however, interesting to examine the distribution of projects and of funds. The CFI has allocated money to universities in fifty-five municipalities.[22]

The post-secondary institutions in the three largest urban centres, with approximately one-third of the projects, received about 50 percent of the funds allocated to individual institutions (there are also seven national projects that received $114,052,782). These three metropolitan areas, Toronto, Montreal, and Vancouver, make up about 43 percent of the Canadian population.[23] There are also clusters developing in smaller urban centres in which different institutions are developing links with the support of CFI funds. One such example of this is Peterborough, Ontario, with Trent University's expertise in water resources as a focus for a wider partnership.[24] Indeed, the CFI president sees a trend towards the formation of clusters around CFI projects rather than development of across-Canada networks financed by CFI funds. This development obviously lends weight to an urban agenda interpretation, in that the geographical location of the project gets the most important economic spin-off. The idea of clusters is an urban-focused development strategy.

The impact of these programs on post-secondary institutions has been the central focus of most of the analysis of these programs (particularly the partnership aspects and the link to the private sector) and certainly not the link to urban policy. However, these programs have invested large amounts of money in the major urban centres according to a relatively clearly defined vision of economic development as being driven by the Castells vision of information technology innovation in world-class cities. The specific sectors are left to the institutions to define in terms of their research priorities, but each university has been required, by the CFI, to articulate its research priorities and to justify each request in terms of these priorities.

There is, therefore, a recognition of the importance of research to innovation, productivity, and economic development; a desire to link post-secondary institutions to other partners; and a desire to see a greater specialization among the post-secondary institutions. There is, therefore, an explicit policy direction, but is it urban policy? Does the policy have to be articulated as urban to be understood as urban? Do federal policy-makers have to agree with Castells about the role of technopoles in the economic development of the twenty-first century in order to consider research support as urban policy?

Having raised these questions, I would argue for the inclusion of these programs as part of Chrétien's urban legacy, although of a very different style of policy from that of the infrastructure programs. The infrastructure programs involved the municipalities and, indeed, gave an important role to municipal decision-makers. The results were, for the most part, very traditional infrastructure relating to a conventional view of municipal activities and responsibilities. The support for research in the post-secondary system is much less traditional, following a model of economic development based on large urban centres. There is no indication that it was seen in an urban context or even as having an urban impact, although, theoretically, the link exists.

One other aspect of policy that is interesting to add at this point is the built form of Canadian cities – has the Chrétien era marked the form of urban Canada? This question is certainly relevant from a world-wide perspective – one needs only to think of Pericles and the Acropolis in fifth-century BC Athens, Pope Julius II and sixteenth-century Rome, Peter the Great in eighteenth-century St. Petersburg, and Napoleon III and the nineteenth-century transformation of Paris under Haussmann to find examples of political leaders who marked, in important ways, the built form of the urban landscape. There are also Canadian examples: Mackenzie King and Jacques Gréber's post-Second World War plans for Ottawa, Pierre Trudeau and the museums in Ottawa-Gatineau in the post-Centennial period. Another example would be Jean Drapeau in Montreal in the 1960s. Drapeau took a personal interest in the architecture of individual buildings and also an interest in ensuring that the Montreal metro was aesthetically significant; his interest in the built form was fully part of his vision for the development of Montreal.

Thinking about the Chrétien era, it is harder to think of any concrete results in terms of buildings or plans that have marked the Canadian urban landscape. The historical waterfront renovation projects (Halifax, Montreal, Québec City, etc.) were prior to Chrétien, as was the Granville market area in Vancouver. A war museum has been built on Lebreton Flats in Ottawa and this was certainly approved and planned during the Chrétien era. The site includes a large festival area which is, at least partly, an attempt to move crowds away from Parliament Hill and to an area easier to control.[25] Perhaps the 2010 Vancouver Olympics, strongly supported by the federal government, should also be included in this list although, again, one will only be able to analyze this in the future.

There was also a short-lived proposal from the National Capital Commission to create a sort of "Champs Elysée" south from the Canadian Parliament buildings. This proposal was widely criticized, in part because it entailed demolishing buildings in the downtown core, in part because the aesthetics of the neo-gothic Parliament buildings were felt to be incompatible with the grand boulevard style of the Champs Elysée. Rumours were rampant in Ottawa that the idea was Jean Chrétien's, as a triumphalist legacy to the country. This may or may not be true and, whatever the origins, the proposal seems to have disappeared under the weight of public criticism.

It is also clear that great buildings are easier to imagine and build in times of prosperity. The earlier years of the Chrétien era were marked by federal budget cutting and expenditure reviews, and clearly this does not lend itself to grandiose architecture.

THE RISE AND (?) FALL OF AN URBAN AGENDA

The first Speech from the Throne of the Chrétien era was that of 10 January 1994. The infrastructure program is described purely in economic terms, as being a measure "to stimulate economic activity." In the Speeches from the Throne, municipal government is never mentioned – clearly an attempt to avoid appearing to interfere with provincial jurisdiction over municipal institutions. The word most often used to refer to cities or to municipal governments is "community," but unfortunately for conceptual clarity, "community" is used not only to refer to cities and municipalities, but also to neighbourhoods, group identities, and/or collective spaces. In the first few years of the Chrétien government, "community" appears in the Throne Speeches as a code for the cutting of government programs. The Speeches reiterate the importance of shared values, often underlining caring and mutual help and the fact that Canadians give time to their communities. All this supports a vision of limited government, of Canadians preferring to look after each other rather than support proactive government policies. "Community" becomes a space for voluntary activity. The 23 September 1997 Speech stated: "Each and every one of us must assume personal responsibility for our community and our country."[26] The idea of community is also linked to the theme of safety: being safe in homes and communities and having safe streets. In the 1997 Throne Speech the government mentions "cities, towns, villages" and from here on, the mention of cities becomes more frequent, although usually coupled with rural communities or, as in 2001, "big cities to small hamlets." Cities become accepted substitutes for communities, although the word "community" is still used.

The 2001 Throne Speech included the first clearly urban thrust, stating that the government "will work with partners across Canada to launch a dialogue on the opportunities and challenges facing urban centres."[27] This led to the setting up of the Prime Minister's Caucus Task Force on Urban Issues, known as the Sgro Task Force, for its Chair, MP Judy Sgro. The Task Force started its work in May 2001, issued an interim report in May 2002, and a final report, *Canada's Urban Strategy: A Blueprint for Action*, in November 2002. The covering letter to the Prime Minister underlined the fact that the 2002 Throne Speech had included recommendations from the interim report of the Task Force and concluded: "Thank you for recognizing the importance of the urban regions to Canada's future prosperity."[28] The report made three major recommendations: programs for affordable housing, for transit/transportation, and for sustainable infrastructure. It called for better co-ordination and collaboration between levels of government, and it emphasized the "overwhelmingly favourable" response to the interim report. Indeed, at the time of the publication of the final report in November 2002, the federal government seemed poised to launch a major urban initiative, but this never really took place under the Chrétien administration.

There are several reasons why this was so: post-September 11 security measures were taking up money, spending on health care was seen to be more politically important than spending on cities, the urban agenda became associated with Paul Martin and was therefore something to be minimized by Jean Chrétien, and, finally, the initial enthusiasm has been dampened by realistically evaluating the federal-provincial context. Whatever the precise reason, or mixture of reasons, the brief moment of an explicitly urban agenda for the Chrétien government faded.

CONCLUDING REFLECTIONS ON CHRÉTIEN'S URBAN LEGACY

The urban legacy of Jean Chrétien is, at best, mixed. Undoubtedly the budget cutting of the early Chrétien years, particularly the elimination of social housing as a federal activity, has been one factor in the increased polarization within Canadian cities and the deterioration of conditions for vulnerable and marginalized groups. On the other hand, the Chrétien government operated a whole series of infrastructure programs which have given significant roles to municipal officials to decide on projects to be funded.

These can be understood in terms of the major priorities of the government during the period 1993 to 2003. The early period was marked by budget-cutting and expenditure reviews and, in this context, it is not surprising that cities were not a policy focus. When money was once again available, urban issues did rise on the policy agenda,[29] but they were trumped by security and health care.

Health care can be seen to be a better fit with the Chrétien image. The "petit gars de Shawinigan" created his public persona as a rural, or perhaps small-town, Canadian, devoted to the enduring values of tightly knit communities. Ready to do battle with the provinces and always happy to pronounce Canada as the best country in the world, this is not an image that fits with the new urban Canada: diverse, metropolitan, heterogeneous, polarized between increasing wealth and increasing poverty, and needing sophisticated and complex solutions to complex problems. And certainly Chrétien had no appetite, and argued that Canadians had no appetite, for formal intergovernmental discussions around the place of cities in the Canadian federal system. He was willing to come to specific agreements around municipal finances (as Paul Martin did after him),[30] but not to raise fundamental questions about the impact of the rising importance of cities on Canadian federalism.

Ironically, the major positive legacy left by Chrétien to Canadian cities may well be the series of policies initiated to support research in the post-secondary education system. If Canada is successful in moving towards an urban, knowledge-based economy and society, the federal expenditure through CFI, CIHR, Metropolis, and the CRC programs will have played a role. What the federal government has not done is articulate a vision of this urban-driven, knowledge-based economy and society and how it relates to the intergovernmental system in Canada. Maybe that is not the role of Jean Chrétien nor perhaps of any federal Prime Minister. If this vision is to be developed, maybe it is more appropriately done by the mayors and elected representatives of Canada's cities.

APPENDIX

Projects approved by the CFI (cumulation to 25 June 2003)

	Maximum CFI Contribution ($)	Number of Projects
TORONTO		
University of Toronto (and affiliated hospitals)	197,803,294	245
York University	10,810,456	46
Ryerson University	303,1251	23
Seneca College	676,035	2
Sheridan College	1,584,492	3
Total	$313,905,528	319
MONTRÉAL		
McGill University	140,988,879	165
Université de Montréal	84,103,270	174
École Polytechnique	37,123,905	24
Concordia University	20,824,542	27
HEC Montréal	1,436,079	2
Université du Québec à Montréal	4,772,718	25
CEGEP Vanier College	140,170	1
Université du Québec Télé-université	1,389,876	4
Total	$290,779,439	422
VANCOUVER		
UBC (and affiliated hospitals)	184,932,274	190
Simon Fraser University	14,742,802	50
BC Institute of Technology	639,990	3
Total	$200,315,066	243
TORONTO	313,905,528	319
MONTREAL	290,779,439	422
VANCOUVER	200,315,066	243
Total	$805,000,033	984
Total provincially allocated	$1,610,697,824	2851

NOTES

Professor, Political Studies, University of Ottawa.

1 Caroline Andrew, "Federal Urban Activity: Intergovernmental Relations in an Age of Restraint," in Frances Frisken, ed., *The Changing Canadian Metropolis: A Public Policy Perspective* (Toronto: Canadian Urban Institute, 1994), 427–58.

2 Manuel Castells and Peter Hall, *Technopoles of the World* (London: Routledge, 1994), 10.

3 For a full discussion of Florida's model, see Betsy Donald and Douglas Morrow, "Competing for Talent: Implications for Social and Cultural Policy in Canadian City Regions," (Report prepared for the Department of Canadian Heritage, 2003).

4 Ibid.

5 Jim Simmons and Larry D. McCann, "Growth and Transition in the Canadian Urban System," in Trudi Bunting and Pierre Filion, eds., *Canadian Cities in Transition: the Twenty-first Century*, 2d ed. (Don Mills: Oxford University Press, 2002), 97–120, 101.

6 Larry S. Bourne, "Urban Canada in Transition to the Twenty-First Century: Trends, Issues, and Visions," in ibid., 26–52, 47.

7 Ibid., 39.

8 Ibid.

9 Damaris Rose, "Making Space for Ethnocultural Diversity Issues in the 'Smart Cities' Discourse" (Conference presentation, Thinking Smart Cities, Carleton University, November 2002): 3.

10 "The new Canada," *Globe and Mail*, 7 June 2003, http://www.theglobeandmail.com/series/newcanada/.

11 Ibid., A4.

12 Ibid., A5.

13 Anne Gauthier, "Conference Presentation" (Paper prepared for the Canadian Social Welfare Policy Conference, Ottawa, June 2003).

14 See Richard S. Harris, "Housing," in Bunting and Filion, *Canadian Cities*, 380–403; and Bourne, "Urban Canada in Transition," 6.

15 Ivan J. Townsend and Ryan Walker, "The Structure of Income Residential Segregation in Canadian Metropolitan Areas," *Canadian Journal of Regional Science* 15 (2002): 25–52; Abdolmohommad Kazemipur, "The Ecology of Deprivation: Spatial Concentration of Poverty in Canada," *Canadian Journal of Regional Science* 23 (2000): 403–26; A. Kaziempur and S.S. Halli, "Neighbourhood Poverty in Canadian Cities," *Canadian Journal of Sociology* 25 (2000): 369–82; and Robert A. Murdie and Carlos Teixeira, "The City as Social Space," in Bunting and Filion, *Canadian Cities*, 198–223.

16 Federation of Canadian Municipalities (FCM), *Infrastructure Backgrounder* (2003).

17 See Caroline Andrew and Jeff Morrison, "Canada Infrastructure Works: Between 'Picks and Shovels' and the Information Highway," in Susan D. Phillips, ed., *How Ottawa Spends, 1995–1996: Mid-Life Crises* (Ottawa: Carleton University Press, 1995), 107–36.

18 Ibid., 134.

19 FCM, *Infrastructure Backgrounder*.

20 Crime prevention, federal land policy – indeed, many of the same areas as in Andrew, "Federal Urban Activity."

21 Harris, "Housing," 397.

22 Information provided by Dr. David Strangway, president of the CFI, July 2003. The full figures for Toronto, Montreal, and Vancouver are given in the Appendix to this article.

23 See "The new Canada."

24 Strangway interview.

25 Some may consider the war museum to make an architectural statement, but its somewhat mixed message of war as tragedy and war as triumphant nation-building leaves a certain ambivalence.

26 Canada, Governor General, *Speech from the Throne* (Ottawa, Minister of Public Works and Government Services, 23 September 1997), 20, http://www.parl.gc.ca/information/about/process/info/throne/index.asp?lang=E&parl=36&sess=1.

27 Canada, Governor General, *Speech from the Throne* (Ottawa: Minister of Public Works and Government Services, 30 January 2001), 15, http://www.pco-bcp.gc.ca/default.asp?Language=E&Page=InformationResources&sub=sftddt&doc=sftddt2001_e.htm.

28 Prime Minister's Caucus Task Force on Urban Issues, *Final Report: Canada's Urban Strategy: A Blueprint for Action* (November 2002) (covering letter), http://www.udiontario. com/reports/pdfs/UrbanTaskForce_0211.pdf.

29 Caroline Andrew, Katherine Graham, and Susan Phillips, eds., *Urban Affairs: Back on the Policy Agenda* (Montreal & Kingston: McGill-Queen's University Press, 2002).

30 See, e.g., Jennifer Lewington, "Gas tax to help cities fund projects," *Globe and Mail*, 2 February 2005.

4

Chrétien and North America

Between Integration and Autonomy

CHRISTINA GABRIEL AND
LAURA MACDONALD

INTRODUCTION

In recent years, politicians on both sides of the border have characterized the relationship between Canada and the United States as one of "family and friends." Prime Minister Chrétien said immediately after the September 11 attacks: "We are not only great friends and great allies, we are family."[1] Two years later, in April 2003, when emphasizing U.S. disappointment over Canada's failure to support the war in Iraq, the U.S. Ambassador to Canada, Paul Cellucci, stated: "There is no security threat to Canada that the United States would not be ready, willing, and able to help with. There would be no debate. There would be no hesitation. We would be there for Canada, part of our own family."[2] The family analogy suggests that the Canada-U.S. relationship is natural, inevitable, and, despite "family feuds," enduring.[3] This rhetoric is misleading on two counts. First, the Canada-U.S. bilateral relationship has not emerged spontaneously but has been constructed, managed, and fostered by successive administrations. Jean Chrétien is just the latest in a series of Canadian Prime Ministers to encounter the perennial Canadian challenge: how to deal with the United States. This challenge took on an additional dimension with the creation of the North American Free Trade Agreement. Consequently, under Chrétien's watch the bilateral relationship was widened to include, in his words, "three amigos" – Canada, the United States, and Mexico. Secondly, the rhetoric is misleading insofar as most Canadians do not feel that Americans, let alone

Mexicans, are part of the family. In fact, a recent survey reported 47 per cent of Canadians consider the U.S. as "friends but not especially close," and only 10 per cent considered them "like family."[4] And it is not immediately evident that Canadians think about Mexicans as part of North America at all. All of these attitudes are framed against a deepening continental economic relationship of which Canadians are even more aware in the wake of September 11.

Throughout their period in office, Jean Chrétien and his administration have had to negotiate the tensions arising from these closer economic ties with the United States, through regional trade agreements such as the North American Free Trade Agreement (NAFTA) and the political sensitivities of the majority of Canadians. The latter see themselves as having very different values than those of their American counterparts and are not necessarily in support of harmonizing social and economic policies, despite fairly broad approval of the existing level of economic ties.[5] This situation has been further complicated by the American government's shift to a more unilateral foreign policy and the use of pre-emptive military action. For these reasons, one of the most difficult elements of the Chrétien legacy to categorize has been his administration's record regarding Canada's role in an increasingly integrated North American region and, most importantly, its bilateral relations with the United States.

Indeed, the start of the Chrétien Liberals' tenure was marked by a strategic retreat. The Liberal Red Book had included a pledge to renegotiate NAFTA. However, upon taking office, Chrétien did an about face and endorsed the agreement. This, coupled with a tight monetary policy, prompted left-wing critics such as Maude Barlow and Bruce Campbell to charge that the Liberal government under Chrétien, "like the Tories under Brian Mulroney, has become the political agent of big business interests and the neo-liberal ideology that sustain them."[6] However, by the end of his watch, the Prime Minister was being hailed by nationalists and excoriated by right-wing critics both for his refusal to sign up Canada for the "coalition of the willing" in support of the United States' war against Iraq and for his endorsement of the role of the United Nations.

How, then, should we analyze Canadian relations with the United States and Mexico and, by extension, Canada's role in North America? Popular assessments of Canadian relations with its southern neighbours often focus on the leader's personality and ideology, and those of his (or very occasionally her) counterparts. We argue, however, that the individual predilections of leaders and their top officials play out in the context of, and are constrained by, dramatic changes occurring in global power relations. Through an examination of some key developments in the Canada-U.S. bilateral relationship, we highlight how accelerating economic integration and the rise in the relative power of the U.S. in the global system (aggravated by the unilateralism of the Bush administration) have had contradictory effects. On the one hand, these trends promoted Canadian economic dependence; on the other hand, they simultaneously stimulated Canadian desires for foreign policy independence in the face of an increasingly powerful and aggressive U.S. partner. These contradictions and concerns have remained on the agenda – in some cases becoming more acute – for the Liberal Party and Paul Martin.

THE NAFTA REVERSAL AND NORTH AMERICAN INTEGRATION: 1993–2000

Over the course of the 1990s, as Andrew Cooper notes, the management of the Canada-U.S. bilateral relationship under the Chrétien administration was characterized as embodying "a considerable degree of calculated ambivalence" insofar as the government maintained and fostered the key policy directions of the relationship, including the ratification of NAFTA, but did so in such a way as to appear to de-emphasize that relationship.[7] In doing so, Chrétien rejected Brian Mulroney's public approach, which emphasized the close personal relationship between the leaders and the active pursuit of harmonious relations in areas of trade, investment, and defence. Chrétien stated that "[b]usiness is business and friendship is friendship ... and the two cannot be confused."[8] Consequently, as Cooper has astutely observed, there was a conscious attempt "to balance Canada's role as a partner to the US with its role as an autonomous actor ... in domestic and international arenas."[9] This "calculated ambivalence" reflected a pragmatic reading of the Canadian electorate and its mixed feelings regarding the U.S. In this part we highlight some of the Chrétien government's key North American initiatives and the way in which these policies were shaped and reshaped in the period 1993–2000. We argue that the pragmatism that marked the Liberal government's approach became more difficult to sustain as the 1990s drew to a close.

One of Chrétien's earliest and most controversial actions upon taking office in 1993 was to accept the North American Free Trade Agreement as negotiated by his predecessor, Progressive Conservative Prime Minister Brian Mulroney. Mulroney's government secured approval for the NAFTA agreement in the House of Commons and the Senate, but chose not to proclaim it into law until the U.S. and Mexico had each achieved congressional approval. The Tories were voted out of office on 25 October 1993, and the Chrétien Liberals took power before approval was proclaimed. Prior to the election campaign, Chrétien's advisors had outlined Liberal policies in a document titled *Creating Opportunity: The Liberal Plan for Canada* (the Red Book). The Red Book said a Liberal government would foster a more independent role for Canada and a "mutually respectful" relationship with the United States,[10] in contrast to the "camp-follower" attitude of the Mulroney government.[11] It committed the party to pursuing greater multilateralism in world affairs. It also called for a review of the side agreements and a renegotiation of both the FTA and NAFTA to obtain:

- a subsidies code,
- an anti-dumping code,
- a more effective dispute resolution mechanism, and
- the same energy protection as Mexico.[12]

Immediately after coming to power, Chrétien caused consternation in Washington by stating that he might not approve the deal before the proclamation date of 1 January 1994 if his demands were not met. He also raised additional concerns about the implications of the deal for water exports.[13] The concerns raised by Chrétien reflected popular opposition to NAFTA among Canadians.[14] However, Chrétien had appointed the strong free trade advocate Roy MacLaren as Trade Minister, and he passed over NAFTA-opponent Lloyd Axworthy for the position of Minister of External Affairs, appointing the more centrist André Ouellet instead. After talks between MacLaren and his U.S. counterpart, Trade Representative Mickey Kantor, Chrétien announced that Canada would proclaim the legislation. While Canadian business leaders praised the agreement, opponents of NAFTA, like Ontario NDP Premier Bob Rae, accused Chrétien of caving in to the Americans on free trade.[15] A *Globe and Mail* editorial declared that the five-year Liberal retreat on free trade was "of Napoleonic proportions: as complete, as abject, as humiliating as the return from Moscow."[16]

How do we explain Chrétien's reversal on this high-profile public policy issue? One major factor was the tight timeline for approval. Given the complex nature of the process of trade policy approval in the U.S., Chrétien had little choice but to approve the deal more or less as Mulroney had negotiated it or to walk away, and the latter option would have guaranteed at least three years of hostility from the Clinton Administration.[17] As well, Chrétien's own position on NAFTA was not entirely clear even during the election campaign, despite his party's positions in the Red Book. He told an anti-NAFTA nursing student that she should support the NDP if she wanted to vote against NAFTA: "You cannot build a wall around Canada as the NDP are proposing. It's not very realistic and it will be self-defeating."[18] Despite his working-class background and early reputation as a left-leaning Liberal, Chrétien had moved toward the right wing of the party on economic issues. This shift was partly a result of his association with his mentor, Mitchell Sharp, an economic conservative by Liberal standards who had supported the continentalist policies of C.D. Howe. Former Chrétien aide John Rae was quoted in Lawrence Martin's biography of Chrétien: "[Chrétien] was very much against the economic nationalism coming out of Toronto. He felt emphasis should be on jobs and employment and investment. Whether it came from outside or inside the country, it should be seen as equal. This reflected his experience in Shawinigan, which had a lot of multinationals."[19]

According to Martin, Chrétien strongly supported cultural nationalism and "the need to build a society different from that of the United States, but he believed it could be done without erecting economic walls."[20] His objection to Mulroney's foreign policy was largely about style, not substance – he criticized the apparently abject and overly cosy nature of Mulroney's relationship with Reagan, not the content of their economic policies. Above all, says Martin, Chrétien was guided by his intense pragmatism. He advised journalists, "Don't try to label me ... Sometimes I side with the Left, sometimes with the Right."[21] Greenspon and Wilson-Smith note, "When it came to politics, Jean Chrétien played defence. He prided himself on being a pragmatist, on eschewing grand plans. The vision thing, as former U.S. President George H.W. Bush might have said, wasn't his thing."[22] Nevertheless, his commitment to Canadian independence was apparently heartfelt. When former adviser and political scientist Donald Savoie pushed him, before his election in 1993, to state what he wanted to achieve as Prime Minister, he listed three priorities: "To keep the country independent from the United States. To keep the International Monetary Fund out. To maintain the unity of Canada."[23] This insistence on maintaining Canadian foreign policy autonomy would resurface in Chrétien's response to the 2003 war on Iraq.

The Liberal government's acceptance of NAFTA both entrenched Canada's economic relationship with the United States and drew it into a new relationship with Mexico. Exports from Canada to the United States increased from almost 75 percent in 1990 to nearly 85 percent in 2004.[24] While much is made of the trading relationship between Canada and the United States – we are each other's largest trading partner – this is a strikingly asymmetrical trading relationship. In 2000, 86 percent of Canadian merchandise exports went to the United States. While United States exports to Canada exceed its exports to the European Union and Japan combined, they still only account for 25 percent of total American exports of goods.[25] Consequently, the American market is vastly more important to Canada than the Canadian market is to the United States. NAFTA has also led to a noticeable increase in the trading relationship between Canada and Mexico. Between 1990 and 2004, Canadian imports from Mexico rose from $1.75 billion to $13.412 trillion, while Canadian exports to Mexico rose from $656 million to $2,994 billion in the same period.[26] Yet despite these impressive figures, overall trade between the two countries, while growing, remains small. The Chrétien government came to accept and embrace NAFTA as one of the keys to economic recovery in Canada, despite ongoing trade disputes with the United States, most notably over softwood lumber.

After the initial controversy around the approval of NAFTA, Canada-U.S. relations under Chrétien became much more low-key and prosaic. Chrétien was careful to distance himself from the sycophantic behaviour Mulroney displayed toward Reagan. For example, he made a point of opening his correspondence with Clinton with "Dear Mr. President," instead of "Dear Bill," the style Mulroney had favoured.[27] Nevertheless, on the surface, relations between Canada and the United States benefited from the ideological similarities between the two leaders.[28]

Chrétien was reputed to have little interest in, or understanding of, foreign policy when he came to office. However, he never lost his instinctual emphasis on independence from U.S. foreign policy priorities. At a 1997 NATO meeting in Madrid, while chatting with other NATO leaders waiting for a late President Clinton, Chrétien was inadvertently caught by an open microphone criticizing Clinton on his policies on Cuba and Haiti, "I like to stand up to the Americans. It's popular. But you have to be very careful because they're our friends."[29] It is suggested that this lack of international experience meant Chrétien "delegated – relegated might be a better word – the direction of foreign policy to the Department of Foreign Affairs and International Trade and his foreign ministers Andre Ouellet (1993–1996) and Lloyd Axworthy (1996–2000)."[30] Andrew Cooper argues, however, that Chrétien's willingness to grant individual ministers considerable room to maneuver was a result of his own experience in various portfolios under the Pearson government: "So long as they did not make mistakes, ministers were allowed ... to run a long way with their own policy initiatives."[31]

Beyond the individual inclinations of Jean Chrétien and his ministers, however, Canada's role in North America has been shaped fundamentally by changes in global structures of political and economic power. In the early period of Chrétien's time in office, the end of the Cold War and globalization appeared to open up new opportunities for Canada as a relatively important, prosperous international actor. In 1996, John Kirton argued that despite the Red Book's traditional liberal internationalist rhetoric (the emphasis on multilateralism and the United Nations), Liberal foreign policy underwent an important shift under Jean Chrétien toward a more "plurilateralist position." This position was marked by the emphasis placed on trade, sustainable development, individual (as opposed to state) security, and the promotion of Canadian culture and values. The traditional emphasis on the United Nations and NATO shifted to "a new generation of plurilateral international institutions in which Canada occupied a position of leader, and its interests and values occupied a predominant place."[32] According to Kirton, the 1997 White Paper on foreign policy painted a picture of the world where power was dispersed, and largely defined in economic terms. Canada occupied a position of leadership because of the advantages it possessed as a result of its geographic location, links with anglophone and francophone countries, membership in important international fora like the G7 and APEC, and as a non-colonial, multicultural power.[33]

After NAFTA was a *fait accompli*, former free trade opponent Lloyd Axworthy's appointment as Minister of Foreign Affairs appeared to confirm Canada's foreign policy independence *vis-à-vis* the United States, and the country's aspirations to play a leading role in the "new world order." To some extent, Lloyd Axworthy's tenure as Foreign Affairs Minister epitomized Canada's contradictory relations with the United States. During his time in office, Axworthy promoted a "human security" agenda that emphasized the importance of the security of individuals, in contrast with the emphasis on state security during the Cold War period. Axworthy championed such causes as an Anti-Personnel Mines Convention, limitations on the use of small arms and child soldiers, an International Criminal Court, and other efforts aimed at promoting international law and human rights. As well, he emphasized greater involvement of non-governmental organizations in foreign policy decision-making in such efforts as the land mines treaty.[34] While the human security agenda clearly bore Axworthy's intellectual mark, the Prime Minister's support was undoubtedly required, and Chrétien's office played an important role in some of these initiatives.[35] Nevertheless, the temporarily fluid and dispersed character of global power relations in the immediate post-Cold War period provided the necessary context for Canada's aspirations to international status, independence, and influence during this period. In pursuing this international agenda Axworthy undoubtedly put strains on the Canada-U.S. bilateral relationship and signaled Canada's foreign policy autonomy. The American administration did not support Axworthy's policy activism. It was not, for example, among the one hundred signatories to the multilateral Land Mines Treaty.[36] As one retired American diplomat put it, "[Axworthy] had every right to express his views and criticisms of our policy; but we exercised our right not to listen."[37]

Indeed, it has been suggested that Axworthy enjoyed "tweaking the Eagle's beak"[38] and paid insufficient attention to the all-important relationship with the U.S.[39] Yet, Chrétien and Axworthy oversaw moves to facilitate U.S.-Canadian trade and promoted a "seamless border." For example, in 1995, Clinton and Jean Chrétien signed the U.S.-Canada Shared Border Accord, designed to promote low-key bilateral measures to improve the day-to-day management of the border and improve the speed and efficiency of cross-border traffic, which increased dramatically after the signing of NAFTA. By the end of the 1990s, the Liberal government had undertaken a number of incremental initiatives directed at the Canada-U.S. relationship in respect to cross-border trade. In addition to the U.S.-Canada Shared Border Accord, the two countries also signed the Canada-United States Partnership (CUSP) in October 1999. Its purpose was to address border congestion and study possibilities of shared border management.[40] Such initiatives were an effort by Canadian officials and private interests to develop bilateral approaches to border management with the United States. These measures would provide the groundwork for additional border initiatives in the wake of September 11. Nevertheless, even through the late 1990s, Canadian officials, business interests, and other interest groups were becoming aware of emerging U.S. security concerns.[41]

Axworthy's approach to a "seamless border" was challenged by rising security concerns in the United States. These revolved around people smuggling, drugs, weapons smuggling, and terrorist threats. Axworthy played a leading role in rallying U.S. interest groups in opposition to 1996 legislation which would impose entry and exit controls at the

Canada-U.S. border under section 110 of the U.S. Immigration Reform Act.[42] This reform was opposed by a broad based coalition on both sides of the border who recognized the implications the measure would have for cross-border trade. It was eventually forestalled.

Chrétien and Axworthy also pioneered some initial forays into improving Canada-Mexico relations. Canada's decision to participate in U.S.-Mexico free trade talks, resulting in the trilateral North American Free Trade Agreement, prompted many Canadians to think about the North American continental space in new ways. Chrétien's first official foreign trip abroad as Prime Minister was to Mexico, signaling the importance to Canada of NAFTA and his apparent desire to cultivate Mexico as an ally in future trilateral negotiations. During his tenure as Foreign Affairs Minister, Axworthy also worked at forging closer diplomatic ties with Mexico. A series of Memoranda of Understanding (MOUs) were signed between Canadian ministries and their Mexican counterparts. Canada also played a role in supporting Mexico's transition to democracy, with the head of Elections Canada, Jean-Pierre Kingsley, acting as an advisor on Mexico's new electoral rules that led to the democratic election of Vicente Fox in July 2000. Mexicans, too, saw the potential of using Canada as a counterweight to American political and economic clout. And, as we shall see in the next section, Mexico and Canada shared similar positions in the post-September 11 period.

But, as *New York Times* journalist Anthony DePalma reports, aspirations for joint Mexican-Canadian diplomacy seemed destined to remain just that. He quotes the Mexican Foreign Minister's observation: "Mexico and Canada cannot possibly make a sandwich.... There is too much meat in between."[43] The dominant tendency within Canadian policy making under Chrétien was to focus on the crucial bilateral relationship between Canada and the United States and attempt to resurrect the much-vaulted "special relationship" that once existed between the two countries. In this respect, Mexico's status within NAFTA or a new North America was frequently downplayed or ignored. As Allan Smith has persuasively argued, those who advocate closer ties with the United States believe Canada and the U.S. share a unique set of affinities that Mexico, given its current development, does not. He writes: "Mexico's role as an indicator of Canadian-American community was demonstrated with special, if unintended, clarity in the work of those who professed to see a North American "experience" or "culture," to the making of which all three societies were contributing. Some of that work did little more than make Mexico an "absent signifier," the very lack of reference to which pointed to the fact that processes of interaction and community-building in view were being seen mainly as matters of Canadian-American concern."[44] Thus, the tendency to either ignore or downplay Mexico's membership within North America remained a hallmark of both Canada's policies in North America and those of proponents of deeper economic integration. Overall, the United States' economic dominance within the continental relationship meant that Canada's economic relationship with the United States was gradually growing in intensity under the Chrétien government, despite both Chrétien's and Axworthy's desires for Canadian autonomy. Chrétien was able to paper over these contradictions while the nature of the post-Cold War era remained unclear, and while the ideologically similar Clinton remained in power. The underlying contradictions in the Canadian position were intensified, however, after the election of George W. Bush in 2000 and the events of September 11.

THINKING ABOUT NORTH AMERICA: 2000–2003

The "calculated ambivalence" and pragmatism that marked the Chrétien administration's handling of the Canada-U.S. relationship in its first two terms meant that the Liberal government entered its third term without a grand vision or long-term plan to manage either its relations with the United States or deepening North American integration. The Prime Minister also had to engage with the new Republican administration of George W. Bush in Washington and the election of Vicente Fox in Mexico. Initially, as this part demonstrates, much was made of the fact that Chrétien and Canada seemed to be the odd ones out when Bush looked southward. However, this concern took a back seat as the attacks of September 11, George Bush's subsequent "war on terrorism," and the U.S. intervention in Iraq profoundly challenged the Canadian government's attempt to balance the tension between economic dependence and a desire for foreign policy independence. Immediately after September 11, the Liberal government announced a number of bilateral measures to address U.S. concerns while simultaneously attempting to assuage Canadian concerns about sovereignty and autonomy. In this respect, as Jean Chrétien moved towards the twilight of his political career, he once again was directly confronted with the question of how close Canada should be to the United States. Here again, he faced the tension between integration and autonomy. Public opinion continued to suggest that the majority of Canadians believed that the Canada-U.S. relationship should not be too close. But Chrétien also had to address the views of a powerful and increasingly vocal group advocating deeper integration. Whereas his predecessor, Brian Mulroney – in line with business and political elites – sought closer ties with the United States in the form of the CUFTA and NAFTA, Chrétien attempted to adopt policies more in line with Canadian public opinion.

The year 2000 saw elections in Canada, the United States, and Mexico. The Canadian electorate gave Jean Chrétien a third majority government. In the United States, George W. Bush came to power in November and was sworn in as President in January 2001, while in Mexico, Vicente Fox came to power, ending seventy-one years of Institutional Revolutionary Party (PRI) rule. This changing of the guard prompted numerous assessments about the personal interactions between the three leaders. Ironically, upon his election Bush was briefed on Canada by "close Bush family friend, Brian Mulroney."[45] Much was made of the fact that George Bush and Vicente Fox had a "warmer" relationship than Chrétien enjoyed with either leader.[46] Indeed, Bush's first visit abroad was to Mexico, breaking the unwritten tradition that the President makes his first foreign trip to Ottawa. There was growing concern in Ottawa that Canada and Canadians were becoming largely irrelevant in Washington.

The U.S. tilt toward Mexico had less to do with the personalities of the individual leaders and more to do with changes in the American political environment. Increasingly, political power and influence were moving southward to states on the U.S.-Mexico border like Texas, California, Arizona, and New Mexico. Four of the last five U.S. Presidents, including Bush, came from the South.[47] But more important was the increasing clout of the Hispanic vote (35.3 million people of which 60 percent were of Mexican background[48]) in the United States.[49] Additionally, as Hampson, Hillmer and Molot note, "by 2005 more Americans will be living in the four states bordering Mexico than in the 13 bordering Canada."[50] It was also projected that Mexico would surpass Canada as the United States' number one trading partner in the following few years.[51] These developments suggested that the kind of bilateral arrangements that Canadian governments and officials have traditionally favoured may not be sustainable over the long haul. Increasingly, the U.S., far from returning to any semblance of the old "special relationship," moved to treat Canada like any other foreign country. Certainly the attempt to pass section 110 – a system of entry and exit control for non-U.S. citizens, including Canadians – and more recent U.S. actions, belie the notion of "family and friends."

Of the three NAFTA members, it was Mexico under the leadership of Vicente Fox that articulated the clearest vision of a "New North America" or a "NAFTA Plus." Fox proposed to his counterparts that the NAFTA agreement be reworked along the lines of the European Union model, with fortified trilateral institutions. His conception called for a common market, free labour mobility provisions, and some variation on the European regional structural and social transfer funds to target the disparities that exist between Mexico and the other two NAFTA partners. Not surprisingly, administrations in both Canada and the United States were lukewarm about this proposal.[52] In the short term, the Fox administration was lobbying Washington heavily to reform American immigration policies to first, legalize undocumented Mexicans living in the United States and, second, to institute a temporary workers' program for Mexicans working in agriculture and the service sector in the United States. On the Canadian side, officials initially appeared to favour a staged model regarding continental relations in which Canada and the United States would pursue bilateral negotiations that would subsequently, at an unspecified later stage, involve Mexico.[53]

Chrétien's approach to the North American partnership was, however, deeply shaken by the events of September 11, 2001. The attacks on the World Trade Center and the Pentagon ended Bush's campaign commitments to isolationism, giving rise to an expansionist and unilateralist foreign policy approach, labeled the "Bush doctrine." The September 11 attacks accentuated the U.S. tendency to prioritize security issues over trade. Increasingly, Canadian officials had to address U.S. perceptions that the Canada-U.S. border was a "sieve" that would permit terrorists access to the United States. New York Senator Hillary Clinton suggested, for example: "We need to look to our friends in the north to crack down on some of these false documents and illegals getting in."[54] These perceptions also informed American television shows such as *The West Wing*, which included an episode featuring terrorists coming across the (non-existent) Vermont-Québec border. Widespread U.S. perceptions of security threats to the north were not corroborated by any evidence that the nineteen hijackers entered the United States from Canada. Nevertheless, such perceptions and fears forced Canadian policy-makers to look for ways to reassure panicked Americans. Even more urgently, Canadian leaders sought to re-establish Canada-U.S. trade, temporarily cut off by the U.S. imposition of a Code Red alert at the border.

The Canadian public initially responded empathetically to the attacks on their neighbours. Canada sheltered tens of thousands of passengers on

U.S. and U.S.-bound airliners diverted to Canadian airports. Canadians decorated the wire fence surrounding the U.S. embassy with flowers, flags, notes, and candles, and 100,000 people gathered at Parliament Hill to commemorate the victims, along with smaller ceremonies across the country.[55] Jean Chrétien, however, like Vicente Fox, was initially criticized for his delayed and tempered response to the September 11 attacks. In the wake of the attacks, Chrétien stressed the need for a "balanced approach" and emphasized Canadian sovereignty, telling the House of Commons "that the laws of Canada, will be passed by the Parliament of Canada."[56] Additionally, in the immediate aftermath of September 11, Mexico's Foreign Minister, Jorge Castañeda, proposed that Canada and Mexico develop a common approach to border issues as the two countries were encountering identical border challenges *vis-à-vis* the United States. Once again, Canada chose the bilateral Canada-U.S. relationship over a North American initiative.[57]

Chrétien's "balanced" approach was difficult to maintain in the face of concerted pressure from a well-organized Canadian business lobby, some provincial premiers, the media, and the general public, as well as the U.S. administration. The Liberal government quickly shifted to adopt a series of measures to improve Canada-U.S. relations. Canada committed 2,000 troops to the war in Afghanistan, under U.S. command, and stated its commitment as a full partner in the "war on terrorism." During the fall of 2001, Chrétien established a high-profile Cabinet committee on anti-terrorism, chaired by then-Foreign Affairs Minister John Manley. He introduced a controversial anti-terrorism act, Bill C-36, that became law in November 2001 and increased spending commitments for border infrastructure and technology. By December 2001, the Immigration and Naturalization Service (INS) in the United States and the Department of Immigration and Citizenship and the Solicitor General in Canada announced that the two countries would seek to co-operate and collaborate in immigration matters.[58]

John Manley and Bush's homeland security advisor (and later Secretary of the U.S. Department of Homeland Security), Tom Ridge, signed a thirty-point Smart Border Action Plan to facilitate cross-border trade in December 2001. The plan included initiatives that Canada had been promoting throughout the 1990s but that had met bureaucratic and political resistance in Washington. After September 11, as a result of renewed anxiety about the Canada-U.S. border in Washington, the Border Task Force established within the Privy Council Office, under Manley's authority, was able to successfully peddle to Ridge the idea of "secure and trade-efficient borders." This approach was based on the concept that greater security could be achieved through rational facilitation of low-risk, cross-border travel and trade, and intensive co-operation in scrutinizing high-risk travelers and goods, than through intrusive and time-intensive scrutiny of all border traffic. In addition, in the 2002 budget, Canada committed $7.7 billion over five years to various anti-terrorist and border control programs.[59]

To some extent, the Canadian government's approach was an attempt to allay U.S. security concerns about the Canada-U.S. border by managing the process rather than facing heavy-handed unilateral U.S. actions. As the Canadian Trucking Alliance stated before the House of Commons Sub-committee on Trade, Trade Disputes, and Investment, "The real loss of sovereignty won't come from working together on a common vision of the border, it would come from having the U.S. decide unilaterally what it would look like."[60] Chrétien's actions during this period need to be framed against the intensive campaign, orchestrated by Canadian business, to prevent a reoccurrence of the extensive delays at the border as a result of the U.S. border shutdown after September 11.[61] Thus his actions, in some ways, typified the style established earlier of adopting gradual, pragmatic, and pro-business policies, while avoiding dramatic statements and commitments that might clearly compromise Canadian sovereignty.[62]

Despite the important policies adopted by the Canadian government after September 11 to accommodate U.S. security concerns, Chrétien's attempt to negotiate Canada's relationship with the United States ran up against the increasingly belligerent, unilateralist foreign policy of the Bush administration. However, the growing conflicts between Canadian and U.S. administrations were not merely the result of the two leaders' differing styles and values, but reflected more fundamental shifts in global power relations.[63] After the temporarily fluid and unclear nature of power in the immediate post-Cold War era, which permitted a limited but important margin for manoeuvre for middle powers like Canada, the post-September 11 period has marked the clear emergence of a new unipolar world system, with the United States as unrivalled hegemon (or "hyperpower," the term coined by French Foreign Minister Hubert Vedrine). As Stephen Brooks and William Wohlforth put it, "the United States has no rival in any critical dimension of power. There has never been a system of sovereign states that contained one state with this degree of dominance."[64]

Despite the fact that U.S. military spending and technological advances had led it to far outpace any other country in conventional military terms, the September 11 attacks caused Americans to feel suddenly vulnerable to "asymmetrical threats" to their "homeland." This new sense of vulnerability empowered hawks in the Bush administration to push the adoption of a radical new military strategy, characterized as the "Bush doctrine." This doctrine, codified in "The National Security Strategy of the United States of America," issued by the White House on 17 September 2002, eschewed multilateralist approaches to international peace and security. Instead, it declared that the United States reserved the right to take unilateral, pre-emptive military action against "unbalanced dictators with weapons of mass destruction."[65] The United States subsequently declared its willingness to lead a "coalition of the willing" into a war against Iraq with or without United Nations Security Council approval.

Given the United States' apparent flouting of multilateralism and Canada's traditional middle-power commitment to the United Nations and international law, it is not surprising that Bush's policies led to an unraveling of Canada-U.S. relations in the last phase of the Chrétien administration. Chrétien spent months waffling and attempting unsuccessfully to broker a compromise between the U.S., France, and Germany over the latter two countries' reluctance to support a U.N. Security Council resolution in favour of military action against Iraq. Eventually, Chrétien opted to refuse to join the "coalition of the willing" in the war against Iraq, choosing to send more troops to Afghanistan instead (a masterful return to the style of "calculated ambivalence").

This decision, however, deepened splits in the Liberal Party between advocates of greater closeness with the U.S. and opponents. It placed the government at odds with a vocal business lobby as well. Even prior to the stand on the Iraq war, the Chrétien administration was accused of being "anti-American"[66] after a Chrétien aide referred to Bush as a "moron."[67] One Liberal Cabinet Minister labeled Bush a "failed statesman," while another Liberal MP, Carolyn Parrish, was overheard by a journalist saying she hated "damn Americans ... those bastards." Chrétien himself came under criticism when he stated, on the first anniversary of September 11, that there was a link between the attacks and the global disparities in wealth and power.[68] Yet in this respect, he was supported by the sentiments of a majority of Canadians who believed that the United States bore "some" responsibility for the attacks.[69] Similarly, prior to March 2003 – when George Bush issued a final ultimatum to Iraq – a full 70 percent of Canadians believed that it was possible to achieve disarmament of Iraq through peaceful means.[70] Chrétien's actions *vis-à-vis* Iraq not only underscored Canada's long-standing commitment to the United Nations and internationalism but appeared to be in tune with public opinion.

United States ambassador to Canada Paul Cellucci retaliated against Canada's position on Iraq by stating bluntly that Ottawa's decision not to participate in the U.S.-led war against Iraq might strain relations between the two countries. Cellucci told a Toronto business audience that "there is a lot of disappointment in Washington and a lot of people are upset" about Canada's refusal to join the coalition of the willing.[71] Canadian business leaders like Thomas d'Aquino, head of the Canadian Council of Chief Executives (CCCE), criticized the Liberals' handling of the issue, arguing that the poor state of Canada-U.S. relations could have a "negative effect" on the $2 billion a day of business between the two countries. The CCCE brought a delegation of business leaders to Washington to try to improve relations.[72] Additionally, Mexico, which was actually a member of the Security Council during the debate on the intervention in Iraq, experienced similar pressures from the U.S. over its refusal to bow to U.S. pressures to support intervention.

At the same time, academics, business leaders, and right-wing think tanks used the events of September 11 and their aftermath as a "window of opportunity" to increase pressure for a recasting of the Canada-U.S. relationship along more neo-liberal lines. Economist Wendy Dobson of the C.D. Howe Institute has rejected the incrementalist approach that characterizes decision-making in Ottawa, and called for Canada to promote a new "Big Idea," based on a "strategic framework" that "links security and defence" with Canada's economic goals. In exchange for concessions to the Americans around security and defence issues, Canada would gain more assured access to the U.S. economy.[73] Variations on this idea have been proposed by former Canadian ambassador to Washington Allan Gotlieb, former Prime Minister Brian Mulroney, and others. More specific suggestions like a currency union or a monetary union have also been floated. In most of these Canadian proposals, Mexican participation is jettisoned (at least for the foreseeable future), since Mexico is perceived either as an unwanted competitor, or insufficiently developed to participate in the new scheme.[74] Reflecting the government's sensitivity to the charge that it has lacked direction in its approach to post-NAFTA integration, the House of Commons Standing Committee on Foreign Affairs and International Trade held hearings on the future of North America during 2002. In December 2002 the Committee issued a report titled "Partners in North America." The report called for the Government "to initiate a detailed review of the advantages and disadvantages of the concept [of a customs union] in the North American context," although it carefully refrained from endorsing such a concept.[75]

Chrétien continued to resist any dramatic attempt to reconfigure the Canada-U.S. relationship until the end of his term. His successor, Paul Martin, came to office promising to develop a more "sophisticated" relationship with the United States. Indeed, Martin put in place a new Cabinet committee on Canada-U.S. relations and participated in the establishment of a new "Security and Prosperity Partnership of North America," signed by the three North American leaders in March 2005 in Waco, Texas.[76] Nevertheless, Canada-U.S. relations under Martin continued to be marked by tensions and conflict. While Martin, given his ties to big business, may have been personally more inclined toward a friendly relationship with the United States, coming to office he faced many of the same conditions faced by Chrétien. The ongoing unpopularity of President George W. Bush among Canadians, along with the apparent vindication of Chrétien's decision to stay out of Iraq in the light of the lack of evidence of the existence of weapons of mass destruction, meant that Martin could not politically afford to move much closer to the U.S. administration. More importantly, however, as the increasing tension over the softwood lumber case shows, it is unlikely that protectionist elements in Congress and the U.S. administration will give in to Canadian demands for more secure market access. And sidelining Mexico may not be politically viable, given the continued growth in the Mexican-American population in the U.S. and the increasing importance of the U.S.-Mexican economic relationship. In this event, caution and pragmatism in future relations with the United States may be Canada's destiny in North America, rather than merely Chrétien's predilection.

CONCLUSION

Under Prime Minister Chrétien, Canada's economic ties to North America dramatically increased, while political relations were tense and unsettled, particularly since the coming to power of George W. Bush. As we have seen, Chrétien attempted to manage relations with both the United States and Mexico in a cautious and pragmatic manner, avoiding major new commitments, while promoting incrementalist reforms to assure market access to the U.S. economy. Chrétien thus reversed his party's campaign promise to renegotiate NAFTA in the interests of maintaining a

smooth relationship with the ideologically-compatible Clinton administration. During the years after the Berlin Wall fell, Chrétien and his activist, liberal-internationalist foreign minister, Lloyd Axworthy, minimized
the importance of the relationship with Washington and sought to maxi-
mize Canada's influence on the world stage through high-profile initiatives like the land mines treaty.

The election of George W. Bush put Chrétien's wily pragmatism to the
test. Even prior to September 11, but particularly after, Americans have
lost their complacency toward Canada and the Canada-U.S. border, and
they increasingly see Canada as a potential source of terrorist threats to
the American homeland. In light of the rise of the United States as
hyperpower and Bush's adoption of an aggressive, unilateralist military
doctrine, older images of Canada and the United States as members of
the same family (albeit unequal members) have been undermined. Canada faces a harsher continental environment, even as it is tied more
closely to the American economy. Chrétien's attempt to reconcile these
pressures by muddling through and cautious pragmatism may have
reached their limit. This approach has also been the subject of harsh criticism from Canada's business community and some political elites. However, Canadians still retain the mixed attitudes toward the United States
that nurtured Chrétien's "calculated ambivalence." Chrétien's successors
will require enormous skill to negotiate these contradictions.

NOTES

Assistant Professor, Department of Political Science and Pauline Jewett Institute of Women's Studies, Carleton University and Professor, Department of
Political Science, Carleton University. We would like to thank the Social
Sciences and Humanities Research Council for their financial support (410
2000 1466), Jimena Jimenez and Malcolm Fairbrother for their research assistance and the anonymous reviewers for their helpful comments.

1 Paul Cellucci citing Jean Chrétien, Speech to IRPP Working Breakfast, 3 April
2003. See Paul Cellucci, "We Are Family," *Policy Options* 24:5 (May 2003):
11–14, 11. Note that this "family and friends" metaphor is not a new theme,
but has a long history in Canada-U.S. relations. See Gordon T. Stewart, *The
American Response to Canada Since 1776* (East Lansing: Michigan State University Press, 1992), 181.

2 Cellucci, "We Are Family," 13.

3 David T. Jones makes a similar point when he writes: "neither the ambassador
nor the prime minister was correct in terming us 'family'. Abstract structures

such as a 'republic' or a 'federation' are political, not biological or social creations." See "Washington Memo: Waiting for Regime Change in Ottawa," *Policy Options* 24:5 (May 2003): 25–9, 28.

4 Robert Sheppard, "Keeping our distance," *Maclean's*, 31 December 2001–07 January 2002, 26–7.

5 See Centre for Research and Information in Canada, "Canadians are protective of their way of life and consider their values distinct from those of their US neighbours," 28 October 2002, http://www.cric.ca/pdf/cric_poll/ borderlines_ca_us/borderlines_press_wayoflife_oct2002.pdf.

6 Maude Barlow and Bruce Campbell, *Straight Through the Heart* (Toronto: HarperCollins, 1995), 3.

7 Andrew F. Cooper, "Waiting at the Perimeter: Making US Policy in Canada," in Maureen Appel Molot and Fen Hampson, eds., *Canada Among Nations 2000: Vanishing Borders* (Toronto: Oxford University Press, 2000), 27–46, 29.

8 Jean Chrétien, cited in John Herd Thompson and Stephen Randall, *Canada and the United States: Ambivalent Allies*, 3d ed. (Montreal and Kingston: McGill-Queen's University Press, 2002), 297.

9 Cooper, "Waiting at the Perimeter," 32.

10 Liberal Party of Canada (LPC), *Creating Opportunity: The Liberal Plan for Canada* (Ottawa: LPC, 1993), 106.

11 Ibid.

12 Ibid., 24.

13 Peter Morton, "MacLaren heads to U.S. to fix NAFTA," *Financial Post*, 27 November 1993, 5.

14 "Canada a big loser if NAFTA proceeds, 63 percent tell poll," *Toronto Star*, 30 November 1993, A2.

15 Tim Harper, "PM accused of breaking election promise on deal," *Toronto Star*, 3 December 1993, A1.

16 "NAFTA plus nada," *Globe and Mail*, 4 December 1993, D6.

17 Edward Greenspon and Anthony Wilson-Smith, *Double Vision: The Inside Story of the Liberals in Power* (Toronto: Doubleday, 1996), 47.

18 Ibid., 38.

19 Lawrence Martin, *Chrétien, Volume I: The Will to Win* (Toronto: Lester, 1995), 171.

20 Ibid., 178.

21 Ibid., 209.

22 Greenspon and Wilson-Smith, *Double Vision*, 25.

23 Ibid., 25.

24 Industry Canada, "Trade Data By Product," http://strategis.ic.gc.ca/sc_mrkti/tdst/tdo/tdo. php#tag.

25 Canada, Report of the Standing Committee on Foreign Affairs and International Trade (SCFAIT), *Towards a Secure and Trade Efficient Border* (Ottawa: SCFAIT, November 2001), 2, http://www.parl.gc.ca/committee/ CommitteePublication.aspx?SourceId= 37058.

26 Industry Canada, "Trade Data By Product."

27 Greenspon and Wilson-Smith, *Double Vision*, 90.

28 See Sylvia Bashevkin, "Rethinking Retrenchment: North American Social Policy During the Early Clinton and Chrétien Years," *Canadian Journal of Political Science* 33:1 (March 2000): 7–36, 11.

29 Anthony DePalma, *Here: A Biography of the New American Continent* (New York: Public Affairs, 2001), 221.

30 Thompson and Randall, *Ambivalent Allies*, 314.

31 Cooper, "Waiting at the Perimeter," 33.

32 John Kirton, "Une ouverture sur le monde: la nouvelle politique étrangère canadienne du gouvernement Chrétien," *Études Internationales* 27:2 (1996): 257–79, 258–9 [authors' translation].

33 Ibid., 260.

34 Fen Osler Hampson, Norman Hillmer, and Maureen Appel Molot, "The Return to Continentalism in Canadian Foreign Policy," in Fen Osler Hampson, Norman Hillmer, and Maureen Appel Molot, *Canada Among Nations 2001: The Axworthy Legacy* (Toronto: Oxford University Press, 2001), 1–18, 3.

35 Donald J. Savoie, *Governing from the Centre: The Concentration of Power in Canadian Politics* (Toronto: University of Toronto Press, 1999), 135.

36 John Herd Thompson, "Playing by the New Washington Rules: The US-Canada Relationship, 1994–2003," *American Review of Canadian Studies* 33 (2003): 5–27, 7.

37 David Jones, "Canada-US Relations After September 11: Back to Basics," *Policy Options* 23 (March 2002): 25–30, 29.

38 Thompson, "Playing by the New Washington Rules," 7.

39 Barry Cooper, cited in Stephen Handelman, "Playing by the new rules," *Time*, 10 July 2000, 26.

40 Canada, Department of Foreign Affairs and International Trade (DFAIT), *Creating Tomorrow's Border Together* (Ottawa: DFAIT, 2000).

41 Christina Gabriel, Jimena Jimenez, and Laura Macdonald, "The Politics of the North American Security Perimeter: Convergence or Divergence in Border Control Policies" (Revised version of a paper presented at the Annual Meeting of the International Studies Association, Portland, Oregon, 2003).

42 Handelman, "Playing by the new rules," 26–7.

43 DePalma, *Here*, 57–8.

44 Allan Smith, *Doing the Continental: Conceptualizations of the Canadian American Relationship in the Long Twentieth Century* (Orono, Maine: Canadian-American Center, 2000), 27.

45 Lawrence Martin, "Comment: Canada-US relations 'snarl-spangled banter'," *Globe and Mail*, 4 July 2002, A13.

46 See John Ibbitson, "Mexico top U.S. partner, Bush says," *Globe and Mail*, 6 September 2001, A10.

47 Andrew Cohen, "Canadian-American Relations: Does Canada Matter in Washington? Does It Matter If Canada Doesn't Matter?" in Norman Hillmer and Maureen Appel Molot, eds., *Canada Among Nations 2002: A Fading Power* (Toronto: Oxford University Press, 2002), 34–48, 39–40.

48 Robert A. Pastor, *Toward a North American Community* (Washington: Institute for International Economics, 2001), 132. However, Hispanic electoral influence is more limited than this figure would suggest since first-generation migrants are not necessarily U.S. citizens.

49 Cohen, "Canadian-American Relations," 39–40.

50 Hampson, Hillmer, and Molot, "The Return to Continentalism," 11.

51 Nancy Gibbs *et al.*, "A whole new world," *Time*, 11 June 2001, 23.

52 Judith Teichman, "Mexico Under Vicente Fox: What Can Canada Expect?" in Hampson, Hillmer, and Molot, *Canada Among Nations 2001*, 270–93, 286–7.

53 Drew Fagan, "Beyond NAFTA: Toward Deeper Economic Integration," in David Carment, Fen Osler Hampson, and Norman Hillmer, eds., *Canada Among Nations 2003: Coping with the American Colossus* (Toronto: Oxford University Press, 2003), 32–53, 48–9.

54 Janice Kennedy, "Blame Canada: Hillary Clinton does it again," *Ottawa Citizen*, 23 August 2003, E5.

55 Thompson, "Playing by the New Washington Rules," 9.

56 Shawn McCarthy and Campbell Clark, "Canada will make its own laws, PM vows," *Globe and Mail*, 20 September 2001, A1.

57 Christopher Waddell, "Erasing the Line: Rebuilding Economic and Trade Relations after September 11," in Carment, Hampson, and Hillmer, *Canada Among Nations 2003*, 54–76, 58–9.

58 Citizenship and Immigration Canada, News Release, "Canada-US Issue Statement on Common Security Priorities," 3 December 2001, http://www.cic.gc.ca/english/press/01/0126-pre.html.

59 Stephen Clarkson, "The View from the Attic: Toward a Gated Continental Community?" in Peter Andreas and Thomas J. Biersteker, eds., *The Rebordering of North America: Integration and Exclusion in a New Security Context* (New York: Routledge, 2003), 68–89, 80–1.

60 RSCDFAIT, *Towards a Secure and Trade Efficient Border*, 7.

61 Christina Gabriel and Laura Macdonald, "Of Borders and Business: Canadian Corporate Proposals for North American 'Deep Integration'" (Paper prepared for Studies in Political Economy Conference, January 2003).

62 Nevertheless, critics of Chrétien's policies asserted that some of these measures did entail a serious infringement of human rights and civil liberties. See International Civil Liberties Monitoring Group, News Release, "Brief to the House of Commons Legislative Committee on Bill C–17: The Public Safety Act, 2002," 28 January 2003.

63 See also Laura Macdonald, "In the Shadow of the Hyperpower: Beyond Canada's Middle Power Image," in Michael Whittington and Glen Williams, eds., *Canadian Politics in the 21st Century*, 6th ed. (Toronto: Nelson, 2004), 291–312.

64 Stephen Brooks and William C. Wohlforth, "American Primacy in Perspective," *Foreign Affairs* 81:4 (July-August 2002): 20–33, 24.

65 Jones, "Canada-US Relations After September 11"; and G. John Ikenberry, "America's Imperial Ambition," *Foreign Affairs* 81:5 (2002): 44–60, 49–55.

66 Gloria Galloway, "Ottawa anti-American, Harper charges," *Globe and Mail*, 23 November 2002, A12.

67 Campbell Clark, "Opposition, U.S. media fan sparks over insult," *Globe and Mail*, 26 November 2002, A4.

68 Shawn McCarthy, "P.M.'s Sept. 11 remarks 'disgraceful,' Mulroney says," *Globe and Mail*, 13 September 2002, A1.

69 An Ipsos-Reid survey of 1003 Canadians found that 69 percent believed that the U.S. bore "some" responsibility with its policies and actions for terrorist action. Cited in Shawn McCarthy, "Majority thinks US partly to blame for Sept. 11," *Globe and Mail*, 7 September 2002, A1.

70 Centre for Research and Information on Canada, "Canadians Differ from Americans on Iraq, United Nations" (9 April 2003), http://cric.ca/pdf/international_affairs_2003/International_%20Affairs_april2003_eng.pdf.

71 Steven Chase and Peter Kennedy, "Business groups warn of big Canada-U.S. rift," *Globe and Mail*, 26 March 2003, B1. See also Geoffrey E. Hale, "The Unfinished Legacy: Liberal Policy on North America," in G. Bruce Doern, ed., *How Ottawa Spends, 2003–2004: Regime Change and Policy Shift* (Don Mills: Oxford University Press, 2003), 23–44, 32, on divisions in the Liberal caucus.

72 Chase and Kennedy, "Business groups warn of big Canada-U.S. rift."

73 Wendy Dobson, "Trade can brush in a new border," *Globe and Mail*, 21 January 2003, A15.

74 See critique by Andrew Jackson, *Why the 'Big Idea' Is a Bad Idea: A Critical Perspective on Deeper Economic Integration with the United States* (Ottawa: Canadian Labour Congress, 2003).

75 Canada, SCFAIT, *Partners in North America: Advancing Canada's Relations with the United States and Mexico* (Ottawa: SCFAIT, 2002), 288, http://www.parl.gc.ca/InfoComDoc/37/2/FAIT/Studies/Reports/faitrp03-e.htm.

76 Canada. Office of the Prime Minister, "Security and Prosperity Partnership of North America Established," 23 March 2005, http://www.pm.gc.ca/eng/news.asp?id=443.

5

Jean Chrétien's Continental Legacy

From Commitment to Confusion

STEPHEN CLARKSON AND
ERICK LACHAPELLE

INTRODUCTION[1]

Assessing a Prime Minister's legacy presents analysts with a logical and empirical minefield. Of the many things that happen during prime ministerial tenures, only some can be attributed to their personal agency. In those international dossiers in which a Prime Minister has taken the lead, assessing the legacy requires making judgments about the foreign partner's contribution to the record. For instance, the contrast between Jean Chrétien's productive rapport with President Bill Clinton and his obvious difficulties with President George W. Bush tells us that any appraisal of the former Prime Minister's management of Canada's *political relations* with the United States would require that as much attention be paid to the goals and behaviour of the two Americans as to the Canadian head of government.

Evaluating Jean Chrétien's stewardship of Canada's *economic relationship* with the United States is more straightforward because of the concentration of power in the hands of the Canadian prime minister in general,[2] and because of the central role Chrétien, in particular, played in causing the Liberal Party's historical *revirement* toward the continental free trade formula that had been its mantra a century before. In 1891, Wilfrid Laurier, the Liberal Party of Canada's aspiring leader, failed to dislodge Sir John A. Macdonald's government in an election campaign focused on trade reciprocity with the United States. Twenty years later, as Prime Minister, Laurier came to political grief trying to convince his electorate of the blessings that the free trade agreement he had negotiated with Washington would bring the Canadian economy.

Laurier's successor, Mackenzie King, learned the bitter lesson of 1911, though he flirted with a new free trade agreement with Washington on the eve of his retirement. King's successors, Louis St. Laurent and Lester Pearson, were on occasion branded continentalist by their critics – the former for such regionally unifying projects as the St. Lawrence Seaway (1952), the latter for signing the sectoral Autopact (1965) – but neither came close to advocating outright economic integration. As for Pierre Trudeau, who was the least interested in the United States of all Canadian prime ministers in the twentieth century, he became identified as a nationalist for endorsing the "Third Option" (1972), which was an effort to reduce Canada's economic dependence on the U.S. by diversifying its trading relationships.

Jean Chrétien's continentalist proclivities were the natural product of his familial roots in Québec's resource-rich hinterland, whose denizens esteemed American investors for developing the region and appreciated the United States as its natural market. The anti-protectionist instincts of the "the little guy from Shawinigan" were politically seasoned through his mentorship within the Liberal government's continentalist wing and through his connecting with the business communities – in Montreal, then Calgary, and finally Toronto – during his tenure of major economic portfolios during the years that Pierre Trudeau was Prime Minister (between 1968 and 1984).

His views were consistent with the fostering of continental economic integration that was advocated by another former Trudeau Cabinet colleague, Donald Macdonald, in his 1985 royal commission report. The "Macdonald Report" declared the Trudeau era's Keynesian and interventionist approach to economic development a failure, warned that Canada was losing ground in an ever-more-competitive global economy, identified growing U.S. trade protectionism as an imminent danger to Canada, and argued that secure and privileged access to the world's largest, most dynamic economy would solve Canada's basic economic problems. The recently elected Progressive Conservative Prime Minister Brian Mulroney implemented Macdonald's proposals with alacrity by negotiating the Canada-United States Free Trade Agreement (FTA) with Ronald Reagan's Administration in 1987. The FTA was signed into force following a dramatic electoral victory in 1988 over the Liberals led by John Turner, who had attacked free trade as the death warrant for Canadian sovereignty.

No sooner had he displaced Turner as Liberal Leader in 1990, than Chrétien repudiated Turner's opposition to free trade in a carefully managed party thinkers' conference held in Aylmer, Québec, in 1991. There, such trade liberalizers as Roy MacLaren exulted for having won the day over nationalists like Lloyd Axworthy.

Practised as he was in the art of politics, Chrétien did not identify himself as a free trader. While Leader of the Official Opposition, he had criticized Mulroney's second venture in continental integration, the North American Free Trade Agreement (NAFTA). His attacks on NAFTA led many to expect him to reject the accord if he managed to defeat the Progressive Conservatives. Indeed, the Liberal Party of Canada's election platform of 1993 tore into the "flawed" FTA and NAFTA for failing to secure access to the U.S. market. It promised: "A Liberal government will renegotiate both the FTA and NAFTA to obtain: a subsidies code; an anti-dumping code; a more effective dispute resolution mechanism; and the same energy protection as Mexico." Actual *abrogation* of the FTA and NAFTA would only "be a last resort if satisfactory changes cannot be negotiated."[3]

Once elected Prime Minister, however, Chrétien showed his true continentalist colours by speedily ratifying the trinational deal. In obvious contrast with his American counterpart, he did not deliver on his promise to seek NAFTA's reform. While Bill Clinton had insisted, once sworn in as President of the United States, on renegotiating NAFTA's labour and environmental provisions, Chrétien was satisfied by a face-saving letter, with no legal weight, that expressed Ottawa's position on some aspects of NAFTA, and that was signed by both the Canadian and American heads of government. Chrétien did not demand that NAFTA abolish anti-dumping and countervailing duties, and so create a real free trade area. Instead, he completed the neo-conservative revolution that Brian Mulroney had begun by entrenching the supra-constitutional framework that restructured Canada's position in the global economy.

The men he appointed as Minister for International Trade – first Roy MacLaren, then Sergio Marchi, and ultimately Pierre Pettigrew – were staunch spokesmen for the trade-liberalization panaceas championed in the Department of Foreign Affairs and International Trade. Even in 1997, when he appointed the nationalist Lloyd Axworthy to be Minister of Foreign Affairs and International Trade, there seems to have been a clear understanding that the left-winger from Winnipeg was to stick to foreign affairs and leave international trade to the ministrations of his free-trading colleagues. Under their evangelistic aegis, the Chrétien government proceeded in 1995 to ratify the World Trade Organization (WTO), to try engineering a Multilateral Agreement on Investment at the Organization for Economic Cooperation and Development, to negotiate a Canada-Chile Free Trade Agreement (CCFTA) in 1997, to participate in continuing liberalization negotiations within the WTO, to play an active role in fostering the Asia-Pacific Economic Cooperation forum, and to interact vigorously on the working groups preparing to create a Free Trade Area of the Americas (FTAA).

In sum, trade liberalization, which was central for the restructuring of Canada's economic position in the global economy, can be directly attributed to Chrétien's leadership. In evaluating it, we first assess NAFTA's narrowly defined economic results in the areas of trade and investment, productivity, and quality of life, and then examine its broader legal, political, and institutional dimensions in the areas of social and cultural policy, labour, and the environment. We will conclude with some reflections on the significance of Chrétien's confused legacy for the future of the economic relationship between Canada and its neighbour, the global hegemon.

ECONOMIC PERFORMANCE

With the United States pursuing an aggressive trade policy in order to protect the intellectual property of its most powerful corporations, and with the consolidation of Europe as a self-contained trade and investment bloc, Canada, as a peripheral country with only one, if giant, neighbour, had focused on securing access to this market of over 300 million people. Ottawa's objectives in negotiating trade liberalization were clear – to reverse a decades-long decline in the Canadian economy's annual rate of growth, to close a widening productivity gap with the United States, and to enhance its citizens' standard of living. The high quality of Canadian statistics should make it comparatively easy to determine to what extent these objectives have been achieved. Whatever these outcomes, it is more difficult to determine what credit or blame the trade agreements deserve.

Trade

An analysis of the trade figures reveals that NAFTA has indeed coincided with a strong increase in bilateral Canada-U.S. merchandise trade. Canada's merchandise exports to the U.S. increased by over 200 percent since the early 1990s[4] (or 12 percent per year), reaching $359 billion in 2000.[5] American merchandise exports to Canada also grew under NAFTA, up 150 percent from 1990 levels,[6] and reached $267 billion in 2000.[7] The resulting $92 billion surplus finances Canada's trade deficit with the rest of the world. The sheer magnitude of Canada-U.S. trade volumes is demonstrated in the estimated $1.9 billion dollars of goods and services that cross the Canada-U.S. border *each day*.[8] Americans trade more with Canada than with the fifteen European Union countries combined,[9] and a total of thirty-eight states have Canada as their primary export market.[10]

Within the context of an overall increase in Canada-U.S. trade, the relative role of FTA- and NAFTA-induced tariff reductions remains unclear. While Daniel Schwanen's analysis of the disaggregated data reveals an increase in America's share of Canadian exports for products that had been liberalized by up to twice as much (139 percent) as for those products that were already liberalized (65 percent) between 1988 and 1995,[11] a Canadian government working paper has shown that only 25 percent of the 200 percent total increase in two-way Canada-U.S. trade between 1989 and 2000 was directly attributable to a reduction in tariffs.[12] An historical analysis of the trade figures reveals that Canada-U.S. trade was already trending upward prior to the free trade agreements. Indeed, the continuing growth of Canada's trade dependency on the U.S. market was what discredited Pierre Trudeau's "Third Option" effort to diversify the country's trade patterns.

Beyond simple tariff reduction, other factors were involved in boosting trade. The steep devaluation of the Canadian dollar, which fell to US$0.63 in 2002, or 16 percent below its 1987 value, provided massive, if invisible, export promotion. Thus, Canadian goods became cheaper in the U.S. market. Since the devalued dollar also made U.S. goods significantly more expensive in Canada, the major increase in U.S. imports and their concomitant loss of Canadian jobs would have been far greater without this veiled protection. Another factor increasing Canadian exports was a burgeoning U.S. economy – which grew in real terms from US$4.9 trillion in 1980 to US$9.3 trillion in 2001[13] – providing additional boosts to Canada's trade performance. With a cooling U.S. economy (2000–2003) and an appreciated Canadian dollar (2003), Canada's overall export performance experienced a modest decline from $360 billion in 2000 to $348 billion in 2002.[14]

Canadian government officials and the business-boosting media rarely miss an opportunity to interpret increased trade volumes as NAFTA's "unconditional success."[15] More trade is assumed to be the engine of economic growth, yet increased trade figures by themselves are not necessarily good news. Despite an increase in merchandise exports, Canadian economic growth rate continued its decades-long decline. The rate of growth had fallen from 5.3 percent in the late 1960s to 3.6 percent between 1975 to 1979, to 2.9 percent in the early 1980s.[16] Under free trade the slide continued to 2.0 percent from 1988 to 1997,[17] down to 1.5 percent in 2001.[18] When the Canadian economy outperformed G-7 countries with a growth rate of 3.4 percent in 2002, it managed the feat despite a decrease in exports, suggesting that Canada's destiny may not be as dependent on trade as proponents of trade liberalization think.

While increased Canadian exports to the U.S. were not enough to increase Canada's share of the U.S. market,[19] they reflect a further increase in the peculiarly open nature of the Canadian economy,[20] and also correspond to an increasing Canadian export dependency on a single market. By 1999, a full 86 percent of Canadian goods were destined for the U.S., up from 77 percent in 1988,[21] accounting for roughly 38 percent of Canadian GDP. As a result, Canada became more vulnerable to protectionist forces in Washington – a point driven home by the unilateral border closures on September 11, 2001, which caused panic in the continent's corporate boardrooms. No longer the unique concern of "dependency theorists," Canada's trade dependence on the U.S. has caught the attention of Canadian business. In a recent report published by the Canada West Foundation, diversifying Canadian export markets was included as one of its top policy recommendations.[22] Similarly, Perrin Beatty, President of Canadian Manufacturers and Exporters, called for a reopening of the debate over diversification.[23] As Beatty put it: "Our strong connection to our North American partners is not an excuse for ignoring the rest of the world. ... To simply hitch your caboose to someone else's train is risky – it can be great when there is a powerful engine pulling you up the mountain, but it provides little protection if things start to go off the rails."[24] If big business was advocating some variant of Pierre Trudeau's Third Option effort to diversify Canada's trade from the United States, Jean Chrétien's trade record cannot be considered unblemished.

Investment

Unlike Canada's trade performance, flows of foreign direct investment (FDI) have not met the expectations of NAFTA. Despite granting foreign

investors the right of establishment, "national treatment," and the right
to claim damages against federal, provincial, or municipal government
measures that diminish their earnings, NAFTA failed to make North
America in general, and Canada in particular, a relatively more attractive
site for FDI. Under free trade, the NAFTA partners' share of global FDI fell
sharply from 44 percent (1984–1988)[25] to just 28 percent (1994–2000).[26]
Within the context of North America's overall decline, Canada's share
declined by 25 percent, from 4 to 3 percent,[27] while Mexico's increased.
In absolute terms, Canada's stock of FDI did increase, but at a *slower* rate
than during the years before free trade.[28] Far from becoming a "magnet"
for FDI as claimed by NAFTA's Trade Commission,[29] the North American
continent seems "destined, through the joint forces of demography and
catch-up, to be a smaller and smaller share of the world economy."[30]

While NAFTA coincided with a strong increase in bilateral flows of FDI
between Canada and the U.S. – particularly in the 1990s – by 2000, the
relative importance of each country as a receiver of each other's FDI
declined. Flows of Canadian direct investment abroad (CDIA)[31] to the
United States increased by over 150 percent, from $60 billion in 1990 to
$154 billion in 2000,[32] but such growth represented a *decline* in Amer-
ica's share of CDIA, from roughly 61 percent in 1990,[33] down to 50 percent in 2000.[34] Since part of the reason for increased CDIA, especially to
the U.S., is the failure of free trade to guarantee secure access to the U.S.,
such a decline may indicate NAFTA's success in assuring Canadian enterprise that it can serve the American market from Canada without actually having to move there. To make this point, persistent anti-dumping
and countervailing duties to protect domestic U.S. steel caused Canada's
relatively more productive steel companies to place all new mills in the
U.S. – to the benefit of American as opposed to Canadian steel workers.
Ironically, this was interpreted positively as Canadian investment
abroad, despite the fact that along with the outward-bound CDIA goes
the high-tech, high-value-added jobs that are the dream of Ottawa's
policy-makers.

Despite an increase in American FDI flows to Canada (which reached
$186 billion in 2000,[35] or double the amount in 1994), Canada declined in
importance as a destination for American FDI. Between 1990 and 2000,
the proportion of total U.S. FDI going to Canada shrank from 16 to 10
percent. This may seem reassuring to those concerned with foreign control of the Canadian economy, but America's share of Canada's overall FDI
stock actually *increased* 8 percent, from 64 to 72.2 percent from 1993 to
1999, while European and Japanese shares declined by 2 and 1 percent,

respectively.[36] In short, Canada represented a smaller part of total U.S. foreign direct investment, but this smaller part nevertheless represented a larger concentration of foreign direct investment in Canada.

Apart from influencing FDI stocks and flows, the impacts of the new rules governing investment under NAFTA have been significant. Canada has benefited from the increase in CDIA, which has supported a devalued Canadian dollar in improving Canada's current accounts,[37] provided government revenue,[38] and given Canada a presence abroad.[39] Theoretically, increased CDIA improved Canadian competitiveness by consolidating links with Canada's trading partners and by stimulating vertical linkages in the form of joint ventures and strategic alliances between foreign-controlled transnational corporations (TNCs) and domestically owned small- to medium-sized enterprises (SMEs). These claims, however, are extremely difficult to prove. By the same token, inward FDI is also supposed to increase Canadian access to technology, capital, and transnational innovation networks, but the secrecy surrounding internal corporate transactions makes verification of these propositions next to impossible.

Notwithstanding such benefits, inflows and outflows of FDI under NAFTA also carry some costs. Given the opportunity for cross-border reorganization and rationalization made possible by the new rules governing trade and investment under NAFTA, some firms have chosen to integrate their Canadian branch plants into the widened economic space of the parent company's production network. Others have chosen to relocate management, production, and marketing functions – along with the associated jobs – to headquarters in the U.S. This prevents the forward and backward linkage effects necessary for regional clustering, since it favours the importing of inputs and exporting of unfinished goods within the global production network of the parent TNC. This model tends to create a maquiladora phenomenon, with an enclave export sector that remains largely disconnected from the local economy.

A second model leads to a "hollowing out" of corporate Canada as the most important corporate functions (e.g., management, research and development) are relocated south of the border, leaving behind mere warehousing operations to distribute imports to the Canadian market. Apart from diminishing final demand linkages for professional and other services, increased FDI leads to increased concentration in the ownership and control of corporations, and oligopolization means less competition, less efficiency, and monopoly pricing.

Ten years after Jean Chrétien's decision to implement NAFTA, the debate over FDI came full circle, with business – which pushed for freer trade and investment in the first place – expressing concern over the potential negative effects of "hollowing out." A report published by the Conference Board of Canada, for example, warned that "the potential consequences of hollowing-out are too significant to ignore."[40] In May 2002, a *Financial Post* poll found 70 percent of Canadian CEOs in agreement that "hollowing out" contributes to the exodus of Canada's top executives and management personnel.[41] Even the Business Council on National Issues (now the Canadian Council of Chief Executives) – a group that masterminded the move to free trade – has expressed concerns about the impact of FDI on corporate Canada. Given the lack of information about corporate decision-making available to the public, however, the debate over FDI and the ultimate shape of corporate responses to NAFTA remains unresolved.

Productivity

In the mid–1980s, advocates of trade liberalization argued persuasively that free trade would stimulate Canadian manufacturing productivity, which, with access to a continental market offering substantial economies of scale, would soon rise to American levels. In the face of global competition, it was held that Canadian firms would be forced to either adopt new technology or fail. Contrary to such predictions, however, the growth of Canadian labour productivity in manufacturing was slower than it had been in the years before free trade and did not even keep up with American productivity growth. While all G–7 members experienced a productivity gap with the United States, only Canada fell further behind. By 1996, Canadian productivity ranked fifth among the G–7, down from second place in 1976.[42]

Within the context of a world-wide productivity slowdown that began in the 1970s, information about Canada's productivity gap with the U.S. is particularly disputed. Most authors point to a growing productivity gap in Canadian manufacturing relative to the U.S. Jeffrey Bernstein, Richard Harris, and Andrew Sharpe, for example, have shown that Canada's productivity gap in manufacturing relative to the U.S. has increased by 17.3 percent – from 12.3 percent in 1994, to 29.6 percent in 2000, to 32.3 percent in 2001.[43] More recently, Andrew Sharpe summarized the economic research as follows: "They all show that output per hour in Canada has always been below that of the United States, that the productivity gap has increased in the 1990s, *particularly since 1994*, and that the current gap is between 11 and 19 percentage points depending on the source of hours data used."[44]

In contrast, University of Toronto economist Daniel Trefler has shown that Canada's manufacturing productivity (defined as total factor productivity) has grown since 1988 at the compound rate of 0.6 percent per year, actually *closing* the gap with U.S. productivity by 0.56 percent per year.[45] While such information may seem reassuring for advocates of liberalized trade, Trefler also shows that Canadian productivity grew at a *slower* rate under free trade than before the FTA was signed. The growth rate of labour productivity was 50 percent higher (0.9 percent per year) in the immediate pre-free trade period (1980–1988) and 150 percent higher (1.5 percent per year) under the previous economic paradigm of Keynesian intervention and import substitution (1961–1980).[46] This, of course, does not deal with the counterfactual argument that the rate of Canadian productivity growth would have decreased even further had Canada not liberalized its economy under FTA and NAFTA.

The persistent lag in Canadian productivity can be explained with reference to several interrelated factors. First, the increase in the Canada-U.S. productivity gap is based on the accelerated growth of output per hour worked in the U.S. (which grew to 4.9 percent per year between 1994 and 2000) and the deceleration in Canada (from 3.7 percent in 1994 to 1.1 percent in 2000).[47] By 2001, output per hour worked in Canadian manufacturing fell to 67.7 percent of the U.S. level, down from 87.7 percent and 70.4 percent in 1994 and 2000, respectively.[48] Second, Canada's lagging productivity gap can be explained with reference to the dominance of foreign-owned and -controlled corporations in Canadian manufacturing industries, which generally perform less R&D than do domestic firms.[49] Finally, "transfer pricing" – i.e., the corporate practice of *over-* or *under-*charging branch plants through technology transfers, royalty, and management fees in order to decrease profits in jurisdictions where taxes are greatest – may themselves explain the putative differences in productivity rates between Canadian and American corporations. This debate is unresolvable, however, since Canadian jurisdictions do not require foreign TNCs to disclose enough data on their pricing policies to produce an accurate productivity profile.

Standard of Living

Relative employment levels and incomes provide good indicators with which to measure worker well-being. Under free trade, the unemployment rate – the number of eligible non-working Canadians actively seeking work expressed as a percentage of the total population – rose from a low of 5 percent from 1960 to 1973,[50] to an average of 9.3 percent between 1990 and 1999.[51] By 2000, the unemployment rate reached its lowest figure since 1974,[52] registering at 6.8 percent, only to increase in 2001 (7.2 percent) and again in 2002 (7.7 percent).[53] Job losses induced by free trade – particularly in Canada's protected manufacturing sector, which lost some 400,000 employees, or 17 percent of its 1988 workforce – combined with a deep, world-wide recession, contributed to the loss of employment prospects experienced in the early 1990s. In the economy as a whole, wages and the number of jobs declined among the lower-skilled, the rate and duration of unemployment rose, and the participation rate by both the youngest and the oldest in the labour force declined.[54]

Between 1994 and 2000, as the Canadian economy adjusted to continental corporate restructuring, employment in Canada's manufacturing sector grew at an annual rate of 3.1 percent per year (compared to only 0.1 percent in the U.S. over the same time period), resulting in the creation of 350,000 new jobs, or fully one-fifth of all net job growth in Canada.[55] According to the Government of Canada, trade and investment helped create roughly 167,000 jobs in 2001, with one out of every four jobs directly or indirectly dependent on trade.[56] But while the impact of NAFTA on employment levels has been close to nil, it has failed to produce the "better" jobs that were expected.[57] Indeed, employment prospects for Canadians are categorically different from their pre-free trade manifestations, most being part-time, low-wage, and service-oriented.

Proponents of economic liberalization argued that "an open trade policy was necessary to prevent the country's average incomes from falling behind those of competitors with more open economies."[58] *Despite* the extreme openness of the Canadian economy under GATT-, FTA-, NAFTA-, and WTO-induced trade liberalization, per capita income for Canadian households actually declined between 1989 and 1996 at an average rate of minus 0.1 percent, while the G–7 figure grew at 1 percent. As was predicted by its critics, real wages stagnated under free trade, reflected in the unchanged median income for Canadian families between 1990 and 2000.[59] Wage stagnation is probably related to the relative decline in the power of Canadian labour. With a restructured Canadian manufacturing sector, many senior-level managerial jobs disappeared, and workers lost bargaining power as companies threatened they would close down and move south. The largest decline in the wage gap occurred for those with less than eight years of education – those most likely to work in the primary and manufacturing industries, where many unionized jobs for men turned into part-time work.

Free trade was meant to ratchet Canadian living standards up to American levels. But wage rates for U.S. production workers are 14 percent higher, whereas U.S. management and professional salaries are 38 percent higher than in Canada.[60] Whatever the cause of this continuing problem, the free trade era – with its increased economic interdependence and accompanying flows of investment – did not achieve a reduction of the gap. It saw the gap grow.

LEGAL, POLITICAL, AND INSTITUTIONAL PERFORMANCE

Though largely an economic agreement supposedly embodying free market principles in the areas of trade and investment, NAFTA rules have had broader political implications. Despite proponents of economic liberalization arguing that free trade would strengthen Canadian sovereignty, NAFTA has entrenched supra-constitutional constraints on Canada's policy choices.[61] In stark contrast to the European model of creating a continental economy managed by continental political structures designed to offset asymmetries of power, the NAFTA negotiators deliberately avoided creating any institutions that might have given Canada (or Mexico) a voice at the centre of North American governance – i.e., in Washington. While its much-touted dispute settlement mechanisms (DSM) theoretically represented movement in this direction, there is little to indicate that they have mitigated existing power asymmetries. Indeed in such cases as the ongoing Canada-U.S. dispute over softwood lumber, Canada became more exposed to U.S. pressure to harmonize provincial public-sector stumpage policies with American private-sector auctioning practices.[62] Moreover, NAFTA actually increased existing power asymmetries. For their part, Canada and Mexico were constrained by new limits on the policy options available to their governments, new rights for foreign investors and their TNCs, and new supra-territorial judicial processes that enforce international commercial law. Although these norms technically applied to all, the continental hegemon was less constrained because the new rules reflected its interests, because the U.S. Congress retained the right to pass trade measures that superseded the agreement, and because American trade representatives proved better able to take advantage of the new rules once they were in place.[63]

Social and Cultural Policy

In the realm of social policy, the impact of NAFTA's free-market norms is indirect, indeterminate, and contradictory. On the one hand, job losses resulting from NAFTA-induced continental restructuring served to *increase* the demands of Canadian citizens for social welfare benefits, including education and training to help displaced workers become part of the knowledge-based economy. On the other hand, trade liberalization has simultaneously undermined the revenue basis for funding such programs. While reduced tariffs decrease government revenue, liberalized rules on trade and investment place significant pressure on Canadian jurisdictions to reduce tax rates, which are declining in the U.S. and are already significantly lower in Mexico. The logic of tax cuts to attract FDI in the context of free trade is complemented by the neo-conservative ideology privileging smaller government with leaner and meaner social policies.

For Canadian cultural policy, the impact of NAFTA has been equally contradictory, if somewhat more visible. When Time Warner decided to launch a Canadian edition of *Sports Illustrated*, for example, the Chrétien government responded with an 80 percent excise tax on the value of advertising revenue contained in every issue of split-run magazines. The legislation was intended to protect the Canadian magazine industry (whose revenues amounted to $850 million in 1992) from American competitors whose larger market ($22 billion in 1992) and reuse of American editorial content subsidized their costs of production in Canada, which allowed them to dump heavily discounted advertising on the Canadian market. Confident that culture was exempted from both FTA and NAFTA rules, Ottawa's cultural policy community believed this new legislation to be compatible with WTO rules – specifically national treatment – because it applied to *any* magazine that had less than 80 percent Canadian content (so was consistent with the principle of national treatment), and because Canada had not committed itself to including advertising under the General Agreement on Trade in Services.

In a striking example of just how little Canadian trade officials knew about the agreements they had signed, Ottawa was wrong every step of the way. Given FTA and NAFTA's grandfathering of existing cultural policies, Washington ignored NAFTA and brought the *Sports Illustrated Canada* case before the WTO's dispute adjudication procedure to set a global precedent. In making their case, they contested not just Canada's excise tax, but also the protective magazine tariff – established in 1965 – as well as Canadian postal subsidies set up in the 1920s. In a single, crushing blow to Canadian cultural policy, the WTO ruled in Washington's favour on each point, declaring Canadian magazine policies – even those developed decades earlier – to be illegal.

Labour and Environment

Although largely about trade and investment, NAFTA included two side agreements wedding trade with labour and environmental concerns. This innovation in trade agreements, however, was not the doing of Jean Chrétien, but of his American counterpart. Responding to the calls of American labour and environmental groups, it was presidential candidate Bill Clinton who declared on 4 October 1992 that he could support NAFTA only if it were accompanied by two supplemental agreements on environmental protection and labour issues whose purpose would be to "require each country to enforce its own environmental and worker standards."[64] Anxious to appease its labour and environmental supporters, a newly elected Clinton administration insisted on supplementary negotiations, resulting in two side deals, which although imperfect, express the need for linking human and environmental rights with trade.

The North American Agreement on Labour Co-operation created a tri-national North American Commission for Labour Co-operation (NACLC) which consisted of a secretariat based in Dallas, Texas, (subsequently moved to Washington, D.C.) and a ministerial council composed of the three national governments' labour ministers.[65] While the NACLC's job was to report on each country's labour laws and to encourage compliance with them, it failed – to the great disappointment of North America's labour unions – to give labour rights any means of enforcement. The NACLC's dispute settlement mechanism did not require domestic law to implement its eleven principles.[66] Nor did it prevent governments from lowering labour protections. In addition, only three of the rights it allegedly protects were sanctionable – minimum wages, child labour, and occupational health and safety – while other fundamental rights – including the rights to organize, bargain collectively, and strike – were not.[67] Beyond the promotion (as opposed to enforcement) of labour rights, the NACLC provided a forum for trilateral labour research and co-operation. Since labour law falls largely under provincial jurisdiction, and since few Canadian provinces signed on to the side agreement, the NACLC has had minimal importance for Canada beyond encouraging some labour unions to co-operate with their Mexican counterparts when working out strategies for negotiating wage agreements with continentally structured corporations.

The North American Agreement on Environmental Cooperation created the North American Commission for Environmental Cooperation (NACEC) in Montreal. This tripartite organization – whose professional secretariat was given supranational standing – constituted the most promising aspect of continental governance under NAFTA, because it incorporated citizens directly into its processes. However, its actual effectiveness has been found wanting. Under article 14 of the environmental agreement, for example, individuals and NGOs are able to submit a complaint that one of the NAFTA partners is not enforcing its environmental law. Of the thirty-five submissions filed since 1995, only three have been made public.[68] Moreover, the NACEC has such a cumbersome dispute settlement mechanism at its disposal that it has never been used.[69]

Despite the promised potential of both side agreements, environmental and labour concerns continue to be subjected to the primacy of trade and economic logic. The NACEC has failed to slow the pace of environmental degradation in North America and its limited success is outweighed by the use of the NAFTA chapter 11 investor-state tribunals to challenge the North American governments' capacity to regulate environmentally harmful products and practices. As demonstrated by chapter 11 cases aborting policies such as Ottawa's ban of the gasoline additive MMT (a dangerous neurotoxin suspected of causing Alzheimer's) and Ottawa's ban on exports of PCB waste, the issue is no longer which level of government, but rather, *whether* any level of government – federal, provincial, or municipal – can initiate environmental legislation at all.[70] At a time when Canadians increasingly want their governments to protect a fragile environment, NAFTA's investor-state dispute mechanism is creating a policy chill that makes this objective much more difficult to achieve.

Institutional Performance

Despite the new trade rules, the biggest issues affecting Canada-U.S. commercial relations have been left unresolved. Indeed, from a Canadian perspective, the single greatest irritant in the Canada-U.S. relationship, as identified in the first Liberal Red Book, has been the failure of free trade to guarantee "secure access." As evidenced by border closures reflecting heightened U.S. security concerns in the wake of September 11, 2001, and in the continuing application of U.S. countervail and anti-dumping actions against Canadian exports, Canada remains no less vulnerable to protectionist forces in Washington than it was prior to "free" trade. The reality of NAFTA's institutional deficit, which prevents it from managing relationships of "complex interdependence"[71] among NAFTA partners, is further complicated by the Agreement's incapacity to evolve in response to changed circumstances. This impotence was reflected in NAFTA's inability to work out a continental solution to the uncertainty surrounding North America's borders when Washington launched its global war on terror, which subsequently challenged the "shared values" of the Canada-U.S. "security community."[72] Nor were the three NAFTA signatories able to work out a common position for the new trade negotiations taking place in either the WTO's Doha Round or in the Free Trade Area of the Americas. In short, despite creating a complex dynamic among its partners, NAFTA was incapable of supporting and massaging their sometimes bumpy evolution.

CONCLUSION

Jean Chrétien's legacy in the Canada-U.S. economic relationship is contradictory and confused. As Leader of the Official Opposition, Chrétien was a critic of both the FTA and NAFTA agreements, and he promised to renegotiate NAFTA to include clear definitions of "anti-dumping" and "countervail." After blatantly betraying his promise, the Chrétien government called NAFTA an "unconditional success"[73] in the face both of statistical evidence attesting to the contrary and of multiple proposals from the business community demanding major repairs to a patently imperfect arrangement. Apart from increases in Canadian imports and exports, which failed to lift Canadian economic growth to pre-free trade levels, NAFTA has not improved North America's or Canada's share of global FDI, has not improved Canada's productivity performance, has not raised real wages, and has not increased employment. NAFTA's labour and environmental side agreements have proven ineffectual, and perhaps most importantly, NAFTA has failed to deliver on its most important objective – securing access to the U.S. market.

When set against such failed objectives, the costs of NAFTA seem disproportionate. Indeed, the constraining effects of NAFTA on Canadian jurisdictions seem to outweigh any benefits of increased commerce, which are not uniquely attributable to NAFTA-induced tariff reductions and which also correspond to an increase in Canada's dependence and vulnerability toward developments happening in the U.S. Under NAFTA, Canada has *lost* much of its capacity to limit or tax exports, to regulate investment in the interests of Canadian workers, to protect the environment, and to assist Canadian corporations to become more globally competitive. In contrast, foreign investors have *gained* greater monopoly rights over such intellectual property as brand-name drugs that cost the public health care system hundreds of millions of dollars.

Jean Chrétien's contradictory legacy in Canada's economic relationship with the U.S. has led to confusion over the future of Canada's economic and political relationship with the global hegemon. While NAFTA increased Canada's export dependence on the American market, it failed to guarantee Canadian industry protection from U.S. protectionist forces. Ironically, the solutions to increased vulnerability under NAFTA proposed by big business in the aftermath of September 11, 2001 aim to increase continental integration, which would further increase Canada's vulnerability to developments in the U.S.

Behind all this confusion, many proposals advocating deeper integration with the Unites States contain an implicit threat. Arguing that Canada must embrace a new "Big Idea,"[74] Wendy Dobson and others suggest that Canada must take a new leap of faith and give up more sovereignty (in immigration and security policy, for example) or else risk being punished by Washington further down the line. The continuing and unresolved controversy about such prescriptions confirms Jean Chrétien's confused free trade legacy, which, while a putative success in terms of increased trade flows, left the Canadian economy insecure in relation to Uncle Sam and still in search of that ever-elusive panacea.

NOTES

Professor of Political Economy, University of Toronto, and Doctoral Student, University of Toronto.

1 A number of sections of this chapter are drawn from Stephen Clarkson, *Uncle Sam and Us: Globalization, Neoconservatism and the Canadian State* (Toronto: University of Toronto Press, 2002).

2 Donald J. Savoie, *Governing from the Centre: The Concentration of Power in Canadian Politics* (Toronto: University of Toronto Press, 1999).

3 Liberal Party of Canada (LPC), *Creating Opportunity: The Liberal Plan for Canada* (Ottawa: LPC, 1993), 23–4.

4 Standing Committee on Foreign Affairs and International Trade (SCFAIT), *Partners in North America: Advancing Canada's Relations with the United States and Mexico* (Ottawa: SCFAIT, December 2002), 59,

http://www.parl.gc.ca/InfoComDoc/37/2/FAIT/Studies/Reports/faitrp03/
faitrp03-e.pdf.

5 Statistics Canada, "Imports, exports and trade balance of goods on a
balance-of-payments basis, by country or country grouping,"
http://www.statcan.ca/english/Pgdb/gbleco2a.htm.

6 SCFAIT, *Partners in North America*, 58.

7 Statistics Canada, "Imports, exports."

8 SCFAIT, *The Canada-United States Economic Relationship* (Ottawa: 2001), 1.

9 See U.S. Census Bureau, "Foreign trade statistics,"
http://www.census.gov/foreign-trade/statistics/.

10 See Michael Kergin, "Canada and the United States, Facing a New World
Reality – Together," Canadian Embassy,
http://www.canadianembassy.org/ambassador/020206-en.asp..

11 Daniel Schwanen, "Trading Up: The Impact of Increased Continental Integration on Trade, Investment, and Jobs in Canada" *C.D. Howe Institute Commentary* 9 (1997): 25, Tables A–1 and A–2.

12 Peter Berg *et al.*, *Canada and the Future of the North American Relationship:
Shaping a Long-term Canadian Agenda*, Parliament of Canada,
http://www.parl.gc.ca/InfoComDoc/37/1/FAIT/Studies/References/
KeyIssuesNA-E.htm, Part V, 1 note 19.

13 Robert Roach, *Beyond Our Borders: Western Canadian Exports in the Global
Market* (Canada West Foundation, May 2002), 7.

14 Statistics Canada, "Imports, exports, and trade balances."

15 See e.g., International Trade Canada, NAFTA Free Trade Commission: Joint
Statement, "A Foundation for Future Growth," Joint Statement (Puerto
Vallarta, Mexico, 28 May 2002),
http://www.dfait-maeci.gc.ca/nafta-alena/Joint_Statement-en.asp.

16 Organization for Economic Co-operation and Development (OECD), *OECD
Historical Statistics. 1960–97* (Paris: OECD, 1999), Table 3.1, 50.

17 OECD, *OECD Economic Survey 1998–9* (Paris: OECD, 2000), Table A3.

18 Statistics Canada, "National economic and financial accounts," *The Daily*, 28
February 2002, http://www.statcan.ca/Daily/English/020228/d020228a.htm.

19 This is a result of American imports from China and Mexico rising at a faster
pace than imports from Canada. See SCFAIT, *Partners in North America*, 59.

20 At approximately 43 percent, Canada's export to GDP ratio ranks highest in
the G–7. Canada's dependence on trade is growing. Exports plus imports as a
proportion of GDP rose from 52 percent in 1987 to 54 percent in 1992 and to
74 percent in 2000. See Biz/ed Business and Economics Service for Students,
http://www.bized.ac.uk/cgi-bin/stats.

21 Canada, *Trade Update 2000: First Annual Report on Canada's State of Trade*, 2d ed. (Ottawa: Department of Foreign Affairs and International Trade, 2000), 7.

22 Roach, *Beyond our Borders*, 20–1.

23 Andrew Cohen, *While Canada Slept: How We Lost Our Place in the World* (Toronto: McClelland and Stewart, 2003), 112.

24 Perrin Beatty, quoted in ibid.

25 Clarkson, *Uncle Sam and Us*, 211.

26 Office of the United States Trade Representative (USTR), *NAFTA at Eight: A Foundation for Economic Growth* (May 2002), 3, http://www.ustr.gov/ assets/Trade_Agreements/Regional/NAFTA/asset_upload_file374_3603.pdf.

27 Schwanen, "Trading Up," 18.

28 The growth rate of Canada's FDI stock slowed from an annual rate of 12.9 percent between 1978 to 1988, down to 9.5 percent from 1989 to 1999. Shawn McCarthy, "Business sounds alarm on vulnerability," *Globe and Mail*, 8 May 2000, B1.

29 USTR, *NAFTA at Eight*.

30 John Helliwell, quoted in David Crane, "Who will stand up for Canadian nationalism?" *Toronto Star*, 17 May 2003, C2.

31 Not all CDIA is "Canadian." CDIA figures include investments made outside Canada by foreign corporations with operations in Canada.

32 SCFAIT, *Partners in North America*, 61.

33 Ibid., 62.

34 Canada, DFAIT, *Third Annual Report on Canada's State of Trade: Trade Update* (Ottawa: Minister of Public Works and Government Services Canada, May 2002), http://www. dfait-maeci.gc.ca/eet/pdf/SOT_2002-en.pdf.

35 SCFAIT, *Partners in North America*, 61–62.

36 DFAIT, *Third Annual Report*.

37 The ratio of CDIA receipts to FDI outflows increased from 97 percent in 1998 to 105 percent in 2002. Derived from Statistics Canada data.

38 Earnings from CDIA, which amounted to $16 billion, or 2 percent of Canadian GNP in 1998, are taxable when claimed by the parent company as income.

39 Having a presence abroad can sometimes be negative, however, since CDIA can reinforce the regressive capacity of repressive regimes abroad. Craig Forcese, *Putting Conscience into Commerce* (Montreal: International Centre for Human Rights and Democratic Development, 1997).

40 Potential consequences of hollowing out listed in the report include "the loss of high-paying senior level jobs and a subsequent decline in the tax base, diminished development opportunities for mid-level individuals, job losses at the support level as positions become redundant, job creation genius leaves the

country – the job drain effect, potentially reduced investment in Canada, reduced corporate donations of both money and volunteer time, diminished prestige for Canada as a global player, possible erosion of distinct Canadian values and standards." Derrick Hynes, *Restructuring in a Global Economy: Is Corporate Canada Being Hollowed-out?* (Ottawa: Conference Board of Canada, May 2001), 6, 15.

41 Andrea Mandell-Campbell, "FP CEO poll: 'Hollowing out' contributes to brain drain," *Financial Post*, 27 May 2002.

42 Andrei Sulzenko and James Kalwarowsky, "A Policy Challenge for a Higher Standard of Living," *Isuma* 1:1 (2000): 125–9, 126.

43 Jeffrey I. Bernstein, Richard G. Harris, and Andrew Sharpe, "The Widening Canada-US Manufacturing Productivity Gap," *International Productivity Monitor* 5 (2002): 3–22, 3.

44 Andrew Sharpe, "Why Are Americans More Productive Than Canadians?" *International Productivity Monitor* 6 (2003): 19–37, 24 [emphasis added].

45 Daniel Trefler, "The Long and Short of the Canada-U.S. Free Trade Agreement," National Bureau of Economic Research Working Paper W8293 (May 2001): 21, 24.

46 Ibid., Figures 1, 4.

47 Approximately 70 percent of the resulting 3.8 percent spread in absolute productivity growth was attributable to the difference in productivity growth rates between the relatively larger and more dynamic high-tech industries in the U.S. relative to Canada, whereas the remaining 30 percent was due to the relative increase in capital intensity growth which accelerated more quickly in the U.S. due to higher labour costs. Jeffrey I. Bernstein, *et al.*, *The Widening Canada-US Manufacturing Productivity Gap* (Ottawa: Centre for the Study of Living Standards, 2002), 4–5, 12–13, 18.

48 Ibid., 3.

49 Foreign firms perform 67 percent less research and development (R&D) than domestic firms – spending 1.2 percent of their revenue on research, compared to 2 percent by Canadian-owned firms – evidence that, with an increase in FDI, the high value-added jobs associated with R&D head south of the border.

50 OECD, *OECD International Statistics* (Paris: OECD Publications, 1999), 45.

51 See the statistical appendix of the International Monetary Fund's website, http://imf.org/external/pubs/ft/weo/weo1098/pdf/1098sta.pdf.

52 In 1974, the unemployment rate was 5.3 percent. Marcel Bédard and Louis Grignon, *Overview of Evolution of the Canadian Labour Market from 1940 to the Present* (Hull: Applied Research Branch, Human Resources Development Canada, 2000), 8, http://www11.hrsdc.gc.ca/en/cs/sp/hrsdc/arb/publications/research/2000–002533/ARB199.pdf.

53 Statistics Canada, "Labour Force Characteristics," http://www40.statcan.ca/l01/cst01/econ10.htm.

54 Schwanen, "Trading Up," 19.

55 Bernstein et al., *The Widening* Gap, 6.

56 Cohen, *While Canada Slept*, 109.

57 See e.g., USTR, *NAFTA at Eight*, 4.

58 Schwanen, "Trading Up," 4.

59 Statistics Canada, A2001 Census of Canada," http://www.statcan.ca/english/census01/release/index.cfm.

60 John Britton, "Is the Impact of the North American Trade Agreements Zero? The Canadian Case," *Canadian Journal of Regional Science* 21 (1998): 167–96, 187–8.

61 Stephen Clarkson, *Canada's Secret Constitution: NAFTA, WTO and the End of Sovereignty* (Ottawa: Canadian Centre for Policy Alternatives, 2002).

62 Despite favourable panel decisions, Ottawa has been forced to impose restrictions on exports to the U.S. Tony Porter, "The North American Free Trade Agreement," in Richard Stubbs and Geoffrey R.D. Underhill, eds., *Political Economy and the Changing Global Order* (New York: Oxford University Press, 2000), 245–53, 249.

63 Clarkson, *Uncle Sam and Us*, 56.

64 Pierre Marc Johnson and André Beaulieu, quoted in SCFAIT, *Partners in North America*, 153.

65 Rafael Fernández de Castro and Claudia Ibargüen, "Las instituciones del TLCAN: una evaluación a los cinco años," in Beatriz Leycegui and Rafael Fernández de Castro, eds., *Socios naturales? Cinco años del Tratado de Libre Comercio de América del Norte* (Mexico: ITAM, 2000): 486.

66 Including: (1) freedom of association and the protection of the right to organize; (2) the right to bargain collectively; (3) the right to strike; (4) prohibition of forced labour; (5) labour protections for children and young persons; (6) minimum employment standards; (7) elimination of employment discrimination; (8) equal pay for women and men; (9) prevention of occupational injuries; (10) compensation in the cases of occupational injuries and illnesses; and (11) protection of migrant workers. See North American Agreement on Labor Co-operation, http://www.naalc.org/english/infocentre/whatisclc.htm.

67 SCFAIT, *Partners in North America*, 156.

68 Ibid., 154.

69 Ibid.

70 Clarkson, *Uncle Sam and Us*, 349.

71 We refer to "complex interdependence" here as the "ideal type" constructed as the opposite of "political realism." See Robert O. Keohane and Joseph Nye,

Power and Interdependence: World Politics in Transition (Boston: Little, Brown, 2001).

72 For an excellent discussion of "security communities" in theory and practice, see Emanuel Adler and Michael Barnett, eds., *Security Communities* (New York: Cambridge University Press, 2001).

73 NAFTA Free Trade Commission, "A Foundation for Future Growth."

74 Wendy Dobson, "Shaping the Future of the North American Economic Space: A Framework for Action," *CD Howe Institute Commentary: The Border Papers* 162 (April 2002).

6

A Passive Internationalist

Jean Chrétien and Canadian Foreign Policy

TOM KEATING

INTRODUCTION

Jean Chrétien and Canadian foreign policy are not often combined in the same sentence. Unlike his predecessors, Pierre Trudeau and Brian Mulroney, who came to be linked rather closely with a particular style and substance of foreign policy, the very idea of a Chrétien approach to foreign policy, let alone a Chrétien foreign policy, seems more difficult to conjure. In spite of more than forty years in elected office, the last ten as Prime Minister, and an extensive record of prominent Cabinet postings including a very brief tenure as Foreign Minister, foreign policy never appeared to be a high priority for Chrétien. As Prime Minister, Chrétien liked to travel, talk to foreign leaders, and participate in numerous summit meetings, yet seldom did he take a lead role on a foreign policy initiative, and beyond the area of trade promotion, he displayed little by way of sustained interest in any particular foreign policy issue. The more prominent and successful foreign policy initiatives that occurred during his time on Sussex Drive, such as the Ottawa Treaty banning anti-personnel landmines or the International Criminal Court, are most commonly associated with his second foreign minister, Lloyd Axworthy, than with Chrétien himself. Outside of his Team Canada sales campaigns, Chrétien's foreign policy legacy is more likely to rest on his refusal to join the American-British invasion of Iraq or his efforts to launch international action to rescue Rwandan refugees or to bring comprehensive sanctions against the Nigerian government at the Commonwealth for executing activist Ken Saro Wiwa and his Ogoni colleagues. One of the highest priorities for Chrétien upon assuming the Prime Minister's office was reducing the substantial deficit that had been accumulating for years under both Liberal and Conservative governments. Despite his rhetorical support for Canada's international commitments it was these very international commitments that became a primary target in the government's attack on the deficit. Foreign aid, defence, and the country's diplomatic service all experienced major reductions during the 1990s. For much of his time in office, foreign affairs portfolios – defence, foreign aid, and the diplomatic corps – were sacrificed in the fight against the deficit rather than deployed to meet global challenges. Throughout his tenure as Prime Minister, Chrétien was torn between the desire and demands to be engaged internationally and the domestic and partisan considerations that had enabled him to survive more than four decades in public office. His instincts and skills were more closely attuned to the latter and thus, not surprisingly, foreign affairs almost always made room for domestic political concerns.

Part of the difficulty in gaining a fair perspective of the Chrétien years in Canadian foreign policy is the stark contrast it presents to the more activist period under his predecessor, Brian Mulroney. As Harald von Reikhoff and Maureen Appel Molot noted: "Though [Mulroney] had had no personal background in international affairs, Mulroney demonstrated a more sustained interest and day-to-day direct involvement in foreign policy than any other Canadian peacetime prime minister."[1] Almost any prime minister would pale in comparison, but especially someone of Chrétien's style and approach. Chrétien did not sing duets with American presidents, nor did he seek to dominate foreign policy-making within his Cabinet. His profile on the international stage was always rather modest at best. Indeed as Nossal has noted, "Chrétien ... came to power ... actively seeking to avoid the kind of activist foreign policy that had been pursued by the Mulroney government."[2] From the start, he was reluctant to commit the country to active participation in foreign ventures, shying away from a more assertive role in both Bosnia and Haiti. In spite of his comparatively low profile, however, it would be wrong to conclude that Chrétien had little influence on foreign policy. Throughout his tenure as Prime Minister, Canadian foreign policy wore the stamp of Jean Chrétien. The stamp has not always been as prominent as that made by previous prime ministers, but it has been no less influential in defining Canada's involvement in the global community. A review of the Prime Minister's speeches on foreign policy reveals a number of persistent themes – the promotion of liberal trade for national and international prosperity, the projection of Canadian values, the reform and support of international institutions, and an ongoing concern with global poverty and inequalities. While Chrétien often spoke of these concerns and Canada's active role in the global community, as Prime Minister he seemed to have a limited interest in these areas, a more modest view of the country's role, and, not unimportantly, a strong belief in the greater importance of domestic affairs. Chrétien was first and foremost concerned with his domestic policy agenda. This agenda was dominated by Québec and the deficit for much of his time as Prime Minister, and these concerns helped to shape his approach to foreign policy.

Of course, not everyone is in agreement with this characterization of Chrétien's approach. John Kirton, for example, has written: "Despite Jean Chrétien's initial instinct to leave foreign policy largely to his trusted foreign and trade ministers, ... both the substance of that policy and the process that produced it came to bear the central stamp of a Prime Minister who had developed clear convictions about Canada's importance and leadership in the world ... which in turn produced a foreign policy distinguished by an assertive, ambitious, highly engaged globalism."[3] While there may have been some support for this notion of "an assertive, ambitious highly engaged globalism" during the period reviewed by Kirton, there is less evidence to support such a view over the full term of Chrétien's reign as Prime Minister.

Looking back on Chrétien's decade as Prime Minister, one is struck by the inconsistencies that surround Canada's foreign policy during this period. Chrétien was initially skeptical of Canada's peacekeeping commitments in Bosnia yet, repeatedly, though primarily rhetorically, supported U.N. peacekeeping. He frequently emphasized the relative importance of the U.N. for Canadian and international security policy, yet Canadian military commitments to the U.N. declined significantly over a decade in power. He asserted the importance of a U.N. mandate before committing Canadian forces to the American-led invasion of Iraq in 2003, yet expressed a willingness to join the Americans and British in attacking Iraq in 1998 without such a mandate, and twice committed Canadian forces to U.S.-led wars in Kosovo and Afghanistan, again with no U.N. mandate. His government continued the move away from formal military commitments to the North Atlantic Treaty Organization (NATO), but significantly more Canadian armed forces served as part of NATO operations than as members of U.N. operations during his governments. He challenged American foreign policy and sought to distance

Canada from the United States, yet developed a close personal relationship with President Bill Clinton; and trade, and later security policy, have drawn the two countries ever more closely together. He championed various regional initiatives in the Pacific, in the Americas, and later on, in Africa, and appointed ministers to look after these regional concerns, but each received only passing attention. When Chrétien addressed foreign policy matters, he often invoked the internationalist legacy of Lester Pearson as the guiding spirit for his Liberal government's approach to the global community. Yet some critics maintain that Chrétien's foreign policy was a far cry from Pearsonian internationalism. "The Chrétien government has been, in practice, if not in word, the most isolationist government since Mackenzie King's in the 1930s, all the while touting the official line that internationalism is still the Canadian doctrine in world affairs."[4] Michael Ignatieff argued: "We are living off a Pearsonian reputation that we no longer deserve."[5] For Andrew Cohen, Chrétien was asleep at the wheel during what he recounts, in considerable detail, as the significant decline in Canada's international presence during the 1990s.[6] For others the "gaggle of Chrétien-era initiatives is eloquent testimony to the degree to which mission diplomacy is alive and well and living in Ottawa."[7] In part, these inconsistencies reflect competing pressures and the uncertainty of the post-Cold War security environment, but they also suggest a Prime Minister without a clear set of priorities or a sufficiently strong commitment to remain highly engaged on foreign policy issues. Lester Pearson once remarked that foreign policy was "domestic policy with its hat on." Perhaps this was never more true than it was during Chrétien's tenure. In a foreign policy that was generally supported by the Canadian public, Chrétien's foreign policy was driven by domestic priorities and foremost among these was the deficit. From his first decision to cancel the Sea King helicopter replacement program for the Navy through a decade of declining support for development assistance, balancing the books always took precedence over the wider world. Thus, and on balance, while a departure from some of his more activist predecessors, Chrétien's approach to world affairs tended to reflect a more passive internationalism than a full-scale retreat to isolationism.

INSTITUTIONAL REQUIREMENTS

A combination of international, institutional, and personal pressures shape the participation of prime ministers in foreign policy making. "When prime ministers assume office, they also assume a wide range of responsibilities that propel even those who might have little interest in world affairs into the international system."[8] The Prime Minister can shape foreign policy not only through direct involvement, but also through powers of appointment, and Chrétien was no different from his predecessors in directing Canadian foreign policy in such a manner. Chrétien's Cabinet appointments set the tone for Canadian foreign policy. In passing over Lloyd Axworthy, "the antithesis of Chrétien," for Foreign Minister and initially appointing Andre Ouellet to this position, Chrétien opted for a more conservative foreign policy during the initial stages of his first government. In doing so, he also demonstrated the clear priority that would be given to domestic considerations, especially economic considerations. The appointment of Ouellet served important national unity objectives in the months preceding the Québec referendum. "The government needed a senior francophone ... in a senior portfolio to strengthen its hand in the anticipated referendum."[9] It was therefore not surprising that Ouellet devoted most of his time and attention to provincial matters rather than to foreign policy. Ouellet's emphasis on Québec also reinforced the view that the more significant foreign policy post, in the Prime Minister's view, was Trade. In this position, Chrétien had targeted Roy MacLaren, an ardent free trader. It was a sign of the inconsistencies to follow. While Chrétien had campaigned with a persistent anti-NAFTA message, the appointment of MacLaren confirmed that the "Liberals once again ... stood for free trade and would ... pursue its attainment with abandon."[10]

The priority given to trade liberalization and trade promotion was clearly evident in the early years of Chrétien's tenure. Axworthy would eventually receive the Foreign Affairs portfolio in 1996 and would use it to promote an agenda geared more to human rights and human security considerations. By this time, however, the economic priorities of the government had been firmly established. Moreover, as many observers have noted, systemic changes in the global political economy and the government's response to them had largely displaced foreign affairs as the key policy portfolio, as trade and finance assumed a greater measure of prominence and influence. In this changing global context, the Foreign Minister had less influence over the general direction of foreign policy.[11] This, however, was more the result of changes in the global political economy than of any decision taken by the Prime Minister. Though given Chrétien's own interests in trade promotion, he was not likely to challenge these priorities, as he made clear in his dealings with China and Indonesia, among others, on human rights. For his part, Chrétien argued that such inconsistencies were defensible: "Yes, we trade with countries whose human rights records are far from perfect. Those who suggest that the choice is "trade versus human rights" pose a false choice. We do not set aside our concerns and commitments on human rights in the pursuit of economic gain for Canadians. Trade and investment, when pursued fairly and with the view to sharing the benefits, also increase income levels and the ability of individuals to provide for themselves and their families."[12]

Chrétien also sought to open the foreign policy process to more parliamentary and public scrutiny. Parliamentary reviews into defence and foreign policy were launched in 1994 and the government's response appeared in a booklet, _Canada in the World_, released in 1995. In addition to this foreign policy review process that now seems to accompany any new government into power, Chrétien sought to institutionalize public consultations to a much greater extent than his predecessors had done. While domestic groups had increasingly gained access to policymakers, and while some elected representatives, such as Joe Clark, had encouraged more regular consultations, Chrétien sought to broaden the range of contacts and increase the amount of consultation. Annual foreign policy forums were initiated in 1995. These were designed to bring Canadians from different perspectives, regions and experiences together to develop policy-relevant recommendations for the government to consider. While the wisdom and democratic character of such gatherings has been widely discussed, _The Economist_ seems to have summed it up best: "What real difference will it all make? In the end, for all the fine words in the old railway station and in committee rooms, foreign policy will probably still be made by the officials around the finance minister, Paul Martin. Which means staying close to the apron strings of the United States."[13] Increased consultations did have the effect of encouraging domestic groups to seek more direct access to policy discussions and generated a number of confrontations between these groups and policy makers, especially on such issues as trade and human rights.

One of the more powerful pressures compelling prime ministers to become involved in global affairs in recent years has been the increasingly common practice of summit diplomacy. Summit diplomacy requires even the most reluctant of political leaders to participate, lest they offend their hosts. Prime Minister Chrétien attended more than fifty summit meetings during his time in office, an average of more than five a year. Some of these summits were set by the Prime Minister himself, for example bilateral meetings with other heads of government, and reflected his personal interests.[14] While these can be used to reinforce one's position on the world stage, Chrétien's "meetings with foreign leaders tended to be more about comparative domestic politics than any exploration of the intricacies of international diplomacy."[15] The majority of summit meetings, however, resulted from Canada's membership in multilateral institutions, such as the Group of Eight (G–8), the Commonwealth, the North Atlantic Treaty Organization (NATO), Asia Pacific Economic Cooperation, and la Francophonie rather than the Prime Minister's discretion. Participating in these institutional summits was, and remains to a considerable degree, an obligation that prime ministers, including Chrétien, could not easily shirk. Summit meetings provide both an opportunity and, at times, a requirement that the Prime Minister express a position on foreign policy matters. Unlike his predecessors Trudeau and Mulroney, who often assumed a high profile at summit meetings, Chrétien's approach was deliberately low key. For example, he tried to minimize the prominence of the first G–8 meeting he hosted in Halifax by describing it as a "Chevrolet" summit. His decision to host his second, shorter, and final G–8 meeting at a relatively remote Alberta resort was motivated both by security concerns and a desire to promote a greater degree of informality to this august gathering. This is not to say that Chrétien refrained from pushing his own priorities at these meetings – reform of international institutions at the 1995 meeting and African development in 2003 – but his approach was somewhat more muted.

Despite the apparent preference for a more modest role, summit gatherings have a tendency of tempting even the most reluctant leaders into the spotlight, and Chrétien was not immune to the pressure. So it was in November 1995 when Prime Minister Chrétien – then attending the Commonwealth Heads of Government Meeting in Auckland, New Zealand – called the Nigerian government to account for its pending decision to execute Ken Saro Wiwa and eight of his Ogoni colleagues. As Black notes: "Chrétien ... distinguished himself by being the only leader to warn in his opening remarks that carrying out the sentence would clearly violate Harare principles" of good governance.[16] In calling attention to the execution, Chrétien appears to have been motivated more by the specific circumstances of the moment rather than a persistent concern with human rights, as these had been routinely ignored at the APEC summit Chrétien hosted in 1993 and in the government's relations with potentially lucrative trade partners, such as China. Yet in taking a stand at the Commonwealth summit, Chrétien moved the Canadian government to centre stage in an effort to promote democratic change in Nigeria. The summit rhetoric was quickly overwhelmed by the necessity of providing the deliverables and, in this and other cases, the Chrétien government sometimes found it difficult to sustain a commitment to making a difference. Black has argued that "an effective human rights-based stand ... needs to be buttressed by a greater degree of consistency than has been manifested in the Chrétien government's foreign policy."[17]

A similar inability or unwillingness to follow through on initiatives plagued the Prime Minister on other issues – for example, when he was motivated to launch a multilateral action to rescue Rwandan refugees threatened by the geographical extension of the Rwandan civil war in November 1994. Motivated in part by the human suffering being displayed by the western media, Chrétien attempted to initiate an international effort to repatriate Rwandan refugees from their camps in eastern Zaire, lest they fall prey to those who sought to use the camps to launch a counter-offensive against the newly installed Tutsi-led government in Rwanda. The Prime Minister's initiative was marred from the beginning by Canada's limited capacities, the reluctance of other parties, notably the United States, to get involved and a limited understanding of circumstances on the ground. The immediate crisis soon ended as developments in the region forced the refugees to risk the return home lest they find themselves in the midst of yet another war zone. This provided an opportunity for the Prime Minister to proclaim a partial success, but the event provided an indication of the uncertainty, if not ambivalence, surrounding the Prime Minister's approach to humanitarian crises. This ambivalence reflected a tendency on the part of the Prime Minister to move from issue to issue with little by way of sustained interest in any particular area. Africa, for example, re-emerged as a major priority for the 2002 summit, by which time foreign aid had declined substantially and Canada's peacekeeping personnel on the continent had been reduced to eight. Andrew Cohen wrote that "cynics could be forgiven for wondering whether Africa was simply the flavour of the month, as Asia was at a summit in Vancouver in 1997.... [F]or Jean Chrétien, who had presided over the hollowing-out of foreign aid, Africa looked equally ephemeral – less a commitment than a caprice."[18] Short attention spans have been evident in other areas. For example, between 1993 and 2003, the Chrétien government demonstrated an interest in developing a more regional approach to its foreign policy, but the interest shifted from Asia, to the Americas, to Africa with little real concentration toward any one of them. Similarly one can see an interest in U.N. reform or in the OAS, or in international financial institutions, but few have been sustained or sup-

ported with a significant commitment of resources. Even bilateral relations seem to rise and fall, for example, with Mexico. This is, to some
degree, a reflection of the position of a lesser power such as Canada having to respond to changing conditions in the global community, but it
also suggests a government and a Prime Minister more concerned with
cutting spending than with supporting foreign policy priorities. Despite
commentaries about the alleged benefits of niche diplomacy as the way
of the future for lesser powers such as Canada, the successive Chrétien
governments dabbled in different niches and moved on to the next without making any clear choices, all the while reducing resources available
for any one of them.[19] While all of this was happening, the only
self-evident priority in Canadian foreign policy, bilateral relations with
the United States, became ever more firmly entrenched.

GOOD – AND NOT COZY

In the spring of 2003, many commentators lamented the deterioration in
Canada's bilateral relations with the United States. Chrétien was criticized for his failure to sanction members of his Cabinet and caucus who
spoke disparagingly of the Bush administration, for his own comments
about American foreign policy, and, most importantly, for his refusal to
support the American-led invasion of Iraq. The American ambassador to
Canada, Paul Cellucci, joined the fray in speeches and comments, and the
conservative media and politicians repeatedly reinforced the idea that
this was a serious disruption in bilateral relations. While many saw the
Prime Minister's actions as an attack on the Bush administration and a
severe and worrisome threat to Canada's economic relations with the
U.S., it was, rather, consistent with Chrétien's long-standing views of the
U.S. and Canada's relations with that country and, more importantly,
obscured the significant degree of support that Chrétien had given to the
U.S. since becoming Prime Minister. The war in Iraq was not the only
issue on which Chrétien parted ways from his American colleagues, having previously challenged the American approach to Bosnia, the U.N.,
and Cuba, among others. Chrétien had assumed office with a commitment to distance Canada from the close bilateral embrace that had
marked Canadian-American relations under the Mulroney government.
Gone were the frequent telephone chats and the fishing trips. In his first
months in office Chrétien sought to avoid meeting President Clinton lest
he give the impression that he was cozying up to the American leader.
Though he subsequently developed a good personal relationship with

Clinton and golf replaced fishing as the recreation of choice, he was not adverse to making snide comments about the American political process and defending anti-Americanism as good domestic politics in Canada. Thus, whatever his personal views of Bush and his administration, Chrétien's opinion of the United States and its political process had deeper roots. It also had little real effect on the bilateral relationship.

Despite these sentiments, Chrétien was not inclined to do much to substantially change the country's increasingly close linkages with the Americans. Nor, despite the occasional differences noted above, did Chrétien regularly challenge American foreign policy interests and priorities. While differences over the war in Iraq, the Ottawa Treaty banning anti-personnel landmines, and the International Criminal Court received a good deal of attention, more often than not, the Chrétien government aligned itself with the United States on many important issues. Among the more prominent, was the government's decision to join the war against Serbia over Kosovo and send troops to Afghanistan as part of the American-led war against terrorism in that country. There were also many other instances where the two countries shared similar views ranging from the Free Trade Area of the Americas to democratization efforts in that region to climate change negotiations (for much of the decade). Overriding all of these issues in bringing the two countries closer together was the deepening trade relationship that continued to flourish during the 1990s. Despite Chrétien's initial reservations about trade with the Americans and many persistent conflicts over issues such as softwood lumber, wheat, beer, and other products, Canada's trade dependence on the United States increased significantly between 1993 and 2003, reflecting not only in the increasing percentage of trade with the United States, but also with Canada's increased dependence on trade for its economic prosperity. Added to this were increased pressures for closer security collaboration in the aftermath of the terrorist attacks of September 11, 2001. While critics were quick to point to Chrétien's comments on global inequality as a source of discontent, his government moved quickly to adopt co-operative border measures – measures that, admittedly, in some areas, the government had been pursuing with the Americans prior to the attacks of 2001. The net result is that Canada is now more closely connected to the United States than at any time in its history – a somewhat ironic condition for a Prime Minister who staked his first term in office on an expressed desire to distance the two countries, and left office amidst cries that his differences with the United States were threatening this most important relationship.

CHRÉTIEN AND CANADIAN TRADE POLICY

Jean Chrétien was elected with a promise to re-open negotiations on the North American Free Trade Agreement (NAFTA) and a parliamentary history of criticism over close economic ties with the United States. Yet the Liberal campaign also highlighted the priority of economic prosperity, and the foreign policy review confirmed this by giving pride of place to prosperity as one of the foremost objectives of the new government. Despite his reservations over NAFTA, Chrétien appointed ardent free trade advocate Roy MacLaren as his Minister for International Trade. Thus, despite the campaign rhetoric, Chrétien displayed little real interest in reversing the course of trade liberalization that had been pursued by his Conservative predecessors. If there was a shift in tone, it was in an attempt to diversify Canada's trade dependence on the United States by pursuing expanded trade opportunities with other countries. Indeed trade promotion and liberalization were perhaps the most (if not only) consistent foreign policy priority pursued by Chrétien during his time as Prime Minister. Prime ministers had acted as salespersons in the past, but Chrétien took the task to a new high with his Team Canada trade missions. Launched in 1995 with much fanfare, Team Canada was a collection of provincial premiers and business executives led by Chrétien, to pry open the markets of China. The visit was marked by numerous public appearances and well orchestrated transactions establishing trade and investment opportunities. The mission's "success" led to subsequent Team Canada excursions to Latin America and South Asia and a favourable assessment from Chrétien. "As you know, promoting Canadian Trade has been a personal priority for me ... I had the honour to lead historic trade missions to Asia and Latin America ... And I was delighted that Canadian businesses got involved in a very enthusiastic [way]. The result was $11 billion in trade and investment deals, and thousands of new jobs for Canadians."[20] Others, such as David Malone suggested that the missions "puzzled our hosts and rapidly outlived their potential."[21] Trade statistics suggest that Team Canada missions were no more successful in changing the pattern of Canadian trade than efforts by previous governments at trade diversification.

Like his predecessors, Chrétien's support of trade liberalization was a reflection of the overwhelming significance of trade for the Canadian economy. As the Trade Minister reported in June 2000: "[E]xports increased by more than 11 percent in 1999 – reaching $410 billion. To put it into perspective, that's 43 percent of our entire GDP. And this growth has been taking place for some time. Ten years ago, our exports represented 25 percent of our GDP, so we've increased exports from 25 percent to 43 percent in one decade."[22] This significant growth strongly reinforced the country's reliance on foreign trade. The government took on an active role in promoting trade liberalization and an expansion in international trade rules to foster this liberalization in a variety of venues. Among the most prominent were its efforts in supporting the Free Trade Area of the Americas (FTAA). Gaining and maintaining access to foreign markets had become even more critically important for the Canadian economy than it had been a decade earlier, but the American market was the one that really mattered, as it accounts for more than 80 percent of Canadian trade.

CHRÉTIEN AND HUMAN SECURITY

One of the more celebrated aspects of Canadian foreign policy during Chrétien's tenure was the Canadian government's involvement in supporting human security. As represented in such high-profile activities as Canadian support for, and involvement in, the treaty to ban anti-personnel land mines and the establishment of an international criminal court, human security became a central feature of Canadian foreign policy, especially under Foreign Minister Lloyd Axworthy between 1995 and 2000. Though human security appeared to become a core principle in Canadian foreign policy with the appointment of Axworthy as Foreign Minister in 1996, it would be difficult to attribute full responsibility for the human security legacy to either Axworthy or Chrétien. For one, the roots of Canada's human security initiative run much deeper than the foreign minister, prime minister, or even Liberal government. Its origins can be traced to the 1970s and lie in a long-standing set of concerns among Canadian non-governmental organizations and officials for issues of human rights, and, more recently, with the Mulroney government's support for good governance and a more interventionist foreign policy.[23] Moreover the human security agenda, while it received a considerable amount of publicity, did not receive much in the way of substantive resources. Good governance received a prominent place in Canadian foreign policy in the early 1990s supporting such initiatives as the Unit for the Promotion of Democracy and the Santiago Commitment in the OAS, and the 1991 Harare Declaration in the Commonwealth. Chrétien, both in opposition and in his early days as Prime Minister, was skeptical of the interventionist character of Mulroney's good governance policy.[24]

His Liberal government eventually moved from good governance to human security and an expanded agenda of concerns. For Chrétien, the decision to pursue human security initiatives appears to have been a response to his sense of Canadian values. For example, in defending the government's support for the air war against Serbia in 1999, Chrétien said: "Our participation in this NATO mission [Kosovo] is just the most recent example of how our foreign policy is dictated not only by our interests but by our values. Our values as Canadians. Our basic human values."[25] What was left unclear was why such values applied in defence of Kosovars but not Liberians, or others suffering from violent oppression. Nor did it explain why such values were not sufficient grounds for adding new resources to the Canadian armed forces and others involved in protecting or promoting such values, or for protecting, let alone expanding, the government's development assistance budget.

Part of the difficulty confronting the Chrétien government, as it pursued foreign policy in the 1990s, were the ambiguities surrounding Canadian security policy in the post-Cold War period. While immediate and direct threats to Canadian interests were not apparent, it was difficult to turn away from horrific civil wars that were destroying lives and societies across the globe. Indifference was made more difficult by a commitment in the foreign policy white paper, to project Canadian values of democracy, civil liberties, and human dignity. There was an expanding array of security concerns, but Canadian interests were often indirect at best. There was, in turn, considerable rhetorical support for the U.N. to assume responsibility for these conflicts, but few states, including Canada, were willing to make the contribution that would allow U.N. operations to be effective. By 2003, Canada contributed only a very small portion of soldiers to U.N. operations (eight out of 12,000 in Africa; thirty-fourth on the list of contributors). There was limited rhetorical support for the continuing relevance of NATO, yet most of our contributions were made under the auspices of that alliance in places such as Kosovo, Bosnia, or in coalitions of the willing in Afghanistan. As Louis Delvoie writes:

The rhetoric of Canadian security policy in the Chrétien years has been: strong support for the U.N., perfunctory recognition of the importance of NATO, great emphasis on human rights and human security, and considerable self-praise for Canada's leading role in the world community. The reality of Canadian security policy in the Chrétien years has been: very little support for the U.N., deep involvement in NATO operations in Europe, a modest measure of success in promoting the human rights agenda, and much less influential a role than we like to think. In politics, a gap between rhetoric and reality is always to be expected. But we may have reached the point where international awareness of the gap between reality and Canadian rhetoric is harming our reputation and effectiveness in the world.[26]

The contradictions are also evident in Chrétien's approach toward human security policy. At times this policy has pursued an expansion of international law and practice into new directions including support for intervention and the use of force. Often this support required a U.N. mandate to win Chrétien's approval. At times, however, such mandates were irrelevant, as seen in Chrétien's support for the landmines treaty, response to Kosovo, military contributions in Afghanistan, and ministerial statements that summed up Canada's willingness to use force in the world in defence of justice and human rights: "with the U.N. if possible, but not necessarily with the U.N."[27] A similar contradiction appeared in 1998, when Prime Minister Chrétien gave his government's support to military action against Iraq that was being considered by the Clinton administration at that time under a rather liberal reading of U.N. resolutions. In a statement in the House of Commons at the time, Chrétien said, "we believe that a military strike against Iraq would be justified to secure compliance with security council resolution 687 – and all other security council resolutions concerning Iraq."[28] The contradiction was brought full circle five years later when the Prime Minister decided to oppose the American and British military assault on Iraq in the spring of 2003, which occurred without a specific U.N. mandate authorizing the use of force. Among the explanations that have been offered for Chrétien's position include: domestic political considerations, especially in Québec; principled opposition to regime change; a renewed concern for the U.N. in light of the Bush administration's actions against that and other institutions; and Chrétien's own reluctance to support the use of force. While the explanation likely lies in a combination of these, it is worth considering the greater significance of Chrétien's own deep-seated reservations over the use of force as an instrument of foreign policy. These sentiments recur repeatedly in the Prime Minister's response to foreign policy problems such as occurred in Bosnia in the mid–1990s. As the Prime Minister stated, there were also profound concerns over the use of outside force to bring about regime change in Iraq. Whatever the primacy of these various motives, it is clear that Chrétien's decision was generally consistent with public attitudes. Lawrence Martin wrote: "Much on the Iraq story has been typical of the Chrétien way. He is a politician who goes to the heart of Canadians' values. He is instinctively there – and this is what has sustained him for so long."[29] The cloud that surrounded the Prime Minister's response to the war in Iraq was, in many respects, typical of his approach – a policy of doing little while invoking the mantra of internationalism.

CONCLUSION

Jean Chrétien seldom missed an opportunity to mention Canada's first place standing in the U.N.'s annual human development index when Canada held that position. He was also always willing to call attention to Canada's internationalist credentials. Yet mere statements were not enough to sustain either one. In reflecting on his government's legacy in foreign policy during a speech in Calgary, Chrétien offered the following comments:

There is a lot of talk these days about Canada's role in the world. Our government has been active in achieving an international land mines treaty. In establishing an international court of criminal justice. With a Canadian as Chief Justice. In promoting the Africa initiative. In the war against terrorism. Canada has earned a unique role in the world. Disproportionate to our population, or the size of our economy, or the size of our military. We have earned this place through an unwavering commitment to the values of democracy, human rights and the peaceful resolution of conflicts. We help our friends most when we are true to that role and the values that underpin it. We have a stake in continuing to strengthen multilateral institutions whether to combat climate change, war crimes, or to make decisions about war.[30]

The record demonstrates the government's efforts to remain engaged with the globe and to make a contribution to a more progressive global order. Yet the record also demonstrates a persistent and significant diminution of the resources necessary to support and sustain this order. In contrast to the country's standing atop the U.N.'s development index, Canada sat at an embarrassing sixteen out of nineteen OECD countries when assessed on its contribution to the welfare of others on this planet. "The government lulled itself into believing that Canada could continue to matter internationally while its foreign policy instruments eroded and while the country's weight relative to others declined."[31] There is little doubt but that Jean Chrétien was strongly committed to the importance of Canadian values as a guiding principle of Canadian foreign policy. He also thought that these values should govern international order and that international institutions, and especially the U.N., should govern this order. Moreover, these values, on more than one occasion, convinced him to support the use of force and commit Canadian armed forces to battle. These ideas can be found consistently in the speeches and statements that the former Prime Minister made on foreign policy during his time in office. This, in itself, reflected a degree of internationalism and a support for a values-based internationalism that was not always shared by his Liberal predecessors. At a more practical level, however, the Prime Minister's commitment to pursuing a values-based foreign policy was not applied consistently, was seldom supported with sufficient resources, and was sacrificed if and when it conflicted with economic interests at home and abroad. Most commonly, there was a tendency throughout the decade to rely on what Foreign Minister Axworthy referred to as soft power – relying on ideas, diplomacy, and one's credentials, but what effectively amounted to trying to pursue this values-based policy without a substantial commitment of the resources necessary to bring these ideas into practice. While the rhetoric and the spirit were unequivocally internationalist, the tangible commitment of resources reflected a passivity not seen for many decades.

NOTES

Professor, Department of Political Science, University of Alberta.

1 Harald von Riekhoff and Maureen Appel Molot, "Introduction: A Part of the Peace," in Harald von Riekhoff and Maureen Appel Molot, eds., *Canada Among Nations 1994, A Part of the Peace* (Ottawa: Carleton University Press, 1994), 12–30, 19.

2 Kim Richard Nossal, "Mission Diplomacy and the 'Cult of the Initiative' in Canadian Foreign Policy," in Andrew F. Cooper and Geoffrey Hayes, eds., *Worthwhile Initiatives: Canadian Mission-Oriented Diplomacy* (Toronto: Irwin Publishing, 2000), 1–12, 4.

3 John J. Kirton, "Foreign Policy Under the Liberals: Prime Ministerial Leadership in the Chrétien Government's Foreign Policy-Making Process," in Fen Osler Hampson, Maureen Appel Molot, and Martin Rudner, eds., *Canadian Among Nations 1997, Asia-Pacific Face-Off* (Ottawa: Carleton University Press, 1997), 21–50, 22.

4 Jean-Francois Rioux and Robin Hay, *Canadian Foreign Policy: From Internationalism to Isolationism* (Ottawa: Norman Patterson School of International Affairs, 1997), 6.

5 Michael Ignatieff, "Canada in an Age of Terror – Multilateralism Meets a Moment of Truth," *Policy Options* 24:2 (2003): 14–19, 18.

6 Andrew Cohen, *While Canada Slept* (Toronto: McClelland & Stewart, 2003).

7 Nossal, "Mission Diplomacy," 4.

8 Kim Richard Nossal, *The Politics of Canadian Foreign Policy* (Scarborough: Prentice-Hall, 1997), 177.

9 Andrew Cohen, cited in ibid., 189.

10 Edward Greenspon and Anthony Wilson-Smith, *Double Vision: The Inside Story of the Liberals in Power* (Toronto: Doubleday Canada, 1996), 103.

11 See e.g., Denis Stairs, "The Changing Office and the Changing Environment of the Minister of Foreign Affairs in the Axworthy Era," in Fen Osler Hampson, Norman Hillmer, and Maureen Appel Molot, eds., *Canada Among Nations, 2001: The Axworthy Legacy* (Ottawa: Oxford University Press, 2001), 19–38.

12 Jean Chrétien, "Canadian Foreign Policy: Basic Human Rights," *Vital Speeches* 65 (1999): 389.

13 "Canada: A few kicks and screams," *The Economist*, 16 April 1994, 50.

14 Among the bilateral meetings with other leaders, perhaps the most important were meetings with the U.S. president, though the one scheduled for May 2003 that did not take place was the most widely discussed.

15 Greenspon and Wilson-Smith, *Double Vision*, 102.

16 David Black, "Canada, the Commonwealth, and Nigeria," in Cooper and Hayes, *Worthwhile Initiatives*, 49–60, 53.

17 David Black, "Echoes of Apartheid?" in Rosalind Irwin, ed., *Ethics and Security in Canadian Foreign Policy* (Vancouver: University of British Columbia Press, 2001), 138–59, 156.

18 Cohen, *While Canada Slept*, 99.

19 Niche diplomacy referred to an attempt to be more selective in choosing foreign policy commitments as a way of reducing demands on resources and concentrating potential influence. See e.g., the discussion in Andrew Cooper, "In Search of Niches: Saying 'Yes' and Saying 'No' in Canada's International Relations," *Canadian Foreign Policy* 3 (Winter 1995): 1–13.

20 Jean Chrétien, "Speech at the National Forum on Canada's Foreign Policy" (Toronto, 11 September 1995).

21 David Malone, "A Shadow of Our Former Selves," *Literary Review of Canada* 11 (2003): 3–6, 6.

22 Pierre Pettigrew, "Notes for an address by the Honourable Pierre Pettigrew, Minister for International Trade, to the Standing Committee on Foreign Affairs and International Trade on the Free Trade Area of the Americas" (14 June 2000).

23 See e.g., Jennifer Ross, "Is Canada's Human Security Policy Really the 'Axworthy Doctrine'?" *Canadian Foreign Policy* 8 (Winter 2001): 75–93.

24 See Nicholas Gammer, *From Peacekeeping to Peacemaking* (Montreal & Kingston: McGill-Queen's University Press, 2001).

25 Jean Chrétien, "Canadian Foreign Policy: Basic Human Rights," *Vital Speeches* 65 (1999): 389–91, 389.

26 Louis Delvoie, "Curious Ambiguities: Canada's International Security Policy," *Policy Options* 22 (2001): 36–43, 36.

27 Defence Minister John McCallum, cited in Gwynne Dyer, "End of History? End of War?" *Queen's Quarterly* 106 (1999): 488–503, 491.

28 House of Commons, *Debates* 055 (9 February 1998), 3589 (J. Chrétien).

29 Lawrence Martin, "Our man in Ottawa," *Globe and Mail*, 9 April 2003, A15.

30 Jean Chrétien, "Address by Prime Minister Jean Chrétien on the occasion of the Calgary Leader's Dinner" (9 May 2003), http://www.pco-bcp.gc.ca/default.asp?Language=E&Page=pmarchive& Sub=Speeches&Doc=calgaryleadersdinner.20030509_e.htm.

31 Malone, "A Shadow of Our Former Selves," 6.

7

Jean Chrétien's Immigration Legacy

Continuity and Transformation

YASMEEN ABU-LABAN

INTRODUCTION

The retirement of Jean Chrétien in December 2003 – after a decade as Prime Minister, and after close to forty continuous years in public life[1] – offers an opportunity to reflect on his impact on Canadian political and social life. This article explores Chrétien's immigration legacy. Immigration policy has been central, both historically and contemporaneously, to the shaping of the Canadian political community. It will be argued that in Chrétien's ten years as Prime Minister, immigration policy underwent a transformation toward greater exclusivity than in the era immediately preceding. Under Jean Chrétien, new stress has been placed on immigrant integration, immigrant self-sufficiency, and continentalization of immigration controls; these themes have continued to reverberate within immigration policy in the post-Chrétien era.

For many observers, both inside and outside Canada, Canadian immigration policy appears to be a model of openness, if not humanitarianism and egalitarianism. Facts can be harnessed to support this interpretation, which primarily rest on comparisons with other countries. According to the 2001 Census, fully 18.4 percent of the Canadian national population are immigrants – a proportion much higher than most other industrialized countries.[2] Since the 1970s, there has been a steady decline of immigrants arriving from the countries of Europe, and an increase of immigrants arriving from countries in the Caribbean, Central and South America, Africa, the Middle East, and Asia, making for greater racial, religious, and cultural diversity in Canada's population. When combined with a pre-existing Aboriginal population, and two European colonizing groups of different power (the British and the French), Canada exhibits a distinct mix of collectivities that may make claims on the state. Moreover, Canada's humanitarian responsiveness to refugees has been recognized at the highest levels internationally. For example, in 1986, Canada was the first country ever to receive the Nansen medal by the United Nations High Commission on Refugees for its policies towards refugees. In 1993, Canada was the first country to formally allow refugees facing gender persecution to enter Canada. Not least, unlike many countries that have historically made use of guest worker programs (such as Germany, Kuwait, and Japan) immigrants who come to Canada are normally able to obtain citizenship relatively quickly – after three years.

While such facts may tell us something about Canada in relation to specific countries, they do not tell the full story of immigration because comparisons can be made in other ways. Another form of comparison can be against an ideal. While it may be hard to imagine a world without countries, there has been lively debate amongst political philosophers on the justifiability of borders and immigration controls in a world where wealth is distributed radically unevenly. Some have argued for eliminating controls on the movement of people.[3] Moreover, comparisons may not be just across geographic spaces, but also over time. Using these alternative benchmarks for comparison, my starting point in this exploration is from a perspective that holds that Canadian immigration policy is *de facto* about exclusion – after all, if people were truly free to move across state borders as they wished, there would be no immigration policy at all. However, the forms and content of the exclusion emanating from immigration policies and selection are historically specific.

When Jean Chrétien entered Parliament in 1963, joining the Liberal government of Prime Minister Lester B. Pearson, Canada's immigration policy was explicitly racist and favoured white, British-origin Protestants as candidates for entry and permanent settlement. This explicitly racist era of policy stemmed from the formation of the modern Canadian state in 1867, and the historic project of creating Canada as a "white settler society."[4] It was only in 1967 that a new era of policy was ushered in with the introduction of a point system of selection, and the source countries of immigrants became much more diverse.[5] The point system, still in place today, numerically assesses all applicants on criteria related to skills and education. While purportedly non-discriminatory, there is ample evidence to suggest that the criteria used in the point system and the practice of immigration selection work to advantage applicants from some countries (e.g., those in the industrialized west) more than others (e.g., those in Africa).[6] Therefore, elements of the racialized forms of exclusion from pre–1967 policy continued into the post–1967 policy, but they reverberated in new ways.[7]

In this article I will suggest that under Prime Minister Chrétien's leadership (1993–2003), yet another distinct era of immigration policy has emerged as a result of neo-liberalism. In contrast to Keynesian inspired ideas which reached their zenith in Canada in the 1960s and 1970s, neo-liberal values include a more limited role for the state, cutting back state policies and programs – especially social programs – a greater stress on individual self-sufficiency, and a belief that the "free market" can efficiently allocate goods and services.[8] Shaped by neo-liberalism, and fortified by the response to the events of September 11, 2001, contemporary immigration policy, while not entirely free of its pre- and post–1967 incarnations, has been shaped by three key new emphases under Prime Minister Chrétien. These are: 1) the promotion of immigrant integration; 2) attracting immigrants who are deemed self-sufficient; and 3) an explicit continentalization of immigration and border security controls. Each of these emphases, and their implications, will be examined in detail below. It will be shown that the emphasis on attracting self-sufficient immigrants, along with post-September 11 responses around security, create new ways in which contemporary policy excludes, despite the strongly stated commitment to better understand and develop policies to integrate and include newcomers to Canada. When Canadian immigration policy is compared favourably against other countries this sometimes breeds complacency. However, when Canadian immigration policy under Jean Chrétien is compared against the ideal of open borders, or compared with the 1967–1993 period, there is less scope for complacency by those concerned with equality.

INTEGRATION

The Canadian approach to diversity strengthens Canada's reputation as a just and fair society. Canada is renowned for its rich cultural mosaic and the Canadian model has become an example for the rest of the world.

– Jean Chrétien, 1999[9]

A hallmark of the Chrétien Liberals' three successive mandates was undoubtedly the emphasis on the "integration" of immigrants. While the use of the term "integration" predates the Chrétien government,[10] there is no doubt that after 1993, integration was increasingly presented to both domestic and international audiences as part and parcel of a larger (uniquely) Canadian "model." An early mention of "integration" is found in a 1994 discussion document released by Citizenship and Immigration Canada, which posits integration as distinct from assimilation and segregation. Hence: "Canada's approach, known as *integration*, encourages a process of mutual adjustment by *both* newcomers and society. This approach sets us apart from many other countries. Newcomers are expected to understand and respect basic Canadian values, but society is also expected to understand and respect the cultural differences newcomers bring to Canada. Rather than expecting newcomers to abandon their own cultural heritage, the emphasis is on finding ways to integrate differences within a pluralistic society."[11] Under Prime Minister Chrétien, the emphasis on integration shaped two distinct areas that impact policy-making: 1) how settlement services are offered and 2) the formation of the Metropolis Project. Each will be examined in turn.

Settlement Services

Federal settlement services for newcomers to Canada include reception, referral, and employment services; language training; and a host program to match volunteers with newcomers. Settlement services are targeted at permanent residents, not Canadian citizens, and so are meant to cover a three-year time frame only.[12] In 1996, the Chrétien Liberals began a process of "settlement renewal" in which the federal government devolved the direct administration and funding of settlement services to lower levels.[13] In this way, immigrant settlement services joined the larger trend of "governance," which Susan Phillips defines as: "a process of governing through collaboration with voluntary, private or other public sector actors in the planning, design and achievement of government objectives in a manner that shares policy formation, risk and operational planning, and that may replace programme delivery by state employees with those of third parties."[14] Not incidentally, this trend has emerged in the context of neo-liberalism and cuts to state spending. The turn towards governance was symbolized by the Chrétien Liberal's commitment of $95 million to a Voluntary Sector Initiative to boost the capacity of this sector, part of which involved a "Strengthening Settlement Capacity Project" begun in 2001 (and ended in 2003). Staff in immigrant-serving NGOs note, however, that such new partnerships carry risks, including the

downloading of deficits to the private sector and challenges to the autonomy and advocacy role of NGOs.[15] Thus, settlement renewal, like the
move towards governance generally, carries still unfolding implications
for the voluntary sector as well as for the private sector, communities,
and families.[16]

The clearest impact of settlement renewal has been evident in the provinces. Since the formation of the modern Canadian state in 1867, immigration has been constitutionally defined as a shared area of federal and
provincial jurisdiction, and since Confederation the relative influence of
the federal and provincial governments has varied.[17] In recent decades,
stemming from the Quiet Revolution in the 1960s, Québec has sought
more control in immigrant selection, starting with the creation of its
own department of immigration in 1968 and culminating in the 1991
Canada-Québec Accord. While the admission of any person to Canada
rests with the Canadian federal state, the *Canada-Québec Accord* gives
Québec sole responsibility for selecting immigrants and refugees abroad
who are destined for Québec, and allows the province to offer its own
settlement services to immigrants, with federal compensation.

A primary consequence of settlement renewal was the extension of
aspects of this arrangement to the other provinces. Indeed, the federal
government subsequently signed agreements (albeit less comprehensive
ones than the agreement with Québec) with British Columbia, Saskatchewan, Manitoba, New Brunswick, Newfoundland and Labrador, and
Prince Edward Island.[18] As Joseph Garcea suggested in the late 1990s,
"[T]he result is an integration system in which the provincial governments will perform the key planning and administrative roles and the
federal government will be limited to setting and enforcing principles and
standards, and providing funding for settlement and integration
programs."[19]

The Metropolis Project

The policy ramifications of emphasizing integration are perhaps most
strikingly found in the national component of the Metropolis Project.[20]
Nationally, the Metropolis Project began in 1996 with a joint effort by
Citizenship and Immigration Canada (CIC) and the Social Sciences and
Humanities Research Council of Canada (SSHRC) to establish four centres of research excellence in the study of immigrant integration. These
four centres, which directly implicate fifteen Canadian universities, are
located in Vancouver, Edmonton, Toronto, and Montreal. The Metropo-

lis Project seeks to bring together academics, policy-makers, and non-governmental organizations with the aim of improving "policy and program development through scientific research."[21] In particular, the objectives of the initiative are to:

- promote innovative, multidisciplinary research on immigration and integration in Canada focusing on key areas of relevance to policy and program development and to service delivery in a variety of sectors;
- develop multidisciplinary research designs and new methodological approaches to the study of immigration and integration issues;
- encourage comparative research from both a domestic and an international perspective which can enhance our knowledge base and inform strategic policy directions and practices;
- promote sustained collaboration among academics, policy-makers, business and labour groups, foundations, community organizations, practitioners, and other interested parties, on research into contemporary issues of mutual interest and on discussions of the implications of this research for policy development, program design, and program delivery;
- provide research training opportunities for students and encouragement for graduate students and researchers in the early stages of their careers to conduct immigration research; and
- disseminate research results widely to policy-makers, practitioners, community organizations, and the general public.[22]

Between 1996 and 2002, SSHRC and the Chrétien government committed $8 million to the four centres of research excellence; indeed, the Metropolis Project has been referred to by SSHRC staff as its "most significant program of targeted research support."[23] In 2002 the Metropolis project was extended for another five years, with the federal government and SSHRC committing a total of $6,615,000 between 2002 and 2007.[24] The emphasis on integration, and the Metropolis Project framework, will continue well past the Chrétien era, making it worthwhile to reflect upon the significance of this emphasis and project for the study and practice of immigration.

Most obviously, under the Chrétien government the term integration emerged as the professed means of "including" those who are newcomers to Canada. Indeed, in a 2003 overview of the work of Metropolis, it is stressed that "the Government of Canada has linked integration of newcomers to the broader goal of building an inclusive society."[25] Relatedly, the Metropolis Project has given not only Canadian policy-makers, but also hundreds of Canadian academics and graduate students, as well as NGOS, a stake in continuing to utilize "integration" in reference to the social inclusion of immigrants. This choice of terminology is noteworthy, since, in fact, integration can be seen to form a less radical alternative to the term – and politics of – multiculturalism.[26] As Peter Li notes, despite the stated definition of integration as involving adjustment on the part of both newcomers and the host society, both policy-makers and academics tend to judge integration as successful when immigrants become similar to the dominant group(s), and thus, ironically, integration has much in common with assimilation.[27] In this sense, there remains continued ambiguity about what the goal of "integration" actually means – despite the fact that it has become intertwined with Canada's approach to handling diversity, and despite the fact that Canada has been described as a "model" to the world – not only by Jean Chrétien, but by non-Canadians as well.[28]

Clearly the Metropolis Project has also served to create a new way of bringing academic research to bear on the policy-making process, and it is anticipated that this will be even more the case in the second phase of the project between 2002 and 2007.[29] Yet the move to establish the university research centres of excellence in the first place should be placed in the context of neo-liberalism, which brought with it shrinking research budgets. Effectively, the Metropolis Project makes use of a highly skilled, salaried professorate who, in contrast to consultants, do not receive personal remuneration for their research efforts.

While it may be the case that Metropolis-based research can lead to better policy practices, for academics, the shift towards targeted research also brings with it the danger of "narrowing the conceptualization and purpose of research to serve particular uses."[30] Arguably, much of the research work, particularly in the first phase of the Metropolis Project, addressed policy practices as they related to the experience of immigrants and their descendants already in Canada, rather than the shifting policies and state practices that governed the entry of would-be immigrants to Canada. Yet, as a result of the turn towards neo-liberalism, immigration selection itself changed markedly once the Chrétien Liberals assumed power in 1993. A distinctive pattern of exclusion can be seen in the increasing emphasis on attracting "self-sufficient" immigrants to Canada. This emphasis contradicts the stated goal of inclusion that permeates discussions of integration.

SELF-SUFFICIENCY

People who know they have to contribute to the cost of the operation are still arriving by the hundreds of thousands. The problem we face is that too many people want to come in and we cannot receive them all

– Jean Chrétien, 1995[31]

In the 1993 election, Jean Chrétien campaigned on the platform articulated in the Liberal Party's Red Book. According to this election manifesto, immigration levels were to be "approximately one percent of the population each year."[32] Yet, it is also worth recalling that when Jean Chrétien came to office public attitudes towards immigration were at an all-time high level of hostility.[33] Moreover, the success of the populist and right-of-centre Reform Party had served to politicize issues relating to racial and ethnic diversity, multiculturalism, and immigration in a distinct way.[34] Thus, it is perhaps not surprising that across three mandates (1993, 1997, 2000) the annual level of immigration never reached as high as 1 per cent of the population under Prime Minister Chrétien.

Instead, shortly after assuming power, between February and November 1994, the Chrétien Liberals carried out a public consultation on immigration. As Janine Brodie and Christina Gabriel note, public consultations have been a central feature of the Chrétien government and, in keeping with consultations in other areas of policy, the one on immigration served to legitimize neo-liberal policies and practices by limiting the parameters of debate and providing the illusion of democratic decision-making.[35] Following these consultations, the hallmark feature of the Chrétien Liberals' immigration selection was the new emphasis on attracting self-sufficient immigrants who could pay the costs of their own "integration" in Canadian society.[36] There are three clear ways that this has become evident under the Chrétien Liberals.

The first way in which the emphasis on self-sufficiency is evident is that there has been a reordering of the mix of immigrants away from the family and humanitarian/refugee classes towards the independent/economic classes. Formally, it is only independent immigrants who are assessed on the criteria of the point system. As Sunera Thobani notes, throughout the 1994 immigration consultation period and its aftermath, the independent category was masculinized and valorized in state discourse, while the family category was feminized and treated as a problem.[37] Specifically, independent immigrants were assumed to be male economic actors who would contribute to the nation, whereas family class immigrants were treated as non-contributory ("wives and children") who would drain social services. However erroneous this representation and this measuring of worth are,[38] by 1994 the Chrétien Liberals had clearly planned not only to lower the annual intake of immigrants but also to give more priority to independent immigrants, since they would be more likely to earn a high income and generate economic growth and less likely to use social welfare.[39] The effects of this shift, inspired by neo-liberalism with its emphasis on reducing social expenditures and promoting self-sufficiency, linger. In 2002, over two-thirds of immigrants came in under the economic/independents category.[40] This can be contrasted with the decade of the 1980s, when the independent category tended to be smaller than the family category.[41]

The second way that attracting self-sufficient and cost-paying immigrants became evident was in the introduction of a "Right of Landing Fee" in 1995. The Right of Landing Fee has been referred to by its critics as a modern form of head tax (in reference to the historic and racialized practice of the federal state charging a tax on every Chinese immigrant to Canada). As originally conceived, the Right of Landing Fee is a $975 fee levied on all adult immigrants, including refugees, entering Canada. In 2000, the federal government repealed this fee for refugees only, and Canada lost its dubious status as the only country in the world to charge a fee to people fleeing persecution and seeking protection.[42] Revenues generated by this fee, according to the Chrétien Liberals, were to off-set the cost of settlement programs and social services used by immigrants, even though incoming immigrants immediately pay taxes, and even though settlement services have been continuously subject to cuts over the 1990s.[43] Moreover, as Peter Li's careful analysis shows, for each year between 1997 and 2001, the amount spent by incoming immigrants on processing fees was higher than the amount spent by the federal government on settlement programs for refugees and immigrants.[44]

The third way the Chrétien Liberals have sought to attract self-sufficient immigrants is by raising the standards and pass marks for eligibility for independent immigrants. Building upon the selection criteria outlined in the 2001 *Immigration and Refugee Protection Act*[45] (which replaced the 1976 *Immigration Act*), new regulations introduced in June 2002 place more emphasis on education and on knowledge of one or both of Canada's official languages in the point system.[46] While the focus on official languages has been framed, in some quarters, as a means to ensure the health of French-language minority communities outside of

Québec,[47] immigrants who know an official language are not going to make use of state-funded language training programs. Indeed, it is important to note that the merit of downloading language training costs from the state to families and individuals was a recurrent theme throughout Chrétien's tenure.[48]

As noted, immigration policy is, by definition, about exclusion. Prior to 1967, Canada's immigration policy was explicitly racist. Canada's policy became officially non-discriminatory only with the introduction of the point system. The criteria used in the point system have long served to favour class-advantaged male applicants in countries with extensive educational opportunities based on the western scientific model.[49] In addition, since independent immigrants must apply from outside of Canada, the uneven distribution of Canadian immigration posts abroad – particularly under-represented on the continent of Africa – suggests how immigration practices can discriminate on the basis of the geographical location (and hence the race/ethnicity) of potential applicants.[50] However, the combined impact of the changes implemented while Jean Chrétien was Prime Minister is to create new and reinforced patterns of exclusion based on race, ethnicity, gender, and class.

The favouring of independent applicants has been coupled with a problematization of immigrant women who are less likely to apply in this category, as well as disfavouring the family class in immigration selection. The imposition of a landing fee imposes financial hardship on would-be immigrants, particularly women and the poor, from many countries in the developing world where this fee might be particularly onerous. Consider, for example, that the $975 Right of Landing Fee is equivalent to about ten months of wages for a nurse in Sri Lanka.[51] The changed criteria in the point system, especially around language, serves to favour applicants from countries where French and/or English is spoken, and/or there are extensive opportunities for learning these languages.

In short, despite the emphasis on "integration" and inclusion that has been a hallmark of the Chrétien Liberals, the practice of immigration selection has actually become more exclusionary since 1993. Since the more exclusionary direction charted in the selection of would-be immigrants has been inspired by neo-liberalism, it is unlikely that immigration policy will be altered fundamentally in the absence of a shift away from these values. Indeed, the September 2003 decision by the Chrétien Liberals to lower the criteria of the point system stemmed less from a change in philosophy and more from a court case launched by would-be immigrants who had applied prior to the change of rules, and who had successfully argued that they should be judged on the old criteria.[52] Moreover, since the events of September 11, public attitudes towards immigration, and immigration controls, seem to be moving in an even more restrictive direction.

CONTINENTALIZATION

Mr. President, you and I met at the White House less than two weeks after 9–11. We understood the urgent need to act ... We recognized that we could create a "smart border," one that was not only more secure, but more efficient for trade.

– Jean Chrétien, 2002[53]

The impact of the September 11, 2001, attacks has affected Canadian public opinion and discourse, and it has opened the possibilities for stricter and more racialized immigration and security controls. Stricter border security and immigration controls have also stemmed from the decision made by the Chrétien Liberals to pursue a continentalization strategy.[54]

In terms of public attitudes, September 11 has "served to make more salient to Americans and Canadians both the real and the more symbolic (*i.e.*, value or cultural) threats that 'foreigners' may pose to their way of life."[55] There are numerous perceived "foreigners" in an immigrant-receiving country like Canada. Indeed, in the immediate aftermath of September 11 citizens provoked violence in cities across Canada against minority co-citizens (including Arab, Muslim, South Asian, and other visible minority Canadians).[56] In addition to this backlash, September 11 led to more negative public attitudes about immigration in both the United States and Canada.[57] It is also clear that in Canada, there has been a shift in public opinion, and perhaps more significantly in the discourse of some political and media elites, towards endorsing ethnic or racial profiling.[58] In the post-September 11 environment, profiling might involve law enforcement and immigration officials differentially targeting those seen to be Arab or Muslim.[59]

In the months following September 11, Jean Chrétien strongly denounced the violence directed at some minority Canadians and advanced a vision of Canada as a culturally diverse country where difference was accepted – arguably preventing the immediate backlash from being much worse.[60] Yet, despite this clear condemnation of racism from Chrétien, there is evidence of a racialization of security threats, and thus immigration control, post-September 11. This is seen in reported practices of profiling by state officials, and the drop in the number of visas granted to applicants from Middle Eastern and predominantly Muslim countries.[61] Stricter border and immigration controls also emerged as a consequence of the deepening economic ties between Canada and the United States, propelling a continentalization of immigration post- September 11.[62]

In contrast to the European Union where nationals of member states enjoy a European citizenship that allows them mobility, residence and other rights within any other member state, the provisions of NAFTA offer only limited mobility rights to business people and professionals. However, there is no question that as a result of the North American Free Trade Agreement the trade between Canada and the United States has been expanded with implications in a host of areas, including immigration.[63]

As a result of the deepening economic ties created by NAFTA, the closure of the U.S. border in the immediate aftermath of September 11 cost Canadian businesses billions of dollars.[64] At the same time, despite the fact that none of the September 11 hijackers came through Canada, and despite the fact that there are relatively few instances of law breaking amongst immigrants, there was a perception on the part of many American policy-makers that Canada was lax on immigration.[65] Combined, these two factors translated into more frequent calls from Canadian businesses and from politicians on both sides of the Canada-U.S. border for a "security perimeter" that would lead to better co-operation, if not harmonization, on border security and immigration policies.[66] The place of Mexico in this vision is unclear. The perimeter call led to the signing in December 2001 of the Smart Border Declaration between Canada and the United States, and its accompanying thirty-point action plan.

The Smart Border Declaration committed the two countries to collaborate to create, in the words of Chrétien, "a border that is open for business, but closed to terrorists."[67] The Accord led to a number of developments that impact immigration. These include: efforts to jointly co-ordinate and standardize biometric identifiers for travelers, efforts to better exchange information on immigration and asylum-seekers, the signing of a "Safe Third Country Agreement" that will allow asylum claims to be heard in only one of the two countries, visa policy co-ordination, and joint co-ordination between immigration officers abroad.[68]

In essence, the Smart Border Declaration met the concerns of the United States about border security and the concerns expressed by Canadian politicians and business leaders about keeping the border open to the flow of goods.[69] The implications of this Accord are far-reaching for Canada. As Satzewich and Wong note, "[C]onvergence and harmonization will most likely put pressures on Canada to move toward a more restrictive immigration policy."[70] This is because the United States has a far greater number of restrictive and inadmissible criteria governing immigration selection and also tends to take fewer immigrants per capita than Canada.

It has been observed that NAFTA created a neo-liberal conditioning framework for the subordinate partners (Mexico and Canada) to the agreement.[71] In tandem, neo-liberalism and regional integration have also impacted immigration. The Chrétien years clearly marked how the paths of neo-liberalism and continentalization have produced, and will likely continue to produce, new forms of exclusion in immigration.

CONCLUSION

There are a lot of things that they can write about, and I will not be there to read my legacy ... For me, I'm satisfied that I've done my best.
– Jean Chrétien, 2003[72]

It is true that future historians will have a lot to cover in any consideration of the life and times of Jean Chrétien, whose nearly forty-year career in public life, and decade as Prime Minister, saw considerable changes in Canadian politics and society. It is future historians who will also have the advantage of time to more adequately gauge what has a lasting impact.

Yet, even relatively soon after Jean Chrétien's retirement from politics, much can already be said about the ways in which immigration policy has evolved. The policy emphasis on integration has brought with it devolved ways in which settlement services are offered, with implications for both the provinces and the voluntary sector. This turn towards governance has also incorporated new modes of policy-making involving academics, as seen in the Metropolis Project. The search for self-sufficient immigrants has reinforced exclusions relating to class, gender, race, and ethnicity that were residual in the officially non-discriminatory post– 1967 immigration policy. Responses to the events of September 11, which have seen Canada working in close alliance with the United Sates, suggest that far from being a borderless world, immigration and border controls are being fortified and harmonized between the two countries and carry the potential for new forms of exclusion to be etched onto immigration policy. In this way, immigration policy has been transformed under Prime Minister Jean Chrétien's leadership in even greater exclusionary directions than the period from 1967–1993.

These emphases on integration, self-sufficiency, and continentalization will shape immigration policy long past the retirement of Jean Chrétien from Canadian public life. Despite the inclusive discourse underpinning integration, and the inclusive character of the "Canadian model," compared to many other countries, growing exclusion is also a factor to be reckoned with in understanding contemporary immigration policy. Whether short- or long-term, this is part of Jean Chrétien's immigration legacy.

NOTES

Associate Professor, Department of Political Science, University of Alberta. For helpful and constructive comments, I would like to thank two anonymous reviewers as well as the guest editors of this volume, Lois Harder and Steve Patten.

1 First elected to Parliament in 1963, Jean Chrétien was in private practice as a lawyer for a four-year period from 1986–1990, before returning to Parliament in 1990.

2 Statistics Canada, "Census of Population: Immigration, birthplace and birthplace of parents, citizenship, ethnic origin, visible minorities and Aboriginal peoples," *The Daily* (23 January 2003), 1–3, http://www.statcan.ca/Daily/English/030121/d030121a.htm.

3 See Joseph H. Carens, "Aliens and Citizens: The Case for Open Borders," *Review of Politics* 49:3 (1987): 251–73; and Teresa Hayter, *Open Borders: The Case Against Immigration Controls* (London: Pluto Press, 2000).

4 Yasmeen Abu-Laban, "Welcome/STAY OUT: The Contradiction of Canadian Integration and Immigration Policies at the Millennium," *Canadian Ethnic Studies* 30 (1998): 190–212, 191.

5 Ibid., 191–2.

6 Yasmeen Abu-Laban and Christina Gabriel, *Selling Diversity: Immigration, Multiculturalism, Employment Equity and Globalization* (Peterborough: Broadview Press, 2002), 47–54.

7 Alan Simmons, "Racism and Immigration Policy," in Vic Satzewich, ed., *Racism and Social Inequality in Canada: Concepts, Controversies and Strategies of Resistance* (Toronto: Thompson Educational Publishing, 1998), 87–114 .

8 Abu-Laban and Gabriel, *Selling Diversity*, 21.

9 Canada, Department of Canadian Heritage, *10th Annual Report on the Operation of the Canadian Multiculturalism Act, 1997–1998* (Ottawa: Public

Works and Government Services Canada, February 1999), iii,
http://dsp-psd.pwgsc.gc.ca/Collection/Ci95-1-1998E.pdf.

10 For example, in 1990, under the Conservative Government of Brian
Mulroney, the Federal Government developed an "Immigrant Integration
Strategy." See Canada, Citizenship and Immigration Canada, *The Issues:
Consultations on Settlement Renewal: Finding a New Direction for Newcomer
Integration* (Ottawa: Minister of Supply and Services Canada, 1995), 2.

11 Citizenship and Immigration Canada, *Discussion Document* (Immigration
Consultations, 1994), 7.

12 Peter Li, *Destination Canada: Immigration Debates and Issues* (Toronto:
Oxford University Press, 2002), 44.

13 See Citizenship and Immigration Canada, *Change and the Management of
Settlement Programs for Newcomers* (Ottawa, 1996).

14 Susan D. Phillips, "More than Stakeholders: Reforming State-Voluntary
Relations," *Journal of Canadian Studies* 35:4 (2000): 182–203, 183.

15 See Tim Owen, "NGO-Government Partnerships," *Journal of International
Migration & Integration* 1:1 (2000): 131–7.

16 Phillips, "More than Stakeholders," 14.

17 See R.A. Vineberg, "Federal Provincial Relations in Canadian Immigration,"
Canadian Public Administration 30:2 (1987): 299–317.

18 A useful overview of these arrangements can be found in Casey Vander-Ploeg,
"Canadian Intergovernmental Agreements on Immigration" (Background
Paper 2 at the Pioneers 2000 National Conference on Immigration, Canada
West Foundation, 2000).

19 Joseph Garcea, "Bicommunalism and the Bifurcation of the Immigration
System," *Canadian Ethnic Studies* 30:3 (1998): 149–72, 165.

20 The international Metropolis Project, of which Canada is also a part, is an
international forum that brings together policy-makers, academics, and
non-governmental organizations in the immigration field. By 2000, twenty
other governments were involved in this project, including the U.S., Argentina,
Austria, Denmark, France, and the United Kingdom; the Commission of the
European Union and UNESCO were also involved. See Abu-Laban and Gabriel,
Selling Diversity, 94–5.

21 SSHRC and CIC, "Revised Program Description," *Memorandum of Understanding Between SSHRC and CIC* (February 2002), Metropolis Canada
website, http://canada.metropolis.net/Renewal/mou_e.htm.

22 Ibid.

23 Norman Vale, "Brave new partnerships: learning how to get along with each
other in the metropolis," *University Affairs* (1998): 11.

24 This figure is subject to possible upward revision (Personal communication with Baha Abu-Laban, co-director of The Prairie Centre of Excellence for Research on Immigration and Integration, University of Alberta, 1 August 2003).

25 Canada, Metropolis Project Team, "Inclusion and Exclusion in Canada," *Metropolis* (March 2003): 1–2.

26 Abu-Laban, "Welcome/STAY OUT," 201–3.

27 Li, *Destination Canada*, 50–3.

28 Abu-Laban and Gabriel, *Selling Diversity*, 121–23.

29 Metropolis Team Project, 1–2.

30 Janice A. Newson, "Presidential Address: Positioning the Social Sciences in a Context of Economic Restructuring," *Society/Société* 19:3 (1995): 1-11, 7.

31 As quoted in House of Commons, *Debates* (5 December 1999) at 1430.

32 Liberal Party of Canada (LPC), *Creating Opportunity: The Liberal Plan for Canada* (Ottawa: LPC, 1993), 87.

33 Victoria M. Esses, John F. Dovidio, and Gordon Hodson, "Public Attitudes Toward Immigration in the United States and Canada in Response to the September 11, 2001 'Attack on America,'" *Analyses of Social Issues & Public Policy* 2:1 (2002): 69–85, 72.

34 See Della Kirkham, "The Reform Party of Canada: A Discourse on Race, Ethnicity and Equality," in Vic Satzewich, ed., *Racism and Social Inequality in Canada: Concepts, Controversies and Strategies of Resistance* (Toronto: Thompson Educational Publishing, 1998), 243–67.

35 See Janine Brodie and Christina Gabriel, "Canadian Immigration Policy and the Emergence of the Neo-Liberal State," *Journal of Contemporary International Issues* 1 (1998): 11–13.

36 Abu-Laban, "Welcome/STAY OUT," 205.

37 Sunera Thobani, "Closing the Nation's Ranks: Racism, Sexism and the Abuse of Power in Canadian Immigration Policy," in Susan C. Boyd, Dorothy E. Chunn, and Robert Menzies, eds., *[Ab]Using Power: The Canadian Experience* (Halifax: Fernwood Press, 2001), 49–70, 59.

38 Abu-Laban and Gabriel, *Selling Diversity*, 37–60.

39 Yasmeen Abu-Laban, "Keeping 'em Out: Gender, Race and Class Biases in Canadian Immigration Policy," in Veronica Strong-Boag, et al., eds., *Painting the Maple: Essays on Race Gender and the Construction of Canada* (Vancouver: University of British Columbia Press, 1998), 69–82, 79.

40 Carsten Quell, *Official Languages and Immigration: Obstacles and Opportunities for Immigrants and Communities* (Ottawa: Office of the Commissioner of Official Languages and Minister of Public Works and Government Services Canada, 2002), 11.

41 Abu-Laban, "Keeping 'em Out," 76.

42 Abu-Laban and Gabriel, *Selling Diversity*, 67–9.

43 Ibid., 68–9.

44 Li, *Destination Canada*, 168.

45 S.C. 2001, c. 27, http://www.canlii.org/ca/sta/i–2.5/whole.html.

46 Peter Rekai, "US and Canadian Immigration Policies: Marching Together To Different Tunes," *C.D. Howe Institute Commentary: The Border Papers* (2002): 4.

47 Quell, *Official Languages and Immigration*, 15.

48 Abu-Laban and Gabriel, *Selling Diversity*, 71.

49 Ibid., 47–54.

50 Abu-Laban, "Keeping 'em Out," 78.

51 Abu-Laban and Gabriel, *Selling Diversity*, 68.

52 Simon Tuck, "Ottawa reverses field, eases immigration rules," *Globe and Mail*, 19 September 2003, A1, A8.

53 "Address by Prime Minister Jean Chrétien on the Occasion of the Canada-U.S. Border Summit" (Detroit, 9 September 2002), http://www.pco.gc.ca/default.asp?Language=E&Page=pmarchive& Sub=Speeches&Doc=border20020909_e.htm.

54 Laura Macdonald, "Turbulence in Global Politics: Beyond Canada's Middle Power Image" in Michael Whittington and Glen Williams, eds., *Canadian Politics in the 21st Century* (Scarborough: Nelson Thomson Learning, 2000), 251–69.

55 Esses, Dovidio, and Hodson, "Public Attitudes Towards Immigration," 75.

56 Yasmeen Abu-Laban, "Liberalism, Multiculturalism and the Problem of Essentialism," *Citizenship Studies* 6 (2002): 459–82, 468–9.

57 Esses, Dovidio, and Hodson, "Public Attitudes Toward Immigration," 33.

58 Abu-Laban, "Liberalism," 449–70.

59 Sujit Choudhry, "Protecting Equality in the Face of Terror: Ethnic and Racial Profiling and s. 15 of the Charter," in Ronald J. Daniels, Patrick Macklem, and Kent Roach, eds., *The Security of Freedom: Essays on Canada's Anti-Terrorism Bill* (Toronto: University of Toronto Press, 2001), 367–82, 368.

60 Abu-Laban, "Liberalism," 470–1.

61 Ibid., 473–7.

62 Vic Satzewich and Lloyd Wong, "Immigration, Ethnicity, and Race: The Transformation of Transnationalism, Localism, and Identities," in Wallace Clement and Leah Vosko, eds., *Changing Canada: Political Economy as Transformation* (Montreal & Kingston: McGill-Queen's University Press, 2003), 363–90, 369.

63 Christina Gabriel and Laura Macdonald, "Beyond the Continentalist/Nationalist Divide: Politics in a North America 'Without Borders'," in Clement and Vosko, *Changing Canada*, 213–40, 214.

64 Abu-Laban and Gabriel, *Selling Diversity*, 62.

65 Yasmeen Abu-Laban and Christina Gabriel, "Security, Immigration and Post-September 11 Canada," in Janine Brodie and Linda Trimble, eds., *Reinventing Canada: Politics of the 21st Century* (Toronto: Prentice Hall, 2003), 290–306, 291.

66 Gabriel and Macdonald, "Continentalist/Nationalist Divide," 222–5.

67 "Address by Prime Minister Chrétien," 2.

68 Canada, Department of Foreign Affairs and International Trade (DFAIT), "Governor Ridge and Deputy Prime Minister Manley Issue One-Year Status Report on the Smart Border Action Plan" (Ottawa: DFAIT, 2003): 2–5.

69 Gabriel and Macdonald, "Continentalist/Nationalist Divide," 225.

70 Satzewich and Wong, "Immigration, Ethnicity, and Race," 369.

71 See Ricardo Grinspun and Maxwell A. Cameron, "The Political Economy of North American Free Trade: Diverse Perspectives, Converging Criticisms," in Ricardo Grinspun and Maxwell A. Cameron, eds., *The Political Economy of North American Free Trade* (Montreal & Kingston: McGill-Queen's University Press, 2003), 3–25.

72 As quoted in Louise Elliott, "Chrétien marks 40 years in politics," *Canadian Press*, 8 April 2003.

8

Looking Forward Without Looking Back

Jean Chrétien's Legacy for Aboriginal State-Relations

MICHAEL MURPHY

INTRODUCTION

Jean Chrétien's involvement with Aboriginal[1] policy began more than three decades ago as a young Minister of Indian Affairs with the Trudeau government. This is a long period, perhaps, by prime ministerial standards, but not so long in comparison to a set of questions whose roots are older than Confederation. Aboriginal policy issues in Canada carry the weight of history. After the balance of power shifted decisively in favour of the European newcomers in the early part of the nineteenth century, Aboriginal peoples were gradually subjected to a paternalistic and colonial relationship with the emergent Canadian state. Since that time, Aboriginal peoples have been struggling to secure the recognition of their basic right to self-determination; to establish their relationships with Canada on a more egalitarian footing; and to restore their communities, cultures, and economies that have been battered by more than a century and a half of displacement, dispossession, and disempowerment. It would be both unrealistic and unfair to expect a single Canadian administration to erase this disruptive policy legacy overnight. It is a process that will take many years, a great deal of resources, and an even greater quantity of political will. It is, however, both realistic and fair to expect a government to seize historic opportunities to establish new, more promising policy trajectories. Faced with opportune political conditions, and with countrywide public and political support for Aboriginal issues at a historic high in the post-Charlottetown period, Jean Chrétien's Liberal government was presented with precisely this sort of historic opening. The former Prime Minister seemed to be the right man for the job, bringing with him to office both a personal and a professional commitment to improving Canada's relations with its Aboriginal peoples. He made a promising start. The shift began with the government's recognition of the inherent right of self-government in 1995. It continued with the commencement of an innovative treaty process in Saskatchewan, and with decisions to follow through on major governance initiatives embarked upon by the preceding government, including the Nisga'a treaty, agreements with Yukon First Nations, and the establishment of Canada's newest territory of Nunavut. The government also signaled its intention to implement the recommendations of the Canadian Royal Commission on Aboriginal Peoples (RCAP), which, in its 1996 *Final Report*, had laid out a comprehensive blueprint for a renewed relationship between Aboriginal peoples and the Canadian state.[2]

For a time, it seemed that the federal government was preparing to make a decisive break with the past, and to move away from a relationship with Aboriginal peoples based on paternalism and government control to a relationship based on co-equality and mutual consent. But the Chrétien government did not live up to this promise and in the latter years of its administration helped reverse much of the initial momentum in favour of lasting change and renewal. What could have become one of Chrétien's most innovative and forward-looking policy legacies ended up looking more like a strategic retreat to the policy past. The follow-through on RCAP was disappointing. In particular, the commissioners' blueprint for transforming the overall relationship with Aboriginal peoples was not implemented, let alone subjected to serious and sustained public debate. This lack of follow-through on the RCAP *Final Report* was compounded by the unilateralist tenor of policy decisions such as the termination of stalled land claim and self-government negotiations, when a co-operative approach would have been preferred. Equally disappointing was the government's determination to forge ahead with the controversial *First Nations Governance Act* (FNGA)[3] over the objections of First Nations leadership and much informed opinion. It is no small irony that Jean Chrétien's history of involvement with Aboriginal policy ended as it began, with an attempt to force through an unpopular change to the *Indian Act*.[4] In the end, the Chrétien government seemed to tire of focusing on the renewal and renegotiation of historic relationships, and it chose instead to focus on more modest efforts to improve the quality of life of the Aboriginal population. These efforts were well-intentioned, and, if successful, would constitute a modest but still laudable policy legacy. However, as the RCAP and many others have warned, there is good reason to believe that the achievement, even of this more modest Liberal objective of improving the economic self-sufficiency, political capacity, and social well-being of Aboriginal peoples will itself be compromised by the failure to develop a relationship that more effectively involves Aboriginal peoples as the authors and initiators, rather than the passive objects, of government policy. In other words, Jean Chrétien may very well be remembered for the fact that his Aboriginal policies were unable to meet even their own more modest standards of success.

This chapter is divided into four parts. Part two briefly describes the history of Aboriginal-state relations in the period between the White Paper[5] of 1969 and Jean Chrétien's election as Prime Minister in 1993. Key policies and transition points and their relation to the new discourse of Aboriginal nationalism are the primary focus. Part three analyzes some of the more important policy initiatives on Aboriginal peoples during Chrétien's tenure as Prime Minister, paying particular attention to their implications for the underlying relationship between Aboriginal peoples and the state. This is followed by a brief conclusion.

SETTING THE STAGE: THE 1969 WHITE PAPER AND ABORIGINAL NATIONALISM

Chrétien's first major foray into Aboriginal policy was his introduction of the Trudeau government's 1969 White Paper on Indian policy. Inspired by ideas of liberal universalism and Trudeau's vision of a just society, the policy sought the assimilation of Aboriginal peoples. The federal government intended to end both its special responsibility for Aboriginal affairs and the differential legal and political status of Aboriginal peoples under the *Indian Act*, in order to more fully integrate them as equal individual members of Canadian society. Treaty rights were characterized as minimal and limited in nature. Inherent Aboriginal rights – those claimed by First Nations on the basis of their original occupation and governance of their traditional territories – received scant attention, but in a speech delivered in August of 1969, Trudeau rejected them outright.[6] The White Paper, which claimed a basis in "a year's intensive discussions with Indian people throughout Canada,"[7] was roundly condemned by Aboriginal people and political organizations across the country, both for its assimilationist tone and for its unilateralist approach to Aboriginal rights and interests. It was formally withdrawn in 1971.

One of the great ironies of this policy, designed to signal the end of "special" status for Aboriginal peoples and their assimilation as equal citizens of Canada, was that it engineered precisely the opposite consequence by inspiring the launch of a more vigorous period of Aboriginal nationalism and political mobilization.[8] From this point onwards, the idea of Aboriginal peoples being passively acted upon as policy clients, or simply being consulted as to the nature and extent of their rights, would be deemed insufficient. Representatives of Aboriginal peoples began to more aggressively assert their right to be the designers and initiators of public policy relating to their rights and interests, and to negotiate their mutual interests and jurisdictional limits on an equal basis with the federal government. Mainstream Aboriginal nationalism and its underlying claim to self-determination was never about separatism. Instead, it articulates the need for a relationship among Aboriginal and non-Aboriginal peoples and governments that acknowledges the need for co-operation and political negotiations to manage their complex interdependence. The essential point is that the negotiating partners are to be accorded equal political status, with neither having the power to dictate terms arbitrarily to the other or to interfere indiscriminately in the other's internal affairs. In other words, Aboriginal nationalism represents a rejection of intergovernmental relationships based on unilateralism and domination in favour of those based on mutual recognition and consent, and the co-equality of Aboriginal and non-Aboriginal governing authorities.[9]

At the moral centre of the Aboriginal nationalist challenge is the argument that, despite the sometimes very different empirical needs, characteristics, and circumstances of Aboriginal and non-Aboriginal peoples,[10] each is entitled to an identical normative right to self-determination. This is the basic democratic right of a people to determine their individual and collective futures and to negotiate relationships with other societies predicated on the principles of equality and mutual consent. Aboriginal peoples may accept that the disruption of their traditional economies, societies, and forms of governance precipitated by colonization will affect how they exercise their right to self-determination, but will not accept that these disruptions have altered their entitlement to the right *per se*. Whatever their empirical circumstances, the point is that the state should not assume an automatic right to act on behalf of indigenous peoples, treating them as the passive objects rather than the active authors of policies relating to their interests.[11]

By the late 1970s the Liberals had dramatically shifted their position on Aboriginal rights. Trudeau's comments at the 1983 First Ministers' Conference on Aboriginal Constitutional issues contrasted sharply with his convictions a dozen years previous: "Clearly, our Aboriginal peoples each occupied a special place in history. To my way of thinking this entitles them to special recognition in the constitution and to their own place in Canadian society, distinct from each other and distinct from other groups."[12] The shift was partly a result of the strength of the opposition to the White Paper, but also to breakthroughs in the judicial recognition of Aboriginal rights in cases brought by the Nisga'a and the James Bay Cree. The latter development led to Chrétien's announcement, again as Minister of Indian Affairs, of a new federal land claims policy and the subsequent negotiation of Canada's first modern land and self-government treaty in James Bay and Northern Québec. Aboriginal-state relations were shifting onto a new trajectory, whose crowning achievement was the entrenchment of Aboriginal rights in section 35 of the *Constitution Act, 1982.*[13] Though not directly involved in either the drafting of the constitutional accord, or in the debates related to its various revisions, Aboriginal representatives were conceded a presence in terms of consultation – a significant gain over past policy processes involving their interests. It is important to recognize that Aboriginal rights were not considered one of the priority issues on the constitutional agenda. In fact, as the minister responsible for the constitutional negotiations, Chrétien initially agreed to delete the Aboriginal provisions to appease provincial concerns over jurisdiction, lands, and natural resources.[14] A diluted version of the Aboriginal provisions made it back into the final draft, not as a result of federal lobbying, but as an indirect result of lobbying by women's groups that helped reopen the draft constitutional accord, and by pressures from Aboriginal peoples, the federal New Democrats, and the NDP government in Saskatchewan.[15]

In 1983, one year after the constitutional entrenchment of Aboriginal rights, a First Minister's Conference on Aboriginal Issues was held, in fulfilment of a mandate set out in section 37 of the *Constitution Act, 1982.* While impressive for its symbolic inclusion of Aboriginal representatives in this key intergovernmental forum, little progress was made on issues such as the definition of Aboriginal self-government or the more explicit clarification and entrenchment of Aboriginal and treaty rights. Three subsequent conferences, the last of which was held in 1987, also failed to produce much in the way of substantive results.[16] Indeed, throughout the 1980s it was left mostly to the courts to define and delimit Aboriginal constitutional rights. They obliged in a number of landmark decisions, although they generally steered clear of the specific issue of the right to self-government.[17] Meech Lake was the next significant policy touchstone. By this time, of course, Chrétien had resigned his seat in Parliament and the Tories, under Brian Mulroney, had taken power, but the ensuing events helped set the stage for Chrétien's return to politics as Prime Minister in 1993. Aboriginal organizations pressed hard to be partners in the Meech process and for the right to self-government to be placed on the agenda. Angered by their eventual exclusion, First Nations seized the opportunity to kill the resulting Accord with the help of Elijah Harper, the lone Aboriginal member of the Manitoba Legislature. Canada's federal political leadership took careful note of the Aboriginal involvement in the demise of the Meech Lake Accord, and in the period leading up to the negotiation of the Charlottetown Accord, Tory Minister for Constitutional Affairs Joe Clark invited leaders of the two territorial governments and the four national Aboriginal organizations to participate. The Aboriginal organizations were regarded as full partners in this process and participated at all levels of the negotiations. This was the first time in Canada's history that Aboriginal peoples were provided with a direct voice in negotiating changes to the Constitution that affected their rights, a development that spoke of a new chapter in the history of Aboriginal-state relations.

The Aboriginal sections of the Accord were the product of a number of significant compromises demanded by the other parties to the negotiations. Nevertheless, its provisions reflected many of the positions adopted by Aboriginal groups over the previous two decades. Most significantly, this included the entrenchment of Aboriginal governments as a third order of government in the Canadian federation, a quantum leap for Canadian politicians who, only a decade earlier, tended to equate the inherent right of self-government with secession and absolute Aboriginal sovereignty. The changes contemplated at Charlottetown were not to be, however, since the Accord was rejected by a majority of Canadians. Nevertheless, both the successful negotiation of the Accord and its eventual defeat yielded key lessons for the future of Aboriginal-state relations. First, it represented a paradigm shift in the willingness of Canadian governments to recognize and constitutionalize an inherent right of Aboriginal self-government. Second, the Accord's demise significantly reduced the enthusiasm among political leadership and the general population for a future round of constitutional negotiations, a trend well-suited to the cautious and pragmatic political instincts of Jean Chrétien – the Prime Minister-in-waiting.[18]

NEW PRIME MINISTER, NEW RELATIONSHIP?

With the decimation of the Tories in the 1993 election and the Chrétien Liberals commanding a large majority in the House of Commons, the stage was set to implement the changes outlined in the Red Book of Liberal policy promises so prominently featured in the election campaign.[19] Aboriginal policy was one of the areas slated for change. Building on the consensus reached at Charlottetown, the first significant change was the announcement of the government's intention to recognize the inherent right of Aboriginal self-government as a departure point for future negotiations with First Nations. True to Chrétien's cautious and pragmatic political instincts, the policy was designed to bypass issues of formal constitutional entrenchment and abstract debates about the nature or source of the inherent right to self-government. The Liberals simply declared that such a right already existed under section 35 of the *Constitution Act, 1982*, adding that the most important thing was to negotiate the specific terms of its implementation.[20] Granted, the outlines of this new policy were not entirely consonant with the relationship among equals sought by First Nations. The inherent right policy retained troubling elements of unilateralism. The government established, at the outset, the scope of policy jurisdictions that were open to negotiation and dictated a set of financial, administrative, and democratic benchmarks that Aboriginal governments were required to meet in order to exercise the right to self-government, subjects that, in a relationship among equals, legitimately belonged to the realm of negotiations. These reservations aside, the Aboriginal policy trajectory seemed set to continue on its new, and more promising, post-Charlottetown track.

Equally promising was the initiation of an innovative approach to treaty negotiations in Saskatchewan, a process described by the Office of the Treaty Commissioner as "[a] paradigm shift ... in relations between the Government of Canada and Treaty First Nations in Saskatchewan, one which could turn the page on the Indian Act approach of the past and build upon the treaty relationship."[21] The process was established to negotiate an integrated First Nations governance system comprising a single province-wide government, an intermediate layer of regional governments based on tribal or treaty areas, and a third layer of local government. In recognition of the increasingly urban character of many Aboriginal populations, the governance model is intended to provide for First Nations jurisdiction both on- and off-reserve. Initially mandated to cover First Nations jurisdiction in education and child and family services, subsequent negotiations are anticipated in relation to justice, lands and resources, hunting, fishing, trapping and gathering, health, and housing.[22] The process exceeds, in important ways, the standards established in the Liberals' own inherent right policy, in that much of the residual unilateralism appears to have been avoided. Of particular note, the process included an Exploratory Treaty Table whose purpose was to produce an agreement among government and First Nations on how the treaty negotiations themselves should be conducted. Representatives of Saskatchewan First Nations were included as full partners at all stages of these discussions, and Canada emphasized that it would not unilaterally alter its policies on treaties prior to the Exploratory Treaty Table discussions, in order to respect the partnership approach with Saskatchewan First Nations.[23]

The Saskatchewan Treaty Process also provided some indication that the Chrétien government intended a serious engagement with RCAP's *Final Report*, whose recommendations and principles were explicitly applied to help structure and guide the Exploratory Treaty Table discussions.[24] RCAP itself was created in response to political events. In the wake of the 1990 Oka crisis, one of the darker chapters in the recent history of Aboriginal-state relations in Canada, Aboriginal peoples across Canada had redoubled their calls for fundamental changes in their socioeconomic and political situations and in their relationships with other Canadian governments.[25] Public sentiment was also running high in favour of a just settlement of Aboriginal claims. In 1991, the Mulroney government responded to these pressures by creating the mandate for RCAP. The seven Commissioners were charged with reviewing the entire history of Aboriginal-state relations, in all of its aspects. The Commission heard testimony from over 2,000 people and organizations, consulted hundreds of experts, commissioned over 200 research studies, and reviewed the recommendations of all of the major previous inquiries and reports on the subject. In 1996, they submitted a blueprint for change: a five-volume *Final Report* containing more than 440 recommendations. The *Report* is a solution to what the Commissioners identify as a social crisis among Aboriginal people, characterized by their economic marginalization and the social disintegration of their communities. This crisis finds its source in the colonial nature of the relationship between Aboriginal and non-Aboriginal peoples over the last 150 years. The solution to the crisis is to change the nature of the relationship, anchoring it in principles of co-equality, mutual respect, and consent rather than subservience, paternalism, and dependency. The commissioners recommended that Aboriginal and non-Aboriginal peoples come together as equals to negotiate the specific terms of this new relationship, which would be codified in secure and mutually binding agreements sealed by the freely given consent of both parties.[26]

The Chrétien government was slow to respond to the *Final Report*, and there was much speculation that it would simply be shelved. This may not have been a difficult task. With the public and the government locked into the new paradigm of debt and deficit reduction, the Commission's call for stiff spending increases over a multi-year period could easily have supplied the noose from which to hang the entire report. Indeed, it is probably not an exaggeration to say that the one thing most Canadians know about the *Final Report* was that it cost more than $50 million to produce. Nevertheless, although fiscal concerns undoubtedly structured the nature and scale of their response, the Liberals did, indeed, respond to the *Final Report* early in their second mandate. This included a statement of reconciliation, presented by then–Minister of Indian Affairs Jane Stewart on behalf of Canada (a ceremony from which the Prime Minister was conspicuously absent). The statement conveyed the government's regrets and an apology for actions of past governments in their relations with Aboriginal peoples. The statement was accompanied by the announcement of a $350 million community healing fund to deal with the legacy of residential schools.[27] The broader outlines of the government's official response to RCAP are found in its 1998 report entitled *Gathering Strength*.[28] The report openly acknowledges that Canada's long history of colonial attitudes and practices played a substantial role in the erosion of Aboriginal societies, cultures, economies, and forms of political organization.[29] In addition to the specific initiative on residential schools, the government conveyed its intention to build a new relationship in partnership with Aboriginal peoples and to focus specific attention both on strengthening Aboriginal governance and fiscal relationships and on repairing the social and economic fabric of Aboriginal communities across the country.

The slimness of the government's thirty-six-page official response to a Royal Commission that issued over 440 detailed recommendations might have been excused on the grounds that, as the Commissioners themselves concluded, the process of repairing the relationship with Aboriginal peoples would not happen over night, but instead required a period spanning many years.[30] However, the Commission was also emphatic that this longer-term process would need to be jump-started in the short term by fundamental changes in the principles and institutions governing Aboriginal policy, and backed up by sufficient political will to see through these fundamental changes in the decades to come. Jean Chrétien did not rise to either of these challenges, and his government failed to move on recommendations considered by RCAP to be central to a renewed relationship with Aboriginal Canadians. In the immediate term, the Commissioners called for a new Royal Proclamation to supplement the *Royal Proclamation of 1763*,[31] as a symbolic turning point in the relationship. This proclamation would supplement the written part of the Canadian Constitution and would form part of the Constitution, as does the *Royal Proclamation of 1763*. The new Royal Proclamation would acknowledge wrongs and harms of the past and the need for redress; would recognize the inherent right of self-government of Aboriginal nations, and the jurisdiction of their governments as one of three orders of government in the federation; would commit governments and institutions to act in the name of the Crown to honour Aboriginal and treaty rights; and would commit the Crown to a reconfigured treaty process. The Royal Proclamation was to be accompanied by five major pieces of federal legislation, and a commitment to establish a forum to negotiate a Canada-wide Framework Agreement for implementing the Commission's recommendations.[32] Granted, the government may have disagreed with the RCAP approach, but if this was the case they should have provided a public account of their reasons for their disagreement and explained why their alternative process for renewing the relationship, if indeed such a process had been conceived, was preferable. No such public accounting was provided, leading one of Canada's most respected political scientists to conclude that the government's response to the RCAP vision of a renewed relationship was at best evasive and at worst "an embarrassment."[33]

In the latter years of his administration, Chrétien fell back on his instincts for smaller-scale and piecemeal reform, announcing modest programs targeting Aboriginal children and youth, education, health, and the needs of urban Aboriginals. In his response to the Speech from the Throne in January of 2001, the Prime Minister stated: "Quite frankly I am concerned that in the case of Aboriginal peoples, *we may be spending too much time, too much energy, and too much money on the past*, and not nearly enough on what is necessary to ensure a bright future for the children of today and tomorrow.... There are never enough resources to do everything. *Our approach will be to focus on the future*. And most important, on the needs of children."[34] Such programs are not to be scoffed at, and indeed they reflect many of the concerns and priorities expressed within Aboriginal communities and by the leadership of Aboriginal political organizations.[35] However, there is a real danger in viewing the redress of historic grievances, on the one hand, and concrete improvements in the lives of Aboriginal people, on the other, as alternative rather than as complementary ends. In fact, the research conducted by RCAP suggests that efforts to improve the quality of life enjoyed by Aboriginal people are crucially dependent on efforts to come to terms with the past and to place the relationship between Canada and Aboriginal peoples on a more positive and mutually acceptable footing. "A renewed relationship is the necessary context and an essential contributor to change in other spheres."[36]

The Liberals, however, soon made good on their intention to look forward without looking back. In October of 2002, Minister of Indian Affairs Robert Nault threatened to shut down as many as thirty stalled land claim and self-government negotiating tables, stating that the government was "not in the business of building an industry for lawyers and consultants" with a vested interest in perpetuating inconclusive negotiations.[37] The first tables were shut down in November of the same year. This policy is disturbing for a couple of reasons. First, leaving aside the issue of the government's own army of lawyers and consultants, the Minister asked us to believe that the self-interested and intransigent "Aboriginal industry," a term with clear resonance among right-wing critics of Aboriginal policy,[38] is the sole explanation for stalled negotiations, when evidence suggests it might equally have to do with factors such as government domination of the negotiations process, their insistence on the policy of extinguishment of Aboriginal rights, or their reluctance to cede final decision-making authority to Aboriginal governments in key policy jurisdictions.[39] Second, and more fundamentally, whatever the obstructing factors might be, Chrétien and his minister once again demonstrated a preference for unilateral and imposed solutions rather than co-operative and consensual approaches to challenging issues in Aboriginal policy.

Nowhere was this approach more apparent than in the government's efforts to force through the FNGA. The historical parallels of this policy initiative with the process surrounding the White Paper of 1969 were not lost on many. Once again Jean Chrétien found himself the champion of a revision of the *Indian Act* that provoked fierce opposition from First Nations. This time, however, the reform was being sold, not as assimilation, but as an interim measure leading up to the negotiation and implementation of the inherent right of self-government. The purpose of the Act was to increase the accountability, accessibility, and transparency of governance on reserves, which, in turn, was intended to facilitate gains in governing capacity and socio-economic performance.[40] Though it is difficult to find critics who disagree that the *Indian Act* is a restrictive and arcane piece of colonial legislation, there were many who disagreed strenuously with the process and substance of the FNGA.[41] In terms of process, unlike the White Paper, the government seems to have made a genuine effort to consult widely with people at the grassroots level. This process met with some success, but it was anything but problem-free. In the first place, the time allotted for consultations (two months) was criticized for being too brief for a substantive digestion and deliberation of the issues.[42] Doubts were expressed as to whether community input would make it into the legislation, particularly where it conflicted with government priorities. The absence of a planned second round of direct consultations on the substance of the draft bill aggravated this concern. Many communities registered extremely low turnout rates while others felt pressured to participate in a process that was the only game in town. For example, the Congress of Aboriginal Peoples (CAP), which fundamentally disagreed with the government's approach to *Indian Act* reform, felt they could not afford to stay outside of a process the government was determined to see through regardless of Aboriginal opinion. CAP's preference, like that of the AFN, is to discuss alternatives to the *Indian Act* and the need to reform federal *self-government* policy.[43]

A more fundamental problem with the FNGA process was the fact that it was based on *consultations*, not *negotiations*. As such, it reinforced rather than reversed the paternalistic nature of the relationship with Aboriginal peoples, who again were treated like special interest groups rather than equal partners in a process of mutual recognition and respect. What should have been clear to governments in the wake of the first failed effort to overhaul the *Indian Act* in 1969 was that Aboriginal peoples are not content to let government define and dominate the policy-making agenda while they are relegated to commenting on what emerges from the other end. As articulated by the AFN, "any initiative dealing with First Nations governance should be designed, driven and ratified by First Nations."[44] This message, repeated emphatically throughout the RCAP report, was not heeded by the Chrétien Liberals. The Liberals responded to criticisms of the FNGA by arguing that the negotiation of self-government agreements to replace the *Indian Act* was going too slowly; hence, reforms to the *Act* were necessary in the interim, particularly in order to respond to a number of challenges to the *Act* before the Supreme Court of Canada.[45] These are legitimate concerns, but they do not explain why the government chose to control the agenda of the interim process itself and to consult with Aboriginal peoples as mere stakeholders rather than as equal partners in the policy process, particularly when the Court itself so frequently endorses a strategy of negotiating the nature and bounds of Aboriginal rights. In fact, the government seemed determined to bypass, and thereby aggravate, First Nations' leadership as part of its process of reform, a departure from their own earlier co-operative approach with the AFN in developing the First Nations Fiscal Institutions, the First Nations Governance Institute, and the Joint Initiative for Policy Development, Lands and Trust Services (LTS).[46] Rather than building on these earlier achievements, the Chrétien government sounded a retreat, a decision with profound implications for the Prime Minister's legacy for Aboriginal-state relations.

Major reservations must also be entered regarding the substance of the FNGA, specifically its intention to increase the legitimacy of Aboriginal governments and their capacity to improve the social and economic quality of life in their communities. This was the message delivered by the architects of the Harvard Indian Project (HIP) in their review of the FNGA. HIP has conducted extensive empirical research on the determinants of economic success among U.S. Indian Reserves, and more recently they have been analyzing Aboriginal governance and economic development on the Canadian side of the border. Their research shows that the three best predictors of reservation economic success are practical sovereignty, capable governing institutions, and cultural match. Practical sovereignty means effective control of reservation institutions, resources, development strategies, etc. "In short, genuine decision-making power over matters of substance has moved into indigenous hands."[47] Capable governing institutions entails the establishment of institutions that facilitate the effective, responsible, and accountable exercise of the jurisdictional authority of Indian nations and usually entails the establishment of an effective and politically independent court system, as well as the separation of politics and business management practices. Cultural match means a "fit" between the formal governing institutions and the community's conception of how authority should be organized and exercised. This "fit" is crucial to establishing the legitimacy of those governing institutions.[48]

The architects of the HIP note that the Canadian government has expressed serious interest in the results of the Harvard Project, but also note that their use of the findings has focused almost exclusively on the dimension of good governance. Neither the dimensions of practical sovereignty nor the dimension of cultural match received much attention in the FNGA. This was a mistake in HIP's estimation, since these different dimensions of governance are crucially interdependent. Their research shows that good governance without sovereign powers is ineffective. Alternatively, HIP concludes that giving tribes primary decision-making powers has the effect of making them responsible, and accountable, for the decisions they make. This, in turn, leads to a dramatically improved quality of decision-making and socio-economic outcomes. Similarly, HIP emphasizes that if there is not a good cultural match between governing institutions and the expectations of the community, there are likely to be problems with the legitimacy of those institutions, particularly if they are to be imposed, as in the case of the FNGA.[49] HIP recommended, instead, that the Canadian government transfer significant constitutional author-ity and decision-making power to First Nations, and invest in the gover-nance capacity-building initiatives designed and chosen by the communities themselves. This conclusion is directly in line with the broader findings of the RCAP report, with the preferences expressed by Canada's Aboriginal leadership, and with the approach that was prom-ised, but ultimately never delivered, by Prime Minister Chrétien.

CONCLUSION

Why did the early promise of the Chrétien government recede as his career as Prime Minster came to a close? Possible explanations for the lack of follow-through include the former Prime Minister's well-known preference for cautious, pragmatic, and piecemeal solutions to political problems, and his corresponding lack of inclination towards bold and visionary public policy. The Liberals may also have been reacting to an intensified right-wing critique of Aboriginal policy from Reform/Alliance on the political front (witness the Reform Party's blistering par-liamentary attack on the Nisga'a Treaty), and from the academic com-munity.[50] Like most previous governments, the Chrétien Liberals were keenly aware that Canadian publics, though generally supportive of Aboriginal peoples and cultures, do not have much sustained interest in, or commitment to, these issues and tend to be even less interested in the dedication of public funds to policies and programs for Aboriginal peo-ples. In his long and successful political career, Jean Chrétien demon-strated a tremendous aptitude for judging what would and would not expend his political capital with the majority of Canadians.[51] In this respect, Aboriginal issues could never compete with marquee policy items such as debt and deficit reduction, the post-September 11 security agenda, and health care, issues with a much more intense and lasting purchase on the minds of the Canadian public. In line with previous Canadian governments, Aboriginal policy in the Chrétien era appears to have been driven not so much by a thoughtful longer-term vision of Aboriginal-state relations as by political events, opportunities and pressures of a more transitory nature. Hence, it is likely that the Chrétien government calculated that it had sufficient political capital early in its administration to pursue a bolder set of Aboriginal policy initiatives, but once this political capital began to diminish, so did the government's will to see these initiatives through to a bold new legacy in Aboriginal-state relations.

Whatever the motivations at work, the failure of the Chrétien Liberals to move decisively to purge the remaining vestiges of colonialism from federal Aboriginal policy is a factor that continues to fuel the dysfunctional relationship between Canada and its Aboriginal peoples. Chrétien was clearly reluctant to accept First Nations' claims to equal status and stature in the federation. He was unwilling to break with the assumption, held by Canadian prime ministers since Confederation, that Aboriginal governments are subordinate political entities. As such, they are not entitled to a share in Canadian sovereignty, but instead enjoy powers that are devolved or delegated from the Canadian state, whose sovereignty must remain comprehensive and undivided.[52] As one commentator sums up the situation, "The federal government won't give up the top rung on the ladder and First Nations insist on a nation-to-nation arrangement."[53] This failure, both of political imagination and political will, has blackened what might have been a brilliant legacy in a policy area in which the former Prime Minister took both a personal and a professional interest. At risk is both the ethical imperative of forging a more just and democratic relationship and also the more concrete improvements to the economies, societies, and lives of Aboriginal peoples that Chrétien increasingly prioritized in the latter years of his mandate.

The end of the Chrétien era provided an interesting contrast with Québec's successes in rebuilding relations through new agreements with the Cree in James Bay and the Inuit of Nunavik. Both agreements, which confer substantial authority for economic and community development upon the Aboriginal parties, are explicitly referred to as "nation-to-nation" partnerships. Though substantial disagreements remain, and much progress remains to be made, the perception amongst many First Nations leaders is that there has been genuine change in the right direction. Pita Aatami, president of Makivik Corporation, which represents Inuit of Nunavik, describes this sentiment following the signing of a wide-ranging agreement on economic development with the province: "In the past, when we signed agreements, we were always dictated to. Now we're dictating together. This is a new beginning, a new era. We're starting to work as partners."[54] It is difficult to assess the closing years of Jean Chrétien's administration with anything remotely approaching the same kind of optimism. Instead, a political career that began with one widely reviled initiative on *Indian Act* reform, in the end, could not avoid foundering on another.

NOTES

Canada Research Chair in Comparative Indigenous State Relations, Political Science Program, University of Northern British Columbia. The author thanks Siobhan Harty and the two anonymous referees for their helpful comments on an earlier draft of this chapter.

1 I will focus most of my discussion on First Nations, although the concerns of other Aboriginal peoples, including the Inuit, off-reserve, and urban populations are also raised at various points in the chapter.

2 Canada, Royal Commission on Aboriginal Peoples (RCAP), *Report of the Royal Commission on Aboriginal Peoples* (Ottawa: Canada Communication Group, 1996), http://www.ainc-inac.gc.ca/ch/rcap/sg/cg_e.html.

3 Bill C–7, *An Act respecting leadership selection, administration and accountability of Indian Bands, and to make related amendments to other Acts*, 2d Sess., 37th Parl., 2002.

4 R.S.C. 1985, c. I–5. The FNGA was scrapped by the incoming Paul Martin government and, as of the January 2006 election, had not been replaced by any comparable initiative to reform the Indian Act.

5 Canada, *Statement of the Government of Canada on Indian Policy* (Ottawa: Queen's Printer, 1969) ["White Paper"].

6 For Trudeau's comments see Peter A. Cumming and Neil H. Mickenberg, *Native Rights in Canada*, 2d ed. (Toronto: The Indian-Eskimo Association of Canada, 1972), 331–2.

7 "White Paper," 5.

8 For background on this period see Sally Weaver, *Making Canadian Indian Policy* (Toronto: University of Toronto Press, 1981).

9 James Youngblood Henderson, "Empowering Treaty Federalism," *Saskatchewan Law Review* 58 (1994): 241–330; Gerald Alfred, *Heeding the Voices of Our Ancestors: Kahnawake Mohawk Politics and the Rise of Native National-*

ism (Oxford: Oxford University Press, 1995); James Tully, "The Struggles of Indigenous Peoples For and Of Freedom," in Paul Patton, Duncan Ivison, and Douglas Saunders, eds., *Political Theory and Indigenous Rights*, 36–59 (Cambridge: Cambridge University Press, 2000); and John Borrows, *Recovering Canada: The Resurgence of Indigenous Law* (Toronto: University of Toronto Press, 2002).

10 These differences relate to factors such as the size, capabilities and independence of indigenous governments. For a discussion of these and related issues see Michael Murphy, "Understanding Indigenous Nationalism," in Michel Seymour, ed., *The Fate of the Nation-State* (Montreal & Kingston: McGill-Queen's University Press, 2004), 271–94.

11 Ibid.

12 Menno Boldt, *Surviving as Indians: The Challenge of Self-Government* (Toronto: University of Toronto Press, 1993), 24.

13 Schedule B to the *Canada Act 1982* (U.K.), 1982, c. 11.

14 Roy Romanow, "Aboriginal Rights in the Constitutional Process," in Menno Boldt and J. Anthony Long, eds., *The Quest for Justice: Aboriginal Peoples and Aboriginal Rights* (Toronto: University of Toronto Press, 1985), 73–82, 78; A.J. Hall, "Making sense of the new Indian Act," *Winnipeg Free Press*, 15 August 2002.

15 Romanow, "Aboriginal Rights," 78–80; and Roger Gibbins, "Canadian Indians and the Constitution: A Difficult Passage Toward an Uncertain Destination," in J. Rick Ponting, ed., *Arduous Journey: Canadian Indians and Decolonization* (Toronto: McClelland & Stewart, 1991), 302–16, 307–8.

16 Gibbins, "Canadian Indians," 311–13. Compare Olive P. Dickason, *Canada's First Nations: A History of Founding Peoples from Earliest Times*, 2d ed. (Toronto: Oxford University Press, 1997), 386.

17 Michael Asch, "From *Calder* to *Van der Peet*: Aboriginal Rights and Canadian Law, 1973–96," in Paul Havemann, ed., *Indigenous Peoples Rights in Australia, Canada, and New Zealand* (Auckland: Oxford University Press, 1999), 428–46; and Michael Murphy, "Culture and the Courts: A New Direction in Canadian Jurisprudence on Aboriginal Rights?" *Canadian Journal of Political Science* 34 (2001): 109–29.

18 It also seemed more in line with the preferences of sectors of the Aboriginal grassroots population who, in definitively rejecting the Accord, appeared unwilling to accept a megaconstitutional framework for Aboriginal self-government negotiated on their behalf by national Aboriginal organizations. Many Inuit, in contrast, voted in favour of the Accord. Caution is essential in interpreting levels of Aboriginal support for the Accord, particularly given the fact that turnout among Aboriginal voters measured less than 8 percent. See

Mary Ellen Turpel, "The Charlottetown Discord and Aboriginal Peoples' Struggle for Fundamental Political Change," in Kenneth McRoberts and Patrick J. Monahan, eds., *The Charlottetown Accord, the Referendum, and the Future of Canada*, 117–51 (Toronto: University of Toronto Press, 1993).

19 Liberal Party of Canada (LPC), *Creating Opportunity: The Liberal Plan for Canada* (Ottawa: LPC, 1993).

20 Canada, Department of Indian and Northern Affairs (DIAND), *Aboriginal Self-Government: The Government of Canada's Approach to Implementation of the Inherent Right and the Negotiation of Aboriginal Self-Government* (Ottawa: DIAND, 1995), http://www.ainc-inac.gc.ca/pr/pub/sg/plcy_e.html.

21 Saskatchewan, Office of the Treaty Commissioner (OTC), *Statement of Treaty Issues: Treaties As a Bridge to the Future* (Saskatoon: OTC, October 1998), http://www.otc.ca/PDFs/OTC_STI.pdf.

22 A richer description and analysis of this initiative appears in David Hawkes, "Re-building the Relationship: The Made in Saskatchewan Approach to First Nations Governance" (Paper prepared for Conference on Reconfiguring Aboriginal-State Relations in Canada, Kingston, 1–2 November 2002).

23 OTC, *Statement of Treaty Issues*.

24 Ibid. at 28, 43, 75–8.

25 The crisis involved an armed stand-off between the Mohawks of Kahnesetake and the Canadian Army in the Summer of 1990 that lasted seventy-eight days. The cost of the standoff was staggering, both in human and economic terms. It left one Québec police officer dead, significantly raised tensions between the Aboriginal and non-Aboriginal communities in the vicinity of Oka, blackened Canada's international reputation as a defender of human rights, and cost the Canadian and Québec governments an estimated $150 million. See Geoffrey York and Loreen Pindera, *People of the Pines: The Warriors and the Legacy of Oka* (Toronto: Little, Brown, 1991).

26 RCAP, *Report of the Royal Commission on Aboriginal Peoples*, Vols. 1–2.

27 Hon. Jane Stewart, "Speech on the occasion of the unveiling of *Gathering Strength – Canada's Aboriginal Action Plan*" (Ottawa, 7 January 1998).

28 Canada, Department of Indian Affairs and Northern Affairs, *Gathering Strength – Canada's Aboriginal Action Plan: A Progress Report* (Ottawa: Minister of Public Works and Government Services, 1998), http://www.ainc-inac.gc.ca/gs/pdf/rprt98_e.pdf.

29 Ibid., 4.

30 RCAP, *Report of the Royal Commission on Aboriginal Peoples*, Vol. 5.

31 R.S.C. 1985, App. II, No. 1.

32 RCAP, *Report of the Royal Commission on Aboriginal Peoples*, Vol. 2, Part 1.

33 Alan C. Cairns, *Citizens Plus: Aboriginal Peoples and the Canadian State* (Vancouver: University of British Columbia Press, 2000), 121–2.

34 See e.g., Jean Chrétien, "Address by Prime Minister Jean Chrétien in Reply to the Speech from the Throne," http://www.pco-bcp.gc.ca/ default.asp?Page= InformationResources&Sub=sftddt&Language=E&doc= sftddt2001_reply_e.htm.

35 See e.g., "INAC On-Reserve Survey: Final Report" (Ottawa: EKOS Research Associates, 5 October 2001).

36 Marlene Brant Castellano, "Renewing the Relationship: A Perspective on the Impact of the Royal Commission on Aboriginal Peoples," in John Hylton, ed., *Aboriginal Self-Government in Canada: Current Trends and Issues*, 2d ed. (Saskatoon: Purich, 1999), 92–111, 97.

37 Kim Lunman, "Ottawa says it may quit stalled land claims," *Globe and Mail*, 7 October 2002, A1.

38 Tom Flanagan, *First Nations? Second Thoughts* (Montreal & Kingston: McGill-Queen's University Press, 2000).

39 R.F. McDonnel and R.C. Depew, "Aboriginal Self-Government and Self-Determination in Canada: A Critical Commentary," in Hylton, *Aboriginal Self-Government in Canada*, 352–76, 359; Frances Abele, Katherine A. Graham, and Allan M. Maslove, "Negotiating Canada: Changes in Aboriginal Policy over the Last Thirty Years," in Leslie Pal, ed., *How Ottawa Spends 1999–2000: Shape Shifting: Canadian Governance Toward the 21st Century* (Toronto: Oxford University Press, 1999), 251–92, 264; and RCAP, *Treaty-Making in the Spirit of Coexistence: An Alternative to Extinguishment* (Ottawa: Canada Communication Group, 1995).

40 Canada, Department of Indian and Northern Affairs, "Speaking Notes for the Honourable Robert D. Nault, P.C., M.P. Minister of Indian and Northern Affairs Canada To Launch Consultations on First Nations Governance" (Siksika Nation, AB, 30 April 2001), http://www.ainc-inac.gc.ca/nr/spch/2001/cfng_e.html.

41 Kathy L. Brock, "First Nations, Citizenship and Democracy" (Paper prepared for the Conference in Honour of Alan Cairns, Vancouver, 11–14 October 2001); Kiera Ladner and Michael Orsini, "De l'"infériorité négociée' à l'"inutilité de négocier': la *Loi sur la gouvernance des Premières Nations* et le maintien de la politique coloniale," *Politique et Sociétés* 23:1 (2004), 59–87.

42 Congress of Aboriginal Peoples, *Final Report, Phase 1 Consultations. Federal First Nations Governance Initiative* (Ottawa: Congress of Aboriginal Peoples, 2002), 7; Speech by Chief Adrian Stimson of the Siksika First Nation, at the Announcement of the First Nations Governance Initiative (Siksika Nation High School, 30 April 2001) ["Speech by Adrian Stimson"]; and Assembly of

First Nations (AFN) "The AFN's Position on the Federal Legislative Initiative on First Nations Governance" (2001).

43 Congress of Aboriginal Peoples, *Final Report*, 4–6.

44 AFN, "The AFN's Position."

45 "Speech by Chief Adrian Stimson." The case of *Corbiere v. Canada (Minister of Indian and Northern Affairs)*, [1999] 2 S.C.R. 203, http://www.canlii.org/ca/cas/scc/1999/1999scc29.html, is particularly important in this regard. For discussion see B. Morse, et al., "*Corbiere* and the Supreme Court's Vision of Governance" (Paper prepared for the Department of Indian Affairs and Northern Development) (Ottawa: B. Morse and Associates, 2001); and B. Morse et al., "Beyond *Corbiere*. Statutory Renewal: Prerequisites and Agendas" (Ottawa: B. Morse and Associates, 2001).

46 AFN, "AFN's Key Messages on the Proposed Legislative Initiative on First Nations Governance."

47 Stephen Cornell, Miriam Jorgensen, and Joseph P. Kalt, *The First Nations Governance Act: Implications of Research Findings from the United States and Canada* (Report to the Office of the British Columbia Regional Vice-Chief Assembly of First Nations) (Native Nations Institute, University of Arizona, July 2002), 4, http://www.udallcenter.arizona.edu/nativenations/pubs/AFN02Report.pdf.

48 Ibid., 4–7.

49 Ibid., 11–12, 15.

50 Peter H. Russell, "Indigenous Self-Determination: Is Canada As Good As it Gets?" (Keynote address at the Conference on Rethinking Indigenous Self-Determination, University of Queensland, Brisbane, Australia, 25–8 September 2001). Examples of this sort of critique include Melvin H. Smith, *Our Home or Native Land? What Governments' Aboriginal Policy is Doing to Canada* (Victoria: Crown Western, 1995); and Flanagan, *First Nations? Second Thoughts*.

51 John Hylton, "Future Prospects for Aboriginal Self-Government in Canada," in Hylton, *Aboriginal Self-Government in Canada*, 445; and Rick Mofina, "3% back native funding as top priority: poll," *The Ottawa Citizen*, 5 January 2003, A4.

52 James Tully, "A Just Relationship Between Aboriginal and Non-Aboriginal Peoples of Canada," in Curtis Cook and Juan D. Lindau, eds., *Aboriginal Rights and Self-Government: The Canadian and Mexican Experience in North American Perspective* (Montreal & Kingston: McGill-Queen's University Press, 2000), 39–71, 42; and Peter H. Russell, "Aboriginal Nationalism: Prospects for Decolonization," *Pacifica Review* 8 (1996): 57–67, 66–7.

53 Paul Barnsley, "Two New Initiatives for Reforming Aboriginal Governance in Canada," *Federations* 1:5 (2001): 11–12.
54 Alexandra Panetta, "Quebec treaty to pump millions into Inuit Region," *Times-Colonist*, 10 April 2002, A6. Jean Charest's incoming Liberal government provided additional cause for optimism with the announcement, on 17 June 2003, of the establishment of a joint council of elected officials from the Québec government and the Assembly of First Nations of Québec. The council, composed of an equal number of Aboriginal and non-Aboriginal elected officials, is designed to promote an exchange of ideas on various subjects, including territory and resources, taxation and economic development, and services for Aboriginal people off reserve. According to Charest, "The signing of the mutual political commitment and the ensuing exchanges represent a major step forward in the political relations between the Government of Québec and the First Nations, and could eventually lead to a permanent space for political exchanges." Information on this new development can be found in a press release on the website of the Secrétariat aux affaires autochtones du Québec, http:www.autochtones.gouv.qc.ca/centre_de_presse/saa_archives_communiques.htm.

9

This whole article is good! (handwritten)

The Chrétien Liberal Legacy and Women

Changing Policy Priorities with Little Cause for Celebration

ALEXANDRA DOBROWOLSKY

INTRODUCTION

For feminist academics and activists, the Chrétien Liberal years can hardly be fêted. The Chrétien Liberals' policy legacy, a smorgasbord spanning ten years, represents more of a famine than a feast when it comes to women's diverse policy needs. Indeed, most collections and leading studies on women and Canadian public policy tell the tale of how the federal government's governing practices in this period consisted of cutbacks and off-loading (onto the market, lower levels of government, or the family), with little regard for the gendered dimensions of such policy preferences. Making matters worse, leading women's organizations were starved of funding over the Chrétien years, and much of their influence wasted away.

good (handwritten)

good (handwritten)

Yet the decisions made and the ideas and actors involved in this period are not as uniform as they first appear. Recent work looks more carefully at the 1990s and early 2000s and notice is made of changing policy orientations, as with, for example, Sylvia Bashevkin's book, *Welfare Hot Buttons*, which details the growth and impact of new, post-conservative rhetoric on social policy (in Canada, as well as Britain and the U.S.);[1] articles on citizenship regimes in transition by Jane Jenson *et al.*;[2] the analyses of Rianne Mahon and Susan Phillips of the repercussions of policies ostensibly directed towards children;[3] and Janine Brodie's identification of Canada's emergent "social cohesion agenda."[4] This chapter draws on these more nuanced accounts. It differentiates between two separate phases in the Chrétien years and considers the consequences that each has had on women. The intent is to provide further food for thought on the Chrétien Liberals' policy legacy *vis-à-vis* women.

The first period is clearly marked by the nature and effects of a *neo-liberal state's* discourses and practices. Phase one peaks in the mid–1990s, but transforms by the tail-end of the decade. By the late 1990s and into the 2000s, the neo-liberal state begins to morph into what has been dubbed the *social investment state*.[5] The two stages cannot be separated neatly by a definitive turning point nor marked by exact time frames. Neither are they mutually exclusive, as strains of social investment can be detected in phase one, and most definitely, elements of the neo-liberal state linger in phase two. It is also important to acknowledge, at the outset, that states and state forms are not determinative. There are complex relationships involved, affecting both the state and civil society, that will be alluded to in this chapter.[6] These provisos aside, the point made here is that the emphases, actors, and networks involved do modify over the two periods.

To be perfectly clear, things did not necessarily get better[7] with the emergence of the social investment state. However, what the following account does underscore is that "the neo-liberal order is neither stable nor impermeable."[8] It is important to re-evaluate the Chrétien years and to recognize that there has been a change in the state form; in the ideas, institutions, and choices of policy instruments at play; as well as in the identities involved, because this transforming terrain generates distinctive opportunities and constraints for collective actors. Thus, while women's activism attempted to effect change in both periods, because of the evolving context, the nature of state/civil society interactionism differed. This makes a close and careful study of shifting discursive frameworks and political priorities in the Chrétien Liberal period of crucial importance.

This chapter will elaborate on these contentions by first comparing and contrasting leading ideas and discourses in phase one (the *neo-liberal state*) and phase two (the *social investment state*). A similar process will be followed in relation to illustrative institutions and policy instruments. Then, changing state/civil society interactionism through an examination of identity politics will be reflected upon. The chapter concludes with an evaluation of evolving opportunities and constraints for women. Throughout, representative Chrétien Liberal policies and priorities will support key contentions.

IDEAS AND DISCOURSES

To begin, a review of the main precepts of neo-liberalism (albeit a cursory one given that its core suppositions have been thoroughly detailed elsewhere[9]) is beneficial. Neo-liberalism, in a nutshell, calls for state streamlining. Cutbacks, contracting out, downsizing, deficit/debt reduction, devolution, and deregulation are dominant discourses and practices.[10] A premium is placed on the role played by the market. The neo-liberal state both elevates the private sphere and exalts in individual solutions to societal problems. Therefore, it not only contracts public space, but eclipses the work of collective actors. In Canada, these notions gained prominence in the 1980s with Brian Mulroney's Progressive Conservative government. Feminist economists, political scientists, and legal scholars have detailed the devastating impact that this neo-liberal agenda and concomitant state restructuring has had on women, for women disproportionately rely upon the state as employees and service recipients of the state, and women thus tend to shoulder the burden of cost-cutting and privatization.[11] As Janine Brodie wrote in the early 1990s, "The rolling back of the welfare state often simply means that vital social services are shifted from the paid to the unpaid work of women ... [and] that the gendered impacts of restructuring are highly uneven exacting the heaviest costs from women of colour and working-class women."[12]

Initially, the Chrétien Liberals held out the promise of an alternative approach. Even though the Liberal Party Red Book, produced for the 1993 election, pledged fiscal responsibility in fine neo-liberal fashion, it also focused on job creation and innovation. Activists and civil servants alike were hopeful that a Liberal win would herald a new era of state regeneration and social policy. The expectation was that the Liberals would revitalize a state demoralized by threats of cutbacks to personnel and programs and by a highly politicized Mulroney administration.[13] In terms of policy, most women took heart at Red Book promises of increased child care spending ($720 million on child care over three years and 50,000 new regulated spaces per year for three years[14]), an area the Liberals had criticized the Tories for ignoring. Many activists also applauded new commitments, such as strengthening employment equity provisions.

After the Liberals' decisive election win, competing concerns became more apparent. Tensions were evident in the government's first year in office with, for example, the Social Security Review (SSR). On one hand, the SSR responded to social welfare mobilization, as it was geared towards unemployment and social assistance, and it even addressed child poverty. On the other hand, it reflected a neo-liberal rationale that maintained that the best way to help those on welfare was to get them off and keep them off welfare. Soon, calls by feminist, leftist, nationalist, anti-racist, and anti-poverty groups to strengthen social programs and uphold universality could not be heard above the din of neo-liberal saving and cost-cutting pronouncements.[15] Any aspirations for bold, new programs were summarily dashed. As Bashevkin recounts, once in office, the Chrétien Liberals wasted little time in asserting that they were "taking seriously the need to control spending, reduce the deficit, and encourage policy flexibility in a diverse federation."[16] Welfare liberal sensibilities were submerged as the right-wing, business agenda took hold, and the Chrétien Liberals would, for instance, "claim that their actions responded to public concerns about overly generous social assistance programs."[17]

As a result, the Liberals' campaign promises regarding child care spending were unfulfilled,[18] and later responses to this need were "both limited and contingent."[19] While there were efforts to expand upon the *Employment Equity Act,*[20] reflecting pressures exerted by groups like the National Action Committee on the Status of Women (NAC), the Women's Legal Education and Action Fund (LEAF), the National Capital Alliance on Race Relations, the Canadian Ethnocultural Council (CEC), and the Canadian Alliance for Visible Minorities, in the end, the Chrétien Liberals' Bill C–64 has been described as "minimalist."[21] Some have suggested that the 1995 *Employment Equity Act* was ultimately innocuous enough to leave even the Conservative government in Ontario, renowned for its anti-employment equity stance, unfazed.[22] As Janet Lum and Paul Williams contend, "In spite of the semblance of more 'teeth,' the new *Act* contains significant omissions, restrictions and ambiguities which substantially limit its 'bite'."[23] Annis May Timpson explains that it shielded employers "against having to introduce measures that would cause economic hardship," reassured them "that they would not be required to develop employment equity targets that were out of line with labour market projections," and essentially insulated the merit principle in the federal civil service.[24] Thus, she concludes that the new *Act* "did not depart fundamentally from the principles of the legislation that was introduced by the Conservatives in 1986."[25]

While the Tories had been roundly condemned for making cuts on the backs of women, and for leaving a weakened women's movement, the situation moved from bad to worse under the Liberals. For example, reductions to social spending (for programs upon which women relied) were much more substantial in the Chrétien years.[26] It became increasingly apparent that the "Ministry of Finance had clearly won the battle over priorities, as extensive cuts to social programs were announced in the name of what was now the overriding goal of eliminating the deficit."[27]

Streamlining extended to the state's "status of women" machinery, epitomized by the 1995 closure of the Canadian Advisory Council on the Status of Women (CACSW), the women's agency set up by the Trudeau Liberals in 1973 for research and advice inside the federal government.[28] There was also less funding for women's organizations outside the state, given the Finance Minister's 1995 budget and its "selective cuts, specifically targeting advocacy groups."[29] Lack of input from feminists in and outside the state might explain why a major policy initiative like the mid–1990s reform to the Unemployment Insurance (UI) system failed to foresee how the new *Employment Insurance Act*[30] (EI) would, on balance, have a devastating impact on women.

In his first budget (1994), Paul Martin declared that unemployment insurance would be slashed by $5.5 billion in 1994–1995 and 1996–1997.[31] Then, when UI became EI in 1996, the Chrétien Liberals, like the Tories before them, priorized the market over social policy as "replacement levels steadily decreased, benefits became more difficult to access and the proportion of the labour force covered ... declined significantly."[32] Qualifying conditions became stricter, periods of benefit were shortened, and ineligibility grew in a context where unemployment rates were high, causing hardship in general, but particularly harming non-standard and part-time workers, most of whom were women.[33] Self-employed workers were not included, and women increasingly found themselves in this category.[34] On the positive side of the ledger, the new hourly-based system meant that more part-time workers would be covered by EI. On the negative side, they would be hurt by new entrant/re-entrant requirements. The change made it more difficult for women to qualify and more likely that women would be disqualified. The new, hourly-based entitlement system (most workers would have to work full-time for twenty weeks or 700 hours of work) affected eligibility.[35] EI encouraged multiple job holding and penalized workers who only wanted, or could get, short hours. These developments posed more of a problem for women than for men.[36] For example, women's family and care-giving responsibilities can often limit both their supply and hours of

paid work.[37] What is more, given that women qualify for maternity benefits under the EI rules, the new system had an impact on these benefits as
well. Many women became ineligible for maternity leave benefits and
some "were obliged to delay childbearing in order to ensure they would
qualify."[38] All this, and in the end the EI overhaul still left inequities
between women and men, as the Canadian Labour Congress (CLC)
reported that "more than half the men on EI drew over $600 a week in
benefits in 1998, though only 18 percent of women did. More than half
of the women on EI ... received less than $400 a week in benefits, 23 per-
cent of what men received."[39]

In spite of this neo-liberal deluge, new ideas began to trickle through as
the context and the actors at play altered. The economy improved, unemployment rates declined somewhat,[40] the deficit crisis was over, and, as
will be discussed below, changes took place due to tempestuous federal-
provincial relations. The debate became one of what to do with a growing surplus. Three options emerged: pay down the debt, lower taxes, or
increase spending. Jean Chrétien portrayed the path chosen as the
"Canadian way,"[41] or a more "balanced" approach, where part of the
surplus would go towards debt repayment and part would reinvest in
social policy. The rationale was that the Liberals would continue to pay
down the debt "because we owe it to our children to do so" but they
would also "invest in the social fabric of the country, particularly in
health care" and "increase investment in learning, research, and innovation."[42] It is here that the *neo-liberal state* begins to give way to the *social
investment state*.

As less has been written on the social investment state, its main features will be examined at more length. Anthony Giddens coined the term,
and since then others have provided both promising (e.g. most notably
British Labour Prime Minister Tony Blair) and more critical assessments.[43] For a start, the social investment state articulates societal goals,
for instance, in adopting the discourse of social inclusion/cohesion. Perhaps most distinctively, whereas the neo-liberal state's main objective is
to cut expenditures, the social investment state will engage in new spending. Indeed, as its name suggests, it promotes *investment* to counterbal-
ance *social* ills in part wreaked by pure, unfettered neo-liberalism. Yet,
unlike the welfare state, the social investment state concentrates its
spending in areas with perceived dividends and pay-back potential, such
as promoting life-long learning, supporting activation, and innovation.
The ultimate goal is a future with greater prosperity for all. In introducing one of the two papers composing Canada's Innovation Strategy in

2002, Jean Chrétien summed up this logic: "In the new, global economy of the 21st century prosperity depends on innovation, which, in turn, depends on the investments that we make in the creativity of our people. We must invest not only in technology and innovation but also, in the Canadian way, to create an environment of inclusion in which all Canadians can take advantage of their talents, their skills and their ideas."[44]

Investments made now must reap future rewards, and thus the social investment state's policies and programs are pragmatically results-oriented. Accountability is emphasized as well, with the use and reporting of indicators that measure outcomes and the setting of goals and targets. In short, the social investment state is more directive than the neo-liberal state, but unlike the welfare state, the social investment state steers more than it rows. Thus, the latter is depicted as "enabling."[45]

To illustrate, education, innovation, health care, and children become focal points for the social investment state, because "investment" in these areas is seen to have returns in both human and social capital. And so, in contrast to its neo-liberal phase, and as a response to growing citizen disquiet, by the 1997 election, the Liberals promised to "cancel planned cuts to health, welfare and post-secondary education."[46] Measures taken in the name of children and youth, in particular, came to play a notable role precisely because they were good bets for the future. By the late 1990s, the Chrétien government began to rearticulate earlier concerns with child poverty and, moreover, it began to direct new spending towards children, especially children "at risk."[47] The Prime Minister announced that the National Children's Agenda would figure prominently in future social policy, and in the Liberals' platform for the 1997 election, the links between children and good investment were made explicit.[48] In the preface to the Liberals' 2000 election pamphlet, Jean Chrétien boasted that "we have invested for the future – in health care, education, innovation, children, the environment, and the social programs that are the foundation of a strong society. In fact, close to 75 percent of our spending since 1997 has been in these areas.... Our purpose will be ... to [continue to] do better for ourselves and our children."[49] To be sure, the proportion of funds directed towards children would be significantly less than those of health, for example; nonetheless, by 2002, the list of initiatives undertaken featuring children and youth included the National Child Benefit (NCB), the Early Childhood Development Agreement (and new measurement and reporting on the learning readiness of children), Aboriginal Head Start on reserves, SchoolNet, financial assistance to the provinces and the territories for the Official Languages in Education Program and the Youth Employment Strategy, and finally, the establishment of Centres of Excellence dealing with children's development and well-being.

There were also changes afoot in relation to the social investment state's approach to collective actors. While the Tories began to adopt the language of "partnerships" in the early 1990s, the Chrétien Liberals extended its usage beyond the private sector.[50] Indeed, the third sector was more readily called upon for policy research, and there were efforts made by the federal government to strengthen the third sector's accountability.[51] A closer examination of the institutions, policy instruments, and identities at play will bear out these claims about the social investment state, and more consideration will be given to what all this means for women. As will be discussed below, although more money for education, health, child/youth-related policies, and child/family services was made available, and even though the "children's agenda" anchors the social investment state, all is not ship shape for women.

INSTITUTIONS AND POLICY INSTRUMENTS

To highlight the changes that take place between phase one and phase two, the gradual move from the *neo-liberal state* to the *social investment state* over the Chrétien years, two political forms and fora are particularly revealing: the civil service and federal-provincial relations.

From 1995 to 1998, through such means as privatization, buyouts, attractive retirement options, and off-loading responsibilities onto other levels of government, and with the logic of what was "affordable," 56,000 federal civil service jobs were eliminated.[52] There were also multiple attempts to "renew" the civil service over the 1980s and 1990s, mostly through new public management (NPM) reorganization. Thus, the bureaucracy's role was confined to service delivery and struggling with shrinking resources, for as Reg Whitaker contends, the "one clear agenda item in the government's first term was deficit elimination, and that was achieved, although at some cost to the public service."[53]

Yet, due to collective actors' efforts around the *Employment Equity Act*, and due to pressures exerted by international mobilization and agreements, the Chrétien Liberals also worked on making the civil service more representative of women and other under-represented groups. In addition, its 1995 document, *Setting the Stage for the Next Century: The Federal Plan for Equality*, the Liberal government outlined a five-year strategy to integrate a "gender lens" into its departments.[54] However, as Louise Chappell concludes, "improvements in numerical representation ... including Francophones and women, have done little to unsettle neutrality as a core bureaucratic value within the Canadian federal public service."[55] Moreover, commitments to mainstream gender throughout departments seemed to work at cross-purposes with neo-liberal actions such as closing down the CACSW and folding the Women's Program into the Status of Women Canada, when all three were meant to monitor and promote women's equality in and outside the state in different ways. Specifically, the CACSW had produced analyses on government policies and kept in contact with women's organizations, whereas the Women's Program had provided women's groups with both operational and project funding. Cuts to funding had predictable deleterious consequences, and the loss of the CACSW created a research void and a breach in communications between women's groups and the federal government.

The neo-liberal state also had a negative impact on federal-provincial relations, not so much because it devolved power and responsibilities onto lower levels of government, but because, in so doing, it significantly reduced its funding to the provinces. This "disengaged" federalism,[56] initiated by Mulroney and augmented by Chrétien, caused dissension. The ultimate "disengaged" solution came with the Chrétien Liberals' 1995 Canadian Health and Social Transfer (CHST). As Bashevkin recounts, the CHST was "devoid of many older provisions, including national entitlements to benefits and services."[57]

Feminist academics and activists expressed their concerns about the repercussions of the CHST – from the lack of national standards it signified to the fact that the off-loading involved would disperse power, making it more difficult for the women's movement to target state officials and organize for change. They were also well aware that women's groups would have to compete for fewer resources. The situation was most dire for low-income women given their reliance on social assistance and the numerous services that the CHST's predecessor, the Canada Assistance Plan (CAP), had funded, from legal aid, sexual assault centres, and women's shelters to homecare and subsidized child care.[58]

Many provinces wanted this freedom, but they did not want it at the cost of less funding from the federal government, which is precisely what happened: the CHST would save a projected 30–35 percent on what the federal government would have had to spend on welfare, health, and post-secondary education,[59] and transfers were reduced by $7 billion between 1996–1997 and 1997–1998.[60] The provinces were outraged, as they were compelled to scale back and, in some cases, to eliminate social programs (as occurred with public housing). Health care also suffered.[61] Lois Harder recounts: "Tensions ... increased as the federal government ... decreased its level of funding and the provinces ... scrambled to cope ... with both levels of government insisting that they respect the desire of Canadians for a universal, public healthcare system."[62] Both the civil service and federal-provincial relations were in trouble given the severity of cuts. The civil service suffered from a "quiet crisis."[63] Downsizing and NPM had created a policy vacuum, since there was less capacity for policy thinking.[64] Policy innovation and expertise were in short supply, and there were gaps in policy design and delivery; thus, the federal government turned to think-tanks and other forms of networking outside the state,[65] including the third sector. Here, for example, the Caledon Institute and its president, Ken Battle (previously of the National Council of Welfare), played a pivotal role in developing federal social policies in relation to child and seniors benefits. Indeed, these two major policy innovations resulted in the Caledon Institute acquiring the nickname of the "godfather of Canadian social policy."[66]

The language of partnership arose in light of the plight of program delivery. The third sector was touted as an alternative to the market. This dovetailed nicely with social cohesion concerns, as not-for-profits could be "portrayed as expressions of community spirit."[67] Consequently, new programs were created like the Voluntary Sector Initiative (VSI), which "received a $90 million budget for five years to increase the sector's involvement in policy making and service delivery."[68]

The push for partnerships extended to the realm of federal-provincial relations, where, unlike in the civil service, the crisis was not so quiet. The shock of the sovereigntist near-win in the 1995 Québec referendum stunned the Chrétien Liberals. Their first response was to take a more "disengaged" approach, but it soon became apparent that greater collaboration and co-operation were necessary. Gregory Inwood points to the new institutions established since 1995 to act on "social union federalism,"[69] such as the Federal/Provincial/Territorial Council on Social Policy Renewal to "develop and coordinate the social-policy renewal agenda."[70] By 1996, the federal government pledged to "not use its spending power to create new shared-cost programs in areas of exclusive provincial jurisdiction without the consent of a majority of the provinces."[71] Herman Bakvis and Grace Skogstad detail what they see as the rise of a more collaborative federalism representing "de facto concurrence in areas of provincial jurisdiction like social policy."[72] The Social

Union Framework Agreement (SUFA) of 1999 illustrates this trend, as it stresses the legitimacy of the federal spending power but also promises consultation and the forging of partnerships with the provinces. Similarly, the National Child Benefit (NCB), discussed in more detail below, is touted as an exemplar of "co-partnership" and social investment state steering and, hence, as a reflection of "a new spirit of negotiation and compromise between the two levels of government."[73]

There are two aspects of these partnerships that should be distinguished from a neo-liberal state's purely disengaged federalism. Whereas neo-liberalism calls for divesting responsibilities, the social investment state's collaboration involves directing as well as devolving. Here, the federal government's role is more apparent. A few examples of this tendency include the Chrétien government's creation of centres of research excellence, a $38.5 million federal fund called the Women's Enterprise Initiative, its $2.5 billion Millennium Scholarship Fund, and the Canadian Biotechnology Strategy (CBS) (meant "to define the role of the federal government in managing the biotechnology industry and the development and use of biotechnology in Canada").[74] Again, the federal government was keen on such initiatives because they were viewed as sound "investments" that would foster future innovation and a knowledge-based economy.

In sum, the neo-liberal state expected everyone to be more reliant on the market. Tax-cutting measures,[75] and the drive to buy Registered Retirement Savings Plans (RRSPS),[76] reflect this expectation, as both promote personal rather than collective responsibility. Individual initiatives, private enterprise, downloading, and offloading were preferred solutions. The social investment state engages in somewhat more direct provision, given that long-term societal well-being becomes an important calculation. Thus, by 2000, the Chrétien Liberals committed to "investing" $21.1 billion through the CHST.[77] This shift, not surprisingly, also coincides with more conventional electoral calculations.[78] The social investment state relies on fiscal measures such as tax expenditures, refundable and non-refundable tax credits, and tax deductions. But it also links its new tax expenditures to children as with its Canada Child Tax Benefit, and opts to increase its investment in this area. For example, in February 2000, Finance Minister Martin proclaimed that the Canada Child Tax Benefit (CCTB) would be increased by $2.5 billion a year,[79] and further boosts were announced in June of 2001 and in July of 2003.[80]

Instead of complete reliance on the private sector, the social investment state fosters more public-private sector co-operation and invokes the vol-

untary sector along with the market. Nonetheless, with its call to partnerships, with either the third sector or lower levels of government, the
social investment state's role becomes more negotiated. For example, in
response to provincial demands (save for Québec) for a "'co-leadership'
role in setting standards and designing social policy,"[81] we see developments like SUFA, where the federal government's choice of policy instruments becomes more contingent. More specifically, new programs
involving federal spending cannot be unilaterally initiated. At the same
time, "[w]hile line departments are responsible for generating policy, the
co-ordinating role played by intergovernmental relations officials can
introduce veto points to the process."[82] Thus, even though policy instruments have changed somewhat, this does not mean that they are uncon-
strained. Further complications with the social investment state can be
addressed with a closer study of its impact on collective actors, and on
women in particular.

COLLECTIVE ACTORS/IDENTITIES

The neo-liberal state shrinks the scope of the political, whether politics is
formal or informal. Collective actors are challenged by neo-liberalism's
individualism and its language of universality. Under the neo-liberal
state, the "rational individual/taxpayer/market player" is characterized
as a "universal social actor whose interests are paramount."[83] If this individualism or universalism does not make it hard enough for collective
actors, the neo-liberal state also depicts them as troublesome "special
interests." Bob Russell underscores the irony here, observing that a special interest becomes: "practically any collective that supports popular
government programs, other than the most powerful elites, who on most
issues support a shrinking state. Indeed, it is both quite telling and surprisingly wrong-headed to concentrate on the power exerted by senior
citizens, the unemployed, students, visible minorities and public-sector
workers, while ignoring the influence of groups such as the Business
Council of Canada and the interests which they represent."[84] Prime Minister Mulroney was renowned for castigating "special interests," and
women's groups, in particular, came under fire during his time in office.[85]
Thus, it was no great stretch to have Prime Minister Kim Campbell subsequently swear off state support for "'advocacy groups' such as NAC
arguing that they should be funded by their private constituencies."[86]

It was somewhat more surprising to have such discourses perpetuated
by the Chrétien Liberals, given that Liberal governments in the 1970s

and early 1980s had considered women's groups like NAC and the National Association of Women and the Law (NAWL) to be legitimate political actors. Although the women's movement certainly had to struggle to be heard in the past, there was still a sense that women's groups' representatives should be consulted in policy-making and that women's issues could be debated at election time.[87] Mulroney, and even his Minister Responsible for the Status of Women, broke with such practices. Then, in 1993, Jean Chrétien also refused to participate in an election debate on women's issues sponsored by NAC. In true neo-liberal fashion, the Chrétien Liberals' first budget in February 1994 reduced group funding by 5 percent, and Chrétien, like Campbell, "promised to consider whether the federal government should get out of the business of funding 'lobby groups' altogether."[88]

These words and deeds went beyond cutting costs to eliminate the deficit. As Mahon and Phillips contend, "the underlying intent was to reduce the influence of advocacy associations."[89] Notably, one of the program areas hardest hit by the neo-liberal state was the Women's Program, which funded an array of women's organizations.[90] The downgrading of women's issues was then made manifest with the handling of the CACSW, and the Women's Program amalgamation with the Status of Women Canada, effectively closing two potential entry points for state/women's movement interactionism. There is no doubt, then, that the neo-liberal state diminished political space for women, metaphorically and literally.

By the late 1990s, however, with new concerns being raised in relation to social cohesion, and the growing emphasis placed on partnerships beyond market players, a change was in the offing. Granted, social cohesion can be viewed as just another problematic form of universalism and, as Brodie cautions, a dangerous national homogenizing identity.[91] However, the social investment state, with even its most glib reference to social exclusion/cohesion, marks a change from the neo-liberal state. With a modicum of recognition for the social, it becomes harder for the state to ignore societal ills and the condition of certain identities, especially the worst-off members of Canadian society. Thus, the Chrétien Liberals chose to "invest" in First Nations with more funding to band councils and to provincial governments for social assistance for Aboriginal peoples. There were also new programs established, mostly for Aboriginal children, as with the Aboriginal Head Start initiative[92] and support for Aboriginal and Inuit child care. While the amount of the "investment" made was not nearly sufficient, it did illustrate a change in orientation from unadulterated neo-liberalism. In addition, compared to the earlier standstill on such issues, the Chrétien Liberals took a few (if halting) steps forward in relation to gay and lesbian rights: introducing the possibility of same-sex marriage and helping to pass New Democrat MP Svend Robinson's private member's bill to extend hate-crimes protection to gays and lesbians.

Because the social investment state's most heralded investments were made in the name of children, however, a consideration of the identity of the child and its implications on other identities is revealing. Increasingly, children and youth are invoked, but they seldom have a gender, ethnicity, race, or other signifier, save for perhaps Aboriginal youth.[93] This silence about identity has an impact on women's groups, for while they are certainly concerned with child poverty, they make explicit the connections between children's impoverishment and gender, race, and class. The feminization of poverty goes hand-in-hand with child poverty, but this relationship remains unacknowledged. As a result, women's groups continue to struggle in the shadows, while experts, think-tanks, and voluntary associations that focus on (undifferentiated) children's problems or their potential find themselves increasingly in the limelight.[94] Consequently, unlike Caledon's Battle, there are few godmothers on the scene. NAC, for instance, does not seem to be one of the "partners" at play.

Furthermore, because the children's agenda crosses policy domains and occurs in the context of collaborative federalism, various territorial identities and political players must be negotiated. At worst, this represents a new guise for the "executive federalism" which women's groups so effectively decried in the 1980s. At best, more actors are being consulted. As Linda White comments, the focus on children: "compounds the number of actors involved in policy design, development and negotiation. Conceivably, policy experts from departments of health, social services, education, and children and families, federally, provincially, and territorially, could be involved, along with officials from finance and intergovernmental affairs."[95] Here, however, White flags the problem that "the multiple actors involved can lead to turf wars."[96] It is also important to consider who gets consulted and who does not. Ironically, as Jane Jenson underscores, children's voices are seldom heard, given that they are citizens-in-becoming, remaining unenfranchised until age eighteen. Children tend not to be linked to representational forms, whether political parties or social movements and, thus, they have low levels of political resources and clout.[97]

Relatedly, what has become more and more apparent is that the social investment state's ethos of co-operation means that the actors involved and the partnerships that are forged are preferably with individuals and groups with whom the state can work, but not with those who challenge the state. Thus, *collaboration* is desirable, especially with organizations that can provide services, as opposed to those that tend to be more confrontational or combative, such as "advocacy groups." This hurts social movements and especially women's groups that usually work on multiple levels, from engaging in public education, research, and service provision to lobbying and protesting. The women's movement has always been a social and highly political movement.

Such tendencies are clearly illustrated in Lisa Philipps' research on new taxation practices. By establishing policies that would give better tax benefits to charitable donors, it is apparent that the Chrétien government has worked to promote voluntary sector growth. However, lawmakers and public servants still decide which nonprofit groups and donations get this support as the former choose who gets charitable registration status. In order to be eligible for consideration, an organization must avoid political activities. As Philipps points out, this effectively rules out "that portion of the voluntary sector dedicated to promoting egalitarian social change."[98] It is difficult for women's groups to get this charitable designation, and if they have it, it is easy for them to lose it. As Philipps contends, "Even groups that refrain from active lobbying and focus on public education are at greater risk of being labelled political if they define themselves as feminist or women centred."[99] She concludes that this "is likely to have a number of domesticating or deradicalizing effects on women's organizations. ... Groups dedicated principally to lobbying and advocacy may switch to educational publishing or other activities that might qualify as charitable."[100]

In these ways and others, the social investment state still fundamentally challenges the women's movement. Optimistically, some of the ideas and practices of the social investment state could potentially create an entering wedge. Indeed, groups like NAC have used the discourse of the child in the past, for example, to lobby for a national child care program.[101] Realistically, the women's movement has been diminished by the neo-liberal cuts. Now, the social investment state's focus on service delivery also puts the squeeze on women's groups. Both have had a negative impact on its mobilizing potential. As Timpson discerned, "in contrast to the governments led by Pierre Trudeau and Brian Mulroney, the Liberal government of Jean Chrétien has not had to face [hard] questions during an era of intense feminist mobilization or in the wake of royal commission reports ... As a result it has been much freer than previous governments"[102] to pursue an agenda that marginalizes, ignores, or has a negative effect on women.

A weakened women's movement outside the state has an impact on how women's issues are dealt with inside the state. For instance, new equality initiatives in the civil service have increasingly relied on professional "experts" rather than representatives of the women's movement. As Pauline Rankin and Jill Vickers contend, whether "feminist experts speaking for women (inspired by the growth of gender-based analysis initiatives) actually results in the needs being heard of women who are not part of the majority"[103] is questionable. A final evaluation of what various social investment state trends mean for women will be made in the following concluding comments.

CONCLUSIONS: THE CHRÉTIEN LIBERALS' SOCIAL INVESTMENT STATE AND WOMEN

While the social investment state's discourses and practices "may have mitigated the politics of welfare state retrenchment,"[104] they are still not without their drawbacks. On the upside, the National Children's Agenda, endorsed by the federal government and the premiers, earmarks billions of dollars for the improvement of the health and well-being of Canada's children. What is more, after twelve years of unfulfilled child care promises, the Liberals under Paul Martin allocated $5 billion for a national system of early learning and child care. Prime Minister Martin proclaimed, in a September 2005 speech, that the aim of this new child care plan was to "give children a head start in the global economy."[105] Three months later, in their first major policy announcement of the campaign leading to the election of 23 January 2006, the Liberals upped this commitment to $11 billion if re-elected (adding $6 billion, in 2009, to the initial $5 billlion child care investment.) These priorities are commendable. Their goal of making children good investments, who are ready to learn and who have skills and knowledge, can be interpreted in different ways, but these objectives do signal a change from a neo-liberal rationale. In the words of Prime Minister Martin, "Creating a nationwide system of early learning and child care is a great national endeavour. It speaks to the good that government can do."[106] Tackling child poverty, promoting life-long learning, and promoting national child care provisions do appeal to many feminist, liberal, and leftist campaigners. This especially holds true for those who have found new leverage with the social investment state's partnering arrangements.

Nonetheless, there are downsides. As we have seen, while the social investment state will spend, its preference is for more individualized, fiscal strategies, or what Bashevkin dubs "taxification" where "tax-based vehicles" become the preferred policy instrument.[107] And although the social investment state delivers new programs, they are highly selective and usually targeted and means-tested. Even though the federal government takes a more dominant role in social policy in the social investment state, this has not meant a return to universalism. Universal programs are still at risk and the likelihood of new universal programs remains slim. Thus, the discourse proliferates in relation to eliminating child poverty, early childhood development, and support for parents, but the Chrétien Liberals did not entertain proposals to reinstate the family allowance or establish a universal national child care system. The former is emblematic of the kind of program that helped women with children in the past, and the latter would certainly help them at present and in the future, particularly given the priorization of paid work (to which we will return below). In fact, as Martha MacDonald observes, "[d]espite the rhetoric about children, we have gone backwards in terms of valuing reproductive labour with the end of universal family allowances and tax provisions that at least minimally recognize the importance of everyone's contribution to caregiving."[108]

These social investment state patterns come to the fore with flagship programs like the National Child Benefit (NCB). In quintessential social investment state style, the NCB is couched in the rhetoric of children, is a tax measure, is targeted, and represents a collaboration between the federal government and the provinces. The Chrétien Liberals' claim was that they were focusing on low-income families and those on social assistance through the CCTB and NCB, in their efforts to combat child poverty and ultimately enhance social cohesion. Both measures ostensibly compensated for the federal government's earlier cutbacks in its contributions to the provinces for social assistance.

However, the NCB does not constitute a universal program, and the less universal benefits there are, the more vulnerable they are. When benefits are not comprehensive, support for them is incomplete. Programs such as this one are selectively targeted in the hopes of reducing child poverty, and yet comparative studies indicate that targeting, in general, is "ineffective as an anti-poverty strategy."[109]

At the same time, there are also fewer strings attached to these new programs, as compared to the cost-sharing arrangements of old. Hence, the NCB does little to respond to child care needs, not only in terms of provision, but also with respect to quality of child care. As opposed to what took place under CAP, now there are no conditions on the type of child care eligible for funding.[110] The NCB epitomizes "enabling," collaborative federalism, but it opens the door to more provincial variability. Provinces can "reinvest" in ways they see fit, ostensibly to benefit poor children, but in practice, as Deena White found, "[m]ost ... provinces reduced welfare payments to children by the whole or partial amount of the CCTB/NCB and used the freed-up funds to 'reinvest' in employability programs or employment incentives for parents, health or social program for children 'at risk' childcare credits for poor working parents or other programs, both old and new."[111] Ultimately, in her view, this amounts to a "miserly" program,[112] and it should come as no great surprise that child poverty levels may have been higher at the end of Chrétien's tenure than they were in the late 1980s.

Certainly, some elements of neo-liberalism were tempered by the social investment state, but vestiges remain that continue to work against women. To illustrate, employability becomes even more of a buzz-word for the social investment state. Many of its directives are tied to labour force activation; thus, for example, new welfare initiatives are geared towards getting people off social assistance and into paid work. The Chrétien Liberals' low-income supplement aimed to keep low-income families in the workforce and was "designed to encourage poor parents to move from dependency on welfare to self-reliance on paid work."[113] The CCTB "favours working poor over non-working (welfare) poor."[114] In these respects, the market is still an important consideration for the social investment state.

Unlike the neo-liberal state, however, labour market participation for women and men is seen as a way of tackling social exclusion and fostering social cohesion. The social investment state's active labour strategy is also linked to its preoccupation with life-long learning, children, and youth. Children and youth are considered due to their long-term potential (as workers and consumers of the future), but also in relation to the impact that they have on the workers of today. This explains new and welcome initiatives to accommodate parent workers and work/life balance, as is apparent with extensions to maternity and parental leaves and increased benefits.

On the other hand, for women in general, and especially for poor, ethnic and racial minority, immigrant, and Aboriginal women, and for women with disabilities, activation usually means being compelled to enter a low-wage, often discriminatory labour market. Here, then, several key questions were not asked of the Chrétien policies. For example, with women's labour force activation, who will take up the unpaid care work in the home? What kind of paid work (typically part-time, temporary, or flexible) is available for women, in what sectors (increasingly in the service industry) and at what rates (usually low)? What profiles emerge regarding who does what types of work (paid or unpaid, in and outside the home), not just in terms of gender, but also of race, ethnicity, class, disability, age, citizenship, and so on?

The fact that single mothers' challenges are not being sufficiently addressed is also paradoxical given that poor children often come from single parent homes, typically headed by women.[115] By the end of the 1990s, 37 percent of single mothers earned less than $10 per hour and two-thirds of single mothers earned less than $15 per hour; concomitantly, "single mothers are heavily over-represented in the most marginal categories of the labour market – namely the unemployed, discouraged workers, part-time employees and full-time temporary workers."[116] With the social investment state, the income of single mothers may be increasing, modestly, but they are still living in poverty. And given their precarious and low-paid work situation, new national programs like the NCB that prioritize "worthy workers" will do little to get single mothers out of poverty.[117] In addition, hard to find and/or expensive child care has more of an impact on single mothers and is more likely to limit their participation in the paid labour force than on mothers in two-parent families.[118] In the end, then, how such social investment state priorities are truly meant to eliminate child poverty or enhance social cohesion becomes the overriding question.

Lastly, the social investment state's glorification of the third sector has a number of negative repercussions for women as well. In the 1990s, even though the Chrétien Liberals gradually increased their support for the voluntary sector, they still shifted funding away from grants that would cover operating and administrative costs, to funding for the delivery of specific programs.[119] This had an adverse affect on organizations like NAC, as it struggled to keep its offices open, and its organization up and running.

What is more, with the ever more prevalent discourse of partnerships, other issues arise. As Jenson and Phillips point out, many of the so-called partnerships are "in fact merely contracts in which the state, as the contracting party sets all the rules"; as a result, these arrangements can change "the nature of third sector partners, especially social movements" and obviously, as was illustrated above, "the current approach is creating a hierarchy of groups with those focused exclusively on service delivery at the top, and those focused on advocacy deemed irrelevant."[120] As we have seen, this is detrimental to the women's movement, as women's groups face stark choices about either providing services or engaging in advocacy. At best, they can expect some support for the former and no support for the latter.

Even when it comes to straight service delivery, there are limitations that must be considered. Fundamental concerns are raised by Mike Burke and encapsulated by terms such as philanthropic insufficiency, philanthropic particularism, and philanthropic amateurism.[121] Philanthropic insufficiency alludes to the fact that the third sector, in comparison to state provision, does not have adequate resources to provide the services needed on a wide scale. Non-profit groups tend to depend on both the state and the work of volunteers, but neither are secure sources of support. Both the nature and extent of state and volunteer support are not constants. Moreover, the strength and number of third sector organizations is not consistent across the country; some provinces/regions have more voluntary organizations and some have less and, thus, service provision will be uneven across Canada. Philanthropic particularism refers to the fact that many of these third sector groups are geared to a certain interest or to a particular identity. This means that other interests or identities may be underserved or overlooked. As has been indicated here, groups oriented towards children have done relatively well out of the social investment state, but the same cannot be said of women's groups, despite the fact that the latter have also mobilized on behalf of children and against child poverty. Lastly, philanthropic amateurism reflects the fact that, because the third sector tends to run on volunteer power, one cannot expect that all volunteers have the requisite skills, training, and capacities.

In sum, philanthropic insufficiency, philanthropic particularism, and philanthropic amateurism highlight some of the costs that come with the social investment state's reliance on the voluntary sector. At the same time, the gendered dimensions are many. For women, the social investment state's offloading onto the third sector flags many of the same difficulties that arose with the neo-liberal state's offloading onto the family. As Burke observes, the limitations are quite apparent in the area of health care, where "[t]he effects of relegating health to the volunteer labour of the third sector are no less severe than those flowing from the relegation of health to the family. The increased use of this sector will ... intensify gender inequalities because new demands for care will fall mostly on women, who form the majority of volunteers in the field of health."[122] With the social investment state, as with the neo-liberal state, women will have to take on responsibilities formerly assumed by the state. However, this assumption is made in a more constrained context. The women's movement was hit hard by the neo-liberal state, not just in terms of funding cuts but also in terms of its personnel. With privatization, groups had to cut back on their paid staff and were increasingly stretched for volunteers as women had to take up even more care work (of children, of the sick, of the elderly). Now the social investment state promotes both paid work as well as service delivery through the third sector. This can only take a greater toll on women as they struggle with "time crunch" issues and juggle family, paid work, and third sector commitments. If a ball must be dropped, the most likely choice would be to cast away women's voluntary involvement. This puts a strain on a critical source of volunteer labour and undercuts the very same third sector upon which the social investment state pins its hopes.

The foregoing discussion illustrates the changes in policy priorities, instruments, and identities over the Chrétien years. Unfortunately, whether the situation for women improved from phase one, the *neo-liberal state*, to phase two, the *social investment state*, is not immediately apparent. There are new opportunities to be had, but there are also new constraints. As Martha MacDonald has acknowledged, while there is increased attention to meritorious issues like child poverty, "full consideration of the gendered system of reproduction in which these poor children are embedded"[123] is still lacking. Again, this reflects the lack of support for the women's movement, and its work in and outside the state.

In the final analysis, then, it is important to remember, as Janine Brodie wrote a decade ago, that "[s]tates ... do not simply reflect gender identities and inequalities, but instead, play an important role in constituting them."[124] This was a critical consideration at the height of the neo-liberal state, and it is no less acute now with the materialization of the social investment state. To return to the feast metaphor used at the outset of this article, there may have been a few tasty tidbits offered up by the Chrétien Liberals' social investment state, with new spending, benefits, and leaves. Women can certainly chew upon these morsels, but they may end up with a bad taste in their mouths; what is worse, some women may be left, literally and not just metaphorically, hungry.

NOTES

Associate Professor, Department of Political Science, Saint Mary's University. The author wishes to thank the anonymous reviewer, the editors, and her social cohesion research team (SSHRC 829–1999–1001) for their comments on an earlier draft of this article. I am particularly grateful for the work of Jane Jenson and Denis St-Martin on the social investment state, as well as the assiduous research assistance of Ian Morrison. All errors and misinterpretations rest with me.

1 Sylvia Bashevkin, *Welfare Hot Buttons: Women, Work and Social Policy Reform* (Toronto: University of Toronto Press, 2002).

2 Jane Jenson, "Fated to Live in Interesting Times: Canada's Changing Citizenship Regimes," *Canadian Journal of Political Science* 30:4 (1997): 627–44; Jane Jenson, "Canada's Shifting Citizenship Regime: Investing in Children," in Trevor C. Salmon and Michael Keating, eds., *The Dynamics of Decentralization* (Montreal & Kingston: McGill-Queen's University Press, 2001), 107–24; Alexandra Dobrowolsky and Jane Jenson, "Shifting Representations of Citizenship: Canadian Politics of 'Women' and 'Children'," *Social Politics* 11 (2004): 154–80; and Jane Jenson and Denis St-Martin, "Building Blocks for a New Welfare Architecture: Is LEGO the Model for an Active Society?" (Paper prepared for the International Research Conference on Social Security, Antwerp, Belgium, 5–7 May 2003).

3 Rianne Mahon and Susan D. Phillips, "Dual-Earner Families Caught in a Liberal Welfare Regime? The Politics of Child Care Policy in Canada," in Sonya Michel and Rianne Mahon, eds., *Child Care Policy at the Crossroads: Gender and Welfare State Restructuring* (New York: Routledge, 2002), 191–218.

4 Janine Brodie, "An Elusive Search for Community: Globalization and the Canadian National Identity," *Review of Constitutional Studies* 7 (2002): 155–78, 172. For more discussion on the nature and effects of the social cohesion agenda, see Deena White, "Social Policy and Solidarity, Orphans of the New Model of Social Cohesion," *Journal of Sociology* 28 (Winter 2003): 51–77.

5 Denis St-Martin, "De l'État providence à l'état d'investissement social: Un nouveau paradigm pour enfant-er l'économie du savoir?" in Leslie A. Pal, ed., *How Ottawa Spends, 2000–2001: Past Imperfect, Future Tense* (Don Mills: Oxford University Press, 2000), 33–58; Alexandra Dobrowolsky and Denis St-Martin, "Agency, Actors and Change in a Child-Focused Future: Problematizing Path Dependency's Past and Statist Parameters" (Paper prepared for the American Political Science Association Annual Meeting, Boston, September 2002); and Alexandra Dobrowolsky, "Rhetoric versus Reality: The Figure of the Child and New Labour's Strategic 'Social Investment State'," *Studies in Political Economy* 69 (2002): 43–73.

6 For a more detailed examination of the role of non-state actors in shaping the directions of the social investment state, see Dobrowolsky and St-Martin, "Agency, Actors, and Change."

7 A pop culture British phrase that the authors toy with in the title of their book evaluating the first term of Tony Blair's government in Britain: Polly Toynbee and David Walker, *Did Things Get Better? An Audit of Labour's Successes and Failures* (London: Penguin, 2001).

8 Linda Trimble, "Women and the Politics of Citizenship," in Janine Brodie and Linda Trimble, eds., *Reinventing Canada: Politics of the 21st Century* (Toronto: Prentice Hall, 2003), 131–40, 147.

9 Ibid. See also Cossman, who offers a recent evaluation, making clear both the distinctions between and the mutually reinforcing nature of neo-liberalism and neo-conservatism. Brenda Cossman, "Family Feuds: Neo-Liberal and Neo-Conservative Visions of the Reprivatization Project," in Brenda Cossman and Judy Fudge, eds., *Privatization, Law, and the Challenge to Feminism* (Toronto: University of Toronto Press, 2002), 169–217.

10 See Mike Burke, Colin Mooers, and John Shields, "Critical Perspectives on Canadian Public Policy," in Mike Burke, Colin Mooers, and John Shields, eds., *Restructuring and Resistance: Canadian Public Policy in An Age of Global Capitalism* (Halifax: Fernwood, 2000), 11–24, 12.

11 Caroline Andrew, "Women and the Welfare State," *Canadian Journal of Political Science* 17 (1984): 667–83; Isabella Bakker, ed., *Rethinking Restructuring: Gender and Change in Canada* (Toronto: University of Toronto Press, 1996); Janine Brodie, ed., *Women and Canadian Public Policy* (Toronto: Harcourt Brace, 1996); Susan B. Boyd, ed., *Challenging the Public/Private Divide: Feminism, Law and Public Policy* (Toronto: University of Toronto Press, 1997); Patricia M. Evans and Gerda R. Wekerle, eds., *Women and the Canadian Welfare State: Challenges and Change* (Toronto: University of Toronto Press, 1997); Sylvia Bashevkin, *Women on the Defensive: Living Through Conservative Times* (Toronto: University of Toronto Press, 1998); Pat Armstrong and M. Patricia Connelly, eds., *Feminism, Political Economy and the State* (Toronto: Canadian Scholars' Press, 1999); Linda Briskin and Mona Eliasson, eds., *Women's Organizing and Public Policy in Canada and Sweden* (Montreal & Kingston: McGill-Queen's University Press, 1999); Julia S. O'Connor, Anne Shola Orloff, and Sheila Shaver, *States, Markets, Families: Gender, Liberalism and Social Policy in Australia, Canada, Great Britain and the United States* (Cambridge: Cambridge University Press, 1999); Yasmeen Abu-Laban and Christina Gabriel, *Selling Diversity: Immigration, Multiculturalism, Employment Equity, and Globalization* (Peterborough: Broadview,

2002); Cossman and Fudge, *Privatization*; and Sylvia Bashevkin, *Welfare Hot Buttons.*

12 Janine Brodie, *Politics on the Boundaries: Restructuring and the Canadian Women's Movement* (Toronto: York University, 1994), 20. See also Janine Brodie, *Politics on the Margins: Restructuring and the Canadian Women's Movement* (Halifax: Fernwood, 1995).

13 Reg Whitaker, "Politics Versus Administration: Politicians and Bureaucrats," in Michael S. Whittington and Glen Williams, eds., *Canadian Politics in the 21st Century*, 5th ed., (Scarborough: Nelson, 2000), 55–78, 67.

14 Linda White, "Child Care, Women's Labour Market Participation and Labour Market Policy Effectiveness in Canada," *Canadian Public Policy* 27 (2001): 385–404, 388.

15 See Mahon and Phillips, "Dual-Earner Families," 203. For more on the Red Book's promises and the Liberal government's contradictory behaviour in the mid–1990s, see e.g., Jane Pulkingham and Gordon Ternowetsky, eds., *Remaking Canadian Social Policy: Social Security in the Late 1990s* (Halifax: Fernwood, 1996); Andrew F. Johnson, "Strengthening Society III: Social Security," in Andrew F. Johnson and Andrew Stritch, eds., *Canadian Public Policy: Globalization and Political Parties* (Toronto: Copp Clark, 1997), 175–81; Stephen McBride, "Investing in People: Labour Market Policy," in Johnson and Stritch, *Canadian Public Policy*, 53–72; and Jane Pulkingham and Gordon Ternowetsky, "Neo-Liberalism and Retrenchment: Employment, Universality, Safety-Net Provisions and a Collapsing Canadian Welfare State," in Dave Broad and Wayne Antony, eds., *Citizens or Consumers? Social Policy in a Market Society* (Halifax: Fernwood, 1999), 84–98.

16 Bashevkin, *Welfare Hot Buttons*, 83.

17 Ibid.

18 Linda White, "The Child Care Agenda and the Social Union," in Herman Bakvis and Grace Skogstad, eds., *Canadian Federalism: Performance, Effectiveness and Legitimacy* (Don Mills: Oxford University Press, 2002), 105–23, 109.

19 Mahon and Phillips, "Dual-Earner Families," 202.

20 S.C. 1995, c. 44, http://www.canlii.org/ca/sta/e–5.401/whole.html.

21 Janet Lum and A. Paul Williams, "Out of Sync with a 'Shrinking State'?" in Burke, Mooers, and Shields, *Restructuring and Resistance*, 194–211, 210.

22 Annis May Timpson, *Driven Apart: Women's Employment Equality and Child Care in Canadian Public Policy* (Vancouver: University of British Columbia Press, 2001), 181.

23 Lum and Williams, "Out of Sync," 198.

24 Timpson, *Driven Apart*, 181.

25 Ibid., 184.

26 Bashevkin, *Welfare Hot Buttons*, 116.

27 Mahon and Phillips, "Dual-Earner Families," 203.

28 Sandra Burt, "The Canadian Advisory Council on the Status of Women: Possibilities and Limitations," in Manon Tremblay and Caroline Andrew, eds., *Women and Political Representation in Canada* (Ottawa: University of Ottawa Press, 1998), 115–44.

29 Jane Jenson and Susan D. Phillips, "Regime Shift: New Citizenship Practices in Canada," *International Journal of Canadian Studies* 14 (1996): 111–36, 124.

30 S.C. 1996, c. 23, http://www.canlii.org/ca/sta/e-5.6/whole.html.

31 Judy Fudge and Brenda Cossman, "Privatization, Law and the Challenge to Feminism," in Cossman and Fudge, *Privatization*, 3–37, 15.

32 Gregg Olsen, *The Politics of the Welfare State: Canada, Sweden, and the United States* (Don Mills: Oxford University Press, 2002), 178.

33 At this time, women constituted 69 percent of part-time workers. See Martha MacDonald, "Restructuring, Gender and Social Security Reform in Canada," *Journal of Canadian Studies* 34 (1999): 57–88, 67.

34 Caroline Beauvais and Jane Jenson, *Two Policy Paradigms: Family Responsibility and Investing in Children*, Canadian Policy Research Networks (CPRN) Discussion Paper No. F/12 (Ottawa: CRPN, February 2001), 9.

35 Jane Beach, Jane Bertrand, and Gordon Cleveland, *Our Child Care Workforce: From Recognition to Remuneration: A Human Resource Study of Child Care in Canada* (Ottawa: Child Care Human Resources Steering Committee, 1998), 59 note 14.

36 MacDonald, "Restructuring," 72. At the same time, however, the shift from the welfare state male breadwinner model to the social investment state's "parent producer" model certainly has had an impact on both women and men. Dufour examines this in relation to both Québec and France. See P. Dufour, "L'État post-providence: de nouvelles politiques sociales pour des parents-producteurs. Une perspective comparée," *Canadian Journal of Political Science* 35 (2002): 301–22.

37 Richard P. Chaykowski and Lisa M. Powell, "Women and the Labour Market: Recent Trends and Policy Issues," *Canadian Public Policy* (Supp.) 25 (1999): S2–25, S3.

38 Lois Harder, "Whither the Social Citizen," in Janine Brodie and Linda Trimble eds., *Reinventing Canada: Politics of the 21st Century* (Toronto: Prentice Hall, 2003), 175–88, 183.

39 Lum and Williams, "Out of Sync," 195.

40 By the end of the 1990s, unemployment rates fell below 9 percent and settled "at about the 8 percent mark by early 1999." Mike Burke and John Shields,

"Tracking Inequality in the New Canadian Labour Market," in Burke, Mooers, and Shields, *Restructuring and Resistance*, 98–123, 107.

41 Liberal Party of Canada (LPC), *Opportunity for All: The Liberal Plan for the Future of Canada* (Ottawa: LPC, 2000), 2.

42 Ibid., 4.

43 For a positive spin, see Tony Blair's guru: Anthony Giddens, *The Third Way: The Renewal of Social Democracy* (Cambridge: Polity Press, 1999). In contrast, see Bob Jessop's critique of what he calls the Schumpeterian, workfare post-national regime: "From the KWNS to the SWPN," in Gail Lewis, Sharon Gewirtz, and John Clarke, eds., *Rethinking Social Policy* (London: Sage, 2000), 171–84. See also Ruth Lister, "Investing in the Citizen-workers of the Future: Transformations in Citizenship and the State under New Labour," *Social Policy and Administration* 37 (2003): 427–43.

44 Human Resources Development Canada, *Knowledge Matters: Skills and Learning for Canadians* (Ottawa: Government of Canada, 2002), 3, http://www11.sdc.gc.ca/sl-ca/doc/knowledge.pdf.

45 E. Bullen, J. Kenway, and V. Hay, "New Labour, Social Exclusion and Educational Risk Management: The Case of 'Gymslip Mums,'" *British Educational Research Journal* 26 (2000): 441–56.

46 Mike Burke, "Efficiency and the Erosion of Health Care in Canada," in Burke, Mooers, and Shields, *Restructuring and Resistance*, 178–93, 191.

47 Beauvais and Jenson, "Two Policy Paradigms," 29; Susan D. Phillips, "SUFA and Citizen Engagement: Fake or Genuine Masterpiece?" *Policy Matters* 2:7 (2001): 1–36, 27.

48 By September 2001, the federal government was willing to give the provinces $2.2 billion over five years on early childhood development: Rand Dyck, *Canadian Politics: Critical Approaches*, 4th ed. (Scarborough: Nelson Thomson, 2004), 435.

49 LPC, *Opportunity for All*, 3.

50 Jenson and Phillips, "Regime Shift," 127.

51 Kathy L. Brock and Keith G. Banting, "The Nonprofit Sector and Government in a New Century: An Introduction," in Kathy L. Brock and Keith G. Banting, eds., *The Nonprofit Sector and Government in a New Century* (Montreal & Kingston: McGill-Queen's University Press, 2001), 1–16 .

52 Whitaker, "Politics Versus Administration," 73.

53 Ibid., 74.

54 Pauline Rankin and Jill Vickers, *Women's Movements and State Feminism: Integrating Diversity into Public Policy* (Ottawa: Status of Women Canada, 2001), 31–2. This concept first appeared in the Report of the Canadian Panel on Violence Against Women. But, as Burt notes, "in the Panel's report, the

word *feminist* was used in place of gender. The wording adopted ... is significant ... [T]he Liberal government identifies a much narrower reform, i.e., counting women in." See Sandra Burt, "The Status of Women: Learning to Live Without the State," in Johnson and Stritch, *Canadian Public Policy*, 251–74, 266.

55 Louise A. Chappell, *Gendering Government: Feminist Engagement with the State in Australia and Canada* (Vancouver: University of British Columbia Press, 2002), 109.

56 Dyck, *Canadian Politics*, 429.

57 Bashevkin, *Welfare Hot Buttons*, 88.

58 MacDonald, "Restructuring," 78; Evans and Wekerle, *Women and the Canadian Welfare State*; and Pulkingham and Ternowetsky, "Neoliberalism and Retrenchment," 94.

59 Bob Russell, "From the Workhouse to Workfare: The Welfare State and Shifting Policy Terrains," in Burke, Mooers, and Shields, *Restructuring and Resistance*, 26–49, 39.

60 Fudge and Cossman, *Privatization*, 16; and Pulkingham and Ternowetsky, "Neo-Liberalism and Retrenchment," 93.

61 Stephen Brooks and Lydia Miljan, *Public Policy in Canada: An Introduction*, 4th ed. (Don Mills: Oxford University Press, 2003), 188.

62 Harder, "Whither the Social Citizen," 182.

63 Jocelyne Bourgon, former Clerk of the Privy Council, made this observation in a report to Prime Minister Chrétien. See Whitaker, "Politics Versus Administration," 74.

64 Peter Aucoin, *The New Public Management: Canada in Comparative Perspective* (Montreal: Institute for Research on Public Policy, 1997); and Denis St-Martin, *Building the New Managerialist State: Consultants and the Politics of Public Sector Reform in Comparative Perspective* (Oxford: Oxford University Press, 2001).

65 See St-Martin, ibid. See also Michael Howlett and Michael Ramesh, *Studying Public Policy: Policy Cycles and Policy Subsystems* (Don Mills: Oxford University Press, 2003), 79.

66 Donald E. Abelson, "Surveying the Think Tank Landscape in Canada," in Martin W. Westmacott and Hugh P. Mellon, eds., *Public Administration and Policy: Governing in Challenging Times* (Scarborough: Prentice Hall Allyn and Bacon, 1999), 91–105, 105 note 42. On the influence of Ken Battle and Caledon, see also "Tearing down Canada's 'welfare wall'," *Globe and Mail*, 19 June 1998, A8. See also Ken Battle and Sherri Torjman, "Desperately Seeking Substance: A Comment on the Social Security Review," in Pulkingham and Ternowetsky, *Remaking Canadian Social Policy*, 52–66. Battle provides an

account of Caledon's "several and varied roles in the National Child Benefit reform" in Ken Battle, "The Role of a Think-Tank in Public Policy Development: Caledon and the National Child Benefit," *Horizons* 6 (2003): 11–15, 15.

67 Allan Tupper, "New Public Management and Canadian Politics," in Brodie and Trimble, *Reinventing Canada*, 231–42, 237.

68 Stephen Clarkson, *Uncle Sam and Us: Globalization, Neoconservatism, and the Canadian State* (Toronto: University of Toronto Press, 2002), 423. See also Kathy Brock, ed., *Improving Connections Between Governments and Nonprofit and Voluntary Organizations: Public Policy and the Third Sector* (Montreal & Kingston: McGill-Queen's University Press, 2000); and Canada, Voluntary Sector Initiative, *A Code of Good Practice on Policy Dialogue: Building on An Accord Between the Government of Canada and the Voluntary Sector* (Ottawa: VSI, October 2002), http://www.vsi-isbc.ca/eng/policy/pdf/codes_policy.pdf.

69 Gregory Inwood, "Federalism, Globalization and the (Anti-)Social Union," in Burke, Mooers, and Shields, *Restructuring and Resistance*, 124–44, 132.

70 Ibid.

71 As quoted in White, "The Child Care Agenda and the Social Union," 111.

72 Herman Bakvis and Grace Skogstad, "Canadian Federalism: Performance, Effectiveness, and Legitimacy," in Bakvis and Skogstad, *Canadian Federalism*, 3–23, 11.

73 Inwood, "Federalism, Globalization and the (Anti-)Social Union," 142.

74 Roxanne Mykitiuk, "Public Bodies, Private Parts: Genetics in a Post-Keynesian Era," in Cossman and Fudge, *Privatization*, 311–54, 327.

75 Lisa Philipps, "Tax Law and Social Reproduction: The Gender of Fiscal Policy in an Age of Privatization," in Cossman and Fudge, *Privatization*, 41–85, 83.

76 Harder, "Whither the Social Citizen," 185.

77 Dyck, *Canadian Politics*, 435.

78 For instance, it was just before the 2000 election that the federal government restored $20 billion in health care funds. Bashevkin, *Welfare Hot Buttons*, 113.

79 Dyck, *Canadian Politics*, 487. On the CCTB increase, see Canada, Department of Finance, *Better Finances, Better Lives: The Budget Plan 2000*, "Investing in Canada's Children," (Ottawa: Public Works and Government Services, 23 February 2000), 123–52, http://www.fin.gc.ca/budget00/pdf/bpe.pdf.

80 See Canada, Department of Finance, "News Release: Canada Child Tax Benefit Increases by $300 a Year per Child in July 2001" (28 June 2001), http://www.fin.gc.ca/news01/01-057e.html; and The National Child Benefit Website, http://www.nationalchildbenefit.ca/.

81 Inwood, "Federalism, Globalization and the (Anti-)Social Union," 135.

82 White, "The Child Care Agenda and the Social Union," 115.

83 Trimble, "Women and the Politics of Citizenship," 47.

84 Russell, "From the Workhouse to Workfare," 46.

85 Alexandra Dobrowolsky, "Of 'Special Interest': Interest, Identity and Feminist Constitutional Activism," *Canadian Journal of Political Science* 31 (1998): 707–42.

86 Brodie, *Politics on the Boundaries*, 34.

87 See Alexandra Dobrowolsky, *The Politics of Pragmatism: Women, Representation and Constitutionalism in Canada* (Toronto: Oxford University Press, 2000).

88 Brodie, *Politics on the Boundaries*, 34.

89 Mahon and Phillips, "Dual-Earner Families," 205.

90 Ibid. See also Jenson and Phillips, "Regime Shift," 122.

91 Brodie, "An Elusive Search for Community," 174; see also White, "Social Policy and Solidarity."

92 Olsen, *The Politics of the Welfare State*, 28.

93 See the repercussions of collective identity erasure in relation to New Labour's social investment state in Dobrowolsky, "Rhetoric versus Reality," 67.

94 Wendy McKeen, "The Shaping of Political Agency: Feminism and the National Social Policy Debate, the 1970s and early 1980s," *Studies in Political Economy* 66 (2001): 37–58; and Ann Porter and Wendy McKeen, "The Politics of Welfare State Restructuring in Canada" (Paper prepared for the Canadian Political Science Association Annual Meetings, Québec City, 29 May 2001). See also Wendy McKeen, *Money in Their Own Name: The Feminist Voice in the Poverty Debate, 1970–1995* (Toronto: University of Toronto Press, 2003).

95 White, "The Child Care Agenda and the Social Union," 115.

96 Ibid.

97 Jane Jenson, "Rethinking Equality and Equity: Canadian Children and the Social Union," in Edward Broadbent, ed., *Democratic Equality: What Went Wrong?* (Toronto: University of Toronto Press, 2001), 111–29.

98 Philipps, "Tax Law and Social Reproduction," 74.

99 Ibid., 73.

100 Ibid., 74.

101 See Dobrowolsky and Jenson, "Shifting Representations of Citizenship."

102 Timpson, *Driven Apart*, 204.

103 Rankin and Vickers, *Women's Movements and State Feminism*, 35.

104 Mahon and Phillips, "Dual-Earner Families," 205.

105 Canadian Child Care Federation, "Champions for Child Care," http://www.cccf-fcsge.ca/pressroom/champions_for_child_care_en.htm.

106 "Liberals to extend child-care plan," CBC News, 6 December 2005, http://www.cbc.ca/story/canadavotes2006/national/2005/12/06/elxn-martin-childcare.html.

107 Bashevkin, *Welfare Hot Buttons*, 9.

108 MacDonald, "Restructuring," 82–3.

109 Pulkingham and Ternowetsky, "Neo-Liberalism and Retrenchment," 92.

110 Mahon and Phillips, "Dual-Earner Families," 208.

111 Deena White, "The Children's Agenda: How New Is It, and How Is It New? (2003), 9 [unpublished, on file with author].

112 Ibid.

113 Timpson, *Driven Apart*, 201.

114 MacDonald, "Restructuring," 81.

115 Bashevkin, *Welfare Hot Buttons*. For an historical case study of single mother's regulation, see Margaret J.H. Little, *'No Car, No Radio, No Liquor Permit': The Moral Regulation of Single Mothers in Ontario 1920–1997* (Toronto: Oxford University Press, 1998).

116 Burke and Shields, "Tracking Inequality in the New Canadian Labour Market," 106.

117 Bashevkin, *Welfare Hot Buttons*, 86.

118 White, "Child Care," 395.

119 Luc Juillet, et al., "The Impact of Changes in the Funding Environment on Nonprofit Organizations," in Brock and Banting, eds., *The Nonprofit Sector and Government in a New Century* (Montreal & Kingston: McGill-Queen's University Press, 2001), 21–62, 36.

120 Jenson and Phillips, "Regime Shift," 127.

121 Burke, "Efficiency and the Erosion of Health Care in Canada," 189–90.

122 Ibid., 189.

123 MacDonald, "Restructuring," 83.

124 Brodie, *Politics on the Boundaries*, 24.

10

La Petite Vision, Les Grands Decisions

Chrétien's Paradoxical Record in Social Policy

MICHAEL J. PRINCE

INTRODUCTION

In Canada, social policy looms large on our political landscape and in our personal lives, It encompasses the largest part of public expenditures at both orders of government, a great deal of the work of public service bureaucracies, and much of the stuff of intergovernmental relations and executive federalism in Canada. Focusing on federal social initiatives of the Chrétien Liberals from 1993 to 2004, therefore, is a far larger subject than this chapter can embrace. Fortunately, several chapters in this book examine aspects of social policy, including those related to Aboriginal peoples, cities and housing, health care, immigration, the role of the third sector, and women. Thus, the analysis here concentrates on three elements of social policy under Chrétien: the politics of budget deficits, surpluses, and intergovernmental transfers; financial assistance to families with children; and intergovernmental agreements on early childhood development, early learning, and child care services. These are among the most significant social policy developments witnessed in at least ten years, and provide an opportunity to reflect on the shift in policy and the practice of politics that transpired over Chrétien's tenure as Prime Minister. Even still, any one chapter will unavoidably pass over many of the nuances, complexities, and contradictions of a government's legacy.

Chrétien is widely regarded as a politician who lacked a striking vision of lofty ideals and ambitious objectives, be they economic, constitu-

tional, or social. There is much academic, media, and public support for
this representation.[1] In a ranking of Canada's Prime Ministers, Chrétien
is described by historians J.L. Granatstein and Norman Hillmer as having "no great abiding vision of the country."[2] Chrétien's biographer,
Lawrence Martin, similarly has written of his political philosophy that
"he never did see the world in terms of blueprints."[3]

My argument is that Chrétien's impact on social policy developments
was, and will continue to be, more substantial than *la petite vision*
implies, due to his political style, the inherent power of the role of the
first minister within Canadian politics, and the cumulative impact of
numerous decisions over time. The chapter proceeds in four sections.
The first section offers a brief overview of the policy preferences and style
of Chrétien, and suggests that he had a strong and ongoing interest in and
influence over federal social policy. The second section examines the all-
important fiscal context, however it is politically constructed, within
which social spending and policy-making must operate. Implications of
the deficit reduction phase and then the fiscal surplus phase are discussed
to display some of the budgetary forces at play during the Chrétien years.
It was through debates over, and decisions about, the deficit and then
spending and tax relief that Chrétien often exercised his power over
social policy. In the third section, I examine a major part of the Chrétien
social policy record, namely improving the quality of life and income
security of Canadian families with children. The Canada Child Tax Benefit, introduced by the Chrétien Liberals, has become the central federal
policy instrument for providing financial support to families with children. In addition, the 2005 intergovernmental agreements on early childhood development and child care represented the federal government's
main partnerships with provinces and territories in investing in services
for families with younger children. The fourth section sets out the overall
conclusions that emerge from the analysis, centred on the paradoxical
nature of Chrétien's record in social policy.

PRIME MINISTER CHRÉTIEN AND SOCIAL POLICY-MAKING

"In relation to prime ministerial policy preferences," Doern and Phidd
note that: "virtually all recent occupants of the office, except perhaps
Brian Mulroney [and, I would add, John Turner], have leaned to the
social policy side of the policy continuum. This is partly because party
conventions seem to prefer leaders who display, or are perceived to have,

a preference for the 'softer' human issues on the not unrealistic expectations that this is where the 'votes' are."[4] Yet, upon assuming the office, Tom Axworthy, former Principal Secretary to Prime Minister Trudeau, makes the point that "Prime Ministers set a framework and juggle competing forces: rarely has a Prime Minister taken up social policy as a personal cause."[5] The reason for this, Axworthy suggests, is that a prime minister has a limited amount of time and resources to respond to all the needs and issues facing the federal government, and so a strategic political approach is essential.

Even with limited time and other resource constraints, a prime minister can influence the process and content of social policy-making in a number of ways: campaigning on social policy values against opposition parties; selecting and shuffling ministers and senior officials; appointing commissions of inquiry; controlling the agenda of Cabinet and the design of throne speeches; reorganizing Cabinet portfolios, Cabinet committees, and executive decision processes; and shaping the overall fiscal framework for the government, which includes allocating budget surpluses among spending, tax cuts, and debt relief.

Jean Chrétien's political base and career experience undoubtedly shaped his leadership style and policy preferences while Prime Minister. Chrétien came to the Prime Minister's Office as a highly experienced Member of Parliament and Cabinet minister, a professional politician who knew how Parliament worked and how to get things done in government. He understood the importance of public opinion and public service advice in decision-making, and he readily used both while placing them in a political perspective. His approach to making policy was pragmatic and moderate, basing decisions on the circumstances rather than on doctrinal positions, preferring to see this as flexibility and adaptability to changing issues and priorities rather than as opportunism. Chrétien practised a partisan and brokerage style of politics in which he was far more interested in, and adept at, "resolving conflicts and finding workable solutions," than in philosophizing or pursuing long-term plans.[6] His ideological instincts were what he himself called progressive, seeing an active role for government in Canada in both the economy and society, and using politics as an instrument for change.

Social policy is an expenditure-intensive area of government. This fact of budgetary life is apparent by the major income benefit programs to the elderly, the unemployed, and families; in the massive transfer payments to provinces for education, health care, social services, and welfare; and in the grants and contributions dispensed to a vast array of community groups and agencies throughout the country. Chrétien keenly understood the politics of budgeting, as a former Minister of Indian Affairs, Industry, and Energy, as well as something of the economics and management of it, as a former Minister of Finance and President of the Treasury Board. Throughout his career in government, Chrétien resolved "to be where the cash is," a principle that he continued to follow while Prime Minister.[7] He also understood the "inherent tension in federalism" between the federal and provincial levels of government, and that "no social problem will fester long without one government moving to deal with it or, at least, to use it to club the other government."[8] Chrétien managed the intergovernmental dimension of social policy by eschewing megaconstitutional reform, holding First Ministers' Conferences rather infrequently and often timing them around his own election and budget cycles.

As Prime Minister, Chrétien's interest in social policy is best understood in the context of his previous Cabinet portfolios, his populist style of politics, and his progressive orientation to governing. Social policy is inextricably linked with federal-provincial/territorial relations, Canada-Aboriginal relations, and the place of Québec within the federation. He therefore invested his time, political capital, and influence on issues considered to be strategic, such as managing the budget surplus, education and research, health care renewal, and transfers to the provinces and territories. The Prime Minister's Office, aided by the Privy Council Office, intervened in a handful of social policy files, including the original size of the Canada Health and Social Transfer in 1995, the $2.5 billion Millennium Scholarship Foundation announced in 1998, the 1999 Social Union Framework Agreement, the national homelessness initiative, and the health accords of 2000 and 2003 reached between Chrétien and provincial and territorial first ministers. These were all *les grands decisions* in federal social policy.

FROM DEFICITS TO SURPLUSES: SOCIAL BUDGETING UNDER CHRÉTIEN

From their first budget in 1994, the Liberals undertook fundamental reconstruction of social programs, emphasizing expenditure restraint and deficit reduction, thus transforming the federal role in the Canadian welfare state and shifting social politics to one of retrenchment and dismantling. The 1995 budget was an epiphany in fiscal federalism and national social policy with the surprise announcement of the termination of the Established Programs Financing (EPF) and the Canada Assistance

Plan (CAP), and their replacement with the more flexible and much smaller Canada Health and Social Transfer (CHST). After years of restraining the growth rate in health transfers to the provinces in the 1980s and early 1990s, the Liberals delivered, through the CHST, sudden and deep absolute cuts in transfer payments to the provinces.

Announced in the February 1995 federal budget (and replaced in 2004 by two new transfers), the CHST was among the most striking and unilateral developments in Canadian social policy and fiscal federalism. The CHST was a child of federal deficit reduction and a cousin of provincial demands for greater autonomy in social policy. Within this national context of spending restraint and flexible federalism, especially in relations with Québec, the CHST had three main elements. First, it was a replacement for, and consolidation of, the previous arrangements of federal transfer payments for social assistance and social services under CAP, as well as for health and post-secondary education under the Established Programs Financing agreement, into a single program. Second, the CHST was a block grant of an amount substantially less than the sum of the earlier transfer programs. In the beginning, the CHST involved a two-year cut of $7 billion over 1996–1997 and 1997–1998. Third, while the five conditions associated with the *Canada Health Act*[9] remain in place and are enforced by Ottawa with respect to social assistance and social services, only one of the five conditions under the *Canada Assistance Plan Act*[10] is retained, the prohibition of a residency requirement by provinces for income benefits.[11]

Given the secrecy, haste, and ministerial bargaining involved in crafting the CHST, the federal government did not decide upon a cash floor for the block grant until six months after the budget announcement. Finance officials favoured a transfer payment floor of $9 billion per year, while some ministers, particularly social liberals, wanted a floor of $12.5 billion each year. The Prime Minister's Office settled for an annual cash floor of $11 billion.[12]

From Restraining to Reinvesting

With the emergence of budget balances and surpluses and, indeed, successive surpluses since 1997, the second and third Chrétien governments faced a far different and far more favourable fiscal context for making social policy. Going into the 1997 election, Chrétien committed his party and successive governments to a 50:50 formula for allocating any future budgetary surpluses. For every billion dollars of fiscal dividend, Chrétien pledged that one half would go to a combination of tax and national debt reduction, and one half would address social and economic needs through program expenditures.[13] The more recent Chrétien governments did inject additional substantial resources into social programs, especially health care, family policy, and post-secondary education. From 1993–1994 to 1996–1997, federal program spending declined in actual terms from $120 billion to not quite $105 billion, an average annual decrease of 4.4 percent. From 1997–1998 to 1999–2000, corresponding more or less to the second term, federal program spending began to increase, though modestly to $111.8 billion, at an average annual rate of 2.2 percent. Then, spanning his third term, from 2000–2001 to 2004–2005, federal program spending grew at a higher annual average rate of 6 percent. Much of this "growth" in social spending, however, was merely catching up after the deep cuts made in the early and mid-1990s.

Chrétien described his final budget of February 2003 as "the most activist social policy budget" since the Liberals took office in 1993.[14] Despite the claims of critics, the 2003 budget did not constitute a return to the tax-and-spend budgets of the Trudeau era. In contrast to previous Liberal regimes, Chrétien's most activist budget was the sixth consecutive balanced budget at the federal level, with surpluses planned for the next two years, cushioned by a contingency reserve and low inflation. Moreover, federal program spending as a share of the Canadian economy was around 12 percent of the gross domestic product, a level last seen in Canada in the early 1950s, with little chance of rising this relatively low level. Despite this activist budget in social policy, the underlying budgetary approach remained prudent, with social investments spread incrementally over several years.[15]

A reparation agenda characterized this later phase of Liberal social policy-making, an agenda that entailed making amends and rectifying programs or transfers felt to be insufficient in scope or underfunded in resources. The partial restoration of previously frozen or cut federal funding was most apparent in health care. The 1993 levels of federal spending on health care were achieved again only in 2004, following Chrétien's retirement. Another major example of restoration was the reintroduction, in the 2000 federal budget, of the full indexation of income tax brackets, numerous tax credits, and income thresholds for receiving benefits. This move reversed a policy of stealth introduced in 1986 by the Mulroney Conservatives and maintained by the first two Chrétien Liberal governments. The restoration of full indexation is immensely significant because it brings to an end the quiet decline in the value of several tax benefits for seniors, families, and persons with disabilities, among others.

In the later years of the Chrétien era, there were signs of going beyond repairing social programs to erecting new social policy approaches. Substantial innovation was suggested by the National Children's Agenda, new tax collection agreements gave the provinces far greater autonomy, and the financing reforms to the Canada Pension Plan and the formation of the CPP Investment Board introduced in 1998.[16] Considerable investment by Ottawa in higher education since 1997 has produced what one analyst has aptly called "a quiet revolution in Canadian public policy," with Canadians and universities looking to the federal government for continued leadership in research and student aid.[17]

CHILDREN AND FAMILIES: A NOTABLE LEGACY

During Chrétien's second mandate (1997–2000) and even more so in his third mandate (2000–2003), as the fiscal situation of Ottawa improved spectacularly while poverty stubbornly persisted, measures to support Canadian families and their children emerged as a prominent policy area. These measures are summarized in Appendix Table 1. In the Throne Speech previewing their third mandate, the Chrétien government observed that "[a] generation ago, Canadians set a national goal to eliminate poverty among seniors," and it boldly promised to "ensure that no Canadian child suffers the debilitating effects of poverty."[18] The Throne Speech articulated three goals for child and family policy at the federal level:

1 To help disadvantaged families with children break the cycle of poverty and dependency;
2 To ensure that all families have access to the services and supports they need to care for their children; and
3 To provide young Aboriginal Canadians with the basic tools they need to take greater advantage of the opportunities Canada has to offer.[19]

The Speech identified potential further action in all three areas. The first was a selective strategy for tackling poverty with a categorical approach to assisting welfare-poor and working-poor families with children. The National Child Benefit (NCB), introduced by Ottawa in 1998, has similar objectives. The NCB seeks to improve the economic security of low-income families with children. Its core goals are to help prevent and reduce the depth of child poverty, as well as to help parents find and keep jobs by providing benefits and services that better support them.

The second action area is also a form of social protection, but one with an awareness of the instability and variety of family forms in contemporary Canada. Here, the Throne Speech indicates that the federal government will "work with [the provinces] to modernize the laws for child support, custody and access, to ensure that they work in the best interests of children in cases of family breakdown," and to "take steps to enable parents to provide care to a gravely ill child without fear of sudden income or job loss."[20]

The third goal expressed a crucial element of cultural recognition and support for Aboriginal peoples. It entails the federal government working with First Nations to improve and expand the early childhood development programs and services available in their communities. Moreover, it has involved expanding the Aboriginal Head Start program to better prepare Aboriginal children for school and help those with special needs. A related move in pursuit of this goal was adopting measures to significantly reduce the number of Aboriginal newborns affected by Fetal Alcohol Syndrome by the end of this decade.

Does this all add up to a coherent package of policies and goals for children and families in Canada? In a federal system that is not the correct question to ask of a single government, especially of the government lacking most of the constitutional jurisdictions pertaining to children and families. What can be asked of the federal government is whether the Chrétien Liberals, on their own and working with other governments, truly placed children and families on the national policy agenda, addressed a range of issues of real significance to children and their families, and committed substantial resources over the longer term. Various stakeholder and interest groups have different answers to these questions, with some disapproving, some detached, and still others commending the measures and plans.

In my view, Chrétien's cluster of policies for children and families, supported by the National Children's Agenda and the National Child Benefit (NCB), represents the most explicit and extensive family policy at the federal and intergovernmental levels in a generation. These policies fall short, however, in the adequacy of income benefits provided to low- and modest-income families and in the adequacy of affordable and quality child care spaces for all families.

good

but remember he is referring to 2nd and 3rd term.

The Canada Child Tax Benefit

The NCB has been hailed as the first new national social program in thirty years. It represents a significant return of federal involvement in social policy making, accompanied by innovative actions on income assistance for low-income families with children.[21] The NCB was developed jointly by Federal/Provincial/Territorial Ministers of Social Services and introduced in July 1998. Its main goals are to reduce the depth of child poverty and to increase labour market attachment of adults on welfare. We see here the quintessential liberal approach to welfare, with an emphasis on relieving poverty and integrating citizens into the labour market as the means for meeting their social and economic needs.[22] Under the NCB, the federal government injected new funds into child benefits through the Canada Child Tax Benefit (CCTB), and participating provinces, territories, and approximately 600 First Nations committed to reinvest the welfare savings into new or enhanced programs of their choosing for low-income families and their children. These reinvestments cover a broad range of initiatives, including child care, child nutrition, cultural/traditional teachings, early childhood development, income-tested child benefits and earnings supplements, and supplementary health care.

The CCTB has significance in determining which groups Ottawa provides family benefits to, by what policy means, and in what amounts. With the adoption of the CHST in 1996, Ottawa moved significantly away from the role of sharing the cost of financial assistance to low-income families provided for through needs-tested social assistance programs offered, designed, and managed by the provinces/territories. Under the old system of federal and provincial income support to low-income families with children, working poor families typically received only about half the level of child-related benefits provided to families on welfare. Through the CCTB, the Chrétien Liberals moved toward equalizing the level of child benefits provided to all low-income families, whatever their sources of income. A core aim of the CCTB, as a social policy reform, is "to raise child-related payments for poor families not on social assistance *up to* the level paid to social assistance families."[23] While the federal government was increasing its child benefits for low-income families, it also made improvements in the level of benefits paid to non-poor families, specifically covering modest- and middle-income families, while excluding high-income families.

The CCTB has two parts: the Basic Child Tax Benefit for low- and middle-income families, and the National Child Benefit Supplement for low-income families. The Basic Child Tax Benefit is available, on a sliding scale, to over 90 percent of Canadian families with children. The National Child Benefit Supplement is a much more targeted payment that is clawed back from families on social assistance in all provinces except New Brunswick and Newfoundland and Labrador. This clawback of money from the poorest of the poor has been a controversial feature of the National Child Benefit initiative, provoking strong objections by numerous social policy organizations.[24]

The CCTB is an example of social policy supported by intergovernmental agreements and a series of expenditure commitments and policy enhancements over many years. By 2006, federal income support for families with children, through the CCTB, was projected to deliver over $10.1 billion in benefits, more than double the amount expended by Ottawa in 1996 just before the introduction of the CCTB. Over this period, the maximum CCTB payable to an eligible family with one child was $1,020 in 1996–1997.[25] It was projected to be $3,243 by July 2007.[26] The Caledon Institute of Social Policy estimated that total federal spending on child benefits will have increased from 1997 to 2007 by 61 percent in real terms; as well, increases to the CCTB announced in John Manley's 1993 budget "more than make up for reductions in expenditures on federal child benefits in the 1980s: By 2007, Ottawa will be spending $2.6 billion or 38.4 percent more than its 1984 expenditure of $6.8 billion on child benefit programs."[27]

The CCTB and the wider National Child Benefit have various effects for families with children, social policy, and federalism. One result is a "federalization" of child benefits, with Ottawa playing a growing role relative to the provinces and territories. For parents of children still on provincial welfare, the mix of their benefit income is shifting toward federal income-tested support, with less coming from provincial needs-tested assistance. When fully implemented, the planned increases to the CCTB would replace child benefits under provincial social assistance programs and actually increase the income of families with children that have relied on such programs, resulting in an integrated benefit for all low-income families. With this federalization comes a modernization of program delivery: unlike provincial welfare, the CCTB is neither as discretionary nor as stigmatizing.

A second outcome is the move back toward universality, last in effect in federal family allowance policy over a decade ago. With increases in the Basic Child Tax Benefit and in its threshold for maximum benefits and a lowering of the benefit reduction rate, the number of families with children who qualify for the CCTB was to grow from around 80 percent in 1996 to 95 percent or more by July 2004, a return to near-universal coverage in federal family benefits. Behind this symbolic universality, however, is a substantial redistribution of benefits from higher to lower income groups.[28]

A third effect is that the CCTB and NCB serve as a political symbol of co-operative federalism. They point to the effectiveness of governments working together. The CCTB represents the most significant and extensive intergovernmental reform to Canadian poverty policy since the introduction of the CAP in the mid–1960s. In mediating the relationship between the state, labour markets, and families, the CCTB offers a level of income security, delivered by Ottawa and the provinces and territories, that is independent of the work status of the claimants.

A fourth effect is that there continues to be strong advocacy for additional major investments in child and family benefits. Although increases are scheduled until 2007, federal child benefits remain far from adequate in alleviating poverty and supporting families with children. As of July 2003, the CCTB was giving income-tested benefits of equivalent value to low-income families, whether they were welfare families or working-poor families. "The next challenge," as the Caledon Institute put it, "is to build the integrated child benefit into an *adequate child benefit* paying substantially larger amounts to low-income families ... and to modest- and middle-income families."[29]

Early Childhood Development

The Early Childhood Development Framework (ECD) agreed to by the First Ministers, with the exception of the Premier of Québec, in September 2000, underscores this renewed federal role in the social union. The main features of the Framework agreement are outlined in Appendix Table 2.

The Communiqué from the First Ministers' meeting provides a context for the ECD Agreement. It explains: "New evidence has shown that development from the prenatal period to age six is rapid and dramatic and shapes long-term outcomes. Intervening early to promote child development during this critical period can have long-term benefits that can extend throughout children's lives. Governments and other partners currently provide a range of programs and services to effectively support early childhood development. The challenge is to build on existing services and supports, to make them more coordinated and widely available."[30]

The Agreement focuses on children and families and their immediate communities, from the prenatal period to age six. The implementation approach echoes several features of the National Children's Agenda. These ideas include the expansion of funding for services and programs, over time, in a predictable and sustained fashion; governments working together and with other institutions, including Aboriginal peoples; governments reporting frequently and publicly on their progress to their respective constituencies; and governments investing in research, knowledge, and sharing effective practices with others. In this instance, the Chrétien Liberals committed $2.2 billion in early childhood development over the five-year period from 2001–2002 to 2005–2006.

While applauded by some, for many advocates, social policy groups, and families, the 2000 Agreement was a grave disappointment, seen as the abandonment of a national child care strategy. The supply of child care spaces had grown far more slowly over the 1990s than in the 1980s, thus aggravating an already-serious shortage of quality child care spaces. In particular, federal funds under the 2000 Agreement were open-ended, rather than dedicated to expanding the number of regulated child care spaces across the country. Consequently, some provinces directed these funds into other activities.[31]

Early Learning and Child Care Services Initiative

In March 2003, ministers responsible for social services agreed to a federal, provincial, and territorial framework called the Early Learning and Child Care Initiative (ELCCI). In part, this initiative finally met a pledge first made by the Chrétien Liberals in 1993 to invest in child care systems across Canada. Under the ELCCI, the shared goal among governments is to improve access to affordable, quality, provincially and territorially regulated child care and early learning programs and services for young Canadian children (ages six and under) and their parents.[32] The federal government allocated $900 million over five years to support provincial and territorial investments in the areas of early learning and child care, especially for low-income and single-parent families. In addition, the federal government allocated $35 million over five years for similar programs for First Nations children, primarily those living on reserves. This built on an investment announced in 2002 of $320 million over five years for Aboriginal children.

The objectives of the ELCCI are threefold: to promote the healthy development of young children, to support the participation of parents in employment or in training, and to strengthen Aboriginal communities throughout the country. The ELCCI builds on the 2000 Agreement on ECD, taking one of the four areas of action identified in that accord (see Appendix Table 2), and directing this new federal investment into settings such as child care centres, family child care homes, preschools, and nursery schools. Further investments in early learning and child care are to be incremental, predictable, and sustainable over the long term. The intended results are to "substantially increase the number of child care and preschool spaces, reduce the cost of child care and preschool services for low- and modest-income families, and improve the quality of child care and preschool services."[33] Longer-term outcomes would include improved employment skills and labour force attachment of these parents, therefore increasing levels of earned incomes. For Aboriginal peoples, long-term outcomes would include robust communities with an enhanced quality of life. The government's commitment of $935 million over five years fell well short of the target of $1 billion a year in federal funding recommended in 2002 by a group of Liberal MPs. By 2007, these MPs had called for annual federal funding of $4.5 billion on regulated, preschool child care spaces.[34]

The Canadian Council on Social Development, an independent social policy think tank, called this federal investment, first unveiled in the 2003 budget, "a historic day for Canada's children and families," with the federal government having "at long last ... showing leadership" on the child care issue.[35] With a quality national child care system estimated at $10 billion annually, the Council hoped that all governments would continue to increase their support for child care.[36] In a similar vein, a leading expert on child care research and policy in Canada, Martha Friendly, has written of the ELCCI that: "this agreement includes several conditions that begin to set out the shape of what observers hope will become Canada's first new national social program of the 21st century. Those of us who have experienced previous unsuccessful attempts to establish a national childcare strategy are cautiously optimistic that this may be the long sought first step."[37] Putting it in an international context, Friendly suggested that this national child care agreement "may signal that Canada is ready to catch up with other countries that have undertaken to make ECEC [early childhood education and care] part of the mainstream fabric of family and public life."[38]

These comments by Friendly and the Canadian Council on Social Development were, by necessity, early responses and by consequence somewhat speculative. Like the reactions of most seasoned advocates to a policy announcement, their remarks mixed praise, cautious optimism, and a message that far more needs to be done. Indeed, if we are ever to realize a national approach to child care in Canada, it will require greater political leadership than that displayed by Chrétien on the issue, as well as substantial financial investments by Ottawa and other governments.

CONCLUSIONS

Two sets of paradoxes have been examined here: 1) the fuzzy image yet focused influence of Jean Chrétien as a policy-maker, and 2) the deconstructing and then rebuilding of social policy through fiscal policies. All government leaders acquire a public image of their real and perceived characteristics. For Chrétien, that image was of a partisan pragmatist, interested far more with short-term calculations and electoral advantages than with rational planning and majestic visions. Chrétien's approach to social policy and social spending, however, reveals a paradox, a set of results that are contrary to the received view of his style. As Chrétien's biographer has noted, "[I]f he wasn't a man of vision, what carried him on a steady course were his values" and, it should be added, his strong desire "to attain and maintain that power."[39]

In federal social policy-making, Chrétien exhibited both a *modus vivendi* of short-term expediency, associated with the public image, and a *modus operandi* of a longstanding set of beliefs about the role of government in society and the place of the federal government in the social union. Chrétien sought to restore the fiscal capacity of Ottawa, and reinvest in key social programs when it was fiscally prudent and politically important to do so, thus reasserting the visibility and authority of the federal government while maintaining the maximum flexibility possible of the federal spending power within the social union. For a first minister of the federal government with an activist orientation, this is a practical and purposeful strategy.[40] When considering the political attributes of social budgeting, one can make further sense of this paradox, and better understand why the notion of Chrétien as a policy activist, with a view to substantial expenditure commitments over the longer term, is well founded.

The largest component of Ottawa's budget, social spending is an area of high visibility for the federal government, containing programs that are well known and important to the well-being of millions of Canadians. Public opinion about social policy is direct, mass-based, and generally supportive of social programs. Federalism, the *Canada Health Act*, and the *Canadian Charter of Rights and Freedoms* are overarching institutions ever present in this policy field, as are the ongoing issues of the principles of Medicare, the mobility of labour, the role of post-secondary education and research in national policy, and social rights of citizenship.[41]

Chrétien's leadership also must be seen in relation to the fiscal situation of the federal government and the broader economic setting of the country. The financial circumstances of governments have been a decisive factor in shaping the policy agenda, moulding public experiences and expectations, and affecting the dynamics of intergovernmental relations. The Liberals inherited an economy in 1993 that was recovering from a serious recession. Over the next decade, improved economic conditions and more or less sustained growth reduced unemployment, eased poverty for some, and boosted government revenues. Behind these financial circumstances lay power, ideology, and policy decisions and non-decisions. In part, these financial circumstances, especially of deficit reductions and then balanced budgets, came to be decisive because of struggles won by the business Liberals in Cabinet and by the Department of Finance in the federal bureaucracy.[42]

The federal spending power took on greater significance as Ottawa went from a record deficit of $42 billion in 1993–1994 to the first surplus in a generation in 1997–1998. This grew in subsequent years to $12.3 billion for 1999–2000, with further surpluses over the following five years. Ken Battle suggests: "Without the success of the anti-deficit campaign, governments never would have embarked on what became such ambitious and far-reaching reforms to social policy."[43] From 1999–2000 to 2004–2005, the amount of new spending devoted to the Canada Child Tax Benefit totalled $14.4 billion, making it one of the most significant trends and elements of tax-spending initiatives by the Chrétien Liberals.[44] With this new spending, the Liberals were making the program available to more middle-income families, edging to a near-universal child and family cash benefit at the national level. Any influence of Chrétien is due in large part to the possibilities for restoration and new construction of social programs flowing from this rolling wave of budget surpluses, for which he can take some credit.

There will be other readings of Chrétien's social policy legacy, at least some of which will be less favourable than the analysis here may appear. I have provided such critiques myself.[45] To take one example, the argument can be made that Chrétien did not solve the tension between the fiscal and social agendas of the federal government nor seriously address the imbalance in resources and responsibilities between levels of government in the federation. On the contrary, recent evidence – revealed in opinion polls, the Liberal leadership race, and continued calls by business interests for further tax cuts and by provinces and territories for further transfer payments – shows that these tensions were never resolved fully or permanently. Moreover, a longer historical analysis than the one presented would show that the Finance Department has long been a major player in bureaucratic politics and a powerful influence on social policy.[46]

The central point of this chapter was to challenge the conventional view of Jean Chrétien – as an indifferent social policy-maker – as superficial and in need of reconsideration. Chrétien was not a weak or wayward Prime Minister devoid of political beliefs and policy preferences about citizenship, federalism, and social policy. Largely, it was through strategic budget choices as well as far-reaching agreements in the intergovernmental arena that Chrétien exercised his influence, expressed a set of values, and affected a set of *les grands decisions* on social programs that will continue to operate over the coming years. Not bad for a politician with *la petite vision*.

POSTSCRIPT

Comparing Chrétien's social policy record to that of his nemesis and successor, Paul Martin, reveals obvious contrasts, some notable changes, and much continuity. This comparison sheds light on both leaders and the times in which they governed.

Unlike Chrétien, Martin's style was characterized by expansive rhetoric, bold concepts, and earnest pronouncements. For many observers, Martin's big visions for his government and the country fell short of initial expectations, no doubt hampered by a minority government and by political scandals. Critics were led critics to dub him more a ditherer than decision-maker. In the social issues that Martin took up as causes while Prime Minister, change was evident, too, specifically his attention to aboriginal affairs and to forging a "new deal" for Canadian cities and communities.[47] On health care, learning, and research, Martin's interests were more an evolving continuity than a change in the national Liberal political agenda.[48]

Enjoying recurrent federal budget surpluses, Martin maintained the broad pattern established by Chrétien of devoting significant shares of annual surpluses to social programs, notably health, education, and child care, as well as to further tax relief and some debt reduction.[49] While

Martin devoted relatively more funds to certain social program areas than Chrétien, social spending remained under the influence of a doctrine of financial responsibility and fiscal prudence as well as shaped, of course, by bureaucratic politics, intergovernmental relations, and contending demands and policy interests.

The Martin Liberals did not significantly add to the Chrétien plan of financial assistance to families with children, though they did substantially enhance expenditures on early learning and child care. Martin did not enrich the Canada Child Tax Benefit (CCTB), possibly because the last Chrétien budget increased the National Child Benefit Supplement by an annual amount of $150 per child in July 2003, with a further $185 per child to take effect July 2006. From 2003 to 2007, spending on the CCTB is projected to grow by nearly $2 billion, largely due to Chrétien-era spending decisions.[50] Talk about leaving a legacy. In addition, the final Chrétien budget introduced the Child Disability Benefit, delivered as an income-tested and indexed supplement to the CCTB, an important, even though imperfect new income support for families with children living with a severe impairment.[51]

Where the Martin Liberals noticeably expanded upon Chrétien's record in family policy is with the Early Learning and Child Care (ELCC) Initiative. In 2003, the Chrétien government announced $900 million over five years to provinces and territories for the ELCC, plus $35 million over five years for First Nations on reserve. In his first budget as Prime Minister, in 2004, Martin accelerated the implementation of the 2003 plan by increasing transfers to the provinces and territories by $325 million over the next two years. In its 2005 budget, the Martin government committed $5 billion to the ELCC over five years to provinces and territories, on an equal transfer per capita basis, plus $100 million for five years to First Nations on reserves. These further investments – described in intergovernmental agreements as incremental, predictable, and sustainable over the long term – represent more than a three-fold increase in annual federal transfers to provinces and territories. By the end of 2005, two years after Chrétien's retirement, the Martin government had signed ELCC agreements with all ten provinces, based on the principles of quality, universally inclusive, accessible, and developmental service provision.[52]

If Chrétien's initiatives on early childhood development in 2000 and 2003 were a first step to a national child care framework, then with these further sizeable investments the Martin Liberals tried to take the next few steps to building such a framework across the country. Still, there is a long way to go in realizing this vision.

APPENDIX

Table 1
An Overview of Initiatives by the Chrétien Governments for Supporting Families with Children

- Aboriginal Programming: Aboriginal Head Start, Aboriginal urban strategy, First Nations and Inuit Health (1997 onwards)
- Caregiver Tax Credit (introduced in 1998 and since increased)
- Child and Family Law: Child Custody, Access and Support Law and Guidelines, Changes to the Criminal Code on abuse and sexual exploitation
- Child Disability Benefit (2003) for low-and modest-income families with children with disabilities
- Compassionate Family Care Leave benefit through the Employment Insurance plan (2003)
- Early Childhood Development Agreement (2000–2005)
- Early Learning and Child Care Initiative (2003–2008)
- Extended Maternity and Parental Benefits (2001)
- Healthy Family Programs: Community Action Program for Children
                              Canada Prenatal Nutrition Program
                              Fetal Alcohol Syndrome/Fetal Alcohol Effects initiative
- National Child Benefit: Canada Child Tax Base Benefit and NCB Supplement (introduced 1997 with increases planned to 2007)
- Research: National Longitudinal Survey on Children and Youth
- Understanding the Early Years
- General Tax Actions and Specific Tax Expenditure Measures: for example, tax relief for low-income taxpayers and an increase in the child care expense deduction for families caring for children with disabilities

Table 2
Early Childhood Development Framework Agreement, 2001–2006

Key Areas of Action	Focus of Supports	Programming Examples
Healthy Pregnancy, Birth and Infancy	Pregnant women New parents Infants Care givers	Prenatal classes and information Infant screening programs
Parenting and Family Supports	Parents/Guardians Care givers	Family Resource Centres Parent Information Home Visiting
Early Childhood Development, Learning and Care	Young children	Child care centres Preschools Developmental programs for young children
Community Supports	Formal Support Systems Informal helping Networks	Community-based planning Service integration Healthy community initiatives

Based on the *First Ministers' Meeting Communiqué on Early Childhood Development* (11 September 2000), http://www.scics.gc.ca/infoo0/800038005_e.html.

NOTES

Lansdowne Professor of Social Policy, University of Victoria.

1 See e.g., Edward Greenspon and Anthony Wilson-Smith, *Double Vision: The Inside Story of the Liberals in Power* (Toronto: Doubleday, 1996); the "Chrétien Legacy" issue of *Policy Options* 21:9 (2000); and Jeffrey Simpson, *The Friendly Dictatorship* (Toronto: McClelland and Stewart, 2001).

2 J. L. Granatstein and Norman Hillmer, *Prime Ministers: Ranking Canada's Leaders* (Toronto: HarperCollins, 1999), 227.

3 Lawrence Martin, *Chrétien, Volume 1: The Will to Win* (Toronto: Lester Publishing, 1995), 376.

4 G. Bruce Doern and Richard W. Phidd, *Canadian Public Policy: Ideas, Structure, Process*, 2d ed. (Scarborough: Nelson, 1992), 120.

5 Thomas S. Axworthy and Howard Aster, eds., *Social Cohesion and the New Liberalism: Perspectives, Policy, and Prospects* (Oakville: Mosaic Press, 2003), 4.

6 Jean Chrétien, *Straight from the Heart* (Toronto: Seal Books, 1986), 211.

7 Ibid., 156.

8 Ibid., 160.

9 R.S.C. 1985, c. C–6.

10 R.S.C. 1985, c. C–1.

11 The five principles set out in the *Canada Health Act*, 1984, are accessibility, comprehensiveness, portability, public administration, and universality. The conditions under the *Canada Assistance Plan Act*, 1966, were that need be the sole basis for determining eligibility for income support, that residency rules were prohibited for receipt of social assistance, that there be an appeals system on social assistance decisions, that the provinces and territories commit to data-reporting and -sharing, and that the federal transfers would go only to supporting nonprofit providers of social services. Under the CHST, like the EPF before it, there are no federal standards for cost-sharing post-secondary education.

12 For details on the origins of the CHST, see Greenspon and Wilson-Smith, *Double Vision*.

13 For further details, see Michael J. Prince, "New Mandate, New Money, New Politics: Federal Budgeting in the Post-Deficit Era," in Leslie A. Pal, ed., *How Ottawa Spends, 1998–99: Balancing Act: The Post-Deficit Mandate* (Don Mills: Cambridge University Press, 1998), 31–56.

14 Quoted in Jane Taber, "PM takes on Martin in speech that touts agenda," *Globe and Mail*, 30 April 2003, A7.

15 For some press commentary, see Susan Riley, "Forget promises, show us the money," *Times Colonist (Victoria)*, 19 February 2003, A14; and Sharon Cordon and Bruce Cheadle, "Chrétien's legacy fulfilled in Manley's first federal budget," *Canadian Press*, 18 February 2003.

16 For further discussion of the range of recent social policy changes, see Michael J. Prince, "The Return of Directed Incrementalism: Innovating Social Policy the Canadian Way," in G. Bruce Doern, ed., *How Ottawa Spends 2002–2003, The Security Aftermath and National Priorities* (Don Mills: Oxford University Press, 2002), 176–95.

17 Allan Tupper, "The Chrétien Governments and Higher Education: A Quiet Revolution in Canadian Public Policy," in G. Bruce Doern, ed., *How Ottawa Spends 2003–2004: Regime Change and Policy Shift* (Toronto: Oxford University Press, 2003), 105–17.

18 Canada, Governor General, *Speech from the Throne* (Ottawa: Minister of Public Works and Government Services, 30 January 2001), http://www.parl.gc.ca/information/about/ process/info/throne/index.asp?lang=E&parl=37&sess=1.

19 Ibid.

20 Ibid.

21 The Government of Québec, while sympathetic to the principles of the National Child Benefit, does not participate, as "it wishes to assume control over income support for the children of Québec." The same applies to the National Children's Agenda. Québec residents benefit from the increased Canada Child Tax Benefit in the same way as other Canadians. "National Child Benefit: Questions and Answers," Social Union website, http://socialunion.gc.ca/ncb/may14qa_e.html.

22 Recall that one of the aims of the National Child Benefit is to ensure that families are better off as a result of working. Thus, the NCB is designed to encourage adults on welfare to seek and accept work by providing child benefits outside of social assistance and offer benefits and services, possibly including earned income supplements and supplementary health benefits, when they take employment.

23 Ken Battle, *Relentless Incrementalism: Deconstructing & Reconciling Canadian Income Security Policy* (Ottawa: Caledon Institute, 2001), 36 [emphasis in original].

24 See e.g., Canadian Council on Social Development (CCSD), "CCSD's Checklist of Key Commitments in the Speech from the Throne" (27 September 2002); and National Council of Welfare, "Clawbacks keep families on welfare in deep poverty," 10 April 2003, http://www.ncwcnbes.net/htmdocument/reportwelfinco2/PressReleaseWI2002_e.htm.

25 Canada, Department of Finance, *Building the Canada We Want: The Budget Speech 2003* (Ottawa: Minister of Public Works and Government Services, 2003), Chapter 4, http://www.fin.gc.ca/budget03/pdf/speeche.pdf [*Budget Speech 2003*].

26 Ibid.

27 Ken Battle, Sherri Torjman, and Michael Mendelson, *The 2003 Budget: Political Legacy Needs Policy Architecture* (Ottawa: Caledon Institute, February 2003), 3. All figures are in constant dollars – that is, inflation-adjusted 2003 dollars.

28 As 2001 Census data show, there has been a significant shift over the past few decades in the redistribution of child benefits to families with the lowest incomes and away from those with the highest incomes. Specifically, "the 10% of families with the lowest incomes received $1,276 on average in child benefits in 1980, while the 10% with the highest incomes received $1,283. In sharp contrast, the 10% of families with the lowest incomes received $2,378 on average in child benefits in 2000. The 10% of families with the highest incomes received only $26." Statistics Canada also suggests that "[a]n important part of redistribution of government transfers to families with lower incomes has been the transition from the 'universal' family allowance to the current income-tested Canada Child Tax Benefit." See Statistics Canada, *Income of Canadian Families*, "Canada," http://www12.statcan.ca/english/census01/Products/Analytic/companion/inc/canada.cfm.

29 Battle, Torjman, and Mendelson, *The 2003 Budget*, 3 [emphasis in original].

30 Canadian Intergovernmental Conference Secretariat, "First Ministers' Meeting Communiqué on Early Childhood Development," (11 September 2000), http://www.scics.gc.ca/cinfo00/800038005_e.html.

31 Norma Greenaway, "Government ready to pay to boost child-care spaces," *Ottawa Citizen*, 14 February 2003, A1; and Margaret Philp, "National daycare plan being hammered out," *Globe and Mail*, 12 December 2002, A4.

32 Not included in this initiative are programs that form part of the public school system. In this and other agreements, the Government of Québec, while supporting the general principles, "did not participate in developing th[e] initiatives because it intends to preserve its sole responsibility on social policy matters. However, Québec receives its share of [such] federal funding and ... is making major investments toward programs for families and children." Federal/Provincial/Territorial Ministers Responsible for Social Services, News Release, "Supporting Canada's Children and Families" (13 March 2003), Social Union website, http://www.socialunion.gc.ca/news/130303_e.htm.

33 *Budget Speech 2003*.

34 Sue Bailey, "Manley delivers more money for working poor," *Times Colonist (Victoria)*, 19 February 2003, A7.

35 CCSD, Communiqué, "A Historic Day for Child Care" (18 February 2003), http://www.ccsd.ca/pr/2003/postbudget.htm.

36 Ibid.

37 Martha Friendly, "Subsidized child care delivers future payoffs," *National Post*, 31 March 2003, FP15.

38 Ibid.

39 Martin, *Chrétien*, 376–7.

40 Alain Noël makes a similar argument in "Power and Purpose in Intergovernmental Relations," *Policy Matters* 2:6 (2001).

41 Part 1 of the *Constitution Act, 1982*, being Schedule B to the *Canada Act 1982* (U.K.), 1982, c. 11.

42 See, for details, Greenspon and Wilson-Smith, *Double Vision*; and Prince, "New Mandate, New Money, New Politics."

43 Battle, *Relentless Incrementalism*, 49. It was only after the federal deficit was eliminated, for example, that the technique of stealth (the partial indexation of benefits and tax rates) was eliminated, in 2000, and full indexation restored.

44 *Budget Speech 2003*.

45 See e.g., Michael J. Prince, "From Health and Welfare to Stealth and Farewell: Federal Social Policy, 1980–2000," in Leslie A. Pal, ed., *How Ottawa Spends 1999–2000: Shape Shifting: Canadian Governance Toward the 21st Century* (Don Mills: Oxford University Press, 1999), 151–91.

46 James J. Rice and Michael J. Prince, *Changing Politics of Canadian Social Policy* (Toronto: University of Toronto Press, 2000).

47 Frances Abele, Russ LaPointe, and Michael J. Prince, "Symbolism, Surfacing, Succession and Substance: Martin's Aboriginal Policy Style," in G. Bruce Doern, ed., *How Ottawa Spends, 2005–2006: Managing the Minority* (Kingston & Montreal: McGill-Queen's University Press, 2005), 99–120.

48 Consider, for example, that Chrétien's 2003 First Ministers' Accord on Health Renewal committed $36.8 billion in federal transfers to the provinces and territories, while Martin's 2004 grandly labeled 10 Year Plan to Strengthen Health Care provided a further $41.3 billion. One could argue this suggests that Chrétien could and should have agreed to a richer transfer package; and one could also argue that Martin was highly motivated to outdo his predecessor on this all-important policy file.

49 James J. Rice and Michael J. Prince, "Martin's Moment: The Social Policy Agenda of a New Prime Minister," in G. Bruce Doern, ed., *How Ottawa*

Spends, 2004–2005: Mandate Change in the Paul Martin Era (Montreal & Kingston: McGill-Queen's University Press, 2004) 111–30.

50 Canada, Department of Finance, *Tax Expenditures and Evaluations 2005* (Ottawa: Minister of Public Works and Government Services, 2005), http://www.fin.gc.ca/toce/2005/taxexp05_pdf.

51 Stephanie Paterson, Karine Levasseur, and Tatyana Teplova, "I Spy with My Little Eye ... Canada's National Child Benefit," in G. Bruce Doern, ed., *How Ottawa Spends, 2004–2005*, 131–50.

52 More specifically, by the end of 2005, the Martin government had signed agreements-in-principle with nine provinces and a final agreement with Québec. For the nine provinces, once they develop action plans, final funding agreements will be determined. Given that Québec has an explicit family policy system in place, the Martin government signed a final agreement with Québec, the first in the country on this initiative. Québec's exclusive authority in the fields of early learning and child care were recognized in this asymmetrical agreement, which was signed not only by social service ministers but also the first ministers. It is also worth remarking that while the Chrétien funds for child care and early learning flow through the Canada Social Transfer, the Martin funds are transferred in a separate and distinct arrangement.

The Chrétien Non-Legacy

The Federal Role in Health Care Ten Years on ... 1993–2003

GERARD W. BOYCHUK

INTRODUCTION

Reform of health care in Canada arguably marks the greatest missed opportunity for the Chrétien government to leave a lasting legacy – a failure ironically tied to Chrétien's greatest legacy, the fiscal record of his government. While his success in addressing budgetary deficits is indisputable, this victory, to some, may seem pyrrhic. Health care was an area where the federal government faced important challenges and seems to have had considerable scope to respond successfully to these challenges. However, under the Chrétien Liberals' watch, an aura of crisis has come to envelope the system and public support for central aspects of the health care system now appear seriously frayed. Chrétien's Health Care Renewal Accord of February 2003 did little to reverse the limited record of achievement in this field. Overall, the Chrétien government left little in terms of a significant enduring legacy in the area of health care.

THE FEDERAL ROLE IN HEALTH CARE

The federal role in health care is, of course, constrained by the limits of its constitutional grant of power in this field. Provinces are granted the preponderance of jurisdictional authority for health care by virtue of section 92 of the *Constitution Act, 1867*,[1] and the central government has little constitutional jurisdictional authority over the direct provision of health care services. However, the federal government has involved itself in the provision of health care primarily through the use of the federal spending power which allows it to make transfers to the provinces attaching whatever conditions the federal government wishes so long as it does not undertake to legislate directly within a field of provincial jurisdiction.

This power has provided the basis for the main federal role in health care – fiscal transfers to the provinces for health governed by the *Canada Health Act* (CHA).[2] There are five federally defined standards comprising the core of the CHA which is the legislative basis for the Canadian health care system: public administration (each provincial plan must be run by a non-profit, public authority accountable to the provincial government); comprehensiveness (provinces must provide coverage for all necessary physician and hospital services); universality (insured services must be universally available to all residents of the province under uniform terms and conditions, with waiting periods for new entrants being limited to a maximum of three months); portability (each provincial plan must be portable so that eligible residents are covered while they are temporarily out of the province); and accessibility (reasonable access to insured services is not to be impaired by charges or other mechanisms, and reasonable compensation must be made to physicians for providing insured services). As a result of the CHA, public intervention in health care provision in Canada is not limited to the public *provision* of hospital and physician care insurance but also the effective legislative *proscription* of the private provision of insurance for services that are covered under the public plan.

However, even this aspect of public health provision has been called into question with the Supreme Court ruling in *Chaoulli v. Quebec*[3] that such proscriptions in Québec violated the Québec Charter of Rights. The Québec proscriptions on private insurance were not found to vilate the Chanadian Charter of Rights and Freedoms, although the Court was evenly split with one justice abstaining from ruling on this issue. This raises the spectre of future challenges to such proscriptions in the remaining provinces on the basis on Charter rights infringements.

Federal achievements must be judged in light of Ottawa's limited constitutional role in health care. While the Chrétien government itself repeatedly promised to use the powers it did have at its disposal to address the challenges facing health care in Canada, it seems difficult to conclude that it has come close to achieving the best it could. Rather, the driving principle underpinning federal action in the health care field appears to have been calculated political gain – either *vis-à-vis* the prov-

inces or electorally – as opposed to a principled commitment to strengthening health care in Canada. The result has been the failure to leave a
lasting legacy in this policy area.

FEDERAL REFORM – PROMISES AND EFFORTS

Health care was a major plank in each of the three election campaigns
waged by the Chrétien Liberals. The Chrétien government emerged from
both the 1997 and 2000 elections with what could reasonably be interpreted as a mandate to undertake health care reform. In both cases, such
efforts were not immediately forthcoming. While the Liberals commissioned three major multi-year, multi-million dollar health care studies
under Chrétien, serious efforts at reform were less in evidence – a hastily
abandoned "plan to save medicare" in early 2000, the Health Accord of
September 2000, and the Health Care Renewal Accord of 2003.

RED BOOK 1993, THE NATIONAL FORUM ON
HEALTH, AND RED BOOK 1997

The Liberal Red Book 1993 raised the spectre of the increasing vulnerability of the Canadian health care system and attributed some of the
immediate pressure on health care to the Conservative government
"steadily withdraw[ing] from health care funding, thus passing costs
onto the provinces."[4] The Red Book 1993 outlined the "unwavering"
Liberal commitment to the five principles of medicare. Furthermore, it
committed a future Liberal government to "the continuing role, in
financing and in other aspects, of the federal government in health care,"
starkly declaring that "[a] Liberal government will not withdraw from or
abandon the health care field."[5] Finally, the Red Book 1993 committed a
Liberal government to establishing a National Forum on Health to
undertake "a thorough study of the health of Canadians and of our
health care system."[6] Struck just under a year later, in October 1994, the
National Forum on Health (NFH) was given a budget of $12 million and
four years to study the Canadian health care system.

In early 1995, the federal health care bomb was dropped. Without
prior consultation with the provinces, the federal government announced
in the 1995 budget that it would be shifting transfers for health care from
their existing basis under Established Programs Financing (EPF) to a new
Canada Health and Social Transfer (CHST). The shift to the CHST marked
a reduction of transfers of $2.5 billion in 1996–1997 and $4.5 billion in

1997–1998. Many observers wondered how the principles of the CHA could be enforced as the cash component of the CHST dwindled.

At the same time, the federal government engaged in a number of skirmishes with the provinces over violations of the CHA including user fees and extra-billing.[7] The federal government penalized British Columbia in early 1994 for allowing extra-billing by physicians. In late 1995, the federal government began levying penalties against Alberta for allowing private clinics to charge facility fees, with the province recanting six months later. Thus, the federal government did face serious and consistent challenges to its stance on health care – an uncompromising adherence to the tenets of the CHA. Had the federal government been less tenacious in its defence of the CHA, it seems likely that the implementation of user fees and extra-billing would likely have been widespread.

By the time it reported, the NFH itself noted the context of increasing public concern about health care and fundamental concerns about the long-term survival of medicare.[8] Itself more optimistic, the report was predicated on three central, clearly enunciated beliefs: "that the health care system is fundamentally sound"; "that in Canada we spend enough money on health care"; and that "the health care system can be improved."[9]

For the NFH what "really matters" in the bigger picture of health is health promotion including particular attention placed on the social and economic determinants of health especially the "impact of poverty, unemployment, and cuts in social supports on the health of individuals, groups and communities."[10] The NFH recommended maintaining the key features of the Canadian health care system including full public funding for medically necessary services, maintaining the single-payer model, and supporting the five principles of the CHA. This would require, according to the NFH, "a significant and ongoing financial contribution through federal transfers" which "must be stable and predictable over time."[11] In the area of primary care, the NFH recommended a "realignment of funding to patients, not services" and "a remuneration method that is not based on the volume of service provided by physicians but promotes a continuum of preventive and treatment services and the use of multidisciplinary teams of providers."[12] In addition, the NFH recommended building a more integrated system by extending universal public insurance coverage to homecare (including post-acute, chronic and palliative care) and universal first dollar coverage for pharmaceuticals.[13] Finally, the NFH recommended the "creation of an evidence-based health system, built on the foundation of a nationwide health information system."[14] At its broadest, this prescription would become the template for future reports which could be argued to provide minor variations on this basic theme (see Appendix).

The Red Book 1997 echoed the NFH recommendation that changes in funding were most urgently required in the areas of primary care, home care, and prescription drugs.[15] The Red Book 1997 committed a new federal government, among other things, to establish a Medicare Transition Fund encouraging provinces to test approaches to reforming primary care, to support the shift to home care, and, more significantly, to develop a "a timetable and fiscal framework for the implementation of universal public coverage for medically necessary prescription drugs."[16] However, it would be eighteen months after the election before significant further federal action – action which would still fall considerably short of the Liberals' major election promises.

THE FEDERAL-PROVINCIAL HEALTH ACCORD, 2000 AND ELECTION 2000

Federal initiatives in the early part of the Chrétien Liberals' second term were largely limited to re-injecting cash and reinforcing the federal-provincial commitment to the principles of the CHA. More fundamental reform was embodied in the federal "plan to save medicare" in early 2000. However, in the face of provincial resistance and mounting electoral pressures requiring that the federal government secure some kind of deal on health care, the federal government abandoned efforts at more significant reform and returned to the formula of a major injection of federal cash in return for a relatively vague provincial commitment to "strengthening and renewing Canada's publicly funded health care services."[17]

The Social Union Framework Agreement

In the Social Union Framework Agreement (SUFA) of February 1999 struck between the federal government and the provincial/territorial governments (with the exception of Québec), the latter committed, as part of a much larger package, to respecting the five principles of medicare.[18] The federal government agreed to limitations on the federal spending power and increased the cash component of the CHST by $11.5 billion – an increase that was earmarked for health.[19] Provincial governments, in turn, provided assurances that they would spend the increased transfers on health care. As part of the initiative, the 1999 federal "health" budget also set aside $1.4 billion for various other health initiatives including funding for developing systems of health information, enriched funding for the Canadian Institute of Health Information (established in 1994), establishing the Canadian Institute of Health Research, and promoting research. The agreement provided enriched funding but little substantive change – in stark contrast to the recommendations of the NFR and the Red Book 1997.

The "Plan to Save Medicare"

Less than a year later, federal Minister of Health Allan Rock announced a new plan to "save" Canada's health care system in January 2000. The plan included a major new matching cost-sharing initiative for home care, reform of primary care, and the implementation of national standards for the delivery of health services.[20] A major program initiative was not surprising given the federal government's fortunate fiscal position and the fact that public opinion polling suggested that homecare enjoyed very strong public support.[21] However, Rock's plan was reported in the national media to have been greeted with "scorn" from various provinces.[22] By July 2000, the home care plan was officially dead.[23] The failure of the plan was rooted in the politics of the CHST. Past cuts had placed the federal government on tenuous ground in resisting provincial claims that reinvestment in health care should automatically be channeled into restoring transfers. Virtually all provinces, even those that supported the plan, agreed that Ottawa would first have to restore CHST funding. However, restoring CHST funding would have provided little in the way of political visibility for the federal government.[24]

The Health Accord, September 2000

As the spectre of an election loomed, the federal Liberals were increasingly pinched between the electoral pressure to do something about health care and their own inability to manoeuvre given the demands of the provinces. In September 2000, the federal and provincial governments reached an agreement on funding for health care providing an increase of $23.4 billion over five years, including a $21.1 billion increase to the CHST, $1 billion of transfers to the provinces for the purchase of diagnostic equipment (including MRI machines and CAT scanners), $500 million to develop information technology, and $800 million of transfers for primary care reform.[25] The Accord included a statement of support for the principles of the CHA as well as commitments to share information, report to Canadians on "health status, health outcomes, and the performance of publicly funded health services," invest in home care and community care, and work together to develop common strategies regarding pharmaceutical assessment.[26]

Rather than being seen as a shift in the federal approach to intergovernmental relations, some observers argued that the Accord was best seen as a "one-off agreement keyed to the 2000 federal election campaign.[27] Despite having had bolder plans, the federal plan to save medicare and introduce home care was, in the end, reduced largely to an initiative to partially restore CHST transfers driven primarily by the immediate imperatives of the pending election: "The federal government simply gave the provinces a pile of new money, with a nod to some renewal, without trying to extend a base of coverage for home care to all Canadians."[28]

The federal government had enjoyed certain successes – albeit only in much more limited initiatives which, while both important and innovative, did not provide the type of political pay off of big-ticket program reform such as a national home care or pharmacare program. The Health Transition Fund established in the 1997 budget was designed to support pilot and evaluation projects in areas identified collaboratively by both levels of government. In June 2000, the federal government launched the Canadian Institutes for Health Research (CIHR), which was announced in the 1999 budget and replaced the Medical Research Council of Canada.[29] The CIHR initiative doubled the research budget over three years and created a series of virtual institutes which would link researchers in new and innovative ways across different areas of health research. However, these initiatives did not have the political visibility of a federal plan to save medicare through major new programs.

The Liberal Red Book 2000

The Health Accord and the brief entente with the provinces which it signaled contributed significantly to the federal Liberals' ability to undercut any immediate electoral threat from other parties on the issue of health. The Red Book 2000 committed the Liberal government to protecting against two-tier health care and implementing the Health Action Plan, 2000, endorsed by the first ministers in September of 2000.[30] Armed with both an "action plan" and electoral endorsement which could be interpreted as a mandate to proceed with health care reform, the federal government appeared poised to aggressively pursue health care reform.[31] Despite this, less than five months later, the Chrétien Liberals announced an eighteenth-month hiatus in its health care reform efforts with the striking of the Royal Commission on the Future of Health Care in Canada – the Romanow Commission.

THE KIRBY COMMITTEE AND THE ROMANOW COMMISSION

Just a year before, federal health minister Allan Rock had stated unequivocally, "we've had enough studies, we've had enough reports, we've had enough commissions. We're now at the stage where by working together we can move from recommendation to action."[32] Not surprisingly, after the announcement of the Romanow Commission, with a budget of $15 million and eighteen months to report, the Chrétien government faced tough questioning in Question Period: "Why on earth by creating this commission is the government making official its immobility for at least 18 months?[33] This was especially the case as the appointment of the commission took place just months before the Senate Committee on Social Affairs, Science and Technology under the chair of Michael Kirby, which had been studying the health care system since December 1999, was to release its interim report on issues and options. Certainly, the timing of the Commission appointment had the benefit of providing the Chrétien government with both time as well as solid ground from which to rebuff provincial demands for enriched transfers. The Chrétien government argued, as it had argued earlier with regard to the National Forum on Health, that the reports of the Kirby Committee in October 2002 and the Romanow Commission in late 2002 would mark the point at which health care reform would be undertaken in earnest.

The final reports of the Kirby Committee and Romanow Commission were considerably more similar than many observers originally anticipated.[34] Broadly, the basic formula of both sets of recommendations was to maintain federal transfers to the provinces for provincially-provided health services (under some variant of the CHST), which would continue to be governed by principles enshrined in federal legislation. Neither report suggests any major change to the national principles of medicare, as enshrined in the CHA. While the Kirby Report recommended that the CHA be left completely unchanged, the Romanow Report suggested adding a new principle (provincial accountability), as well as expanding the

CHA to include diagnostic services and priority home care services (see Appendix).[35] Both recommended the establishment of a broader national philosophic framework for health care. In the Kirby Report, this would take the form of federal enforcement of a national health care guarantee (guaranteeing timely access to health care) through federal- provincial agreement, or, if not, through federal legislation with financial penalties similar to those of the CHA. The Romanow Commission recommended the establishment of a "Canadian Health Covenant," which would symbolically outline the rights and responsibilities of citizens in health care provision, as well as those of both levels of governments. Finally, both recommend a set of new, more limited federal-provincial programs targeted to specific issue areas – with a two-year period of transition in the case of Romanow. In both cases these would include, for example, catastrophic drug coverage and specific forms of home care.[36]

The reports reflect a relatively similar view of the appropriate federal and provincial roles in health care: "Both recommend highly centralized solutions with federal cash attached by strings designed to 'buy change'."[37] Both, in fact, use this very language. In order to "buy change," both reports recommend shoring up federal transfers. The Kirby Report recommends shifting the basis for existing federal health funding under the CHST to an earmarked tax comprised of a stipulated proportion of the Goods and Services Tax (GST) in order to insulate federal transfers from the caprice of federal budgetary politics while still maintaining leverage to enforce national principles such as those enshrined in the CHA. For its part, the Romanow Commission proposed that the health portion of the CHST be enriched, converted to a dedicated cash-only transfer, and modified to include the requirement that an escalator be negotiated and then established for five-year periods.[38] Both reports recommended that the federal government use funding to leverage specific federally identified models of health care delivery in areas primarily falling under provincial responsibility, including, for example, hospital remuneration, organization of health authorities, and primary health care delivery. In order to achieve these innovations, both reports recommend new programs for federal-provincial matching conditional cost-sharing, including programs for catastrophic drug coverage, some aspects of home care, and primary care reform, although Romanow recommended that these be time-limited.

The reactions to the reports were, for the most part, predictable. Provinces complained that spending for new programs should come after increased funding for more pressing needs, that cost-shared programs would divert cash from other crucial areas, and that, in some case, the priorities identified by the reports did not adequately represent the specific challenges faced by individual provinces. Provincial reactions provide little evidence that the release of the reports did anything to shift the provinces away from a business-as-usual approach to federal-provincial wrangling.

The political dynamics generated by the reports made it basically impossible for the Chrétien government not to act and make some increased commitment, even if a limited one, to health care funding. Secondly, the insistence in both reports that the federal government use increased funding to "buy change" generated expectations that it would do something beyond simply enriching existing unconditional transfers. At the same time, the clock was ticking down on Chrétien's tenure. A new, more accommodative stance had been signaled by the federal government in its proposal, formally agreed to in April 2002, for a CHA dispute resolution mechanism by which either government could refer an issue to a third-party panel. At the initial meeting of federal and provincial ministers of health after the reports were tabled, "it was clear the feds were signaling sympathy for provincial concerns."[39] This relatively accommodating federal stance was argued by some observers to be "proof that Ottawa truly wants a deal."[40]

THE HEALTH CARE RENEWAL ACCORD, 2003 AND THE CANADA HEALTH TRANSFER

In February, the first ministers announced the Health Care Renewal Accord, 2003 which marked the second major intergovernmental health accord in two-and-a-half years and the third in four years. The Accord committed the federal government to increasing federal support for health by $17.3 billion dollars over the first three years rising to $34.8 billion over five years.[41]

The Health Care Renewal Accord, 2003, draws heavily on the Health Accord, 2000. The broad philosophical underpinning of the Accord is a restatement of the five principles of the CHA with a renewed focus (also emphasized in the Health Accord, 2000) on timeliness of access, quality of services, and sustainability of the system. While the Accord commits government to many of same principles as outlined in the Health Accord, 2000, in many cases, the specific commitments are more clearly laid out and targets are set including a more specific commitment to the provision of access (24/7) and home care as well as a commitment to catastrophic drug coverage that was not part of the 2000 agreement. The main contribution of the 2003 agreement is to establish the five-year Health Reform Fund (block transfers for health reform in any of the three priority areas – primary health care, home care, and catastrophic drug coverage) which, after five years, would be integrated into the general transfer for health. The second major change is to rename the health proportion of CHST as the Canada Health Transfers (CHT) creating a nominally dedicated health care transfer. However, the structure of the transfer would not be changed and would include both cash and tax point transfers, nor would it include a fixed escalator.

The clearest example of fleshing out the specifics of the more general commitments undertaken in the 2000 Accord is in the area of performance indicators. The indicators, which were outlined in relative detail in the 2000 Accord, are detailed in specifics in Annex A of the Accord, 2003, despite the fact that one might expect that this level of detail would be left to health ministers as opposed to detailed in a first ministers' agreement. The commitment in the two accords to reporting to Canadians and the specific manner in which this is detailed may turn out to be one of the most significant achievements. Such reporting may ultimately contribute, over the long term, to increased public pressure for more substantive reforms.

Not surprisingly, the Accord delivers on some of the recommendations outlined by the three commissions over the past decade and fails to deliver on others (see Appendix). The Accord achieves the goal of a dedicated health transfer but fails to restructure the transfers (by failing to remove tax point transfers as recommended by the Romanow Commission) or to structure the transfer such that future increases are not determined unilaterally by the federal government (as recommended by both the Kirby Report and Romanow Commission). The transition funding provided in the Accord, which allows provinces to spend funds within the broad areas of primary health care reform, home care, and catastrophic drug coverage, is less highly targeted or conditional than the suggestions in either the Romanow or Kirby reports. In this sense, the Accord falters in gearing new spending to "buying change." Issues central to primary health care provision, including physician and hospital remuneration, remain largely outside the purview of the agreement. The commitment to provide first dollar coverage for short-term home care at some minimum level to be determined by health ministers, and to "take measures to ensure reasonable access to catastrophic drug coverage" are a movement in the general direction proposed by both Kirby, Romanow, and, to a lesser degree, the NFH in this area. However, at the same time, neither does this represent a commitment to establish a national home care or catastrophic drug coverage plan. Finally, the Accord stipulates that the Health Council report through health ministers as opposed to directly to Canadians (as suggested by all three reports) and leaves the reporting of performance indicators to individual provincial governments.

The Health Care Renewal Accord did not mark a significant resolution of the challenges facing health care provision in Canada over the Chrétien term. Initially, various aspects of the Accord such as the creation of a Health Council were implemented only haltingly. In the 2004 elections, it was the Conservative Party, ironically, that campaigned on the basis that the 2003 Accord should be put fully into effect while the Liberal Party under Paul Martin argued that a new agreement to fix health care for a generation was required. A new agreement, superseding the 2003 Accord, was reached in September 2004.[42]

ASSESSING THE LEGACY

Of course, the Chrétien Liberals also had a number of important achievements in the field of health. In its first term, the Chrétien government vigorously defended the principles of the CHA against pressures from the provinces. The supporters of those principles may see the Chrétien legacy as shepherding the Canadian health care system through a decade of serious fiscal restraint relatively intact. As outlined above, there have also been a number of improvements especially in the area of health information and research, including the creation of CIHI; the Health Transition Fund; CIHR; the specific reporting commitments outlined in the Health Accord, 2000; and Health Care Renewal Accord, 2003. The contributions of the NFH, Kirby Committee, and Romanow Commission to a broader understanding of the health care system and the challenges it faces are, in fact, a significant achievement in and of themselves. Finally, the agreement on a CHA dispute resolution mechanism seemed to herald a turn towards more constructive relations in this area.

However, these achievements must be weighed relative to the federal role in contributing to the pressures on the health care system – especially financial ones. Real (constant dollar) per capita federal cash transfers declined significantly in the mid–1990s. While they increased in the late 1990s and early 2000s, they did not reach real per capita 1993 levels until well after Chrétien's tenure of office (see Figure 1). The cumulative

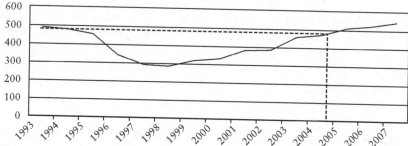

Figure 1
Federal Cash Transfers for Health, 1993–2007
Sources and Notes
Federal cash transfers for health from 1993 to 2003–2004 are calculated as 62 percent of actual CHST cash transfers (using the Department of Finance estimate of the proportion of GST going to health). Federal cash transfers for health after 2004 are comprised of the cash component of the Canada Health Transfer (CHT).

Transfers per capita were calculated by the author using population data from CANSIM I Matrix 00001. Adjustment of transfers per capita to constant dollars (2003) was calculated by the author using CANSIM I Series P100000 and CANSIM II Series V735319. Constant dollars for 2004–2007 are estimated using the three-year average CPI increase for 2000–2003. Population figures for 2004–2007 are estimated from Statistics Canada population projections, CANSIM II, Table 052–0001.

federal shortfall in cash transfers over time (in comparison to what the federal cash contribution would have been if maintained at 1993 levels) by the time Chrétien left office was over $26 billion in 2003 dollars.

Three crucial effects were generated partly as a result of federal transfer restraint. The first is the illusion of health care as a rapidly growing fiscal burden relative to the ability of governments, as a whole, to bear this burden. Public health care expenditures did not constitute a higher proportion of GDP by the end of the Chrétien era than they did at the outset. Yet, as a result of federal transfer restraint, provincial health care expenditures have been increasing significantly as a proportion of provincial expenditure budgets. Provincial governments now make a compelling case that public health care as it currently exists is no longer affordable. Secondly, in part as a result of federal transfer retrenchment, the federal government's fiscal position is disproportionately bright relative to the provinces. The situation in which surpluses are held at the federal level (which has limited direct involvement in the delivery of health care services) and deficits or near deficits are held at the provincial level of government (whose most important single program responsibility is health care) contributes to the political construction of a strong linkage between health care and the issue of debts and deficits. Finally, provinces face limited incentives to forcefully combat public perceptions regarding the declining quality of health care and, rather, leverage their demands for greater federal funding by allowing such perceptions to flourish. Provinces also have an incentive to focus on a lack of financial resources as an explanation for problems in the health care system. This provincial approach has culminated – somewhat predictably – in claims that the current public health care system is unsustainable.[43] These dynamics have contributed to relatively stable and well-documented trends in public opinion including the increasing perception that the health care system is in crisis, declining perceptions regarding the quality of health care provision, and declining public confidence in the health care system.[44] Overall public perceptions of the health care system are increasingly frayed and there is growing public frustration with the leadership of both levels of government in this policy field.[45]

CONCLUSION

The Chrétien government failed to deliver on its oft-repeated promises of major reform of health care. This failure must be judged in the context of the difficult – often intractable – problems facing health care in Canada and the limited federal role in this field. To be fair, the Chrétien government relatively vigorously defended the principles of the CHA, and perhaps its greatest legacy in the health care field is to have largely preserved the status quo in the face of significant pressures to back away from those principles.

At the same time, the Chrétien government contributed to the aggrandizement of health care to a pre-eminent position in federal-provincial relations. This development raises concerns regarding the deflection of attention at the most senior levels of federal-provincial interaction from the overall management of the federation to the nitty-gritty of a specific policy field. Agreements such as the 2003 Health Care Renewal Accord ought to reasonably raise the question of why relatively mundane issues in a specific policy field warrant the attention of first ministers. It highlights the radical politicization of health care as both as an electoral and intergovernmental issue. There is little evidence to suggest that this development will be beneficial in terms of the quality of health care provided in Canada.

Over its decade in power, the Chrétien government had limited impact in the health care field. For advocates of bolder reform on both sides of the health care debate, this modest legacy is likely to be seen, in the broader historical context, as no legacy at all.

APPENDIX

	National Forum on Health	Kirby Committee	Romanow Commission	Health Accord, 2000	Health Care Renewal Accord, 2003
Canada Health Act	Leave unchanged	Leave unchanged		Leaves unchanged	Leaves unchanged
Statement of Values	No formal recommendation	Enforceable health care guarantee	Expand to include "accountability" Canadian Health Covenant (unenforceable) outlining responsibilities and entitlements of governments, individual Canadians and health care providers	Outlines "covenant" – responsibilities of governments (unenforceable)	Outlines commitments of governments (unenforceable)
Funding — Long-term	Stabilize funding – no specific recommendation re: transfer mechanism	Stabilize federal transfers by earmarking a tax source; CHST (slightly amended)[1] to remain as transfer mechanism	Stabilize funding through dedicated cash-only transfer	Funding increase – structure of CHST funding left unchanged	Funding increase and shift to dedicated health transfer – structure (tax points and cash, no fixed escalator) left unchanged
Funding — Transition	Multi-year transition fund to support evidence-based innovation in primary care reform	Earmarked Fund for Health Care (permanent)	Two year targeted funding for rural and remote access, diagnostic services, primary health care, home care, catastrophic drug coverage	Targeted funding for diagnostic equipment ($1B), primary health care reform ($.8B), and development of information technology ($.5B)	Health Reform Fund ($16B over 5 years) – not targeted except generally to primary care reform, home care and catastrophic drug coverage -diagnostic and medical equipment ($1.5B) -electronic health records/telehealth ($.6B)

Appendix (cont'd.)

Primary Health Care					
Physician Remuneration	Fund patients not services, move from fee for service	Adopt alternative to fee for service – either capitation or blended formula	Fee for service as obstacle, encourages movement away from fee for service but does not recommend a specific alternative approach	N/A	N/A
Primary Health Care Delivery	Promote prevention and use of multi-disciplinary teams	Promote use of multidisciplinary teams	Promote use of multidisciplinary teams	Stated commitment (no specifics) to promote use of multidisciplinary teams	Stated commitment (no specifics) to promote use of multi-disciplinary teams commitment to 24/7 access to "appropriate" health care provider within 8 years
Hospitals	No specific recommen-dation	Replace global funding with fee for service funding for hospitals	No specific recom-mendation	N/A	N/A
Public Health Insurance Coverage	Expand to home care and pharmacare (e.g. full public funding)	National home care and catastrophic drug coverage plan	National home care and catastrophic drug coverage plan	Commitment by provinces to a "strengthened investment" in home care (to be determined by individual provinces)	Commitment to first dollar coverage for short-term (acute and palliative) home care – minimum service level to be determined by health ministers (Sept 2003) Commitment to "take measures to ensure reasonable access to catastrophic drug coverage" by 2005/06

Appendix (cont'd.)

Information	Promote evidence-based decision-making through National Health Information System	National Health Care Council and National Health Care Commission	Promote evidence-based decision-making through Health Council of Canada	Commitment to "strengthen" Canada-wide health infostructure	Health Council to monitor implementation of Accord reporting through Ministers of Health
Institutional Infrastructure	Promote evidence-based decision-making through National Health Information System	National Health Care Council and National Health Care Commission	Promote evidence-based decision-making through Health Council of Canada	Commitment to "strengthen" Canada-wide health infostructure	Health Council to monitor implementation of Accord reporting through Ministers of Health
Reporting and Accountability	National Population Health Institute	As above	As above	Reporting undertaken by each government using jointly agreed comparable indicators	Reporting undertaken by each government using jointly agreed comparable indicators
Patient Information	N/A	Establish personal electronic health records	Establish personal electronic health records	Develop personal electronic health records	Commitment to "place priority" on implementation of personal electronic health records Increased support for Canada Health Infoway

1 Rather than being on a per capita basis, provincial share determination would include weighting for percent of the population over 70. Vol. 6, 294.

NOTES

Associate Professor, Department of Political Science, University of Waterloo.

1 (U.K.), 30 & 31 Vict., c. 3, reprinted in R.S.C. 1985, App. II, No. 5.

2 R.S.C. 1985, c. C–6. The federal government plays a role in five aspects of health care: the financing of health services provided by the provinces, research and evaluation, the provision of health infrastructure, the promotion of health in the population, and the direct provision of health services to specific population groups such as armed forces personnel and Aboriginals on reserves in remote locations.

3 *Chaoulli v. Quebec (Attorney General)*, [2005] 1 S.C.R. 791, 2005 SCC 35, http://www.lexum.umontreal.ca/csc-scc/en/pub/2005/vol1/html/2005scr1_0791.html.

4 Liberal Party of Canada (LPC), *Creating Opportunity: The Liberal Plan for Canada* (Ottawa: LPC, 1993), 80 [Red Book 1993].

5 Ibid., 77.

6 Ibid., 81.

7 For a good overview, see Joan Price Boase, "Federalism and the Health Facility Fee Challenge," in Duane Adams, ed., *Federalism, Democracy, and Health Policy in Canada*, (Montreal & Kingston: McGill-Queen's University Press, 2001), 179–206.

8 National Forum on Health, *Canada Health Action: Building on the Legacy, The Final Report of the National Forum on Health* (Ottawa: National Forum on Health, 1997), 9.

9 Ibid., 11–12.

10 Ibid., 14.

11 Ibid., 21.

12 Ibid., 23.

13 Ibid., 11–12.

14 Ibid., 28.

15 LPC, *Securing Our Future Together: Preparing Canada for the 21st Century* (Ottawa: LPC, 1997), 72 [Red Book 1997].

16 Ibid., 75.

17 Canadian Intergovernmental Conference Secretariat (CICS), *First Ministers Meeting: Communiqué on Health*, News Release, 11 September 2000, http://www.scics.gc.ca/cinfo00/800038004_e.html.

18 For an overview of SUFA and subsequent federal-provincial agreements to early 2001, see Duane Adams, "Canadian Federalism and the Development of

National Health Goals and Objectives," in Adams, *Federalism, Democracy, and Health Policy*, 61–105.

19 Canada, Department of Finance, *Strengthening Health Care for Canadians* (Ottawa: Finance Canada, 1999), 7.

20 Camille Bains, "Provinces greet new federal health care proposals with cynicism," *Canadian Press Newswire*, 27 January 2000.

21 It has been reported that 80 percent of Canadians "believe that home care should be a free, universal health care program" and that 83 percent "felt public coverage for prescription drugs should be expanded (up from 73% in 1998)." See PricewaterhouseCoopers, *Health Insider* (Toronto: PricewaterhouseCoopers, 2000), 3.

22 Anne McIlroy, "Scorn greets Rock's health plan: Ontario and Quebec say Ottawa's cutbacks caused the problems," *Globe and Mail*, 28 January 2000, A1.

23 Anne McIlroy, "Liberals dump homecare plan in try for deal: billions at stake as health ministers begin meeting to address Canada's ailing system," *Globe and Mail*, 19 July 2000, A4.

24 For an elaboration of this argument, see Gerard W. Boychuk, "Federal Spending in Health...Why Here? Why Now?" in G. Bruce Doern, ed., *How Ottawa Spends, 2002–2003: The Security Aftermath and National Priorities* (Don Mills: Oxford University Press, 2002), 121–36 .

25 Canada, Department of Finance, *Economic Statement and Budget Update 2000* (Ottawa: Minister of Public Works and Government Services, 18 October 2000), http://www.fin.gc.ca/ec2000/pdf/ecooe.pdf.

26 CICS, *First Ministers Meeting*.

27 Roger Gibbins, "Shifting Sands: Exploring the Political Foundations of SUFA," *Policy Matters* 2:3 (2001), 9, http://www.irpp.org/pm/archive/pmvol2no3.pdf.

28 Terrence Sullivan and Patricia M. Baranek, *First Do No Harm: Making Sense of Canadian Health Reform* (Vancouver: University of British Columbia Press, 2002), 35.

29 Health Canada, "Health Minister launches Canadian Institutes of Health Research," News Release, 7 June 2000, http://www.hc-sc.gc.ca/ahc-asc/media/nr-cp/2000/2000_chir-irsc_e.html.

30 LPC, *Opportunity for All: The Liberal Plan for the Future of Canada* (Ottawa: LPC, 2000), 15 [Red Book 2000].

31 Gibbins, "Shifting Sands," 9.

32 Allan Rock, "Canada's Health Care System" (Speech delivered to the University of Calgary, Faculty of Medicine, Calgary, March 2000).

33 *House of Commons Debates*, 045 (6 April 2001), 2912 (André Bachand).

34 Jeffrey Simpson, "Proud parents of health-report twins," *Globe and Mail*, 3 December 2002, A25. See Standing Senate Committee on Social Affairs, Science and Technology, *Highlights, Volume Six: Recommendations for Reform, Final Report on the State of the Health System in Canada* (Ottawa, October 2002) (M. Kirby), 24 [Kirby Report]; and Royal Commission on the Future of Health Care in Canada, *Building on Values: The Future of Health Care in Canada, Final Report* (Ottawa, November 2002) (Roy J. Romanow) [Romanow Report].

35 Romanow Report, xxiv.

36 The Kirby Report also recommended increased federal investment in a number of areas more clearly within the federal ambit, including health care technology, human resource development, health promotion, and disease prevention. The Romanow approach was to recommend matching conditional cost-sharing to achieve these various objectives under the rubric of various transitional funds: Rural and Remote Access Fund, Diagnostic Services Fund, and Primary Health Care Transfer. See Romanow Report, 71–2.

37 Simpson, "Proud parents."

38 Romanow Report, xxv.

39 John Ibbotson, "Why Roy will sing the blues," *Globe and Mail*, 7 December 2002.

40 Ibid.

41 Health Canada, "First Ministers Agree on 2003 First Ministers' Accord on Health Care Renewal," http://www.hc-sc.gc.ca/hcs-sss/delivery-prestation/fptcollab/2003accord/nr-cp_e.html.

42 For an overview, see Gerard W. Boychuk, "How Ottawa Gambles: Rolling the Dice and the Politics of Health Care Reform in 2004" in G. Bruce Doern, ed. *How Ottawa Spends, 2005–2006: Mandate Change in the Paul Martin Era* (Kingston: McGill-Queen's University Press, 2005), 41–58.

43 See e.g., The Mazankowski Report, which was couched precisely in this language. Alberta, Premier's Advisory Council on Health for Albertans, *A Framework for Reform: A Report of the Premier's Advisory Council on Health for Albertans* (Edmonton, December 2001) (D. Mazankowski).

44 For overviews of public perceptions of the Canadian health care systems, see Health Care in Canada (HCIC), *Health Care in Canada Survey 2001: A National Survey of Health Care Providers, Managers and the Public* (HCIC, 2001); Matthew Mendelsohn, *Canadians' Thoughts on Their Health Care System: Preserving the Canadian Model Through Innovation* (Commission on the Future of Health Care in Canada, June 2002); and Stephen Vail, *Canadians' Values and Attitudes on Canada's Health Care System: A Synthesis of Survey Results* (Ottawa: Conference Board of Canada, 2001).

45 For an interpretation linking these public opinion trends to the politics of
federal provincial relations see Gerard W. Boychuk, *The Changing Political
and Economic Environment of Health Care in Canada*, Discussion Paper No.
1 (Commission on the Future of Health Care in Canada, July 2002); and
Gerard W. Boychuk, "The Changing Economic and Political Environment," in
Greg Marchildon, ed., *Health Care in Canada: Fiscal Issues* (Toronto: University of Toronto Press, 2004), 320–9.

12

The Devil's in the Detail

The Chrétien Legacy for the Third Sector

KATHY L. BROCK

INTRODUCTION

When the Liberals won a resounding victory in the 1993 federal election, the quality and nature of Canadian democracy was undergoing a transformation. Both governments and public interest organizations were caught in this process as antagonists and victims. On the one side, the Mulroney government had entered office in 1984 promising open government, but by 1993 had become distrustful of public interest groups, denouncing them as "special interests" after the Meech Lake and Charlottetown constitutional failures and the budget wars of the 1980s and 1990s. The government perception was that these organizations were advancing policy agendas that conflicted with the general public interest. On the other side, public interest groups castigated the Mulroney government as unresponsive to citizen needs and elitist. At the same time, the public was becoming increasingly skeptical of both government and public interest groups, demanding more accountability and transparency and questioning their ability to serve the public needs in an efficient and effective manner. Public trust was reaching new lows.

The public criticism of government and public interest organizations reflected the increasingly complex relationship between the two sectors. In the area of policy implementation and service delivery, the two sectors had become increasingly intertwined. As government had largely divested itself of program delivery in an effort to streamline and rationalize government, public interest organizations had assumed new functions as joint partners or independent agencies in service delivery. These relations tended to be more co-operative, although not without tensions, as government funding became constrained and demands for service climbed. In the area of policy development, the relationship was more strained. Valuing the expertise of public interest organizations, particularly in specialized areas of policy, government officials were increasingly skeptical of the value of unsolicited policy advocacy by many groups. While this tension has always existed between the two sectors, it became especially pronounced in the 1980s and 1990s as government attempted to redefine its role in society and as public interest organizations grew in number. The relationship between the voluntary sector and government became more antagonistic as a more educated and sophisticated public demanded more public engagement, directly and through interest organizations, in questions of governance.

The Liberals had sensed this shift in democratic governance. In 1993, the Chrétien Liberals were promising to meet the challenges posed by change through extensive consultations on "hot" issues like the economy, the environment, trade, and foreign policy. They built a governing plan firmly anchored upon the belief that "governing is about people, and that government must be judged by its effectiveness in promoting human dignity, justice, fairness and opportunity."[1] Citizen or public interest groups, as they were more commonly called, were integral to this process.

Did the Liberals deliver on the promises of promoting human dignity? Justice? Fairness? Opportunity? Were consultations effective? Meaningful? Did they achieve the goal of "a country whose governments are efficient, innovative, and cooperative not only with each other but with business, labour, the learning sector, environmentalists, and volunteer groups"?[2] Have the Liberals managed the relationship effectively and balanced the tensions inherent in their relationship with the voluntary sector? The legacy is mixed. The Liberal government made some truly significant advances with citizen organizations through a joint process with the sector, known as the Voluntary Sector Initiative (VSI). This initiative culminated in the signing of a bi-sectoral accord to regulate their relationship and codes of good practice for policy development and funding. However, the Chrétien government remained uneasy with the larger questions of policy advocacy and funding for the sector as a whole, largely leaving those issues unsettled. And the proverbial devil is indeed in the details – the issues remained unsettled even in the Paul Martin administration.

This chapter examines the legacy of the Chrétien Liberals for the third sector in Canada. This sector includes charitable, nonprofit, and voluntary organizations as well as civil society movements. At approximately 165,000 organizations, the sector touches most areas of life including religion, education, health, sports, culture, social services, legal services, human rights, and more. Organizations are usually self-governing although they might rely upon government funding, are not profit-distributing bodies, are voluntary but usually have paid staff, and are organized or institutionalized to some extent.[3] Given the size and diversity of the sector, the analysis is constrained to the sectoral level rather than attempting to document relations between particular organizations and government departments or to characterize developments at the subsectoral level. The Liberal promises touched the very heart of this sector, often euphemistically called the caring sector, by affecting the core mandates of organizations as well as drawing them further into the policy orbit through the proposed consultations and engagement. The chapter explores the successive Liberal promises to the third sector; the process of engagement through the Voluntary Sector Initiative, which attempted to redefine their relationship; and the products of this dialogue, including the Accord signed by the federal government and voluntary sector leaders, as well as the attendant codes of good practice. It concludes with an evaluation of their achievements. Since the vsi became the focal point of the relationship between the two sectors, much of the description and analysis will focus on it. However, the final evaluation extends outwards to assess whether the principles endorsed by the Liberal government in 1993, 1997 and 2000–2001 and captured in the accord, are evident in the active relationship between the two sectors.

THE PROMISES

The 1993 platform, *Creating Opportunity: The Liberal Plan for Canada*, was filled with hope and promises to the Canadian public. This "Plan" was premised on "an integrated and coherent approach to economic policy, social policy, environmental policy, and foreign policy";[4] a view of government as "a force for good in society";[5] and "a profound optimism about Canada's future."[6] To achieve a better future for Canada, the Liberals emphasized "the notion of partnership with all sectors of society,"[7] focusing efforts on strengthening society, and "evaluation, innovation, and finding best practices."[8] Although no one section of the Plan was addressed specifically to the voluntary and nonprofit sector, implicit in these ideas was a commitment to working with community and citizen organizations in the pursuit of human dignity, justice, fairness, and opportunity.

Partnership, collaboration, and consultation were emphasized throughout the document, opening the door to third sector organizations. For example, the education, childcare, jobs, and economic development proposals rested, in part, on the involvement of community groups.[9] The environmental and healthcare proposals incorporated national forums to allow individual and group access.[10] And perhaps owing to the looming presence of Lloyd Axworthy, the section on foreign policy included an endorsement of an open foreign policy-making process at home and an independent policy abroad.[11] One section specifically addressed lobbying, a key activity of organizations. While the section affected all groups engaged in lobbying government, it was seen as a response to criticisms that the previous Conservative government had been too open to the powerful business lobby. In an effort to ensure an open process in which individuals and groups of many different interests were able to represent views to government officials, the Liberals proposed stronger regulation of lobbyists, a code of conduct for public officials, and an ethics officer to monitor relations. The proposals were designed to create a more open, efficient, and ethical climate for government business.

In office, the Chrétien Liberals began to consult broadly with interest organizations, particularly in the areas of the environment, health care, and foreign policy, through the creation of special forums. They invited representatives from organizations to address critical issues in each area but also solicited broader public opinion. In this process of consultation, the Liberals, like the Tories before them, began to ask questions about the representativeness and legitimacy of many of the organizations engaged in these policy forums. Were these groups representing the public interest? Were they placing special interests ahead of the general public interest in recommending certain policy outcomes? Inviting groups into the policy development process obscured the line between organizations and government. When organizations were on the outside lobbying government, their roles were clear: organizations represent interests and governments aggregate and broker them. Now that interest organizations were becoming more integrated into the regular policy process and expected to see their views reflected in policy, the nature of their representation became more important and governments expected them to assume a stance that balanced their particular interest against the general public interest. Mindful of the public and media criticisms that too many organizations were private and closed to public scrutiny, the government began to listen to demands that organizations be more transparent and accountable whether they were engaged in policy advocacy or service delivery.

To foster the further involvement of organizations in policy development and to ensure that those organizations were accountable, the federal government began a series of regulatory reforms at the request of the Voluntary Sector Roundtable (VSR). The VSR was an unincorporated group of leaders of national voluntary sector organizations, formed by those leaders, to promote the concept of voluntary organizations as comprising a sector, in an effort to provide a counterweight to the business sector in the policy process. After consulting with the VSR, the government revised the tax and regulatory structures to allow organizations more latitude to raise revenues, build capacity, and create jobs. This was the first time, since they were introduced in the 1960s as a means of regulating the sector and providing revenue to government,[12] that the taxation measures were revised in a meaningful manner to assist charities and nonprofit and voluntary organizations labouring under increased demands for services from the public, due in part to government departure from social and community programs.[13] The progressive reforms were continued in the 1997 budget, with the ceiling for donations as a portion of income becoming more generous, and the limit on capital gains loosened to encourage larger donations of capital to charities. The government also ensured that Revenue Canada had sufficient resources to monitor charities more effectively. The dialogue for reform and partnership at the sectoral level had begun in earnest, with the tensions in the relationship simmering below the surface.

These reforms, made during the Liberal government's first term in office, were significant advances that enabled charities to raise revenues more efficiently. However, the 1997 Liberal election platform proposed expanding this dialogue vigorously, beginning with the recognition of the third sector as an actor in its own right in a new section of the platform entitled "Engaging the Voluntary Sector." In this section, the Liberals announced that: "This government has already moved to enhance the capacity of the voluntary sector and is involving it more fully in the public policy process. We are actively strengthening our partnerships with voluntary organizations in the knowledge that Canadians will benefit from this more collaborative approach."[14]

Not only did the document recognize the sector as a coherent unit of society, it went so far as to label the sector the "third pillar of Canadian society and its economy."[15] As if to underscore the importance of the sector in the governance process, third sector agency reports were cited throughout the report to support government policies and actions. However, the government's tendency to understand the sector in terms of particular relationships between departments and organizations, rather than as a whole sector, was reflected in its candid admission that government did not understand the nature, size, functioning, value added, or challenges of the sector and thus had foregone opportunities for partnership in the past.

The 1997 Liberal platform contained specific measures for building the collaborative relationship with the voluntary sector.[16] The platform encouraged federal government employees to volunteer time and energy to the sector or engage in personnel exchanges to promote cross-sectoral understanding of the roles, cultures, and nature of government and organizations.[17] It proposed continuing efforts at tax and regulatory reform through a structural review and modernization of Revenue Canada's Charities Division to enhance the capacity and public accountability of charities.[18] The platform also proposed building the technical capacity of voluntary sector organizations through Industry Canada and Voluntary Sector Supports, by extending support to agencies and providing access to computer equipment, new technologies, the Internet, information technology, network support, and training.[19] If re-elected, the Liberal government planned to expand its efforts to engage the voluntary sector in stimulating local entrepreneurship and in fostering economic development.[20] The 1997 platform treated the sector as an important social and economic ally in creating a better future for Canadians. These proposals were to form the basis of a comprehensive overhaul of the relationship between the government and the voluntary sector that occurred over the Liberal government's second and third terms in office.

In the 2000 election, the Liberals downsized their election platform. Given that the measures for the voluntary sector outlined in the 1997 platform had been achieved or were in the process of being attained, the Liberals could afford to pay the voluntary sector little attention except where it was subsidiary to other policies.[21] Upon election, the Liberal government used the 2001 Throne Speech to explicitly recognize the role of the sector in building Canadian culture and the importance of volunteers in the community.[22] However, in practice, the newly elected government largely adopted the attitude that it had "been there, done that." The voluntary sector agenda had been addressed successfully in the eyes of government. But had it? What had been accomplished or left undone and what do these reforms portend for the future? Was the federal government relationship with the voluntary sector more collaborative and harmonious or were the tensions still present? To these questions, we now turn.

THE PROCESS AND PRODUCTS

The VSR was quick to act upon the opportunity presented by the 1997 Liberal platform. The leaders had learned from the previous 1996 experience with tax and regulatory reform that a proactive alliance would be necessary and that context was important. In 1996, concern over the representativeness, legitimacy, and public accountability of nonprofit and voluntary sector organizations had erupted prominently with the publication of the Ontario Law Reform Commission's review of charities, and with Member of Parliament John Bryden's more sensational and damning report on these "special interests."[23] The upshot was that the Department of Finance commissioned a review of grants to so-called special interest groups, cutting their funding by $300 million within a year, and reformed the *Income Tax Act* to ensure greater transparency within the sector.[24] With the 1997 government pledge to ensure greater accountability in any tax or regulatory reform process, the VSR had to act. The leaders created the Panel on Accountability and Governance in the Voluntary Sector (PAGVS) under the chairmanship of Ed Broadbent, a highly respected former leader of the New Democratic Party and professor. PAGVS consulted broadly with the sector and government officials and reported in February 1999 with extensive recommendations on improving accountability, governance, and service in the voluntary sector.[25] In a shrewd move, PAGVS did not limit its suggestions to the voluntary sector but also addressed what government and the private sector could do to strengthen the sector. The Report inspired the federal government to act on its promise in the 1997 platform with the creation of a collaborative commission comprising equal representation from the public service and voluntary sector.

This collaborative commission, known as the Government of Canada and Voluntary Sector Joint Initiative, and commonly called the Joint Tables in reference to the three collaborative tables set up to examine the government and sector relationship, reported in August 1999. Like PAGVS, the Joint Tables made extensive recommendations, calling for changes within the sector to enhance good government practices and changes to the regulatory and political framework governing interactions between the two sectors.[26] Both recommended further discussion and dialogue between representatives from the two sectors on the implementation of the recommendations. The words of PAGVS and the Joint Tables were heeded a few months before the November 2000 election when the federal government, jointly with members of the voluntary sector, announced the VSI in June.

The $94.6 million VSI was designed to deliver on the 1997 Liberal promises incorporated into the recommendations of the PAGVS and Joint Tables over a five-year period. The VSI website explains that the "long-term goal of the VSI is to strengthen the sector's capacity to meet the challenges of the future, and to enhance the relationship between the sector and the federal government."[27] More specifically, the VSI was intended to strengthen the collective voice of the voluntary sector to express common needs, to streamline government rules and regulations for the sector, to increase the opportunities for voluntary sector organizations to participate in public policy development, and to improve the access of organizations to new technologies, training, and research. Tangible outcomes for Canadians would include enhanced programs, more volunteers who are better supported, more responsive public policy, and more opportunities for civic engagement. The work was to be done by seven joint tables comprising senior public officials and sector leaders who reported to a Reference Group of Ministers and to a Voluntary Sector Steering Group, respectively. The tables were named according to their mandates: the Joint Coordinating Committee, the Joint Accord Table, the Joint Awareness Table, the Joint Capacity Table, the Joint Information Management and Information Technology Table, the Joint Regulatory Table, and the National Volunteerism Initiative Table.

The VSI was intended to achieve specific outcomes and outputs, or deliverables.[28] The VSI vision document reveals five major outcomes with specific deliverables (outputs). First, the VSI was intended to improve and sustain a dialogue or collaboration between the federal government and voluntary sector in areas of mutual interest, with the broader goal of improving quality of life for Canadians. The specific deliverable was an Accord signed by representatives of both sectors on 5 December 2001, with subsidiary implementation agreements in the form of codes of good practice in the areas of policy dialogue and funding, annual reporting requirements, and ongoing mechanisms to ensure a continued relationship. Given that these documents are the centrepiece of the VSI and a critical piece of the Chrétien legacy, they deserve attention.

Modelled upon the United Kingdom idea of compacts, the Accord is a framework agreement that will set the tenor of future relations between the two sectors.[29] The document outlines a shared vision and common principles, and a mutual commitment to future collaboration. The Accord is intended to strengthen the relationship between the two sectors by encouraging better partnering practices, fostering consistent treatment of voluntary organizations across government, and promoting a better understanding within each sector of the constraints, operations, and practices of the other.[30] The Accord underscores the separate accountability requirements of each sector and then promises transparency, high standards of conduct, and sound management as they work together, as well as monitoring and reporting on the results.[31] A narrow construction of this section of the Accord could justify limited performance evaluations. However, a more robust reading would impose evaluation standards consistent with the values identified as underlying the Accord – democracy, active citizenship, equality, diversity, inclusion, and social justice.[32] Contributing to the realization of these values in daily operations will be the benchmarks of the work of the two sectors.

The *Codes of Good Practice* attending the Accord are operational documents. For example, the *Code on Policy Dialogue* is intended to implement the Accord's provisions by establishing an ongoing dialogue between the sectors in the development and design of policies and programs.[33] To facilitate this, "[b]oth sectors will provide feedback to their respective constituencies on the full range of views expressed, and clearly communicate how this input has been considered in the public policy process."[34] In addition, the voluntary sector is expected to provide feedback to government on policies and processes with an eye to improving performance.[35] Similarly, the *Code on Funding* pledges to sustain the capacity of voluntary organizations to serve Canadians through direct funding as well as indirect mechanisms such as taxation measures.[36] The *Code on Funding* commits the voluntary sector to sound financial, board, ethical, administrative, and monitoring practices, and the federal government to flexible application and accountability standards subject to effective protection of public money, consideration of alternative monitoring mechanisms, agreement on measurable results and clear roles, and respect for diversity. The two sides will develop the processes and evaluation tools together.

The second intention of the VSI was to strengthen the capacity of the voluntary sector to serve Canadians well. This was realized in the development of strategic approaches to building human resources, financial management, information technology, and management capacities with the necessary resources, as well as in the experimental Sectoral Involvement in Departmental Policy Development (SIDPD) aimed at building policy and research capacity in the sector. Through a competition, funds were allocated to departments to flow to their sector partners to: enhance their capacity to collaborate with government; develop, implement, and evaluate policy; represent citizens more effectively; mobilize participation in the sector; and ensure accountability. The purpose of the program is to prepare sector organizations to be more capable policy partners for government departments. While SIDPD is limited in scope, it represents an opportunity for changing the policy-making process and for ensuring that the principles of the VSI penetrate to the operational levels of government activity. The test will be whether the changes become permanent and extend to other areas of government. Immediately following the first phase of the VSI, relationships remained in flux and seemed to be developing towards a more co-operative relationship between the two sectors. However, SIDPD is based upon the idea of invited sector participation in policy and does not endorse advocacy or unsolicited policy advice by organizations. As a result, the effect of SIDPD seems confined to the departments that were already converts to greater voluntary sector involvement in the policy development process; however, the wheels of government turn slowly and the effects may yet spread to other departments.

Third, the VSI was intended to increase awareness of the contributions made by volunteers and of the role of the voluntary sector in Canadian society. The VSI was much more successful in recognizing volunteer activities during the International Year of the Volunteer (2001). The media and awareness campaigns for the voluntary sector have been more limited in effect.

Fourth, the VSI addressed the need for more information about the sector and its role in Canadian life with the creation and funding of ongoing mechanisms such as the Canadian Survey on Giving, Volunteering and Participating, the Statistics Canada Satellite Account to the System of National Accounts, and the National Survey of Nonprofit and Voluntary Organizations (NSNVO). These data collection devices will provide the longitudinal data so desperately required to map the sector and its trends and to inform policy decisions about the sector, as well as to provide more exact information on the contribution of the sector to the nation's social and economic life. This information allows for a more profound understanding of the nature and development of the sector both within Canada and in comparative international studies. They coincide with the Capacity Table funding for the inclusion of Canada in the high-profile

Johns Hopkins comparative country studies of the third sector – a significant omission over the past twenty years. Further, the NSNVO provides insight into the collective state of financial, human, and administrative capacity of organizations for the first time.[37] The qualitative portion of the NSNVO was released in spring 2003[38] and the quantitative study was relased in the fall of 2004.[39]

Finally, the VSI envisioned a streamlined regulatory framework, a revised tax form with clarified definitions of allowable activities for charities, and a review of liability for members of the boards of directors of organizations. A further objective of achieving clarity, consistency, and transparency in the funding relationship between the sector and state was undertaken through the federal funding review, the *Code on Funding* and a strategic funding approach. Although the federal government consulted the sector on these reforms, it retained control over the final shape of the reforms. While the federal government has reviewed the definition of charities and shortened the tax form, further regulatory reforms continue to be discussed between the two sectors.

The VSI did not come to terms with two of the most important issues for the sector. Many organizations had expected that the VSI would clarify and expand the right of organizations to engage in policy advocacy, public education, and political activity. Under Revenue Canada guidelines, organizations may not engage in partisan political activities, may only devote 10 percent of their revenues to nonpartisan political activities, and must be devoted to charitable activities. Thus, while an organization might deliver an essential service like shelter for the homeless, it cannot have, as its purpose, the intention to lobby government to change housing legislation. Organizations had hoped that these restrictions would be loosened to allow them a greater voice as advocates of policy change. Similarly, organizations had argued for a redefinition of charities that would expand the number of organizations able to issue tax receipts for charitable contributions as well as for a more liberal funding regime. The federal government agreed to review these items internally but would not discuss them jointly, which almost caused the Regulatory Table to collapse. Strategic interventions on both sides prevented a crisis and provided an impetus to the government process for reforms. However, these areas signify the inability of the government to reconcile the tension between a desire to have organizations involved more fully in policy design and delivery and to accept organizations in a critical, policy advocacy role.

THE POTENTIAL OR PRATFALL

The VSI embodies the most significant aspect of the Chrétien legacy for the third sector. Taking life from the Liberal campaign platforms and the throne speeches that signalled an openness to reforming the policy process, the VSI engaged the federal government and voluntary sector representatives in a protracted dialogue culminating in the Accord and the Codes as well as other reforms to the benefit of the sector. But are these changes significant and lasting? An assessment of the legacy must begin with the VSI and then extend to the relationship between the state and the sector more broadly as well as to the impact on the sector and its ability to serve Canadians.

Without doubt, the VSI was an impressive achievement with lasting effects for Canadian political, social, and economic life. For the first time in Canadian history, the government engaged in a protracted dialogue with representatives from a sector in a comprehensive review of their relationship. This had not even been attempted, for example, with the private or business sector. On an international level, the Canadian VSI model of reform has become a focal point for other nations interested in building a better relationship between the state and sector and in building capacity within the sector itself.[40] Analysts in other nations often express surprise at the extent of the negotiations, the efficiency of the process, and the scope of co-operation between the two sectors. On a national level, the initiative set a powerful precedent for shared decision-making and policy development. This precedent is unlikely to be forgotten in the future.

An equally impressive accomplishment of the VSI has been one of understanding and definition. The VSI increased understanding between sectors as well as knowledge of how each sector operates. While this knowledge is most concentrated among the actors sitting at the Joint Tables, it has spilled over into those actors' organizations and departments and to other attentive policy actors. Further, the process mobilized the voluntary sector as a sector, raising the consciousness within the sector of cross-cutting issues and interests at the national level. The process has encouraged both sector representatives and government officials to develop policy and define issues on a macro level for the sector as a whole.

The VSI is important for establishing a set of best practices that may have lasting effects for the federal, provincial, and other interested governments. Experiments like SIDPD will reinforce the policy impact of the

VSI process but provide tangible models of co-operative policy decision-making at the departmental level. In some ways, the SIDPD experiments are likely to be even more compelling than the VSI process, since the involvement of the sector organizations in policy is occurring within the regular policy process rather than through an external process created by mutual agreement. However, changes in the policy-making process towards a more inclusive format will depend very much upon the conditions, the policy issues, the actors, and sustained good will between the two sectors.

Another consequence with lasting effect was unintended. The VSI generated debate on the extent to which the federal government is the appropriate locus of activity of the nonprofit and voluntary sector given that primary constitutional responsibility for the sector rests with the provincial level of government and the federal government is restricted to action through its revenue-raising jurisdiction. Thus, a spin-off effect has been the generation or encouragement of the formation of coalitions of nonprofit and voluntary organizations at the provincial and regional levels of government that are beginning to press for reforms at that level of jurisdiction. For example, provincial organizations have encouraged their governments to examine the regulatory environment for nonprofit organizations, to consider standardizing their regimes and to encourage volunteerism through educational and community oriented programs. In the case of Québec, the community sector tended to largely dissociate itself from the VSI and national experience, defining itself even more strongly within that province.[41]

To some degree, the legacy of the VSI rests upon the new structures that the voluntary sector and federal government have chosen to oversee implementation of the Codes on policy and funding. The VSI steering group transformed itself into a new body called the Voluntary Sector Forum, composed of nine leaders from the original group and ten new leaders from the voluntary sector who had not served on any of the VSI Tables. Subsequently, additional individuals have been added to ensure representation from the major regions, national and regional organizations, large and small organizations, different ethnic and racial backgrounds, and various interests in the voluntary sector, among other things. The federal government initially assigned responsibility for implementation to a line department, Canadian Heritage, but retained a ministerial committee as a consultative body. A steering committee of senior officials was struck to oversee horizontal co-ordination of the initiative in departments, with the Privy Council Office as the final checkpoint.

When Paul Martin assumed the office of Prime Minister, however, responsibility for the initiative was largely allocated to a new department, Social Development Canada. The implementation goals of the vsi have been overshadowed by the focus on the social economy, but voluntary sector leaders have continued to press Social Development Canada to ensure that the gains of the vsi are not lost. One incentive to activity lies with the proposed joint annual meetings to review the progress on the implementation of the Codes. For the first two years, these meetings culminated in a progress report, but in December 2005, the publication of a third progress report is in doubt, removing one of the most powerful incentives for further implementation in abeyance. Another incentive within the federal government is provided by the letters of mandate for deputy ministers requiring them to report annually on their department's progress on the implementation of the Accord and Codes. However, as the letters of mandate contain many items, this incentive remains a weaker check. Despite these disappointments, at a minimum, the Accord and Codes will serve as a conscience to both sectors in future interactions.

The legacy of the vsi is not limited to process or relationship issues. Knowledge about the sector and its impact on the Canadian economy and society provides a basis for more fertile interaction between the state, the private sector, and the nonprofit sector. The national surveys and the satellite accounts, mentioned above, will provide longitudinal knowledge of the health of volunteering, giving, and participating in Canada, thus enabling policy actors to accurately assess the importance of those activities to our national social and economic health and to intervene where necessary. For example, the Chrétien government devoted significant funds to computerizing the sector and bolstering the technological capacity of organizations. The survey on capacity and the satellite accounts will provide the requisite information to continue the development of the sector in this area, particularly where there are broader benefits to society, such as the more efficient delivery of services. With more accurate knowledge of the strengths and weaknesses of the third sector, public, private, and nonprofit organizations may be able to build stronger and more effective alliances to address polycentric policy issues.

One of the big question marks in assessing the legacy of the Chrétien government rests with Treasury Board and Finance. The tax forms, new definitions, and revised monitoring and registration mechanisms for charities will have tangible results but will continue to affect different charities to different extents, and most nonprofits will not be directly affected in daily operations.[42] As noted above, the issues of advocacy and funding remain outstanding, although the President of the Treasury Board did indicate a need to address the issues. The new administrative guidelines on political activities by charities released by the Canada Customs and Revenue Agency in the fall of 2003 have failed to meet the expectations of both charities and nonprofit organizations. The sector is committed to achieving further reforms in the future, while the commitment of government to future reforms remains vague at best. Thus, a core area of the relationship between the third sector and government remains unchanged and the effects of reform are likely to be limited if not contentious.[43] The fundamental tension between government and the sector over the political and advocacy role of third sector organizations remains unresolved.

A final legacy of the Chrétien government involves the greater use of consultations in the regular policy process. Government sector engagement may take place through regular or special consultations, policy engagement, service development, and implementation or even citizen juries. Human Resources is renowned for its extensive links with the third sector. Heritage regularly reaches out to key constituent groups. Industry Canada has broadened its consultative base. Justice reaches beyond the legal community to include groups representing victims and concerned citizens. Under Paul Martin, Finance formalized the process of consultations in the budget process. Indian Affairs has engaged in extensive consultations with both First Nation governments and citizen organizations in effecting changes in that community, albeit with very mixed reviews. And perhaps most significantly, government efforts to go online and to make information broadly available provides valuable access points and information to citizen groups and individuals. Once the halls of government are opened, it is difficult to close the doors to participation and so this might be one of the most important developments of the Chrétien years for citizen organizations. If the principles of the Accord take root, then these relations will be more systematized and standardized across government.

Does citizen engagement make a difference in terms of policy output? Here the legacy is uncertain. The impact of consultations or other forms of engagement on policy decisions is very difficult to measure. For example, in the case of the latest First Nations consultation on governance, the federal government has been widely criticized for pursuing its predetermined agenda and not listening to First Nations' criticisms. However, some organizations representing Aboriginal peoples living off reserve think their voices have been heard.[44] Similarly, in the case of the citizen engagement and community consultation strategy used by Human Resources Development Canada in the implementation of the Supporting Communities Partnership Initiative (SCPI) to alleviate homelessness, organizations have criticized the process for diluting the voices of organizations with extensive experience with the issues by inviting broad public participation. In a review of the process, Alan Bentley argues that a balance of larger and smaller organizations is essential for a fully developed policy and found the impact of organizations on the policy process and output mixed.[45] While a cynic might suggest that policy engagement and consultation are just legitimation devices for predetermined policies, an optimist might suggest that there is merit in requiring public officials to vet and justify policy reforms in public where an exchange of ideas occurs, since those ideas may influence current or future policies. One point remains clear: the tension between advocacy and policy inclusion is unresolved in practice.

The world is not entirely rose-tinted for the third sector in the policy process, as the example of Foreign Affairs reveals. On the one hand, Foreign Affairs made significant efforts to involve citizen organizations in the policy process, both at home and abroad, particularly under Lloyd Axworthy, but also subsequently. In the 1980s, Foreign Affairs began using roundtable consultations regularly, but in the later 1990s, in response to citizen group pressure, Canada was instrumental in securing access for citizen groups to forums and information involving multilateral trade, tariff, investment, and global governance negotiations.[46] Foreign Affairs established a forum to facilitate citizen input through the internet and townhalls, resulting in the Dialogue on Foreign Policy held in 2003.[47] However, this method of consultation is more conducive to individual input than to organizational input. And in the aftermath of September 11, 2001, the Canadian government, like its allies, has passed legislation on terrorism that has had a chilling effect on organizations.[48] Provisions in the new anti-terrorism legislation have affected advocacy and funding activities of Arab and Muslim organizations in particular, but also citizen organizations more broadly. These trends may have a paralyzing effect on the legacy of the Chrétien government for third sector organizations.

CONCLUSION: THE SECTOR WAITS

And so, what is the overall Chrétien legacy for the third sector? First and foremost, the Chrétien government mobilized the sector and, along with key actors in the sector itself, created an awareness of a "third sector" consisting of diverse organizations with crosscutting issues. Second, it increased the policy voice of organizations both for the sector as a whole and for organizations within particular policy subsectors. Organizations are more cognizant of the need to build and sustain a relationship than ever before. Third, it began the process of addressing hard capacity issues particularly in the area of human resources, internal governance, and technology. Fourth, it began a process of change to policy formulation. The policy development process has become more open and transparent with third sector organizations involved more regularly. The prospects for further change are promising. Fifth, it signed an historic agreement with the third sector, providing a basis for a more productive relationship with the broader goal of improving quality of life for Canadians. Sixth, it has been a friend to the third sector on the international scene, supporting more open and transparent global governance, although that has been curtailed in the wake of September 11, 2001.

The legacy is sadly lacking in two key areas. While the government has improved access of invited organizations to the policy process and made the policy process more open to the public, it failed to address the critical question of advocacy. The definition of charities remains restricted to a limited group of organizations within the third sector. Groups with non-partisan political activities including public education and policy change as their missions remain outside the ambit of the benefits accorded to charitable organizations. Funding issues also remain unresolved. While the benefits of articulate, critical organizations to parliamentary democracy are widely extolled, the government failed to act decisively to resolve these two important aspects of third sector activity.

Is this legacy a lasting one? Certainly the Accord between the federal government and the voluntary sector has the potential to frame a new relationship to the benefit of Canadians. In a similar vein, a more open and transparent policy process, whether domestic or global, is consistent with a globalized society and economy where capital, humans, and goods flow across borders, and where citizens are sufficiently informed to ask intelligent questions of their governments. And members of the voluntary sector are rising to the challenge of becoming more committed and engaged policy players than ever before. However, under-resourcing of the sector continues even as this new dimension of activity opens up new policy doors. Organizations large and small are facing increasing challenges as: citizen demands increase; government support for services declines; the competition within the sector for funds, contracts, and contribution agreements intensifies; the nonprofit sector moves into direct competition with the profit sector for goods, services, and contracts; and attempts to meet the demands for more accountability consume more time and resources. Further, the government commitment to meaningful consultations remains tentative at times. And organizations question the extent to which the spirit of the Accord will penetrate into the inner and upper recesses of government administration, while the government questions the extent to which the Accord will be embraced by organizations that were not immediately involved in the vsi.

Although many leaders in the nonprofit sector and government continue to press for policy engagement and appreciation of a more robust role of the third sector in Canadian social and economic life, the impact of the changes initiated by this administration is yet to be known. The devil is always in the level of commitment to the details of implementation. While some elements of the Accord and the Codes inexorably embed themselves in the process of policy development, the general level of commitment has been attenuated in the new focus on the social economy introduced by the Martin administration. The sector waits for the promises of the vsi to be realized across government but is not sitting idly by. Change is inevitable, but to what extent? That is the unresolved question for the vsi and the Chrétien legacy for the voluntary sector.

NOTES

Associate Professor, School of Policy Studies, Queen's University. I would like to thank John Ronson, Steve Patten, and the two anonymous reviewers for their helpful suggestions in improving this chapter.

1 Liberal Party of Canada (LPC), *Creating Opportunity: The Liberal Plan for Canada* (Ottawa: LPC, 1993), 5.
2 Ibid., 10.
3 Lester Salamon and Helmut Anheier, *The Emerging Sector Revisited: A Summary, Revised Estimates* (Baltimore: Johns Hopkins University, Institute for Policy Studies, Center for Civil Society Studies, 1999), 1.
4 LPC, *Creating Opportunity*, 10.
5 Ibid., 10–11.
6 Ibid., 10.
7 Ibid., 11.
8 Ibid., 12.
9 Ibid., 30, 36, 39–40, 58.
10 Ibid., 69, 80.
11 Ibid., 105.

12 Ontario Law Reform Commision, *Report on the Law of Charities* (Toronto: The Commission, 1996), 261–65; and Patrick J. Monahan and Elie S. Roth, *Federal Regulation of Charities: A Critical Assessment of Recent Proposals for Legislative and Regulatory Reform* (Toronto: York University Press, 2000), 11.

13 For a review of practices and reforms, see Carl Juneau, "Revenue Canada Practices and Procedures Affecting Charities," in Canadian Tax Foundation, *Report of the Proceedings of the Forty-Ninth Tax Conference* (Toronto: Canadian Tax Foundation, 1998), 29:1–12.

14 LPC, *Securing Our Future Together: Preparing Canada for the 21st Century* (Ottawa: LPC, 1997), 69.

15 Ibid., 67.

16 Ibid., 67–9.

17 Ibid., 68.

18 Ibid., 67.

19 Ibid., 68.

20 Ibid., 69.

21 LPC, *Opportunity for All: The Liberal Plan for the Future of Canada* (Ottawa: LPC, 2000).

22 Canada, Governor General, *Speech from the Throne* (Ottawa: Minister of Public Works and Government Services, 30 January 2001), 16, 18.

23 Two of the most trenchant criticisms of the voluntary sector were by the Ontario Law Reform Commission in its *Report on the Law of Charities*; and John Bryden, *MP's Report: Canada's Charities: A Need for Reform* (Ottawa: House of Commons, 1996).

24 Chris Miller, "Tough Questions Avoided: The Broadbent Report on the Voluntary Sector," *Policy Options* (October 1999): 75–9, 76.

25 Panel on Accountability and Governance in the Voluntary Sector, *Building on Strength: Improving Governance and Accountability in Canada's Voluntary Sector* (Ottawa: PAGVS, 1999).

26 Al Hatton, et al., *Working Together: A Government of Canada/Voluntary Sector Joint Initiative* (Ottawa: Privy Council Office, 1999).

27 Canada, Voluntary Sector Initiative (VSI), "Sectoral Involvement in Departmental Policy Development," http://www.vsi-isbc.ca/eng/policy/sidpd.cfm.

28 See Joint Coordinating Committee, "Progress to Plan" (Ottawa: VSI, 5 September 2002).

29 Canada, VSI, *An Accord Between the Government of Canada and the Voluntary Sector* (Ottawa: Privy Council Office, December 2001), http://www.vsi-isbc.ca/eng/relationship/pdf/the_accord_doc.pdf.

30 For detailed analyses of the birth and content of the *Accord*, see Susan D.
   Phillips, "In Accordance: Canada's Voluntary Sector Accord From Idea to
   Implementation," in Kathy L. Brock ed., *Delicate Dances: Public Policy and
   the Nonprofit Sector in Canada* (Montreal & Kingston: McGill-Queen's
   University Press, 2003), 17–62; and Susan D. Phillips, "A Federal Government
   – Voluntary Sector Accord: Implications for Canada's Voluntary Sector"
   (Toronto: Voluntary Sector Initiative Secretariat, 2001).
31 VSI, *Accord*, 9.
32 Ibid., 7.
33 VSI, *A Code of Good Practice on Policy Dialogue* (Ottawa: Privy Council
   Office, 2002), 2.
34 Ibid., 7.
35 Ibid., 8–9.
36 VSI, *A Code of Good Practice on Funding* (Ottawa: Privy Council Office,
   2002), 2–4.
37 Consortium members include Canadian Centre for Philanthropy, Alliance de
   Recherche Universités–Communautés en Economie Sociale at UQAM, the Canada West Foundation, the Canadian Council on Social Development, the
   Capacity Development Network at the University of Victoria, the Community
   Services Council of Newfoundland and Labrador, Queen's University School
   of Policy Studies, the Secretariat on Voluntary Sector Sustainability of the
   Manitoba Voluntary Sector Initiative, and Statistics Canada.
38 The results of the CSGVP are available the Imagine Canada website,
   http://www.givingandvolunteering.ca. For the qualitative results of the NSNVO,
   see Michael Hall, et al., *The Capacity to Serve: A Qualitative Study of the
   Challenges Facing Canada's Nonprofit and Voluntary Organizations*
   (Toronto: Canadian Centre for Philanthropy, 2003).
39 Michael Hall et al., *Cornerstones of Community: Highlights of the National
   Survey of Nonprofit and Voumtary Organizations* (Ottawa: Statistics Canada,
   2004), http://www.statcan.ca/engish/freepub/61-533-XIE/2004001
   /61-533-XIE2004001.pdf
40 There was a level of curiosity expressed through requests for information on
   the VSI and at international conferences, particularly with practitioners and
   academics from Britain, India, and Australia.
41 Throughout the process it was difficult to engage representatives from the
   Québec sector and to popularize the initiative within that province. One of the
   best examples of this problem was the translation of the slogan "I volunteer"
   for International Year of the Volunteer. "Je suis là" just "did not resonate ...
   to the same extent that 'I Volunteer' did...." Canada, Department of Canadian
   Heritage, Corporate Review Branch, *Evaluation of the 2001 International*

Year of the Volunteers Initiative (Ottawa: Department of Canadian Heritage, 28 May 2003), 25, http://www.pch.gc.ca/progs/em-cr/eval/2003/2003-pdf/IYV_03_eval_e.pdf

42 For a superb review of the current state of regulations and analysis of what needs to be done, see A. Paul Pross and Kernaghan Webb, "Embedded Regulation: Advocacy and the Federal Regulation of Public Interest Groups," in Brock, *Delicate Dances*, 63–121.

43 Finance did provide a powerful check on the VSI and was often viewed as more difficult to persuade to accept reforms leading to a more open decision-making process especially where any money decisions were involved throughout the VSI. See for example, Kathy Brock, "A Final Review of the Joint Coordinating Committee of the Voluntary Sector Initiative 2000-2002 by the Official Documentalist and Occasional Advisor" (Ottawa: VSI Background Papers, 2002).

44 Kathy L. Brock, "First Nations, Citizenship and Democratic Reform," in Gerald Kernerman and Philip Resnick, eds., *Essays in Honour of Alan Cairns* (Vancouver: University of British Columbia Press, 2004), 257–72

45 See Alan Bentley, "SCPI Consultation Report Issues: Final Report to the Policy Internship and Fellowships Program" (Ottawa: PIAF, 2003).

46 See Maxwell A. Cameron, "Democratization of Foreign Policy: The Ottawa Process as a Model," *Canadian Foreign Policy* 5:3 (1998): 147–65; Elizabeth Smythe and Peter Smith, "NGOs, Technology and the Changing Face of Trade Politics," in Brock, *Delicate Dances*, 297–339; and Kim Nossal, "The Democratization of Canadian Foreign Policy: The Elusive Ideal," in Maxwell Cameron and Maureen Appel Molot, eds., *Canada Among Nations 1995: Democracy and Foreign Policy* (Ottawa: Carleton University Press, 1995), 1–28.

47 For a result of the consultations and information on the process, see the Hon. Bill Graham, Department of Foreign Affairs and International Trade (DFAIT), *A Dialogue on Foreign Policy: Report to Canadians* (Ottawa: DFAIT, June 2003), http://www.dfait-maeci.gc.ca/cip-pic/participate/FinalReport.pdf.

48 See Ann Capling and Kim Nossal, "The Third Sector Meets the National Security State: The Anti-Globalization Movement in Canada after 9/11," in Brock, *Delicate Dances*, 275–96.

13

The Chrétien Ethics Legacy

IAN GREENE

INTRODUCTION

A central promise in the Liberal Red Book, or campaign platform of 1993, was to "govern with integrity." Chapter Six of the Red Book was devoted to ethics reforms designed to overcome "cynicism about public institutions."[1] The key promises were to strengthen the *Lobbyists Registration Act*,[2] to develop a Code of Conduct for public officials in their dealings with lobbyists, to establish an independent ethics counsellor to advise on the application of this Code, to introduce "tough" election financing and spending rules by limiting "the role of special-interest groups in election campaigns,"[3] to reduce the influence of patronage on order-in-council appointments, and to keep election promises. In 1996, the Liberal Party published a self-evaluation of its Red Book promises, and concluded that most of the promises had been kept, with the exception of the new election financing rules.[4] In the introduction to the self-evaluation report, Prime Minister Jean Chrétien wrote that "of all the Red Book commitments we have kept, none gives me greater pride than our living up to our pledge to govern with integrity."[5]

As the Liberal mandate extended through three terms, ethics scandals gradually but steadily tarnished the government's integrity record, until in May of 2002 the Prime Minister announced an eight-point "ethics package" to polish up the government's integrity record. The package included legislation to limit contributions to parties by corporations, unions, and individuals, and a bill to create a truly independent ethics commissioner for Parliamentarians. Prior to the Liberal convention in November 2003 that chose Paul Martin to succeed Chrétien, the party financing bill became law, but the ethics commissioner bill stalled in the Senate. In Chrétien's farewell speech to party faithful at the November 2003 Liberal convention, the integrity agenda was not on the list of accomplishments that the retiring Prime Minister boasted about. The sponsorship scandal, which had been brewing since news reports in 2000, blew up into a political storm of hurricane proportions in February of 2004, thanks to a report of the Auditor General. The end of the Chrétien era coincided with one of the worst ethics scandals in Canadian history. What went wrong?

A review of the ethics controversies that plagued the Chrétien government suggests that the Prime Minister and his supporters had failed to keep up with the waves of ethical reforms in provincial governments that had so successfully reduced the incidence of ethics scandals in provincial politics.[6] In particular, Chrétien was reluctant to create legislation to prevent conflicts of interest among Cabinet ministers, other MPs, and Senators that would be enforced by an ethics commissioner independent of the Prime Minister. In fact, had the government introduced legislation to create an independent ethics commissioner early enough in its mandate, it is quite possible that the commissioner could have provided the kind of advice needed to keep the government out of much of the hot water it encountered. Moreover, the judgments of an independent ethics commissioner about allegations of ethical improprieties would have had a great deal more legitimacy than the judgments of an official reporting to the Prime Minister, and so decisions exonerating Cabinet ministers would likely have put an end to particular controversies. However, until 2002 the Prime Minister clung to the old-style approach to ethical politics that had been found to be unworkable in the provinces and territories. He claimed that, as Prime Minister, he had ultimate responsibility to decide what was ethical and what was not, and that to cede the adjudication of an ethics law to an independent official would be a dereliction of duty.[7] As well, the Prime Minister and some of his key Cabinet ministers apparently believed that the idea of an independent ethics commissioner was too "legalistic," transferring to a quasi-judicial official the discretion of Cabinet ministers about how to resolve ethics dilemmas.

But it was not just the Prime Minister who was skeptical about creating an independent ethics commissioner in 1993. It was clear to me when testifying before the Special Joint Committee of Parliament on a Code of Conduct in 1995, and the House of Commons Standing Committee on

Procedure and House Affairs on a draft Parliamentary Code of Conduct in 2002, that a number of Liberal backbenchers also had cold feet. The fear was that Cabinet ministers and government MPs would find themselves victimized by an opposition constantly complaining to the independent ethics commissioner about trumped-up charges, and that even if the commissioner found that the rules had not been breached, the negative publicity could do serious damage. However, the academics present at the hearings assured MPs that such negative consequences have not befallen the governments of provinces that have had independent ethics commissioners for a decade or more, and perhaps this testimony reassured the MPs so that they could finally support the legislation in 2003.

This chapter will begin by summarizing the ethics scandals encountered by the Chrétien government. The analysis will show that some of the controversies could have been avoided if an independent ethics commissioner had been in place. Other ethical lapses could have been prevented if the Prime Minister had placed greater emphasis on impartiality rather than partisanship by creating impartial inquiries in some cases, or attempting to make impartial, merit-based appointments in others. The achievements of the Chrétien government in the ethical politics arena will then be catalogued, and finally, the overall ethics record of the Chrétien government will be evaluated. Although the Chrétien government had a far better ethics record than that of the Mulroney government, even in light of the sponsorship scandal, it became mired in ethical quagmires because of its reluctance to embrace tougher conflict-of-interest rules until the end of its term, and higher standards of impartiality. Even so, the Chrétien government has left the country with a healthier set of ethics rules because of an improved lobbyist registration regime, greater Parliamentary scrutiny of some order-in-council appointments, and tough legislation limiting political contributions. As well, because the legislation to create an independent ethics commissioner passed the House of Commons when Chrétien was still Prime Minister, the Martin government felt it had the momentum to reintroduce similar legislation in 2004, and this legislation made it through the Senate prior to the 2004 election.

SCANDALS

There were eleven prominent episodes of ethics scandals that were weathered by the Chrétien government during its decade in power. This is a far better record than that of the Mulroney government, which was faced with no fewer than fourteen serious allegations of conflict of interest during its first two years in office alone, including the infamous Sinclair Stevens affair, which led to an inquiry by Mr. Justice William Parker. In 1987, the inquiry found that Stevens, while a Cabinet minister, had been in a real conflict-of-interest situation on at least six occasions,[8] though in December 2004, Stevens obtained a ruling from the Federal Court that found that Parker had operated outside his jurisdiction by creating his own definition of "conflict of interest," as the conflict-of-interest guidelines for Cabinet ministers did not contain one.[9]

Michel Dupuy, 1994

The first ethics problem was relatively minor, but being the first, it attracted attention. When it became public knowledge that Heritage Minister Michel Dupuy had sent a letter to the Canadian Radio-television and Telecommunications Commission (CRTC) to support the license application for a Greek-language radio outlet in his constituency, Chrétien apologized for the error.[10] However, the Prime Minister stressed: "There is no scandal here. No violation of integrity. No breach of the public trust." What happened was an "honest mistake."[11] To prevent such mistakes from occurring in the future, the Prime Minister issued "supplemental guidelines" to make it absolutely clear the ministers must not attempt to influence the decisions of judges or administrative tribunals.

In provinces such as Ontario and British Columbia, which had independent ethics commissioners at the time (Gregory Evans, former Chief Justice of the High Court of Ontario, and Ted Hughes, a former superior court judge), the commissioner meets with new Cabinet ministers and other elected members individually. They make the ethics rules very clear to these officials – for example, the rule that they must not have any dealings with judges or quasi-judicial tribunals.[12] These commissioners issue annual reports that summarize the inquiries that the commissioners have received from Cabinet ministers and other elected members (without mentioning the names of those making the inquiries), and the complaints that they have investigated. Since the advent of the Ontario regime in 1988, and B.C. in 1991, there has been only one incident in which a Cabinet minister was alleged to have interfered with a judicial or quasi-judicial process, an ambiguous case where an Ontario minister tried to mediate a dispute that was already before the courts. The Prime Minister, however, had relied on ethics counsellor Howard Wilson, a public servant who reported to the Prime Minister, and his personal ethics advisor, Mitchell Sharp, to explain the Prime Minister's ethics guidelines to members of Cabinet. This approach, however well-intentioned, was not as likely to be as successful as counselling by an independent ethics commissioner who also has the power to investigate allegations of a breach of the ethics code.

David Collenette, 1996

The shortcomings of the Prime Minister's system of enforcing his code were illustrated again in 1996, when Defence Minister David Collenette was forced to resign because he had sent a letter to the Immigration and Refugee Board asking it to speed up its consideration of the case of a relative of one of Collenette's constituents.[13] The importance of ministers leaving quasi-judicial tribunals alone had still not sunk in. And although the Prime Minister appears to have taken this breach seriously by demanding or accepting Collenette's resignation, it should be remembered that Collenette had been the subject of a fair amount of criticism for his handling of the defence portfolio. Thus, the resignation may have served a strategy to remove Collenette from the hot seat, while at the same time the Prime Minister could stress the importance of respecting the impartiality of an independent agency.

The Pearson Airport Cancellation, 1993–1996

A major issue at the end of the 1993 election campaign concerned the decision of the Mulroney government to lease Pearson Airport in Toronto for fifty-seven years to a private firm with strong connections to Mulroney. Three weeks prior to the election, Prime Minister Kim Campbell signed the final documents to proceed with the deal, in spite of the promise of then Opposition Leader Jean Chrétien to review the plan and to cancel it if the review so recommended. One of Chrétien's first acts as Prime Minister was to appoint Robert Nixon, former Liberal treasurer of Ontario, to review the arrangement. Nixon recommended that the contract be cancelled because of flaws in the tendering process, and undue influence from lobbyists. The Chrétien government cancelled the contract, and in 1994 introduced a bill to limit the government's liability to out-of-pocket expenses incurred by the Conservative-friendly firm, as recommended by Nixon. The real trouble began for the Chrétien government when this bill reached the Senate. Conservative Senators were still in the majority, and their view was that the 1993 deal had been a good one, and was cancelled for purely partisan political reasons.

The Senate established a special committee to hold public hearings into the original contract and its cancellation, and the report was released in December of 1995. The Conservative majority report stated that the privatization contract had been fairly negotiated and was financially advantageous to Canada, while the Liberal minority report painted a picture of rampant undue influence on the part of lobbyists close to former Prime Minister Mulroney. In June of 1996, the Senate defeated the compensation bill, thus allowing the firm to which Prime Minister Campbell had given the contract to sue for loss of profit, as well as out-of-pocket expenses.[14]

In hindsight, from an ethics perspective the Chrétien government mishandled the Pearson Airport affair in two ways. First, it would have been far better if Chrétien had appointed a politically neutral party to review the Pearson airport deal in 1993. The findings might well have been the same, but they would have been more difficult to attack as partisan. Second, rather than leave it to the Senate to investigate the Pearson saga, it would have been better for the government to have appointed an impartial commission of inquiry.

The Airbus Affair, 1994–2003

The Airbus affair dates to the late 1980s, when Airbus Industrie, a European consortium, was hoping for a large contract to sell airliners to Air Canada in order to establish its credibility in the world market against its major competitor, the Boeing corporation. Airbus hired prominent Ottawa lobbyist Frank Moores, a close friend of Brian Mulroney and a former Conservative premier of Newfoundland. In 1985, Mulroney appointed Moores to the Board of Air Canada. Although Moores claimed that there was no conflict of interest, public pressure forced him to resign his Air Canada Board seat later in 1985. In 1988, Airbus got the contract for a new Air Canada fleet, and shortly after this decision the government-owned airline company was privatized.

In 1985, the Mulroney government began a consultation process prior to drafting Canada's first *Lobbyists Registration Act*. Some claim that this legislation was forced on the Mulroney government because of Moores' lobbying activities.[15] The Liberals were critical of the *Act* for not going far enough, and in 1993 promised that they would strengthen it if elected.

But this was to be only the beginning of the Airbus story. In 1994, journalist Paul Palango alleged that prior to Air Canada's privatization, Brian Mulroney had pressured Air Canada to pay several million dollars in consulting fees to Moores' lobbying company, a charge denied by both Mulroney and Moores. In March of 1995, both the CBC and the German media revealed the possibility that Airbus may have paid bribes to prominent members of the Canadian government to secure the Airbus sale.[16] In September of 1995, officials in the federal Department of Justice requested Swiss authorities to assist in an RCMP investigation of possible bribes in the Airbus sale, and the request implicated Brian Mulroney. Mulroney, along with Karlheinz Schreiber, a German businessman who acted as a go-between in international contract negotiations, found out that they, along with Frank Moores, were being investigated by the RCMP, and Mulroney launched a lawsuit for $50 million against the federal government. To begin with, the government defended itself against Mulroney's suit, but in January of 1997 it abandoned its defence, apologized, and agreed to pay Mulroney's legal and public relations expenses, which came to over $2 million. Apologies were also addressed to Moores and Schreiber, but they received no compensation.[17] The total cost to the federal government of the investigation and the settlement was pegged at $6.4 million.[18] Justice Minister Allan Rock and Prime Minister Chrétien were both accused by the opposition and the media of having wasted public funds in a witch-hunt directed against former Prime Minister Mulroney and his friends. Rock, however, refused to confirm that the probe of the Airbus affair had ended.

Just prior to Chrétien's retirement as leader of the Liberal Party in mid-November of 2003, the Airbus affair once again monopolized the front pages of the national media for several days. On 7 November, *The Globe and Mail* covered the front page with a story about its success in co-operating with the CBC in getting evidence unsealed in a previously *in camera* court proceeding that had been going on in Toronto for more than three years.[19] The proceeding concerned allegations that bribes were paid by a German helicopter firm, Messerschmidt-Bolkow-Blohm, to facilitate sales to the Canadian government. One alleged go-between was Karlheinz Schreiber, represented in this proceeding by lawyer Edward Greenspan. Three days later, it was revealed that Brian Mulroney made a post-retirement deal worth $300,000 with Schreiber to "provide advice and open doors" regarding an international pasta company of Schreiber's.[20] This payment from Schreiber was not reported during negotiations between Mulroney's lawyers and the federal government regarding the lawsuit that was settled in 1997. Donald Savoie, an expert on Canadian public administration, commented that for some reason, the question of whether Mulroney had been paid by Schreiber "was not asked."[21] If it had been, it is possible that there would not have been offer from the Canadian government to settle the lawsuit. Most likely, even if there had been a settlement, it would have been a different one.

The continuing Airbus affair leads to two main conclusions. First, legislation to control the activities of lobbyists to prevent undue influence needs to be tough enough to match the wits of lobbyists intent on abusing the public interest. Second, the litigation process is sometimes inadequate when trying to get to the bottom of potential undue influence involving lobbyists. A public inquiry might have been the preferred route. A public inquiry can shed light on all relevant factors of an important public issue, but inquiries can also mean delays in criminal and civil litigation, and sometimes the possibility of a criminal prosecution can be weakened as a result. On the other hand, a criminal prosecution is focused on particular individuals rather than on the entire context of a situation, and it is unlikely to result in the holistic exposition of a problematic situation.

The Promise to Replace the GST, 1993-1996

During the 1993 election campaign, the Liberals promised to replace the Goods and Services Tax (GST) imposed by the Conservative government. By 1996, the Liberal government concluded that the GST was needed to collect revenue to reduce the deficit – thus, the "replacement" of the GST would actually be a harmonization of the federal sales tax with provincial sales taxes in provinces that were willing to blend the two taxes. For Chrétien, and for the Liberal self-evaluation of 1996,[22] this approach fulfilled the Liberal promise of "replacement," though few believed that the Liberals had not broken a key campaign promise. However, Deputy Prime Minister Sheila Copps had made a campaign promise to resign if the Liberals were elected and did not "abolish" the GST.

When the government's plans to continue the GST with only minor modifications were revealed in 1996, Copps was reminded by the opposition of her promise. At first, she simply blamed her "big mouth" in 1993. Under continued public pressure, Copps did eventually resign her seat in the Commons, then contested it in a by-election that she won (and in which she avoided discussion of the tax). John Nunziata, the flamboyant Liberal MP for York South-Weston, voted against his government's

1996 budget because of its continuance of the GST, and for his stand he was kicked out of the Liberal caucus.

These episodes drew attention to the ethical issue of being accountable for election promises.[23] Canadians favour politicians who think through their election promises clearly, and then do what they promised to do after election. Although the Red Book was an important step toward greater accountability for election promises, it would have been more honest, and more courageous, to have the degree to which the election promises were kept evaluated by an impartial tribunal, rather than by the Liberal Party itself.

Pierre Corbeil, 1997

In March of 1997, Human Resources Minister Pierre Pettigrew became aware that a Liberal fundraiser, Pierre Corbeil, had cited his government connections when approaching companies that might be seeking grants under the Transitional Jobs Fund program. Pettigrew forwarded these allegations to the RCMP for investigation, and in October the police laid charges against Corbeil. Corbeil was eventually convicted and fined $34,500. Pettigrew acted with integrity, but this event underlines the need for political parties to conduct internal education campaigns about ethics rules and the importance of the impartial administration of the law.

The Auberge Grand-Mère Affair and the Business Development Bank, 1999–2004

As a result of an investigation by *National Post* journalist Andrew McIntosh, who had learned his research techniques from veteran investigative journalist Stevie Cameron, a potential conflict-of-interest situation involving Prime Minister Chrétien came to light in 1999. In 1993, when Jean Chrétien was settling his private business affairs in preparation for his new public office role, he and two business associates sold their shares in Auberge Grand-Mère to Yvon Duhaime. Chrétien had also held shares in an adjacent golf course, and he attempted to sell his shares in the golf course to Jonas Prince, a Toronto businessman.

The first problem Chrétien encountered was that Prince reported that he had not followed through with the sale. There were embarrassing moments when Prince claimed to members of the media that he had only had an option on Chrétien's share in the golf course, an option he had never followed through with. Chrétien maintained that the sale had been final, and Prince still owed him money. Eventually, another buyer was found for the unwanted shares.

There is nothing wrong with a Prime Minister owning shares of a golf course, unless those shares are likely to get him involved in a conflict-of-interest situation. On the advice of the Ethics Counsellor, Chrétien had put assets that might get him into a conflict-of-interest situation into a "blind trust."[24] So after Prince failed to follow through with his purchase of the golf course shares, they sat in the blind trust with other non-personal assets of the Prime Minister.

Meanwhile, Yvon Duhaime, the new owner of the Auberge, wanted to renovate and enlarge it, and he applied for a $2 million loan from the Business Development Bank (BDB), a federal government enterprise. Duhaime apparently could not raise the funds from a private institution because of the risk, and the BDB was also skeptical. Duhaime asked his friend and MP, Jean Chrétien, for help, and Chrétien telephoned François Beaudoin, president of the Bank, on behalf of Duhaime. Later in 1996, Chrétien met Beaudoin at his residence and again spoke on Duhaime's behalf. In spite of Chrétien's intervention, the BDB turned down Duhaime's application. In 1997, Duhaime applied for a smaller loan from the BDB for $615,000 and also for an HRDC grant of $164,000. This time, after another intervention from Chrétien on Duhaime's behalf, he was successful in obtaining the smaller grant.

The story gradually unfolded during 1999 and 2000, and the Ethics Counsellor was asked to investigate on three occasions, the last time just before the 2000 election. Each time, he found that the Prime Minister had not been in a conflict-of-interest situation. He ruled that the Prime Minister had not been aware that he still owned the golf course shares until 1999, and so his interventions on behalf of Duhaime, which might have resulted in a more attractive Auberge and therefore might have increased the value of the golf course shares, did not really constitute a conflict of interest. As with previous conflict-of-interest events, the Ethics Counsellor could well have been right in his conclusions, but because of his lack of independence, his conclusions were not terribly persuasive. Later, Wilson recommended that the Prime Minister's conflict-of-interest guidelines should be amended to prohibit a Cabinet minister from lobbying a government agency on behalf of a constituent.

Also just before the 2000 election, François Beaudoin complained that he had been let go as head of the BDB because he had attempted to recall the $615,000 loan to the Auberge. Beaudoin's allegations kept the

Auberge scandal in the limelight throughout 2001 and 2002. Progressive Conservative leader Joe Clark continued to press for legislation to create an independent ethics commissioner right up until May of 2002, when Chrétien announced legislation creating an independent ethics commissioner. Meanwhile, Beaudoin launched a lawsuit against the federal government, claiming that his removal as head of the BDB was politically motivated. In February of 2004, Beaudoin scored a major victory in the lawsuit. The judgment of Justice André Denis of the Québec Superior Court "completely vindicated" Beaudoin and criticized Michel Vennant, Beaudoin's replacement as head of the BDB, for misleading the BDB Board. In March of 2004 the Martin government fired Vennat in an attempt to distance itself from the Chretien government's handling of the situation.[25]

Had an independent ethics counsellor been in place from 1993, someone with the authority to review thoroughly all of the Prime Minister's non-personal assets to ensure compliance with ethics rules, it is quite possible that the Auberge Grand-Mère scandal could have been avoided.

The APEC *Inquiry and Solicitor General Scott, 1997–2000*

In the fall of 1997, Canada hosted the Asian-Pacific Economic Cooperation (APEC) summit in Vancouver. Representing Indonesia was its authoritarian president Suharto, whose human rights record was anything but stellar. Suharto had apparently been promised by Prime Minister Chrétien that he could be shielded from seeing protesters while in Vancouver, and the Prime Minister's Office was in contact with RCMP security services in Vancouver to keep the Prime Minister briefed on security arrangements. Security services attempted to keep legitimate protesters as far away as possible from Suharto, and television footage indicated that police may have used excessive force against demonstrators whose only fault was that they happened to possibly be within Suharto's range of vision. Civil suits were filed by protesters against the RCMP, and some formal complaints were lodged.[26]

Complaints against the RCMP with *prima facie* validity are considered by the Public Complaints Commission, which strikes three-member panels to investigate such complaints. The panel for the APEC affair was headed by Gerald Morin, who scheduled a hearing for early October, 1998. In the meantime, criticism of the Prime Minister over the APEC affair grew because of reports that the Prime Minister's Office may have helped to orchestrate the harsh treatment of the protesters, because the government refused to cover any of the cost of the lawyers hired by the protesters, and because the Morin inquiry was limited to the actions of the RCMP, excluding the possible role of the Prime Minister's Office. In September, Chrétien issued a weak apology for the way the protesters had been treated, but this only increased demands for a judicial inquiry. On the eve of first session of the Morin Public Complaints Commission inquiry, Solicitor General Andy Scott, while flying out of Ottawa, was overheard by an NDP MP discussing what he expected the Morin inquiry to find. When the MP made Scott's remarks public, there were calls for Scott to resign because of prejudicing the results of the inquiry. Scott claimed that his remarks would not prejudice the inquiry, and Chrétien initially supported him.

Pressure continued on Scott to resign, which he did on 23 November. As well, Gerald Morin was overheard saying that he thought that two RCMP officers had acted improperly during the APEC protest, and so lawyers representing RCMP officers tried to shut down the Morin panel because of the perceived bias of the chair. In early December, Morin resigned, and the other two panel members followed his example. On 21 December, Ted Hughes was appointed to head a one-man Complaints Commission inquiry. Hughes was a retired superior court judge from Saskatchewan, and the former ethics commissioner for British Columbia. His credibility meant that the inquiry process could resume, and because of Hughes' background, it had the trappings of a judicial inquiry.

The Hughes inquiry lasted for well over one hundred days in 1999 and 2000, hearing evidence that indicated that security arrangements were established with the goal of keeping protesters far away from the authoritarian leaders attending the conference. However, individual officers testified that they had not been pressured by the PMO to act in the way they did. In 2001, Hughes issued his report, which was critical of the PMO for intervening in the affairs of a police force whose mandate it was to administer the law impartially. On the other hand, Hughes wrote that there was no evidence that the Prime Minister was personally involved in trying to direct the RCMP operations.

The APEC affair put the spotlight on the ethical question of whether the Prime Minister had been respectful enough of the need for an arms-length relationship between the government and the police in a rule-of-law democratic regime. As well, it once again pointed to the importance of the impartiality principle when establishing a public inquiry process.

Human Resources Development Canada, 1999–2000

In 1999, the report by Auditor General Denis Desautels was full of praise for the government's attempts to promote accountability and transparency. At the same time, he was critical of practices where the protocols for tendering contracts had been ignored, and especially where contacts were awarded without soliciting bids. He was particularly critical of the practices of Human Resources Development Canada (HRDC), which was already in the spotlight because of an internal audit that highlighted shoddy practices in allocating grants to businesses and individuals.

The deficiencies of the practices of HRDC continued as front-page news during the first part of 2000. Human Resources Minster Jane Stewart had ordered an audit of the $3 billion Transitional Job Fund, and when she released the report it showed that about 80 percent of the files had problems. More than 70 percent of the applications for funds did not have proper business plans, as required. Police investigations eventually took place, and numerous charges were laid.[27] Auditor General Desautels conducted another review of HRDC and reported systemic discrepancies in the department's management of grants.

According to a senior public servant I interviewed, the HRDC scandal resulted from the philosophy of new public management (NPM), a public administration movement which began in the early 1990s as a means of making government less "bureaucratic" and more efficient and responsive.[28] NPM evolved into an approach that advocated that public services ought to act more like businesses in order to become more efficient, and ought to cast off unnecessary red tape. This approach was adopted with enthusiasm by many neo-liberal and neo-conservative governments in the western world,[29] but sometimes the fact that NPM did not advocate abandoning accountability was overlooked. The way in which NPM was implemented by HRDC opened the door to abuse by those who saw the government as an easy source of money, and by those who viewed political connections as a means to enrich themselves. During 2000, the HRDC put back into place traditional controls to prevent fraud and abuse, measures subsequently applauded by the Auditor General.

Public Works Canada and Alfonso Gagliano, 1999–2004

Later in 2000, Public Works Minister Alfonso Gagliano was attacked by the opposition for awarding advertising contracts to companies that had close ties either to the Liberal Party or to members of his family (or both).

The contracts were awarded in the wake of the narrow victory of the "no" side in the 1995 Québec referendum, when the Chrétien government instituted a pro-federalism advertising campaign in Québec. For example, in 1999, a company called Groupaction was awarded a $615,000 contract to report on the impact of government contracts for sponsorship of recreational events, and for this fee produced only a twenty-page report. An internal audit of Public Works indicated that proper controls were not in place regarding the advertising contracts, and Gagliano was accused of being in a conflict-of-interest position for awarding contracts to companies that subcontracted their printing to a company in which Gagliano's son was prominent. In 2001, Ethics Counsellor Howard Wilson cleared Gagliano of the conflict allegations, but the Ethics Counsellor's review was not taken seriously by many because of the Counsellor's lack of independence. Early in 2002, Gagliano resigned from the Cabinet and was appointed as Canada's ambassador to Denmark. Don Boudria took over as the new Minister of Public Works.

The scrutiny of Public Works Canada continued, and in May of 2002 the new Auditor General, Sheila Fraser, issued a report claiming that bureaucrats dealing with Groupaction had broken "just about every rule in the book."[30] This investigation led to a more detailed report released by the Auditor General in February 2004. This report indicated that the scale of abuse was far worse than originally suspected. After the 1995 Québec referendum and up to 2004, the federal government spent $250 million to sponsor events to promote Canada, particularly in Québec. Much of the money was paid out through Liberal-friendly advertising agencies that held back tens of thousands of dollars for commissions. A good deal of the money that actually got to the programs it was intended for seemed wasted. Fraser said the scale of the misappropriation was "outrageous." Prime Minister Martin recalled Gagliano from Denmark, fired the heads of several Crown agencies involved in the scandal, established an independent inquiry headed by Justice John Gomery to investigate the affair, and took steps to recover the misappropriated funds. In spite of these commendable actions, the Liberal Party's image was badly tarnished, support for the party plummeted, and the party lost its majority in the election of June 2004.[31]

Justice Gomery released his first report on 1 November 2005, and in it he blamed Jean Chrétien and his Chief of Staff, Jean Pelletier, for making serious errors in administrative judgment that set the stage for the sponsorship scandal. Gomery did not find the former Prime Minister guilty of any corrupt practices, but criticized him for allowing the sponsorship program to be run out of the Prime Minister's Office, where the usual bureaucratic controls to ensure value for money could more easily be circumvented.

Prime Minister Martin was not implicated by Gomery. Soon after the report's release, Martin banned for life from the Liberal Party ten party officials who were severely criticized by Gomery, and he ordered the party to repay the $1.14 million that Gomery found was illegally funnelled into party coffers from the sponsorship program. Gomery also found that Alfonso Gagliano played a major role in perpetuating the irregular way in which the sponsorship program was run. He noted that Chuck Guité, a bureaucrat working for Mr. Gagliano, used the sponsorship program to reward friends as well as Liberal-friendly advertising firms. (In his testimony at the Gomery inquiry, Guité reported that these kinds of practices had also gone on during the Mulroney period, except it was the Conservative-friendly advertising firms that reaped the benefits.) As well, Gomery wrote that Jean Corriveau, who was a good friend of Jean Chrétien, ran a "kickback scheme" that resulted in sponsorship funds going into his own pocket, as well as the Québec wing of the Liberal Party of Canada.[32]

The rule of law, which can be regarded as a key principle of ethical politics, implies the impartial administration of government programs – a concept that is sometimes hard to grasp for "old style" politicians who may prefer to view them more as a means of advancing partisan and personal agendas than as services established for the sole purpose of promoting the public interest.

Don Boudria, Art Eggleton, Lawrence MacAulay, and the Irvings, 2000

May of 2002 was not a good month for the government's ethics record. On 20 May, it was revealed that the new Public Works Minister, Don Boudria, had accepted hospitality in the form of a luxury ski weekend for himself and his family at the home of a Québec advertising executive with interests in government contracts. After consulting with the Ethics Counsellor, Boudria admitted that accepting the hospitality created the perception of conflict of interest, and he resigned as Public Works Minister, to be replaced by Ralph Goodale.

A few days later, it was revealed that Defence Minister Art Eggleton had hired a personal friend to do work for which she had few qualifications. Eggleton was accused of conflict of interest, and also resigned after consulting with the Ethics Counsellor.

At the end of May, Solicitor General Lawrence MacAulay was accused of a conflict of interest for contacting RCMP Commissioner Giuliano Zaccardelli to support a $3.5 million grant for a college in Prince Edward Island for which MacAulay's brother was applying. Pressure mounted for MacAulay to resign, which he did in October after Ethics Counsellor Howard Wilson ruled that he had violated the government's ethics guidelines.

The Boudria, Eggleton, and MacAulay affairs indicate the poor understanding of the nature of conflicts of interest possessed by some Cabinet ministers. As a result, there was intense pressure from the public and the official opposition for the government to legislate an independent ethics commissioner with the authority to try to ensure that Cabinet ministers understand the nature of conflicts of interest and why they are unacceptable. The need for such an official became even more apparent in October of 2003, when several federal Cabinet ministers, including Labour Minister Claudette Bradshaw, Fisheries Minister Robert Thibault, Industry Minister Alan Rock, and Environment Minister David Anderson, admitted that they had accepted free plane trips and other substantial hospitality favours from companies owned by the Irving family, one of the wealthiest families in the Maritimes.

ACHIEVEMENTS

In spite of the ethical lapses of the Chrétien administration, some progress was made toward establishing rules and procedures for promoting higher ethical standards among Cabinet ministers. The Prime Minister and his Liberal supporters were likely sincere in 1993 when they promised to govern with integrity. The essential problem, according to a former Chrétien Cabinet minister who spoke to me anonymously, was that the Prime Minister was an "old-style" politician who believed that the use of a certain amount of political influence to help friends and supporters was simply part of the political game. From that perspective, there is nothing ethically wrong with helping political supporters, as long as politicians do not line their own pockets, and as long as these supporters act in the broad public interest. But it was not just Chrétien who held these kinds of views. It is likely that a number of Liberal Cabinet ministers and backbenchers also believed that a certain amount of "greasing the wheel" was ethically acceptable, and politically unavoidable. What needed to be avoided was the excessive granting of favours and the use of public office for personal gain.

From the perspective of democratic theory, however, we need to move beyond this "old style" of politics. Democracy demands equality, the rule of law, and the impartial application of the law. These principles imply that the law ought to be applied even-handedly, and that no one – especially public office-holders and their associates and supporters – should use public office either for personal gain or to reward friends or colleagues.

Every provincial and territorial legislature has now enacted conflict of interest legislation that prohibits any elected member from continuing in a real conflict of interest situation, or a situation in which a member could potentially make a personal gain from involvement in a public office decision. In recent years, "personal gain" has been interpreted more broadly to include providing favours to friends and political supporters.[33] In nine provinces, an independent ethics commissioner has been appointed to help to educate elected members about the conflict-of-interest rules, to advise on appropriate measures to handle non-personal assets so as to avoid conflicts of interest, and to investigate alleged breaches of the rules.

The Chrétien government, however, remained opposed to the concept of an independent ethics commissioner until the series of ethics scandals described above finally forced a change of heart in 2002. The government then proposed legislation to create a Code of Conduct for Parliamentarians similar to the conflict of interest legislation in place in the provinces and territories. The legislation would also establish an independent ethics commissioner, appointed for a term of five years, who would report to Parliament. The commissioner or his or her officials would communicate with MPs and Senators to explain the Code of Conduct, arrange for appropriate public disclosure of non-personal assets, and advise on disposal of assets likely to result in conflict-of-interest situations.

The legislation had some flaws. Decisions about appropriate ethical behaviour of Cabinet ministers would continue to be made by the Prime Minister rather than by Parliament, although the Ethics Commissioner would have the power to investigate allegations that ministers had violated by the Prime Minister's guidelines for Cabinet ministers (which would continue to operate) and report to the Prime Minister. Spouses and close family members would not be covered by the new Code. And the legislation would not require face-to-face meetings between the Ethics Commissioner's office and MPs or Senators. In November of 2003, the legislation was amended by the Senate so that the upper house would be able to choose its own internal ethics officer, and the bill died when Parliament prorogued just prior to the November Liberal leadership convention. Legislation to create an independent ethics commissioner or commission had also been introduced in 1988, 1992, and 1997, and these previous attempts also died on the order paper.

Prime Minister Paul Martin, however, was committed to the idea of independent ethics commissioners as part of his plan to reduce the "democratic deficit," legislation creating an independent Ethics Commissioner for the House of Commons and Cabinet as well as an independent Ethics Officer for the Senate was enacted prior to the 2004 election.[34] The first Ethics Commissioner for the House of Commons – Dr. Bernard Shapiro, former Principal of McGill University – was nominated by Prime Minister Martin in May of 2004. The Prime Minister is supposed to consult with opposition leaders regarding the appointment, but the consultation was, to say the least, rushed, thus creating a sour note for the new office to start on.

A second thrust in ethics rules in Canadian politics in recent years has been lobbyist registration legislation. The Mulroney government was the first to enact such legislation, perhaps in response to the lobbying activities of Frank Moores mentioned above. In 1993, the Liberals promised to toughen up the Conservative legislation by making the ethics counsellor in charge of the *Lobbyists Registration Act* more independent and by requiring registered consultant lobbyists to disclose their lobbying methods and targets. They carried out this promise in 1995. As well, the government promoted a Code of Conduct for lobbyists (and gave the Ethics Counsellor the power to investigate alleged violations), and a Code of Conduct for public officials when dealing with lobbyists.[35] Reform of the *Lobbyists Registration Act* is also an important step forward in promoting ethical government, although even tougher legislation would require lobbyists to disclose their fees and would require fees to be "fair and reasonable."[36]

A third method of promoting ethics in politics is to place limits on the amount of money that can be donated by individuals or organizations to political parties and candidates. The purpose of such limits is to prevent the possibility or the perception that donations are made with the expectation of public office favours in return. If limits are low enough, it is unlikely that they will impact, or be perceived to impact, decisions by elected members. Ontario and Québec have tried to combat undue influence by limiting contributions to political parties. Ontario permits contributions from individuals, unions, and corporations, but limits donations to $750 per candidate, with a limit on the number of candidates who can receive donations from a single source. (This amount is doubled in an election year.) Québec limits contributions to individuals, with a maximum of $3,000. In 2000, Manitoba's legislature also enacted legislation to limit political contributions.

Perhaps because of the attempts of some individuals and corporations to influence public policy through large political donations while he was Prime Minister, Chrétien announced, as part of his 2002 ethics package, that legislation would be introduced to limit political contributions as well as to ban contributions from corporations, associations, and unions. When the legislation was tabled, the annual total limit on individual contributions was set at $5,000. However, corporations, unions, and associations were allowed to make contributions of only $1,000 annually, and these contributions were limited to constituency associations, candidates and their campaigns, and local nominations; contributions of these groups to the national party or leadership campaigns were outlawed. At the same time, the bill increased government contributions to registered political parties to cover 60 percent of their expenses (up from 22.5 percent) up to certain limits, and to cover 50 percent of the expenses of individual candidates as long as they received at least 10 percent of the popular vote (down from 15 percent). As well, there is a payment to parties of $1.75 for each vote received in the previous election. Furthermore, the legislation covers leadership conventions and candidate nomination campaigns. (Separate limits apply to these events, but the legislation requires such donations to be made public, for the first time.) The legislation, which received royal assent in June of 2003, represents a major step forward in combatting undue influence in politics.[37]

A fourth way in which ethics in politics can be promoted is to curtail as much as possible the influence of patronage in making order-in-council appointments. As part of the Red Book promises in 1993, the Liberals promised to improve the system of federal judicial appointments to superior courts by making appointments more transparent and less open to political influence. The promise was kept in part when the judicial appointments advisory committees that had been set up by the Mulroney government were mandated to encourage applications for judgeships from outside the political process, and they publicized the judicial appointments process on the government's website. However, the promise to make the process more transparent by making public the names of persons on the appointments advisory committees was not kept.

The Chrétien government did only a little to combat patronage in other areas. Thanks to reforms introduced by the Chrétien government, many order-in-council appointments are now subject to scrutiny by Parliamentary committees. This is a step in the right direction, but does not eliminate the need for a selection system for members of administrative tribunals, boards, and agencies based on merit rather than political connections. The revelations about the misspending and mismanagement of George Radwanski, who had been the Chrétien-appointed Privacy Commissioner until forced to resign in 2003 under threat of removal by Parliament, underlines the inadequacy of the current patronage-based appointments system. And although Chrétien appears to have made fewer patronage appointments as rewards to loyal followers when leaving office than most of his predecessors, the dozens of patronage appointments made by Chrétien during November of 2003 just before his retirement, supports the portrait as Chrétien as an "old-style" politician with only slightly higher standards than his predecessors.

The promotion of higher ethical standards in the public service had been a priority of the Chrétien government, though it is difficult to determine whether this commitment came primarily from Red Book promises, rather than from urgings by the Auditors General Desautels and Fraser, and concerns raised by officials in the Treasury Board Secretariat. Nevertheless, the continuing set of initiatives to highlight public service ethics,[38] culminating in the government's *Revised Values and Ethics Code for the Public Service* (which also establishes a Public Service Integrity Officer who can investigate complaints of ethical breaches by public servants)[39] announced in 2003, is to be commended.

The Red Book itself made an important contribution to the principle that parties should be accountable for the promises they make in election campaigns. The Red Book was likely, at the time, the most comprehensive election platform ever set out by a Canadian party, and the Liberal Party attempted to hold itself accountable by publishing an audit of its performance after three years. The problem was that the Party was not willing to submit its Red Book promises to an independent audit, and so the internal audit lacked credibility.

CONCLUSION: A BETTER ETHICS RECORD THAN MULRONEY, BUT ONLY MEDIOCRE GRADES

The ethics record of the Chrétien government was better than that of its predecessor. On the legislative front, the Mulroney government's only significant contribution was the first *Lobbyists Registration Act*. In comparison, the Chrétien Liberals not only introduced important enhancements to that legislation to prevent undue influence by lobbyists, but they also enacted legislation to limit campaign contributions from single sources and gave a much higher profile to ethical practices in the public service. As well, the Chrétien government came very close to having conflict-of-interest legislation passed that would have created an independent ethics commissioner, and it paved the way for later legislative efforts in this area. Had the ethics commissioner legislation been enacted at the beginning of the Chrétien era, however, it is possible that a number of the ethics scandals endured by the Chrétien government could have been avoided, such as those involving Dupuy, Collenette, Gagliano, Boudria, Eggleton, MacAulay, the Cabinet ministers who accepted hospitality from the Irvings, and the Prime Minister himself regarding the Auberge Grand-Mère affair and the sponsorship scandal.

The other major shortcoming of the Chrétien government was its unwillingness to apply the impartiality principle to the resolution of ethics controversies. Had an impartial commission of inquiry been appointed to review the Pearson Airport deal, or the Airbus fiasco, or the APEC affair right from the beginning, the ethics legacy of the Chrétien government would most likely have been brighter. The legacy would also have been more positive had the government gone further to reduce patronage appointments and instead promoted appointments based solely on merit for federal boards, tribunals, and commissions, and if the government had taken steps earlier on to ensure impartiality in the distribution of funds from HRDC and Public Works Canada.

Like his precedessor in the Prime Minister's Office, Paul Martin has made ethical government one of the cornerstones of the agenda for his administration. Hours after being sworn in as Prime Minister on 12 December 2003, Martin described the core principles of his government as "transparency, accountability and ethical conduct."[40] In pursuing his ethics agenda, Martin's starting point was the Chrétien ethics legacy – both its contributions and shortcomings. Martin announced that one of his priorities was to ensure passage of the legislation establishing independent ethics commissioners for the Senate and House of Commons prior to the 2004 election. He succeeded in doing so, although the process of appointment of the first Ethics Commissioner for the House of Commons left something to be desired. Chrétien can at least be thanked for belatedly establishing the groundwork for this long-overdue reform.

NOTES

Professor, Department of Political Science, and Associate, Centre for Practical Ethics, York University.

1 Liberal Party of Canada (LPC), *Creating Opportunity: The Liberal Plan for Canada* (Ottawa: LPC, 1993), 91-5.

2 R.S.C. 1985, c. L-12.

3 LPC, *Creating Opportunity*, 94.

4 LPC, *A Record of Achievement: A Report on the Liberal Government's 36 Months in Office* (Ottawa: LPC, 1996).

5 Ibid., at 9.

6 Ian Greene and David P. Shugarman, *Honest Politics: Seeking Integrity in Canadian Public Life* (Toronto: James Lorimer, 1997), 52–4.

7 During the seventeenth century, the Stuart Kings of England made a similar argument as to why they would not allow judges to be independent. The fear, then as now, was that independent officials sometimes make decisions that politicians do not like.

8 Greene and Shugarman, *Honest Politics*, 51.

9 "Sinclair Stevens," *Wikipedia*, http://en.wikipedia.org/wiki/Sinclair_Stevens.

10 According to the Prime Minister's conflict of interest guidelines, Cabinet ministers are not supposed to use, or appear to use, their influence to sway judges or members of administrative tribunals, such as the CRTC. The Dupuy oversight was made worse by the fact that Dupuy was the minister responsible for the CRTC. As well, it was revealed that several other ministers had sent letters to the CRTC on behalf of constituents.

11 Susan Delacourt, "New guidelines for Ministers promised in wake of Dupuy affair," *Globe and Mail*, 1 November 1994, A1, A2.

12 Greene and Shugarman, Honest Politics, Ch. 6.

13 Jeffrey Simpson, "What are these ethical guidelines that brought down Collenette?" *Globe and Mail*, 8 October 1996, A18.

14 Greene and Shugarman, *Honest Politics*, 112–25.

15 Peter Cheney and Dale Brazao, "Moores king of movers, shakers," *The Toronto Star*, 3 December 1995, A18.

16 Carolyn Abraham, "Bribes rampant in aerospace industry," *Southam News Internet Report*, 22 December 1995.

17 Robert Everett, "Parliament and Politics," in David Mutimer, ed., *Canadian Annual Review of Politics and Public Affairs, 1997* (Toronto: University of Toronto Press, 2003), 11–53.

18 Simon Tuck, "Airbus probe's tab at least $6.4-million, papers reveal," *Globe and Mail*, 26 December 2003, A1.

19 Kirk Makin, "Special: Secret trial revealed," *Globe and Mail*, 7 November 2003, A1.

20 Daniel Leblanc, "Critics assail Mulroney over deal with Schreiber," *Globe and Mail*, 11 November 2003, A1.

21 Ibid., A8.

22 LPC, *A Record of Achievement: A Report on the Liberal Government's 36 Months in Office* (Ottawa: LPC, 1996).

23 Greene and Shugarman, Honest Politics, 19–21.

24 Justice William Parker, who headed the inquiry into Sinclair Stevens in 1986, had warned of the weaknesses of blind trusts. Unless trustees are empowered to sell all assets in a blind trust and buy others instead, the owner still has knowledge of what is in the "blind" trust, and could still get involved in a conflict situation where the owner could use public office to enhance the value of his or her assets.

25 Margaret Wente, "Couldn't happen to a nicer guy," *Globe and Mail*, 13 March 2004, A23.

26 See W. Wesley Pue, *Pepper In Our Eyes: The APEC Affair* (Vancouver: University of British Columbia Press, 1999).

27 Robert Everett, "Parliament and Politics," in David Mutimer, ed., *Canadian Annual Review of Politics and Public Affairs*, 2000 (University of Toronto Press, forthcoming).

28 David Osborne and Ted Gaebler, *Reinventing Government: How the Entrepreneurial Spirit Is Transforming the Public Sector* (Reading: Addison-Wesley, 1992).

29 Janice Gross Stein, *The Cult of Efficiency* (Toronto: House of Anansi, 2002).

30 Canada, Office of the Auditor General, *Report to the Minister of Public Works and Government Services on Three Contracts Awarded to Groupaction (Ottawa: Minister of Public Works and Government Services, 8 May 2002)*, http://www.oag-bvg.gc.ca/domino/reports.nsf/html/02sprepe.html/$file/02sprepe.pdf. For a summary of the Groupaction affair, see "Origin of a scandal," CBC News Online, 12 August 2004, http://www.cbc.ca/news/background/groupaction/timeline_origin.html.

31 Campbell Clark and Daniel Leblanc, "Fraser puts heat on PM," *Globe and Mail*, 11 February 2004, A1.

32 Canada, Commission of Inquiry into the Sponsorship Program and Advertising Activities, *Who is Responsible? Phase 1 Report* (Ottawa: Minister of Public Works and Government Services, 2005), http://www.gomery.ca/en/phase1report/.

33 Greene and Shugarman, *Honest Politics*, ch. 4.

34 *An Act to amend the Parliament of Canada Act (Ethics Commissioner and Senate Ethics Officer)*, S.C. 2004, c. 7, http://www.canlii.org/ca/as/2004/c7/whole.html.

35 Ian Greene, "Principle Versus Partisanship: The Chrétien Government's Record on Integrity Issues," in Gene Swimmer, ed., *How Ottawa Spends 1997–98: Seeing Red: A Liberal Report Card* (Ottawa: Carleton University Press, 1997), 287–307.

36 A clause requiring lobbyists' fees to be fair and reasonable was deleted from an early draft of the legislation.

37 *An Act to amend the Lobbyists Registration Act*, S.C. 2003, c. 10, http://www.canlii.org/ca/as/2003/c10/whole.html.

38 Eleanor D. Glor and Ian Greene, "The Government of Canada Approach to Ethics: The Evolution of Ethical Government," *Public Integrity* 5 (2002): 41–67.

39 Treasury Board of Canada Secretariat, *Values and Ethics Code for the Public Service: Democratic, Professional, Ethical & People Values* (Ottawa: Minister of Public Works and Government Services, 2003), http://www.hrma-agrh.gc.ca/veo-bve/code/alternate/vec-cve_e.pdf.

40 Andrew McIntosh, "Martin's new ethics rules include ban on private jets," *National Post*, 13 December 2003, A6.

14

Could the Rebels Find a Cause?

House of Commons Reform in the Chrétien Era

DAVID DOCHERTY

INTRODUCTION

Jean Chrétien's three consecutive majority governments stand as a testament to his political acumen. While his success was certainly assisted by the lack of a viable national alternative, there can be no denying the fact that Chrétien managed what only three other Prime Ministers have done, to win three successive majorities. Pierre Trudeau served longer, Brian Mulroney had a bigger majority, but neither of these predecessors could manage to hold majority governments for over ten years in a row.

Given our Westminster Parliament, leaders of majority governments are granted nearly unlimited powers. The authority of a prime minister under such conditions is overwhelming. And Jean Chrétien was certainly willing to embrace and, indeed, expand the power of his office. Political observers have not hesitated to use terms such as "friendly dictator" to describe his style and the control he and his office exerted.[1]

What is the impact on the Canadian House of Commons of Jean Chrétien's use of power? What is the parliamentary legacy of Jean Chrétien? From one perspective it will not reflect well on the former Prime Minister. He did not embrace reform of Parliament and, in fact, treated his own caucus much like the cliched cohort of "yes" men and women. His was not Parliament-centred government, nor even executive- centred, but evolved into prime ministerial-centred government. He used party discipline effectively and at times ruthlessly. But from a different perspective, the Chrétien parliamentary decade might be looked upon as the catalyst for subsequent reform of Canada's lower chamber. Not because the Prime Minister embraced a relaxing of party discipline and a greater role for MPs, but rather his consistent refusal to listen to his members eventually led them to rebel.

This chapter examines the Parliament of Canada during the thirty-fifth, thirty-sixth, and thirty-seventh Parliaments. It argues that most democratic reform that came about during the Chrétien era was a reaction against the Prime Minister. Jean Chrétien did not instigate reform so much as his actions toward his own caucus inspired backbench Liberals to embrace it on their own. In doing so, government backbenchers have taken a brave step toward fundamental reform within Parliament. Chrétien's muscular use of party discipline may have prevented meaningful reform while he led his government, and subsequent Prime Ministers may see Chrétien as a leader who pushed the line too far and eventually felt the backlash from his own caucus. In doing so, Chrétien unwittingly encouraged the desire for reform among the group that really mattered, the government backbench.

SETTING THE CHRÉTIEN STAGE: THE HOUSE OF COMMONS PRIOR TO 1993

Observing parliamentary reform in Canada can be trying. With every new government comes the promise of "greater participation" for private members, increased debate on Private Member's Business, greater freedom for committees, and the standard promise to loosen party discipline and allow for more free votes.[2] Of course the promise and the reality are often quite at odds. Changes tend to take place at the margins, and some are often found to have less than desirable effects. When the latter occurs, new governments are quick to revert to previous practice, instead of looking at different alternatives to solve long-standing problems. Yet despite the perhaps glacial pace of change in the House of Commons, the direction of movement has always been toward greater democratization of the assembly.

Canada's Parliament is executive-centred.[3] On this there is little debate. Westminster systems encourage party solidarity and cohesiveness. Prime ministers cannot properly lead their Cabinet, party, and government if the threat of loss of confidence is constantly surrounding them. As a result, the need for strong leadership (and the need to keep members supporting their leader) is a natural part of Canada's system of government. Of course, prime ministers must be sensitive to their members. Members of the governing caucus who are not in Cabinet must be allowed to both represent their constituents and participate in decisions affecting the national interest. The trick is in balancing party discipline with participation.

When Brian Mulroney won his overwhelming majority in 1984 he was faced with just this problem. He had a huge caucus – 211 MPs in a House of 282. Even after appointing the largest Cabinet in Canadian history (forty members) he was left with a large and potentially unwieldy backbench. Included in his caucus were supporters of former leader Joe Clark, veteran Conservatives who believed they should be in Cabinet, new Québec MPs who had sympathies for a more nationalist Québec, and new Conservative MPs from the west who were supporters of a much more right-wing approach to governing. The trick in managing this disparate group was to keep them busy!

Early on in the thirty-third Parliament, Mulroney appointed the McGrath committee – a special committee of the House of Commons – to examine how the roles of Members of Parliament might be improved.[4] The genesis for the committee originated during the thirty-second Parliament, under the chairship of Tom Lebrevre. The Lebrevre Committee had begun a major report on modernization of the House that died when the thirty-second Parliament ended.[5] Picking up on the work of Lebrevre, McGrath provided a detailed and forward-looking approach to opening up the legislative process to greater backbench participation.

Mulroney, who had little history in the House of Commons, and was by no one's definition a parliamentarian, embraced some, but not all, of the significant changes proposed by McGrath and the other members of the committee. Notable among the accepted recommendations were changes to the introduction of Private Member's Business, the secret ballot election of the Speaker of the House of Commons, and changes to the committee structure.

The move to secret ballot election of the Speaker was the greatest change. In fact, the move away from a prime ministerial selection (albeit endorsed by other parties) may be the single largest reform to the Canadian Parliament in the past thirty years in Canada.[6] For the first time, members had true control over who was to be both their steward and their servant. While some feared that the move to election would lead to MPs campaigning for the position, it was clear that would-be Speakers no longer had to limit their campaigning to the head of government.[7] Second, the fact that all provinces were quick to follow the federal lead suggests the reform was popular and lasting. Once members had the ability to choose their Speaker, there was no turning back.

The third large reform, creating legislative and standing committees, giving the former jurisdiction over specific legislation and the latter domain over policy fields, had unintended consequences. The rationale behind the split was laudable. Legislative committees could concentrate on bills before the House, while standing committees would be free to investigate matters of their own choosing. This autonomy was seen as a way of allowing committees to more freely and effectively engage in their accountability function. No longer were they limited to mandates imposed by the House; now they could determine their own agenda and investigate policy or departments at their own choosing. This move, again part of the McGrath recommendations, was strongly supported by government and opposition backbench MPs.

And to some degree it was successful. For example, the Standing Committee on Finance and Economic Affairs was, at times, an effective thorn in the side of the government. The chair of the committee, Progressive Conservative Don Blenkarn, was unafraid to scrutinize his own government. In doing so, Blenkarn managed to develop a strong national profile that was, no doubt, the envy of many junior Cabinet ministers. Reports of the committee were taken seriously by the press and the government.

Over the course of the remainder of the thirty-third and throughout the thirty-fourth Parliaments, however, it became apparent that many of the standing committees were engaging in interesting and important investigations that held little interest or import to members of the executive. The result was a large pile of reports gathering dust and a large cohort of MPs growing frustrated at an executive unwilling to acknowledge their efforts. In many cases the issues examined by committees were not pressing matters to the Cabinet.[8] On those occasions where the executive did have an interest, they also had an agenda, which did not always overlap with that of the committee.

More importantly, there was the problem of resources. Members with expertise in a particular policy field were stretched to serve on both a legislative committee and a standing committee looking at similar issues. Committees were essentially doubling up on the same members. This experiment would be scrapped and standing committees would once more examine legislation. Even advocates for a greater role for private members argued that this move was healthy. Some committees do have freedom to examine issues of their choosing. Special committees could be struck to examine particular matters or particular mandates could be given to standing committees. Although this limits some of the freedom of the committees, it does insure that they will be more likely to investigate relevant matters.

In terms of parliamentary reform, Brian Mulroney's biggest successes were his earliest. He did not embrace sweeping change, and certainly did not decrease the historic importance of party discipline in the House of Commons. By the end of his term, the Reform Party of Canada was poised to replace the Conservatives as Canada's party of the right. One of their main platforms was large scale institutional reform, including a Triple-E Senate and wholesale changes to our traditional understandings of what constitutes confidence in the House of Commons. It was into this scenario that Jean Chrétien inserted his 1993 election campaign pledges, in the form of his now-famous Red Book. Included in the Red Book's policy announcements and promises was Chrérien's commitment to enhance the role of the private member and loosen party discipline.

THE THIRTY-FIFTH PARLIAMENT OF CANADA AND THE PROMISE OF CHANGE

If there was one Parliament in recent history that held the tools to break with tradition it was the thirty-fifth Parliament. True, the Liberal Party had returned to their almost-assumed position as the government of the day. But that was about the only expected result of the 1993 election. Canada's other founding party, the Conservatives, had gone from two consecutive majority victories to a mere two seats. The New Democrats had been reduced from over forty seats to nine. Neither of these two traditional parties had enough members to garner recognized status in the House of Commons. But this was hardly the most bizarre result of the day.

The Bloc Québécois (BQ), arising out of the failure of the Meech Lake constitutional accord and the collapse of the Tories in Quebec, was now the second most successful party in the land, in the first general election they contested. The Reform Party, which had not elected a single member in the 1988 election, was now the third-largest party in the country in terms of seats.[9] The change was historic.

Some of the problems with high levels of turnover have been documented in greater detail elsewhere.[10] For our purposes it is important to note that in terms of experience and institutional memory the thirty-fifth Parliament was a House of neophytes. If ever there was a chance to challenge the prevailing norms of legislative life it was in the aftermath of the

1993 election. Two of the traditional parties were all but gone, and there existed within the new parties a desire for policy, constitutional, and parliamentary reform. The lack of institutional attachment and the huge influx of new blood set the stage for possible transformation.

What were the attitudes of these rookie members? Most, including members of the governing Liberal Party, arrived in Ottawa seeing themselves as agents of change. Certainly the Reform caucus was dedicated to altering the rules (both written and unwritten) that stressed party cohesion even at the expense of representing constituents. But even the new Liberal cohort saw themselves as constituency representatives first and party representatives second. Three-quarters of the rookie class in 1993 responding to a survey indicated that they would follow their constituents over their leader and party. The Reform Party had a higher total indicating constituency loyalty (over 90 percent), but nearly two-thirds of rookie Liberals answered in this manner.[11]

Of course, for Reform members such an attitude is almost a prerequisite to candidacy. For Liberals, there was at least some signal that such an approach to representation would be tolerated. After all, the Red Book, outlining the Liberal Party's plans for the thirty-fifth Parliament, talked of improving the role for private members. BQ members represented a much wider ideological spectrum than other parties, although they were predominately united by their views on a nationalist Québec. All the preconditions for a new understanding of party discipline and the role of private members were in place.

Yet this new understanding never emerged. Why? Despite the existence of these preconditions, it was never clear that a fundamental challenge to existing legislative norms was going to develop. First, while the Reform Party operated under a very relaxed notion of party discipline, there was considerable homogeneity among their elected cohort. They were, with few exceptions, neo-conservatives from western Canada who shared similar views on the economy and on most social issues. They may have represented a broader cross-section within their respective ridings, yet the actual Reform caucus was not ideologically diverse.[12] On most issues they voted together because they agreed with each other.

Second, Chrétien took advantage of his huge majority and actually magnified the experience gap. Off-setting the demands of new and enthusiastic members did not turn out to be a huge problem for the Prime Minister. Chrétien largely turned to veteran members to sit in Cabinet. This is hardly radical and made good strategic sense. Experience in the House of Commons is not a prerequisite to a successful Cabinet career, but there are few members who can quickly grasp the nuances of parliamentary life while grappling with large and complex government departments. Certainly some of the difficulties faced by, for example, Allan Rock early in the thirty-fifth Parliament might be attributed to his lack of understanding of legislative norms and roles. But in selecting, where possible, seasoned MPs for Cabinet duty, the Prime Minister created a large gap in experience between his Cabinet and virtually the rest of the House.[13]

At the beginning of the thirty-fifth Parliament, nearly all legislative experience rested with the Cabinet. The average years of experience among Cabinet members at this time was eight years of federal service, or two full terms. Among government backbenchers it was just over three years, or less than one term. Among opposition members is was barely over a year. In fact, when the New Democrats and Conservative MPs are pulled from the opposition cohort, the experience dropped to less than one year.[14]

The net result of this gap in experience was that new members were simply unable to keep the government accountable. Rookie MPs arrived in Ottawa thinking that within months they would be fully cognizant of all the formal and informal rules of the House of Commons. Most of these individuals later admitted that it took far longer than they initially thought before they felt they were working efficiently. For most of the first session of the thirty-fifth Parliament, rookie MPs on both sides of the Speaker's dais were finding their way around, both literally and figuratively. Many were uncomfortable asking questions during question period, particularly when veteran Liberals including Jean Chrétien, Herb Gray, Lloyd Axworthy, Sheila Copps, and Paul Martin – old hands at hard-core debate – were responding to their queries.

Third, well-intentioned moves by the Reform Party turned into strategic mistakes. The Reform Party's initial idea of discussion groups instead of a well-defined shadow Cabinet was an attempt to encourage a policy dialogue over a partisan debate. However within the naturally adversarial confines of the House of Commons, all this did was confuse lines of responsibility. Reform MPs did not know who in their party were critics for which departments and, more often than not, the government sidestepped accountability. In addition, there was a reluctance from members of the Reform caucus to turn to experienced politicians for advice.[15] The more experienced New Democrats were regarded with skepticism by many in the Reform Party despite the western-based party's desire to move beyond partisanship. The same was true for those experienced Liberals not in Cabinet and some members of the BQ who were former Tories. As a result, there was less opportunity for cross-party consensus on less contentious matters. Ironically, in campaigning for office by running against Parliament and the traditional parties, Reform actually increased party solidarity.

Fourth, as the first term unfolded, it became increasingly clear that from a member's perspective, party discipline can be a desirable beast. Given the difficulty in actually determining what constitutes a majority consensus in a constituency, and given that members often have access to greater information than most citizens, party solidarity provides a safety valve for many MPs. It is far easier for members to tell their constituents that "while they share their concerns, after much debate the party has decided to vote in a particular manner and that collective decisions must be honoured."

It might make good politics to indicate that as a Member of Parliament you would always place the constituency ahead of the party, but such a stance is risky. First, what might be in your constituency's interest may not lie in the national interest. As a member of Parliament you must often choose between competing interests, and depending upon the nature of the issue, the national interest may be far more consequential. The difficulty for members is informing voters that the national interest coincides with the stance of their party.

Further, even if members adamantly maintained their "constituency first" policy, rookie MPs in 1993 soon learned that taking the pulse of the riding on many matters was an impossible task. On uncontentious issues, there may be little public debate in the riding. On more divisive matters, the so-called "silent majority" may well be silenced and only the forceful advocates on either extreme are heard. For the most part, rookies in the thirty-fifth Parliament did not use any truly innovative ways of gathering the views of their citizens. Town hall meetings, following local debates, and household mail-outs asking residents to return a form soliciting views have been used by members of Parliament for years. It was not clear that these members were any more in touch with constituents than were their predecessors.

One particular piece of legislation in the government's first term highlighted the problem. Bill C-68 was the controversial gun control legislation. Under the direction of rookie Justice Minister Allan Rock, the Bill enjoyed widespread support across most of the country, but also met with staunch and vehement opposition within different regions. The Prime Minister had decided to stake out a strong position on this issue and was not willing to harbour internal dissent. However, Liberal MPs from rural ridings were facing strong and organized opposition to the bill at home. For other parties, the matter was less contentious. The BQ favoured the bill and the Reform Party opposed it, while eight of the nine New Democrats were opposed. One Reform MP, Jim Silye, supported the bill after he conducted a scientific poll in his Calgary riding that found the majority of his voters supported stricter gun laws. But in breaking with his party to vote with his constituents, Silye acknowledged that determining constituents views with accuracy on every issue was simply beyond the resources of members of Parliament.[16]

One further outcome of Bill C-68 resulted for the nine Liberal MPs who voted against it at third reading. While they may have received some kudos at home, the reception on Parliament Hill was much different. Despite the Red Book promise of relaxed party discipline, on some issues at least, Jean Chrétien was not below punishing those who broke ranks with their party. It was a strong signal that Jean Chrétien saw his government as executive-centred in the extreme. Matters of confidence would be decided by the Prime Minister, and those who strayed from the party lines would expect a very cold reception from the Prime Minister's Office. Loyalty to the party (and more importantly the leader) took priority over constituency representation. In this sense, nothing had changed, despite campaign pledges. The Prime Minister was determined to govern according to the Sam Rayburn congressional motto: to get along you go along.

Perhaps more interesting and telling was the reception that the Liberal caucus had for their dissenting brethren. Party solidarity helped to breed a sense of cohesiveness within the caucus, at least among those who took an unpopular local stance. Many urban Liberal MPs remarked that they held rural Liberal MPs who supported Bill C-68 in high regard. These members supported a bill they believed to be in the nation's best interest, despite opposition at home. By contrast, dissident Liberal MPs voted against a bill they knew would pass, knowing they would be treated as outspoken representatives of the public interest within their own ridings. The implied message was clear: solidarity reinforces itself; dissent leads in the other direction.

THE THIRTY-SIXTH PARLIAMENT AND THE PROBLEM OF NUMBERS

The second Chrétien majority was far more tenuous than the first; his majority was reduced to nine seats. If his first government had the luxury of a large majority and could afford some dissident backbenchers, the second could not. Yet for most of the second term, the Prime Minister governed as he did the first, knowing that, when necessary, he could force his members to rally behind the party banner. In some ways this was more easily accomplished in times of tighter majorities. When facing a united opposition, there is a greater tendency to band together. At the same time, the Prime Minister must also be cognizant that it requires fewer dissidents to defeat a bill, and thus must be more sensitive to the demands of his or her backbench. In fact, less than a half dozen Liberals voting with a united opposition could force the government into an unwanted election.

The largest problem facing the thirty-sixth Parliament, however, was not party unity but workload. The results of the 1997 vote meant that all five parties in Parliament enjoyed full party status. The New Democrats and Progressive Conservatives managed to win twenty-one and twenty seats, respectively. This allowed them to fully participate in all House of Commons activities on a regular basis, including question period and committees. The first problem encountered here was how to effectively manage the time of the Chamber.

A unique solution was found by agreement of all parties and the Speaker. A set order of questioners (including the use of supplementaries) was established and a strict adherence to time for both questions and responses was also determined. The result was not only greater participation from all parties, but a greater number of questions being posed. During the thirty-fifth Parliament, the forty-five-minute Question Period would typically see anywhere from thirteen to fifteen questions asked by ten or twelve different members. By contrast, in the thirty-sixth Parliament, Question Period would more typically have over twenty-three questions raised by anywhere from fifteen to eighteen members.[17]

In terms of accountability, this approach to Question Period was a qualified success. It was true that the new rotation did include more room for questions from the government backbenches and that these questions were more likely to solicit soft pro-government responses. But the shortening of questions did mean that every party, including the Official Opposition, increased the total number of questions asked. Further, there were questions regularly being posed by four distinct opposition parties. In terms of public discourse this was a marked improvement. In terms of scrutiny, the additional parties resulted in less cohesion in Question Period. Unless it is an issue that dominated all headlines, parties are less likely to focus their collective attention on one minister or policy. As a result, the new question period may be more participatory but it is also more disjointed.

There was also greater participation at the committee level, as New Democrats and Progressive Conservatives could now fully participate in committees. Yet the smaller number of government members and greater opposition party representation necessitated a change in committee size. Committees in the thirty-fifth Parliament typically had eleven voting members. In the thirty-sixth Parliament this was increased to sixteen. More critical was the actual party representation on committees. With committees of sixteen, the Liberals had nine members and the combined opposition seven. But, typically, one of the nine Liberals was the Chair, who only voted to break ties. This meant that full attendance at committee meetings (or at least for votes) was a priority. As a result, there was an increased emphasis on voting and attendance over substance, and substitutions were increasingly common.

But while some changes in the five-party Parliament were positive and some were rather neutral, others can be seen as adversely impacting the ability of private members to more fully participate in the legislative process. In particular, the thirty-sixth Parliament brought about an increase in the use of time allocation. The process, implemented under Standing Order 78(3), permits the government to limit the time that a bill can be debated. The process is viewed as less drastic than closure (which essentially kills debate and forces a vote) but is, nonetheless, regarded as a method to decrease, rather than foster, debate.

In the thirty-fifth Parliament, with three recognized parties, time allocation was used twenty times on 152 passed pieces of legislation. In the thirty-sixth Parliament, it was imposed twenty-nine times on ninety-five passed pieces of legislation.[18] This represents over a doubling in the rate of use of time allocation.

The cause for an increase in the use of time allocation is unclear. However, time allocation was often used on major, and occasionally controversial pieces of legislation. In some cases, there was support by some opposition parties for the use of Standing Order 78(3). Usually this occurred when opposition parties were split, with some supporting the legislation and others opposing it. Bill C-20, otherwise known as the *Clarity Act*, is a case in point. This legislation, introduced in the House on 13 December 1999, was supported by the Alliance and the New Democrats but opposed by the BQ and the Progressive Conservatives. Time allocation was used on three occasions for the *Clarity Act*, at second reading, at committee, and again at third reading. It was also used when extending benefits to same-sex couples and in ratifying the treaty between British Columbia, the Government of Canada and the Nisga'a nation.[19]

The thirty-sixth Parliament also saw a continued increase in the concentration of power in the Prime Minister's Office (PMO). The PMO used its authority extensively and it came not just at the expense of private members on the government side but also from Cabinet.[20] Canada's traditionally executive-centred Parliament was, indeed, increasingly becoming prime ministerial-centred.

Perhaps the most extreme use of this power was the decision of the Prime Minister to whip all Liberal MPs into line on the vote to limit compensation to Canadians who contracted Hepatitis C through blood transfusions. The action came after the federal government had announced that compensation would be available to Canadians who contracted Hepatitis C between 1986 and 1990. Those who contracted the disease prior to 1986 would not be eligible for compensation. To say that this decision sparked controversy would be an understatement.

While the government may have had the law on their side, the politics of the issue was certainly against them. As columnists, critics, editorialists and victims indicated, the government had offered broader compensation to many other Canadians without the seemingly arbitrary cut-off date.[21] Many members of the Liberal caucus were equally, and in some cases openly, concerned with the decision. While the actual decision may have come from Health Minister Allan Rock's office, the call to Liberals to rally around the government despite public criticism was headquartered in the PMO.

The matter came to a head when the Reform Party moved a motion in the Commons committing the government to provide compensation for all victims of Hepatitis C. Some Liberal MPs, taking flak at home for the government's position, were sympathetic to the motion. As a motion, it was non-binding. Some Liberal MPs even met to discuss the possibility of voting with the opposition.[22] In a somewhat surprising move, the Prime Minister declared the motion to be a matter of confidence in his government, even though the actual motion did not indicate non-confidence in the government.

This heavy hand of the Prime Minister seemed to mark a turning point in the relationship between Chrétien and his backbench. Political observers noted that many Liberals were voting against an opposition motion they would have preferred to endorse. Further, there was a growing resentment over the manner in which they were forced to support the

Cabinet. They were on the wrong side of a political issue, the opposition was united and the Prime Minister was demanding total loyalty to the party over political considerations at home. This was one issue where a healthy cadre of government members did not want to hide behind the comfort blanket of party discipline, yet they eventually did.

It is difficult to measure the precise impact of this event. Certainly the issue of compensation for Hepatitis C victims did not end with the defeat of the Reform Party motion. It continued on past the next election. But so, too, did the problem of demanding party loyalty. Chrétien's next – and last – Parliament, would see a remarkable change on a far less public and contentious motion placed by the very same opposition.

THE THIRTY-SEVENTH PARLIAMENT AND CHALLENGING PARTY SOLIDARITY

The re-election of Jean Chrétien and the Liberal Party on 27 November 2000 was an historic victory. Not since Mackenzie King had a prime minister won three consecutive majority governments. Further, the victory reversed a federal and provincial trend of winning re-election but with reduced seats. Of course, given the narrow margin of the previous win, any further reduction would have made a minority government a reality. Nonetheless, the continued split on the right assured the Prime Minister of another term in office. Further, the increase in seats came largely at the expense of the fourth- and fifth-place parties. The New Democrats and Conservatives barely hung on to recognized party status. The five-party "pizza" Parliament continued, but the pressure of resources was particularly felt by these two smallest parties.

Within the Liberal caucus, a series of events also laid the final preconditions necessary for a successful caucus revolt. First, it was increasingly clear that the Prime Minister was not going to run for a fourth term, despite his less than cryptic signals that he might. As a result of this, the unofficial leadership race began soon after the election was over. Although then-Finance Minister Paul Martin had long had a healthy list of supporters in caucus, many were more willing to be more open in their support for the Minister after the November vote.

Second, many Liberal backbenchers – even those who were not strong Martin supporters – by this time came to understand that the game of "to get along you go along" was not working in their favour. The Prime Minister who had come to power promising that "no Cabinet job" was safe was, in fact, quite reticent to shuffle his front bench. Many rookies from

1993 had been rotated through parliamentary secretaryships, committee chairs, and vice-chairs, and they felt there was no real career ladder, just a roller coaster that never hit the heights of power and inevitably ended up where it started.

Third, it was less clear that the punishment of earlier rebels had any lasting impact on their careers. Nine members broke ranks on Bill C-68 during the first Chrétien government. While they were punished at the time, most enjoyed successful careers despite their failing to adhere to the party line. Seven of the nine were re-elected in 1997, and one did not run. Six of the nine were still members of Parliament in the fall of 2003. Three of the nine were serving as parliamentary secretaries in the thirty-seventh Parliament. While they may have been stripped of positions in 1995, these were only temporary setbacks.

Fourth, there developed among some of these members a more subtle and sophisticated understanding of confidence and party discipline. Specifically, members were now more willing to challenge some forms of party discipline, feeling that if done under the appropriate conditions, it would not constitute a lack of confidence in the government. Time in office had allowed their views on party discipline and representation to mature. In 1993, nearly three-quarters of rookie members of Parliament surveyed thought that party discipline prevented them from properly representing their constituents. By 2002, over half of MPs felt that they could work around party discipline and still properly represent their constituents.[23] Once members were less intimidated about party discipline, there was less reason to heed its call.

The combination of these events meant that government private members were more vocal in their resistance to government legislation than they had been in the two previous Chrétien administrations. The criticism from within was restricted neither to Paul Martin supporters nor to the long-time advocates for House of Commons reform, such as Roger Gallaway and Reg Alcock. As Jonathan Malloy suggests, internal opposition greeted the government on many bills, from anti-terrorism legislation to the *Species at Risk Act*.[24] In the case of the latter, Liberal private members attacked it from both sides, some thinking it too stringent, others arguing it was too lax.[25] Importantly, these discussions and disagreements were no longer contained within caucus.[26] They were now being played out in Parliament, in committees, and in the national media.

Matters came to a head over the most unlikely of issues, the selection process for committee chairs. In November 2002, the Canadian Alliance introduced a motion calling for the secret election of committee chairs.[27]

Open votes might be more transparent, but for many government back-benchers this practice was used to elect a chair that was the choice the party leadership.[28] A secret vote would actually provide more freedom for private members to elect their own choices and not the dictated choice from above.

As the days to the vote got closer it was apparent that many government MPs were willing to break ranks with the party leadership. Fully fifty-six members of the government party voted with the opposition and the motion easily passed. While the size of the rebellion was noticeable, it was, perhaps, not surprising. As far back as the summer of 2001, Liberal private members were pushing for just such a change. An internal Liberal caucus report called for increasing democratic changes to House of Commons practices to make the role of MP "more meaningful."[29] Among the recommendations of the report was for committees to select chairs through secret ballot. Two years after the report, Liberal private members had their way.

While the actual motion was a rather obscure piece of parliamentary procedure, the fallout for the government was enormous. It made front pages in national newspapers and led most major newscasts.[30] Much of the debate focused on the "lame duck" Prime Minister and the impact this would have on the Liberal Party and Paul Martin's fortunes. Had the opposition tried to paint the government as unstable, they might have forestalled the opportunity for greater rebellion. As it turned out, the opposition was quick to portray the rebels not as anti-Chrétien but rather pro-Parliament. It was, perhaps, ironic that the crucial challenge to the party leadership occurred over an opposition motion, given that the defeat of a previous opposition motion (on Hepatitis C) in the thirty-sixth Parliament had led to the seemingly extreme use of the party whip.

The process of rebellion was far from over. However, Chrétien was not about to face a further defeat at the hands of his own caucus. In one of his final major legislative moves, the Prime Minister introduced major changes to campaign finance rules. In tabling Bill C-24 – *An Act to Amend the Canada Elections Act and Income Tax Act* – the outgoing Prime Minister signaled that he was willing to leave – or stay – with a bang, not a whimper.[31] The scope of the legislation was impressive.

The changes drastically reduce the amount of money that corporations and unions can donate to political parties. Further, it introduce broader public funding of election campaigns. This bill represented the first major internal challenge to the outgoing Prime Minister since the Alliance motion on the selection of committee chairs.

Many Liberal MPs were openly opposed to the thrust of the proposed new laws. There are many factors that might have caused some government MPs to speak out against the legislation. The Prime Minister had already announced his retirement date. The Prime Minister was creating rules he would not have to live under. The further irony is that the Prime Minister was a master at corporate fundraising, but would be limiting the ability of his successor to draw from the same well. In addition, the *Act* as introduced (and as subsequently passed) limited the ability of individual members of Parliament to raise and spend money locally. In this manner, a bill limiting large corporate and union donations actually centralized more authority with national political parties at the expense of local candidates. Even Liberal Party President Stephen LeDrew described the Act as "dumb as a bag of hammers."[32]

In response to internal and external dissension, the Prime Minister indicated that the legislation would be considered a matter of confidence. In a move just short of absurd, the Prime Minister was threatening to call an election if Bill C-24 was defeated. The spectre of the Prime Minister touring ridings of rebel Liberal MPs, and exhorting the crowd to vote for these members to give the Prime Minister a mandate to punish them for voting against him, might be viewed as the type of Alice in Wonderland approach to politics usually seen in U.S. elections. It was, however, a signal that prime ministers could no longer take their private members for granted. The only way the Prime Minister could get the rebels in line was to threaten to stick around longer.

As Chrétien's slow march to retirement entered its final summer, one last, but critical parliamentary drama was played out. If the rebels had found a cause in the selection of committee chairs, all members – rebels and loyalists – were willing to use the committee system to demonstrate the strong role that committees can play in the accountability process. The Standing Committee on Government Operations, created during the thirty-seventh Parliament, was given the authority to examine and comment on the annual reports of the Privacy Commissioner.[33]

In the spring of 2003, the Committee was unanimous in its criticism of Privacy Commissioner George Radwanski, his reports to Parliament, and his testimony to the Committee. The Committee felt that Radwanski had not only spent public monies inappropriately, but that his testimony to the Committee was at best evasive and at worst misleading.[34] In a remarkable show of solidarity, the Committee reported to the House that it had lost confidence in Radwanski and that he should no longer serve as Privacy Commissioner. The Privacy Commissioner is an Officer of Parliament and, as such, reports to all members through the Commons, rather than through a Cabinet minister. The role of the Privacy Commissioner is that of a watchdog on government, hence the role of the office is to complement Parliament's scrutiny function. As a result, the Commission and the Committee are not natural adversaries. This action was not a political vendetta, but rather driven by the actions of the Commissioner.

While the specific case against Radwanski was clear, the longer term implications of the affair suggest a renewed vigour for House of Commons committees. A unanimous report carries far greater weight than those that have dissenting views attached to them. Further, the Committee sent a strong signal that members of Parliament could not be bullied by officers of Parliament. Indeed, in the fallout of the Radwanski episode, the Committee called for a greater role in the appointment of officers and for the officers to provide greater transparency to Parliament. Having lost some of the power to undertake independent investigations ten years earlier, committees were greeting Chrétien's farewell by renewing their authority as instruments of accountability.

THE LESSONS OF REBELLION

By the end of the Chrétien era it was clear that the elected men and women who came to power in 1993, or who joined the team along the way, had changed their views on caucus solidarity, the need for party discipline, and the role of private members in the House of Commons. With the early promises of a greater role in public policy broken, Liberal private members witnessed their leader leave the public stage with little of the command he held ten years prior. The Prime Minister, in his heavy-handed use of discipline, helped to create a cohort of rebels within his caucus. All they needed was a cause, and the selection of committee chairs provided the best opportunity to flex their muscles.

It is true that the rebels backed down on a more substantial policy issue, campaign financing, but even here the irony abounds. The Prime Minister who was elected to office in 1993 pledging to free up members ended up using party discipline as a sledgehammer and not a means to effective co-operative governance. In order to ensure he would have a lasting impact on future governments and elections, he had to threaten members with not retiring unless they supported his plans. This is not the type of legacy advocates of parliamentary reform (or even adherents to parliamentary democracy) envisioned.

Nonetheless, the longer-term parliamentary legacy of the former Prime Minister might not be as critical as imagined. The use of the party whip and the tendency to punish rebel members, coupled with the unwillingness to promote backbenchers, led to the creation of more – not less – rebellious members. It was the former Prime Minister's actions and the reactions of strong, but frustrated backbenchers that eventually stimulated demands for the relaxation of party discipline. In terms of parliamentary reform this was the single biggest change of the Chrétien tenure in office. Further, there was little sign that these demands would go away under Prime Minister Martin's leadership.

Chrétien's successor openly stated his support for less party discipline and his willingness to create opportunities for more meaningful participation from private members. As Minister of Finance, Paul Martin made effective use of pre-budgetary consultations with the Standing Committee on Finance. Martin also supports a move to the British three-line whip system. Under this system, the status of legislation in terms of confidence in the government is transparent, and members have more freedom to vote against their party on matters that are not critical to a government's electoral mandate. While not a radical move for many parliamentary democracies, it certainly is for Canada.

Martin's experience as Prime Minister with a minority government after the 2004 election produced mixed evidence on his ability to follow through with these commitments. The fact that he had a minority meant that party unity was even more critical. However, his first Speech from the Throne produced criticism from within his own ranks that he did not consult his caucus. Further, his back bench had to learn the painful realities that in minority government, opposition parties and even independent members have the ear of government as much as the Prime Minister's caucus. Yet, there were signs that the move for reform was not ignored by the new Prime Minister. Committees were very effective and the whip was used with less intensity than in the Chrétien era. Minority governments encourage strong discipline, but they also make every vote critically important. This means listening not just to opposition parties by to the government caucus. Martin learned that lesson.

Yet even if there was not support for reform from leadership hopefuls, it is hard to imagine the move from within the governing caucus receding. In forcing Prime Minster Chrétien's retirement announcement in the summer of 2002, members went through a painful exercise that was about more than simply supporting one leadership hopeful over an incumbent Prime Minister. It was about power and the democratization of both the Liberal caucus and the Commons itself. And having survived, the rebels' appetite for more meaningful involvement, and for taking ownership over their own agenda (such as selecting committee chairs), has been whetted.

This may be the real irony of the Chrétien legacy. Paul Martin might actually believe in a more democratic lower house. But whether he or his successors are true believers in reform, it will be hard to turn back the clock. Meaningful reform of legislatures must originate from within the governing caucus. Opposition parties can advocate change, and they may find a supportive public behind them. But change will only take place when a prime minister either initiates it or faces the possibility of mutiny from his or her followers. Jean Chrétien more than tapped all of the goodwill and partisan cohesiveness in his caucus. Even if he had wanted to, Paul Martin could not impose the type of discipline his predecessor practised. The rebels and their successors will not soon abandon their cause.

NOTES

Associate Professor, Department of Political Science, and Dean of Arts, Wilfrid Laurier University. An earlier version of this article was presented at the annual meeting of the Canadian Political Science Association in Halifax in June 2003. In addition to the two *Review of Constitutional Studies* anonymous reviewers, the author wishes to thank the following individuals for their helpful comments and suggestions on the earlier drafts of this paper: Steve Patten, Jon Malloy, Bob Williams, Bill Blaikie MP, John Godfrey MP, Roger Gallaway MP, and James R. Robertson of the Library of Parliament. Some of the data used in this paper was collected as part of a larger SSHRC-funded study. The author thanks SSHRC for their continued support of social science research.

1 Jeffrey Simpson, *The Friendly Dictatorship* (Toronto: McClelland & Stewart, 2002). See also Donald Savoie, *Governing from the Centre* (Toronto: University of Toronto Press, 1999).
2 Private Member's Business includes both Private Members' Bills and Motions.
3 C.E.S. Franks, *The Parliament of Canada* (Toronto: University of Toronto Press, 1987).
4 Canada, *Report of the Special Committee on Reform of the House of Commons* (Ottawa: Queen's Printer, 1985).
5 Canada, *Report of the Special Committee on Standing Orders and Procedure* (Ottawa: Queen's Printer, 1982).
6 Gary Levy, "The Evolving Speakership," *Canadian Parliamentary Review* 21:2 (1998): 7–11.

7 Gary Levy, "A Night to Remember: The First Election of a Speaker by Secret Ballot," *Canadian Parliamentary Review* 9:4 (1986): 10–14.

8 Jean-Robert Gauthier, "Accountability, Committees and Parliament," *Canadian Parliamentary Review* 16:2 (1993): 7–9.

9 The Reform Party won its first seat in a 1989 by-election. Deborah Grey became the first Reform Party Member of Parliament.

10 See David C. Docherty, *Mr. Smith Goes to Ottawa: Life in the House of Commons* (Vancouver: University of British Columbia Press, 1997).

11 Ibid.

12 David Laycock, *The New Right and Democracy in Canada* (Toronto: Oxford University Press, 2002), 14–17.

13 The New Democrats did have a cohort of veteran MPs including Bill Blaikie, Vic Althouse, and Svend Robinson. But with less than the requisite twelve members, they lacked the formal recognition required to fully participate in many House activities, including Question Period. As a result, this experience was partially neutralized, and the Liberals faced even less accountability from veteran legislators.

14 Docherty, *Mr. Smith Goes to Ottawa*, 54.

15 Ibid.

16 Ibid.

17 These figures were based on a sampling of Question Periods in the fall of 1996 and 1997. See David C. Docherty, "It's Awfully Crowded Here: Adjusting to the Five Party House of Commons," *Parliamentary Perspectives* 2 (1998): 3–20.

18 Yves Pelletier, *Time Allocation in the House of Commons: Silencing Parliamentary Democracy or Effective Time Management* (Ottawa: Institute on Governance, 2000), 8.

19 Ibid., 13.

20 Savioe, *Governing from the Centre*.

21 Rex Murphy, "Hep-C and vote of confidence," *CBC: The National*, 28 April 1998.

22 Canadian Press, "Liberals squirming on hep-C," 24 April 1998.

23 Figures are taken from both a 1993 survey of MPs and a 2001–2002 survey of members undertaken by the author as part of a larger project: see David C. Docherty, *Legislatures: A Democratic Audit* (Vancouver: University of British Columbia Press, 2005).

24 S.C. 2002, c. 29, http://www.canlii.org/ca/sta/s-15.3/whole.html. See Jonathan Malloy, "The House of Commons under the Chrétien Government," in G. Bruce Doern, ed., *How Ottawa Spends, 2003-2004: Regime Change and Policy Shift* (Don Mills: Oxford University Press, 2003), 59-71, 65.

25 As Malloy points out, those thinking it too stringent were rural MPs concerned about the potential implications for farmers. Ibid.

26 Malloy, "The House of Commons."

27 Paco Francoli and Mike Scandiffio, "Scrambling Grits working on Commons reform package," *The Hill Times*, 11 November 2002, 1.

28 Angelo Persichilli, "Political parties must be democratized, not Parliament," *The Hill Times*, 11 November 2002, 4.

29 Graham Fraser, "MPs want meaningful work," *Toronto Star*, 21 June 2001, A8.

30 Shawn McCarthy, "Key vote fractures Liberals," *Globe and Mail*, 6 November 2002, A1.

31 S.C. 2003, c. 19, http://www.canlii.org/ca/as/2003/c19/whole.html.

32 Abbas Rana, "Liberals rake in $13.2 million in 2002," *Hill Times*, 7 July 2003, 8.

33 As well as some other officers of Parliament – see Standing Order 108.2(c)(vii).

34 Campbell Clark, "Committee calls for Radwanski's resignation," *Globe and Mail*, 18 June 2003, A1.

15

Jean Chrétien and a Decade of Party System Change

STEVE PATTEN

INTRODUCTION

When Jean Chrétien assumed the leadership of the Liberal Party of Canada in June 1990, the Canadian party system was entering a period of turmoil. The pan-Canadian, two-party-plus system of partisan competition that had matured under Lester Pearson, Pierre Trudeau, and Brian Mulroney was in tatters as constitutional politics, regionalism, ideological debates, and public cynicism undermined the Mulroney coalition of the 1980s. The Reform Party, which was less than a year away from making its decision to "go national," was represented in Parliament by its first elected MP, Deborah Grey. A popular federal Cabinet minister, Lucien Bouchard, was about to break from the government to establish himself as leader of the newly formed Bloc Québécois. And the popularity of the Mulroney Conservatives was on a downward trajectory that would eventually devastate the "Party of Confederation." Indeed, the 1993 election that brought Jean Chrétien to power and saw the Progressive Conservatives reduced to just two seats in the House of Commons also established the fledgling Bloc Québécois and Reform Party as Canada's principal opposition parties. It's small wonder, then, that this tumultuous election has been characterized as a classic example of a "critical election" – that is, an election in which both popular support for parties and the terms of political debate are dramatically altered.[1] The Chrétien Liberals replaced the governing Conservatives at a turning point in Canadian party politics. The three-decades-old "system" of partisan politics to which Canadians had grown accustomed was unraveling. Not surprisingly, then, the ensuing years were to be a period of uncertainty, experimentation, and change. The Chrétien-era party system was a system in transition.[2] Thus, the character and practice of partisan politics during the Chrétien years will, one day, seem out of step with the party system as it existed before and after Jean Chrétien's tenure as Prime Minister.

Of course, the task of examining Chrétien's role in a decade of party system change requires some clarity regarding what is meant by the term "party system." At bottom, electoral competition between party organizations produces competitive patterns and interrelationships that constitute the core of what is meant by the party system. But to appreciate fully the character of a party system one must look beyond matters such as the number and relative competitiveness of Canada's political parties – these factors are only the most obvious and observable dimensions of any party system. Party competition is itself shaped by a number of factors that combine to constitute the party system. These include the organizational character and operation of parties as democratic institutions; the public rules governing party financing, elections, and the parliamentary party system; and the norms and practices that shape campaign behaviour and techniques. Added to these are the ideologies and discursive framework that define the core issues, interests, and identities of politics. Finally, there is the relationship between political parties and other processes and institutions of representation, including interest groups, social movement organizations, and lobbyists. Each of these factors has an independent and unique influence on the character of the Canadian party system and the process of party system change.

It would be wrong to identify a decade of changes in the Canadian party system as Jean Chrétien's *personal* legacy. While the Chrétien era will be viewed as a period of significant changes in the character and practices of partisan politics, one should not attribute too much responsibility for these changes to Prime Minister Chrétien himself. Very few of the changes in the Canadian party system over the past decade can genuinely be called the "Chrétien legacy." Jean Chrétien was caught up in processes shaped by multiple political actors, social forces, and economic conditions.

All the same, in what follows, I will explore party system change during the Chrétien decade under three broad headings – the changing contours of party competition, ideological change, and party leadership and organization. Examined first are the processes of "regionalization" that have resulted in multiparty competition, regionally segmented campaigns, and Liberal electoral dominance. Second, emphasis will be placed on the extent to the which Jean Chrétien, in partnership with Paul Martin, emphasized the market liberal face of Canadian Liberalism. Together, these two leaders facilitated the emergence of a loose consensus regarding the privileged place of market liberal ideological orientations in political debate. In essence, after a breakdown in the consensus that underpinned the previous party system, the orientation of Chrétien's governments helped to establish market liberalism as the new "centre" of brokerage politics in Canada. Finally, it will be argued that Jean Chrétien and, even more so, Paul Martin, raised the bar in terms of the financial and organizational requisites of a successful campaign to lead Canada's "government party." In doing so, it has become increasingly evident that the supposed democratization of the rules for electing party leaders is not enough to ensure open and meaningfully democratic leadership selection processes.

Chrétien's leadership style and the nature of recent Liberal leadership campaigns have contributed to the further "hollowing out"of Canada's already leader-dominated and ideologically flexible cadre parties. Following Reg Whitaker, this is tied to the rise of the "virtual party" and a lowering of the quality of democracy.[3] In addition, the Liberal Party's dominance of Canadian politics during the Chrétien years stimulated an unprecedented interest in electoral system reform, and Chrétien's iron-fisted leadership style caused a restiveness within the parliamentary wing of his party and calls for the democratization of the parliamentary party system. When combined with the surprise decision to reform the rules governing party financing, the Chrétien era concluded with glimmers of democratization in the party system existing in tension with multimillion dollar leadership campaigns and leader-dominated virtual parties. While the long-term implications of the Chrétien reforms to election and party financing are still being assessed, there is no doubt that the former Prime Minister's decision to ban the very corporate contributions that allowed him to win the leadership and three successive elections will have far-reaching significance. Moreover, as this was a prime ministerial initiative with, at best, mixed support from the government caucus, party financing reform may, more than anything else, qualify as Chrétien's *personal* legacy for political parties.

THE CHANGING CONTOURS OF PARTY COMPETITION

Regionalization, a new multiparty dynamic of partisan competition, and the electoral dominance of the Liberal Party were perhaps the most striking features of partisan politics in the 1990s. Obviously, regional identities and cleavages have a long history as a defining feature of Canadian politics. It has been argued, however, that from the 1960s through to the late 1980s, the dominant discourse of partisan politics was pan-Canadian.[4] This is not to say regionalism and regionally based partisan support were unimportant. The Pearson and Trudeau Liberals, for example, governed on the basis of support rooted in eastern Canada's Catholic populations and a virtual electoral monopoly in Québec.[5] But Pierre Trudeau's articulation of a vision of a bilingual and multicultural Canada, in which individual rights served to underpin a quintessentially liberal political community, was a direct challenge to subnational political identities, be they western, Québécois, or otherwise. Mulroney rejected much of Trudeau's vision of Canada, opting to support greater decentralization and the possibility of a more asymmetrical federalism. But Mulroney's acceptance of bilingualism and multiculturalism, and his determination to broker subnational identities within the context of a pan-Canadian conservative coalition, evidenced his desire to maintain his Liberal predecessor's pan-Canadian focus.

As the importance of television news and select "national" news sources – in particular, the CBC and the *Globe and Mail* – increased from the 1960s onward, the contest between national party leaders came to define partisan competition. Party leaders competed to set the national policy agenda, and political legitimacy was narrowly equated with being nationally competitive. Indeed, following the behaviour of the news media, campaign strategies and tactics ensured that "the local" and "the regional" took a back seat to "the national." Being strategic and "on message" was equated with maintaining a pan-Canadian focus. There was, in essence, one campaign being waged, and strategists came to accept that this required consistent tactics and messaging from coast to coast.

In contrast, Jean Chrétien won three majority governments in elections that were marked by regional fragmentation of the party system. In terms of the patterns of party competition and, therefore, campaign strategies, the striking success of Reform and the BQ in the 1993 general election resulted in something akin to a number of regional "party subsystems" replacing the pan-Canadian party system. The Progressive Conservatives were reduced to a party of Atlantic Canada, fighting for survival in an electoral battle with Liberals (or, in Nova Scotia, both the Liberals and New Democrats). In Québec, a partisan struggle pitting the nationalist Bloc Québécois against a federalist Liberal Party virtually eliminated any possibility of other parties having a meaningful electoral presence.[6] Indeed, the reality of this new two-party competition in Québec was reinforced by Reform's inability to nominate and run more than a handful of Québec candidates in 1993 and 1997. During the Chrétien era, Ontario was, with the exception of a handful of seats, a virtual Liberal fiefdom. The Reform Party and, later, the Canadian Alliance typically earned the support of between one-fifth and one-quarter of Ontario voters.[7] But Canada's single member plurality electoral system awarded the Liberals approximately 97 percent of Ontario's 103 seats. In the prairie provinces of Manitoba and Saskatchewan, there was a fairly competitive three-way race for seats during the Chrétien years – the Liberals and the Reform/Alliance were out in front, winning, on average, the same number of constituencies, but the NDP won a respectable number of ridings as well. It was in the final party subsystem – Alberta and British Columbia – that the Reform/Alliance party found its real strength. The NDP was only able to win two or three B.C. seats, and the PCs were uncompetitive throughout Canada's two most westerly provinces.[8] With the Liberals earning approximately 25 percent of electoral support in Alberta and B.C., the governing party was notably weaker here than in other regions. All the same, the Chrétien Liberals were the only rival capable of mounting a meaningful challenge to the Reform/Alliance party, which, under the single-member plurality electoral system, won just over 80 percent of the seats in the region.

Clearly, while the Chrétien Liberals were competitive in all the party subsystems of the 1990s, the differentiated nature of electoral competition required segmented, rather than truly national, campaigns. Regional variation in the nature of strategic appeals increased for very practical reasons: "Given this balkanization in party competition, no party could effectively campaign on the same message in each part of the country."[9] But strategic regionalization of campaign messages was not the extent of segmentation. In the campaigns of 1997 and 2000, even the Liberals – the only party with the legitimate claim to being nationally competitive – recognized the strategic wisdom of writing off any chance of winning Alberta and British Columbia constituencies outside of Edmonton, Vancouver, and Victoria. Regionalization, then, had a significant impact on the character and public image of Canada's political parties during the Chrétien years. The BQ was, unquestionably, a party of francophone Québec, the Reform/Alliance party symbolized western political interests, and the character of the governing Liberals was often shaped by the overwhelming size of the party's Ontario caucus. While I am in agreement with David Laycock in believing that observers typically overstate the "westernness" of the Reform/Alliance ideology and policy agenda,[10] there is no doubt that the party's Western roots have been significant to both the party's policies and voter attitudes toward the party. Indeed, former Prime Minister Chrétien revealed the extent of party system balkanization when, during a campaign stop in 2000, he joked to the national media that he was more comfortable in and preferred visiting Atlantic Canada in contrast to the west.

With the NDP low in the polls, the Tories limited to an Atlantic Canadian base, and the unique regional competitiveness of the BQ and Reform/ Alliance parties, the Liberals were, under Chrétien, able to dominate electoral politics. Clearly, Canada's simple plurality electoral system and unevenness in the size of the populations of the various party subsystems served to inflate Liberal victories. But these uncontrollable institutional causes of Liberal domination only reinforced growing public frustration with the situation. Given the character of Canada's Westminster-style parliamentary party system, the inevitability of Liberal majorities and the lack of a credible one-party opposition fueled the spread of rhetoric regarding Canada's status as a "one-party state." And Chrétien's apparent lack of concern for the antidemocratic consequences of Liberal domination in a multiparty system frustrated those interested in electoral democracy. By the summer of 2000, a multipartisan citizens' group with impressive support from partisan luminaries, including former NDP leader Ed Broadbent, emerged to campaign for electoral system reform. Fair Vote Canada has now established a media presence and has won support for the consideration of a form of "proportional representation" from numerous commentators, including the editorial board of the *Globe and Mail*.

Of course, governing parties have seldom taken electoral reform seriously. The Mulroney Conservatives kept consideration of the issue off the agenda of the Royal Commission on Electoral Reform and Party Financing, only to find their own survival as a party called into question as a result of the disproportionate outcomes of the simple plurality electoral system. But, during his decade in power, Chrétien's smug refusal to consider electoral system reform may have served the cause of reform. The complacency of the Prime Minister bolstered the determination of the reformers. While Chrétien has not supported such reforms, their current popularity is, in a sense, an unintended legacy of his success as Liberal leader in a regionalized multiparty system of partisan competition.

THE CHRÉTIEN LIBERALS' "MARKET LIBERALISM" AND THE NEW DISCURSIVE FRAMEWORK OF BROKERAGE POLITICS

As many of the contributions to this volume confirm, Jean Chrétien was never a policy visionary. While he cared about governing and held certain personal priorities, he cared most about winning elections. After losing to John Turner at the 1984 Liberal leadership convention, Chrétien and his supporters worked tirelessly to ensure victory would be theirs in 1990. Although originally viewed as a somewhat left-leaning social liberal, Chrétien's policy orientation in government was to be determined by a combination of strategic electoral calculations and a series of political debates and power struggles within his Cabinet. Indeed, nothing was more important to defining the policy and ideological orientation of the Chrétien years than the early power struggles within Cabinet that solidified the influence of Finance Minister Paul Martin, and thus also of Martin's orientation towards market liberalism.[11] As Martin secured his place of pre-eminence among ministers, he and Chrétien formed a unique political partnership. It was, without a doubt, a partnership of ambitious rivals, and one that could only be sustained until Chrétien's continued tenure as leader began to threaten the possibility of Martin succeeding him as Prime Minister.

The Chrétien-Martin partnership did more than ensure Martin's privileged position within Cabinet. It also solidified the power of the Department of Finance as a central agency with the capacity to shape the government's agenda and limit the scope of policy innovation throughout the line departments. But more than anything else, this partnership gave priority to one policy goal above all others: slaying the deficit. The parameters established by this goal gave substance to the dramatic project of social policy reform and government restructuring that was undertaken during Chrétien's first mandate. Under Chrétien and Martin, the Liberal Party of Canada moved to the right, adopting many aspects of the market liberal agenda of the Mulroney Conservatives. In essence, this meant that fiscal and economic priorities would trump social priorities. Early in his first mandate Chrétien moved to embrace economic globalization and confirm his support for continentalization under the North American Free Trade Agreement (NAFTA) – an agreement that his party had campaigned against in both 1988 and 1993. While balking at American priorities, particularly after the election of George W. Bush in 2000, and rejecting the overblown neo-conservative rhetoric of the

1980s, Chrétien and Martin pursued a policy agenda in keeping with neo-liberal restructuring, free trade, and continentalization.

In political terms, this rather dramatic shift was made easier by the position of the Reform/Alliance party as the Liberals' primary challenger in English Canada. The Liberals could pursue an agenda that satisfied business interests and the conservative press, while reminding more moderate Canadians of the Reform/Alliance policy of going "further and faster" in terms of economic liberalization and shrinking government. The Liberals were able to move to the right while appearing relatively moderate. Moreover, by continuing to embrace multiculturalism, inclusiveness, and the principles of the *Canadian Charter of Rights and Freedoms*, as well as demonstrating a willingness to act on gun control, same-sex rights, and other progressive issues, Chrétien maintained a degree of social liberalism that allowed the Liberals to claim they were continuing the party's tradition of governing from the ideological centre. There is no doubt that this pacified those voters – particularly urban and Ontario voters – who were uncomfortable with the growing influence of the new right.

Not long after the 2000 election the Martin team intensified their efforts to ensure Paul Martin could soon replace Chrétien as leader of the Liberal Party. As signs of the Martin team's activity grew more obvious, Chrétien was forced to reflect on his future: Should he run again? If not, what would his legacy be? Then, in the summer of 2002, the politics of party leadership came to a head. Chrétien was feeling pressure to retire from members of both the parliamentary and extra-parliamentary wings of the Liberal Party, and there was no doubt that Martin supporters were behind the move to oust the Prime Minister. Thus, in June 2002, Chrétien removed Martin from Cabinet, ended their partnership, and prepared to do battle. But two months later, in a dramatic turn of events, the former Prime Minister announced his plan to retire prior to an anticipated 2004 general election. Politically wounded, Chrétien then turned his attention to the matter of his policy legacy. The political press was abuzz with stories of Chrétien's desire for a more explicitly social liberal legacy than would result from historical reflection on the policies of the Chrétien-Martin partnership.

Given the eventual decision to hold a Liberal leadership convention in November 2003, Chrétien *sans* Finance Minister Martin would have little more than a year to put the finishing touches on his legacy as Prime Minister. The Throne Speech that opened the second session of the thirty-seventh Parliament in September 2002 laid the groundwork for

Chrétien's legacy agenda.[12] That speech promised that Canada would increase development assistance, push for comprehensive free trade on all products from the least-developed economies, and focus on the challenge of African development.[13] It promised action on health care, particularly Aboriginal health care.[14] It committed the government to advancing the 1997 children's agenda and taking action for families in poverty, particularly with regard to closing the gap between the quality of life for Aboriginal and non-Aboriginal children.[15] With regard to the environment, there were commitments to developing new parks and wilderness areas and to implementing a strategy to meet the commitments associated with ratifying the 1997 Kyoto Protocol on climate change.[16] Themes associated with the global competitiveness of the Canadian economy were not absent, but reducing the debt-to-GDP ratio, lowering taxes, and focusing on skills development and "smart regulation" all took a back seat to the social themes. The first full budget of Paul Martin's successor, John Manley, built directly on the language and priorities of the Throne Speech.[17] After a decade of Martin-inspired budgets, political columnists emphasized the extent to which Chrétien's priorities – his "fingerprints" – were particularly obvious in this budget.[18] Indeed, the *Globe and Mail* declared that Chrétien's final budget marked a return to a style of "activist government" that would cast a shadow over governments to follow.[19]

But time was running short. Leadership politics were distracting the government caucus. The apparent inevitability of Paul Martin soon succeeding Chrétien as prime minister was slowing progress on policy initiatives that Martin had not willingly endorsed. And provincial premiers were not particularly willing to trust Chrétien and facilitate the quick implementation of his policy agenda. Thus, by the fall of 2003, the extent of real policy change had been limited, and commentators searching for an identifiable legacy of Chrétien's decade in power could only conclude that the former Prime Minister's defining achievement was slaying the deficit – a legacy he would have to share with Paul Martin.

Chrétien's inability to define a policy legacy beyond constraining public spending is significant. In contrast to the neo-Keynesian nationalist policy orientation of Trudeau's final term as Prime Minister (1980–1984) and to the anti-free trade policy platform that informed the final election campaign of the Turner Liberals (1988), Jean Chrétien, in partnership with Paul Martin, led the Liberal Party to the right: privileging market liberalism and marginalizing the post-war Liberal tradition of social liberalism. But the full importance of a more right-wing Liberal Party rests in its relationship to the reshaping of the ideological and discursive framework of partisan debate and political competition. Chrétien first assumed the leadership of his party at a moment of significant ideological turmoil. The 1988 election had been uncharacteristic in the extent to which the voting decision of Canadians came down to how they felt about a single issue of far-reaching importance: free trade. The Meech Lake Accord died on the very day – 23 June 1990 – that Liberals selected Chrétien as their leader, and the subsequent Canada round of constitutional negotiations vastly expanded the constitutional agenda. With Canadians waking up to the legitimacy and magnitude of First Nations' grievances, this new constitutional agenda included, among other issues, the recognition of the right of Aboriginal self-governance. At the same time, polling showed that environmental concerns were nearing the top of issue priorities for voters. And social movement organizations related to the environment, feminism, and anti-racism were demonstrating a level of political activity and sophistication unprecedented in the post-war era. Moreover, with Prime Minister Mulroney's popularity plummeting and Bob Rae's NDP elected in Ontario, there were, in 1990, reasons to wonder whether the final decade of the twentieth century might be characterized by a rejection of the neo-conservative vision that motivated the Mulroney Tories.

Uncertainty and ideological turmoil were, then, the order of the day. With this in mind, it should be clear that the significance of the 1993 election was not merely the emergence of multiparty competition – 1993 was also important because it was marked by a rejection of brokerage-style consensus politics. Most obviously, the nationalist BQ and the ideological Reform Party both rejected the policy-averse politics of consensus that is so central to brokerage party systems. But, beyond that, it was still apparent that, as in 1988, the Liberals and Progressive Conservatives were not merely offering "more or less" of the same policy package.[20] The Liberal Red Book emphasized the stimulative power of the state and the importance of infrastructure and public spending to job creation,[21] while the Tories focused on the fiscal deficit and hinted at a plan to dramatically downsize the public sector. In sum, it can be argued that Jean Chrétien ascended to the Prime Minister's Office at a moment when policy visions clashed to an extent that is not characteristic of moments of brokerage-style partisan competition.

By the mid 1990s, however, a new consensus *was* emerging. In February 1995, Paul Martin introduced what was arguably the most economically conservative budget of the post-war era. His budget attacked the federal deficit through "structural change" that set in motion major reforms to government spending (including the introduction of the Canada Health and Social Transfer) and public sector restructuring (overhauling "not only *how* government *works* but what government *does*").[22] Indeed, according to Stephen Harper, the Liberal government of the mid-1990s was "more conservative on most issues than the previous Progressive Conservative government."[23] But the Liberals were certainly not alone in moving to the right. The Conservatives, devastated by the 1993 election results, were going through a process of grassroots policy consultations and political soul-searching that resulted in an election platform – their 1997 platform – "that marked the zenith of market liberalism's influence within the Conservative Party."[24]

What did all this mean for the ideological and discursive framework of partisan politics in Canada? Essentially, by the turn of the century, policy debate was increasingly organized around the provision of "more or less" of a market liberal agenda at a "faster or slower" rate. Red Tories who had once cautioned against overstated market enthusiasm were taking their final gasps within the Progressive Conservative Party, social liberals were marginalized within the Liberal Party, the new Canadian Alliance was downplaying Reform-style social conservatism in favour of market liberalism, and Canada's party of social democracy, the NDP, was increasingly treated as irrelevant by observers, including the political press. Credit for this transformation of the discursive framework of the Canadian party system must be shared. Clearly political leaders like Preston Manning, Mike Harris, and Ralph Klein were important, as were non-partisan policy think tanks such as the Fraser and C.D. Howe institutes.[25] But Chrétien's partnership with Paul Martin drew the governing Liberals to the market liberal right, and its consequences for the Canadian party system are, indeed, a part of the Chrétien legacy.

THE CHANGING POLITICS OF PARTY LEADERSHIP AND PARTY ORGANIZATION

Between 1984, when Jean Chrétien first ran for the leadership of the Liberal Party, and 2003, when he was replaced by Paul Martin, the accepted thinking regarding democratic leadership selection changed considerably. The trend during this period was inspired by grassroots democracy, it involved embracing various methods of one member/one vote, party-wide leadership selection. An examination of leadership selection within the Liberal Party shows, however, that democratizing the rules governing voting processes does not guarantee truly open and meaningfully democratic leadership selection.

The 1984 Liberal leadership selection process involved a traditional delegated convention. John Turner won on the second ballot with just shy of 55 percent of the vote. Jean Chrétien was second with 40 percent. Following the convention, Chrétien's supporters did not willingly accept Turner's leadership. Not only did they maintain the hope of one day putting Jean Chrétien in the leadership, but at times they openly challenged Turner. There was, for example, an open but unsuccessful challenge to Turner during the regular leadership review process at the party's 1986 party convention. As the 1990 leadership convention approached, the Chrétien team left nothing to chance. With a nationwide organizing network and a healthy "war chest" to finance the campaign, the Chrétien organization literally "captured the party in the few months before the convention."[26] They ensured, in other words, that the convention results would be a foregone conclusion – the leadership would be won at delegate selection meetings, not on the campaign trail or the convention floor. Indeed, so slim was the room for leadership aspirants to enter the race and mount a respectable campaign that senior Liberals like Lloyd Axworthy considered the hurdles to a respectable showing to be insurmountable.[27]

The rules for the race to replace Chrétien were changed so that the thousands of Liberal members who attended the delegate selection meetings two months prior to the convention would *directly* control the outcome of the first ballot voting. But these new rules did not really change the nature of the process. In fact, like any good apprentice, Paul Martin adopted and perfected the Chrétien formula. Martin took control of the party's constituency associations in the years prior to 2003. He never hid his intention to run, and in 2002 he used his strength within caucus, the party executive, and local constituency executives to challenge Jean Chrétien's continued tenure as party leader. When the Martin strategy became clear, Chrétien announced his intention to stand up to the challenge. Plans were put in place for a full-fledged "campaign" to rally Liberals behind their leader as the 2003 party convention and leadership review vote approached. Key national organizers were put in place and, according to one report, Jean Chrétien "forked over about $100,000 of his own money" to finance the launch of the campaign.[28] But, facing the Martin juggernaut, the Chrétien campaign crumbled. It was clear that Jean Chrétien had lost control of his party. The national campaign organizers failed to mobilize a network of regional and constituency-based supporters. Fundraising – intended to repay Chrétien and finance the campaign – faltered. Before long, Jean Chrétien was announcing his planned retirement as a means of avoiding the anticipated 2003 leadership review vote.

Paul Martin had beaten Chrétien at his own game. But he also extended the Chrétien strategy to such an extent that the politics of Liberal leadership selection has been fundamentally transformed. In 1984, many observers were shocked by the suggestion that Turner may have spent over $2 million to win the leadership. In the lead-up to the 1990 convention, there was notable comment on the fact that leading Liberals like Axworthy felt a credible run at the top job was impossible without an early start at building a campaign war chest. As the results were counted and Jean Chrétien won on the first ballot at the 1990 convention, it was noted that this was the first time since the 1950s that a leader had secured a majority of delegates prior to the opening of the convention. Today, this record of big spending and sophisticated campaign strategy pales in relation to Paul Martin's spending and campaign accomplishments. Under Chrétien's watch, Martin raised over $11 million to secure the leadership. He managed to put such a lock on local Liberal associations that ambitious potential candidates like Brian Tobin chose not to run, and one potentially significant challenger, John Manley, opted out of the race after months of campaigning. When the convention was held, a Paul Martin coronation was supported by over 90 percent of the delegates. The rules structuring the translation of grassroots preferences into convention results had been democratized, but the process was, in the end, far from truly open and meaningfully democratic. Martin's only remaining challenger, Shelia Copps, campaigned as a "voice for the voiceless" – but at the end the Chrétien era there was very little room for the voiceless in the process of selecting the leader of the Liberal Party of Canada.

Liberal leadership politics reveals something significant about the changing character of party organizations in Canada. Regardless of the apparent success of moves to democratize Canadian political parties, party organizations are, increasingly, hollow shells with little in the way of an ideological or policy "essence" and little organic connection to civil society. Of course, there is something quite familiar about the virtual party. Canadian political parties have long been characterized as cadre-style organizations that revolve around their leaders. Most of Canada's parties emerged out of Parliament and the parliamentary wing has remained dominant. Prior to 1919, party leaders were selected by secretive and undemocratic negotiations within the parliamentary caucus. Prior to the 1960s, the extra-parliamentary party bureaucracy was notably rudimentary. There were fairly vibrant local party networks in the nineteenth century, but these were tied to the constituency-based patronage networks that financed campaigns and ensured sustained patterns of political support for local candidates. Throughout the twentieth century, local party organizations were, for the most part, electoral machines that went into hibernation when not needed to staff campaign offices, canvass the voters or attend rallies. Between the early 1960s and the 1980s, central party bureaucracies grew in size and strategic importance. But it was also during this period that advertising professionals, public relations consultants and pollsters were drawn in to guide national political campaigns and advise party leaders. The gradual professionalization of strategic advice from the Pearson era to the Mulroney era influenced the character of party organizations and presaged the emergence of virtual parties in the 1990s.

According to Reg Whitaker, the Chrétien years witnessed the rise of the "virtual party," an organization that forms around a politician and the coterie of advisors and strategists who colonize the shell of the party and use it like one would a franchise with brand recognition.[29] Two features distinguish the virtual party. First, the virtual party is, at bottom, little more than an empty vessel waiting to be filled with a political and ideological character by a leader and his or her appointed advisors. Think of the small group of ideological party activists who coalesced around Mike Harris to transform the hollowed-out shell of the once-powerful Ontario Tories from a party of tory pragmatism into a programmatic party of neo-liberalism. Second, the virtual party is little more than a convenient franchise, a marketable brand. Think of the "re-branding" exercise that created the Canadian Alliance out of the Reform Party in the hope that the new brand could be successfully sold in the formerly impenetrable Ontario market. While the Liberal Party is not so clearly a virtual party as were the Harris Tories and the Canadian Alliance, Whitaker describes the party under Chrétien as "neither the elite-run 'ministerialist' party of the King-St. Laurent era, nor the 'participatory' party of the Pearson-Trudeau era," because both Cabinet ministers and the grassroots became less important than they once were.[30] What matters now is polling analysis, media strategy, and the agenda of the leader's coterie of policy advisers. Of course, in the era of the Chrétien-Martin partnership the Liberal Party was something of a "two-headed" virtual party, but it was a virtual party nonetheless.

In the final year of Chrétien's leadership, the supporters of various leadership aspirants actively worked to build the party organization. By July 2003, the Liberal Party had over 530,000 members, more than any other party in Canadian history. Key operatives, particularly from the Martin campaign, were abuzz with excitement about the party's new vitality. In September, when party members had their opportunity to select delegates to the leadership convention and determine the outcome of the first ballot, a mere 52,000 members participated.[31] The subsequent convention to install Paul Martin as leader was a poorly attended media extravaganza designed to say a fond farewell to Jean Chrétien, to prepare the way for the Martin entourage to seize the reins of power, and to present the Liberal Party of Canada to the Canadian public as a different party than it was just months previously. This is the essence of leadership transition in the virtual party.

Elsewhere in this volume, David Docherty reveals how the power of the leader in Chrétien's virtual Liberal Party caused considerable unrest within its parliamentary wing. While Paul Martin and the powerful Ministry of Finance set the core of the governing agenda for much of the decade that Chrétien served as Prime Minister, Jean Chrétien used the power of the Prime Minister's Office and the Privy Council Office to manage his caucus and Cabinet in a manner that was both understated and controlling. Chrétien demanded that the Liberal caucus respect the principle of party discipline as the defining feature of the parliamentary party system. The result was prime ministerial government. Interestingly, however, after Chrétien's departure, a restive Liberal backbench demanded that Paul Martin commit himself to democratizing caucus and Parliament. Martin made promises but failed to take action.

In the final months of his term as Prime Minister, Jean Chrétien initiated a dramatic reform of the rules governing political party financing. Regulation of party financing was originally modernized with the *Election Expenses Act* of 1974. That legislation took an important step toward recognizing political parties as quasi-public institutions of democratic governance. The Liberal government of Pierre Trudeau was declaring simultaneously that parties are not merely private voluntary organizations and, very importantly, that there is a "public good" associated with putting parties on a more level playing field in terms of financing and spending. These values were affirmed by instituting campaign spending limits, requiring public disclosure of contributions, providing for public funding through tax credits for political contributions, and the partial reimbursement of campaign expenses. At one level, it could be argued that Chrétien's party finance legislation, Bill C-24, simply aimed to extend the logic of the Trudeau legislation and tighten up the rules and procedures. But, at the time, several political observers claimed partisan politics simply "won't be the same after Bill C-24."[32] Indeed, the extent of opposition to the changes – from within both opposition *and* Liberal Party ranks – was evidence that politicians and campaign strategists agreed with this latter assessment.

The Bill C-24 amendments to the *Canada Election Act*[33] have two broad sets of consequences for the character of the Canadian party system.[34] First, the legislation further entrenches the notion that political parties are "public institutions" that, by definition, are the legitimate target of both public regulation and public financing. In the first instance, parties are redefined as public institutions by extending the range of party activities to be covered by public regulation. Since 1 January 2004, spending limits have been placed on local candidate nominations. Secondly, corporations and unions are forbidden from donating to leadership campaigns, while the extent of public financing of political parties will be increased. Registered political parties now receive an annual allowance equivalent to $1.75 for each vote the party received in the last general election. The extent of the tax credit that Canadians receive for political contributions was also increased.

The second set of consequences pertains to the source and size of political contributions. The 1974 legislation put in place spending limits for local and national campaigns. Bill C-24 tackled the other side of the party financing equation. Individual Canadians may contribute up to $5,000 annually to registered political parties, the campaigns of candidates running in a federal election, local party constituency associations, and contests to nominate local candidates. Individuals can also donate up to an additional $5,000 to party leadership campaigns. Corporations, trade unions, and associations, on the other hand, are forbidden from donating to registered political parties. These entities can donate at the local level, but their contributions are limited to a maximum of $1,000 annually to local candidates, party constituency associations, and contests to nominate local candidates. At bottom, then, the 2004 rules of party financing place limits on individual donations and, perhaps more significantly, they prevent corporations and unions from donating to the national-level activities of registered parties and leadership campaigns.

The long-term implications of placing limits on individual contributions, prohibiting corporate sources of party financing, extending the regulatory reach of the *Elections Act* to local nominations and leadership campaigns, and, finally, shifting to greater public financing are not yet entirely clear. There are, however, at least three observations that can be made. First, the federal ban on corporate and union donations will force renewed effort to solicit funds from individual contributors. Second, relying on a per-vote system of public funding will make it difficult for smaller and new parties to compete with established parties. Indeed, it was publicly acknowledged in the fall of 2003 that one of the perceived benefits of the agreement to merge the Progressive Conservative and Canadian Alliance parties was the increased public funding associated with the two parties' combined vote. Third, the new party financing rules will alter the character of leadership campaigns, particularly those for the leadership of parties that have a realistic chance of victory in a general election. Within the Liberal Party, for example, the Chrétien/Martin strategy of developing a multi-year campaign to capture the party organization from the constituency level upwards is now widely accepted as the only way to assume the leadership of the "government party." But such campaigns are costly, and it may be virtually impossible for future aspirants to match the $11 million Paul Martin raised en route to the Prime Minister's Office.

Of course, the fact that Martinites within the Liberal Party joined Progressive Conservatives and members of the Alliance in attacking Bill C-24 seemed to suggest there might be some appetite for new amendments to the *Elections Act* following the 2004 general election. The opposition conservative parties were highly critical of the uneven playing field created by a per-vote system of public funding – indeed, the Canadian Alliance was critical of any legislative move toward further entrenching the notion that parties are public institutions. And Liberals, such as party president Stephen LeDrew, were highly critical of making any distinction between corporate and individual donations.[35] Martin, however, did not move to undo this aspect of the Chrétien legacy. Indeed, given Martin's rhetorical commitment to democratization, it would be difficult for him to entirely reverse Chrétien's move to reduce corporate financial leverage within the Canadian party system.

CONCLUSION

Jean Chrétien came to power in a "critical election." There is little doubt that 1993 marked a turning-point in terms of the structure of partisan competition and the terms of partisan discourse. The previous party system had come apart. The Chrétien era, then, was destined to be a tumultuous period of uncertainty, experimentation, and change in the Canadian party system. On the surface, a powerful process of regionali-

zation – one that resulted in multiparty competition, regionally segmented election campaigns, and the apparent guarantee of overstated
Liberal electoral victories – dominated the course and character of party
system change during the Chrétien years. It has been argued, however,
that there were also important changes to the discursive character of the
Canadian party system, as well as to the character of party leadership
and organization.

Jean Chrétien, in partnership with Paul Martin, moved the Liberal
Party of Canada to the market-liberal right. At times over the past decade
there was evidence suggesting this was not the legacy Chrétien wished to
leave. But the privileging of deficit elimination combined with Martin's
pre-eminence among Chrétien's ministers served to ensure that economic
and fiscal priorities would trump social priorities during the decade that
Chrétien was Prime Minister. Beyond the importance of these fiscal priorities to how Canadians were governed, it is also clear that the Chrétien-
Martin partnership paved the way for the establishment of a discursive
framework that placed market liberalism at the "centre" of a new era of
brokerage politics in Canada. After coming to power at a moment that
lacked the sort of loose consensus that structures brokerage-style partisan debate, Chrétien helped to establish the ideological focal point of
brokerage in the emerging party system.

Interestingly, while Jean Chrétien came to power when populist
democracy was all the rage and governed during a period in which there
was considerable experimentation in democratizing the rules governing
Canadian political parties, his style of leadership and developments in
the politics of leadership within the Liberal Party marked, if anything, a
retreat from democracy. I have argued that this contributed to the further
"hollowing out" of Canadian political parties, thus creating space for the
rise of "virtual parties" that are little more than shells waiting to be given
political and ideological character by a leader and the appointed advisors
who will market the party "brand" to the electorate. Of course, in politics, most actions generate reactions, and the combination of Liberal
Party electoral dominance and increased leader dominance of political
parties has renewed interest in electoral system reform and democratization of the parliamentary party system. There is, as of yet, no certainty
that we will see a more proportional electoral system any time in the near
future, let alone the type of democratization of Parliament that Paul
Martin has promised. But Jean Chrétien's surprise changes to party
financing regulations were also unexpected, so the talk of democratization that amounted to very little of substance in the 1990s may, indeed,

come to shape the post-Chrétien party system more than the Chrétien legacy would suggest it will. What is clear is that the experimentation and change that marked partisan politics in the Chrétien era are indicative of a transition in party practices and the party system – even if it may take a few electoral cycles before the full impact of this transition is understood and appreciated.

NOTES

Associate Professor, Department of Political Science, University of Alberta.

1 A. Brian Tanguay, "Canada's Party System in the 1990s," in James Bickerton and Alain-G. Gagnon, eds., *Canadian Politics*, 3d ed. (Peterborough: Broadview Press, 1999), 324–54. On "critical elections," see Walter Dean Burnham, *Critical Elections and the Mainsprings of American Politics* (New York: W.W. Norton, 1970); and Walter Dean Burnham, "Great Britain: The Death of the Collectivist Consensus?" in Louis Maisel and Joseph Cooper, eds., *Political Parties: Development and Decay* (London: Sage Publications, 1978), 267–308.

2 R. Kenneth Carty, "Three Canadian Party Systems: An Interpretation of the Development of National Politics," in George Perlin, ed., *Party Democracy in Canada* (Scarborough: Prentice-Hall Canada, 1988), 15–30; and R. Kenneth Carty, William Cross, and Lisa Young, *Rebuilding Canadian Party Politics* (Vancouver: University of British Columbia Press, 2000).

3 Reg Whitaker, "Virtual Political Parties and the Decline of Democracy," *Policy Options* 16 (2001): 16–22.

4 See R. Kenneth Carty, "Three Canadian Party Systems."

5 James Bickerton, Alain-G. Gagnon, and Patrick J. Smith, *Ties That Bind: Parties and Voters in Canada* (Toronto: Oxford University Press, 1999).

6 The one, partial exception to this was in 1997 when the Progressive Conservatives won 22 percent of the vote and five seats under the leadership of the current Liberal Premier of Québec, Jean Charest.

7 The Progressive Conservatives typically earned the support of approximately 17 percent of the Ontario electorate during the Chrétien years, while the NDP sat at about 8 percent.

8 Of course, one important exception was the victory of PC Leader Joe Clark in Calgary Centre in 2000.

9 R. Kenneth Carty, William Cross, and Lisa Young, "A New Canadian Party System," in William Cross, ed., *Political Parties, Representation, and Electoral Democracy in Canada* (Toronto: Oxford University Press, 2002), 15–36, 27.

10 David Laycock, *The New Right and Democracy in Canada: Understanding Reform and the Canadian Alliance* (Toronto: Oxford University Press, 2002).

11 Edward Greenspon and Anthony Wilson-Smith, *Double Vision: The Inside Story of the Liberals in Power* (Toronto: Doubleday Canada Limited, 1996).

12 Canada, Governor General, *The Canada We Want: Speech from the Throne* (Ottawa: Minister of Public Works and Government Services, 30 September 2002), http://www.pco-bcp.gc.ca/sft-ddt/docs/sft2002.pdf.

13 Ibid., 3.

14 Ibid., 4–5.

15 Ibid., 5–6.

16 Ibid., 6–7.

17 Canada, Department of Finance, *Building the Canada We Want: The Budget Speech 2003* (Ottawa: Minister of Public Works and Government Services, 2003), http://www.fin.gc.ca/budget03/pdf/speeche.pdf.

18 Hugh Winsor, "'People's budget' has Chrétien's fingerprint," *Globe and Mail*, 19 February 2003, A11.

19 "Mr. Chrétien's return to activist government," Editorial, *Globe and Mail*, 19 February 2003, A28.

20 According to Brodie and Jenson, a defining feature of brokerage politics is the limiting of ideological debate to offering "more or less" of an essentially identical policy package. Janine Brodie and Jane Jenson, "Piercing the Smokescreen: Brokerage Parties and Class Politics," in Alain-G. Gagnon and A. Brian Tanguay, eds., *Canadian Parties in Transition* (Scarborough: Nelson Canada, 1989), 24–44.

21 Liberal Party of Canada (LPC), *Creating Opportunity: The Liberal Plan for Canada* (Ottawa: LPC, 1993).

22 Canada, Department of Finance, *Budget Speech 1995* (Ottawa: Department of Supply and Services Canada, 27 September 1995), 6, http://www.fin.gc.ca/budget95/speech/speech.pdf.

23 Stephen Harper and Tom Flanagan, "Our benign dictatorship," *Next City* (Winter 1996/97): 34–41, 39.

24 Steve Patten, "'Toryism' and the Conservative Party in a Neo-Liberal Era," in Hugh G. Thorburn and Alan Whitehorn, eds., *Party Politics in Canada*, 8th ed. (Toronto: Prentice Hall, 2001), 135–47, 140.

25 Indeed, it should be noted that changes to tax laws governing charities and Liberal cuts to the funding of public interest groups in the early and mid-1990s helped silence left-leaning voices of dissent just as these right-wing think tanks were gaining in prominence.

26 Carty, Cross, and Young, "Three Canadian Party Systems," 78.

27 Ibid., 79.

28 Campbell Clark, "Chrétien spent own funds to save leadership," *Globe and Mail*, 22 October 2003, A4.

29 Reg Whitaker, "Virtual Political Parties." Tom Kent offered the following observation: "The Liberals have abandoned the democratic role of a political party, of an association of people actively concerned about the aims of public policy ... The life has gone from such an association." Tom Kent, "There's Still a Chance for Jean III," *Inroads: A Journal of Opinion* 9 (2000): 59–64, 61.

30 Whitaker, "Virtual Political Parties," 18–19.

31 Campbell Clark and Shawn McCarthy, "Martin plans to move fast, but Chrétien's in no hurry," *Globe and Mail*, 23 September 2003, A1.

32 Hugh Winsor, "Politics won't be the same after Bill C-24," *Globe and Mail*, 16 April 2003, A8.

33 S.C. 2003, c. 19, http://www.canlii.org/ca/as/2003/c19/whole.html.

34 Canada, Library of Parliament, Parliamentary Research Branch, *Bill C-24: An Act to Amend the Canada Elections Act and the Income Tax Act* (Political Financing), Legislative Summary LS-448E (Ottawa: Library of Parliament, June 2003).

35 Irving Gerstein, "A cure worse than the ailment," *Globe and Mail*, 23 April 2003, A1; Stephen LeDrew, "Liberals and Tories can agree: Bill C-24 needs some work," *Globe and Mail*, 28 April 2003, A11.